MySQL Database Service Revealed

Running MySQL as a Service
in the Oracle Cloud Infrastructure

Charles Bell

Apress®

MySQL Database Service Revealed: Running MySQL as a Service in the Oracle Cloud Infrastructure

Charles Bell
WARSAW, VA, USA

ISBN-13 (pbk): 978-1-4842-8944-0   ISBN-13 (electronic): 978-1-4842-8945-7
https://doi.org/10.1007/978-1-4842-8945-7

Managing Director, Apress Media LLC: Welmoed Spahr
Acquisitions Editor: Jonathan Gennick
Development Editor: Laura Berendson
Coordinating Editor: Jill Balzano

Cover photo by Pawel Czerwinski on Unsplash

Distributed to the book trade worldwide by Springer Science+Business Media LLC, 1 New York Plaza, Suite 4600, New York, NY 10004. Phone 1-800-SPRINGER, fax (201) 348-4505, e-mail orders-ny@springer-sbm. com, or visit www.springeronline.com. Apress Media, LLC is a California LLC and the sole member (owner) is Springer Science + Business Media Finance Inc (SSBM Finance Inc). SSBM Finance Inc is a **Delaware** corporation.

For information on translations, please e-mail booktranslations@springernature.com; for reprint, paperback, or audio rights, please e-mail bookpermissions@springernature.com.

Apress titles may be purchased in bulk for academic, corporate, or promotional use. eBook versions and licenses are also available for most titles. For more information, reference our Print and eBook Bulk Sales web page at http://www.apress.com/bulk-sales.

Any source code or other supplementary material referenced by the author in this book is available to readers on GitHub. For more detailed information, please visit http://www.apress.com/source-code.

Printed on acid-free paper

I dedicate this book to my younger brother Ronald who is battling cancer.

Table of Contents

About the Author

 **Charles Bell** conducts research in emerging technologies. He is a member of the Oracle MySQL Development team and is one of the principal developers for the MySQL Database Service (MDS) team supporting MySQL as a service in the Oracle Cloud Infrastructure (OCI). He lives in a small town in rural Virginia with his loving wife. He received his Doctor of Philosophy in Engineering from Virginia Commonwealth University in 2005. Dr. Bell is an expert in the database field and has extensive knowledge and experience in software development and systems engineering. His research interests include 3D printers, microcontrollers, three-dimensional printing, database systems, cloud systems, software engineering, Internet of Things, and sensor networks. He spends his limited free time as a practicing Maker, focusing on microcontroller projects and refinement of three-dimensional printers.

About the Technical Reviewer

Andres Sacco has been a professional developer since 2007, working with a variety of languages, including Java, Scala, PHP, Node.js, and Kotlin. Most of his background is in Java and the libraries or frameworks associated with it, like Spring, JSF, Ibatis, Hibernate, and Spring Data. He is focused on researching new technologies to improve the performance, stability, and quality of the applications he develops.

In 2017, he started to find new ways to optimize the transference of data between applications to reduce the cost of infrastructure. He suggested some actions, some of them applicable in all the microservices and others in just a few of them; as a result of these actions the cost was reduced by 55%. Some of these actions are connected directly with the bad use of the databases.

Acknowledgments

I would like to thank all of the many talented and energetic professionals at Apress. I appreciate the understanding and patience of my editor, Jonathan Gennick, and managing editor, Jill Balzano. They were instrumental in the success of this project. I would also like to thank the army of publishing professionals at Apress for making me look so good in print with a special thank-you to the technical reviewer for his wise counsel. Thank you all very much!

Most importantly, I want to thank my wife, Annette, for her unending patience and understanding while I spent so much time with my laptop.

Introduction

The new era of cloud computing is here. Gone are the days when "cloud" simply meant something was connected to the Internet. Now companies like Oracle are providing complete suites of resources and tools for organizations to build their computing infrastructure without having to purchase hundreds of pieces of hardware, numerous equipment racks, and a small army of computer engineers to install, configure, and manage the many components that make up the infrastructure for hosting applications for use by their customers.

One such resource provided by Oracle is the MySQL Database Service – a fully managed MySQL service that you can use as your database backend. Yes, you no longer must install MySQL and configure it yourself! Now, you can create a MySQL database server in the Oracle Cloud Infrastructure (OCI) with a few clicks of a mouse. Best of all, you can configure the resource to meet your business needs such as tailoring the system to use a minimal computing, memory, and disk size, which will permit you to reduce your overhead costs. The MySQL Database Service (MDS) is a brand new chapter in the long legacy of the world's leading open source database server.

Intended Audience

I authored this book to share my passion for MySQL and to continue the legacy of MySQL that I have been fortunate to have been a part. I especially wanted to show how anyone can use MDS in OCI even if you do not have a systems engineering background. OCI is really that easy to use. The intended audience therefore includes anyone interested in learning how to leverage MySQL in the cloud such as hobbyists and enthusiasts, and more importantly systems engineers and IT planners who want to learn how MDS can expand their infrastructure with significant lower costs than on-premise solutions.

How This Book Is Structured

The book was written to guide the reader from a general knowledge of MySQL and OCI to creating MySQL servers in OCI and connecting them to their applications. The following is a brief overview of each chapter included in this book:

- *Chapter 1, "Getting Started with MySQL in the Cloud"*: This chapter introduces the Oracle Cloud Infrastructure and MySQL Database Service Oracle. It also presents an overview of Cloud Infrastructure and the resources you will be working with so that you can take advantage of the MySQL Database Service.

- *Chapter 2, "Oracle Cloud Infrastructure"*: This chapter goes deeper into the OCI and includes a tour of some of its features. You will also see how to get started with a special free account that you can use to learn how to use OCI.

- *Chapter 3, "A Brief Tutorial of MySQL"*: This chapter is a tutorial on MySQL. You will learn the basics of how to use MySQL including an overview of its major features and how to use the basic, frequently used structured query language (SQL) commands to perform basic database operations.

- *Chapter 4, "MySQL Database Service"*: This chapter dives even deeper into learning OCI as you learn how to set up and use an MDS database system including a short tour of the MDS service and a DB System via the cloud console.

- *Chapter 5, "Backup and Restore"*: This chapter discusses the recovery features of MDS including how to back up your database (data) and restore it should you need to do so. The chapter also discusses the importance of including backup and restore into your recovery plan.

- *Chapter 6, "Point-in-Time Recovery"*: This chapter discusses an advanced recovery feature in MDS called point-in-time recovery which allows you to recover your data to within a five-minute window. This feature makes using MDS safer for those who have data that can change frequently and those who want to ensure the most recent recovery can take place should the data become compromised either through human error or system failures.

- *Chapter 7, "Data Import and Export"*: This chapter presents several ways you can migrate data to/from MDS beginning with the concepts, strategies, and tools for data import and export.

- *Chapter 8, "High Availability"*: This chapter presents an advanced feature of MDS – the ability to create a system that is fault tolerant and thus highly available. You will discover what high availability is and how it can be achieved in MDS. The chapter begins with a brief tutorial on high availability.

- *Chapter 9, "OCI Command-Line and Application Programming Interfaces"*: This chapter introduces an alternative mechanism for accessing and interacting with OCI and MDS through the command-line and application programming interfaces available for OCI. The chapter presents an overview of the capabilities of the command-line interface (CLI) and application programming interface (API) for working with OCI and MDS including demonstrations of each.

- *Chapter 10, "Migrating to MDS"*: This chapter is for those who are planning to move their infrastructure to OCI. The chapter presents strategies for planning and migrating your existing MySQL installations to MDS as well as some of the deeper topics such as getting more details about MDS features or troubleshooting tips should something go wrong. This chapter will prepare you to begin planning and designing your MySQL infrastructure using MDS.

How to Use This Book

This book is designed to guide you through learning more about OCI and MDS, discovering the power of both, and learning how to build your own OCI MDS solutions.

If you have experience with OCI, you can skip those portions that present tutorials on the minimal OCI technologies needed for use with MDS. Similarly, if you have experience with MySQL, you can skip the introductory chapter on MySQL and focus on how to get started using MDS. Either way, there is something for everyone interested in leveraging MySQL in the OCI cloud.

Downloading the Code

The code for the examples shown in this book is available on the Apress website, www.apress.com. You can find a link on the book's information page on the Source Code/Downloads tab. This tab is located in the Related Titles section of the page.

Contacting the Author

Should you have any questions or comments—or even spot a mistake you think I should know about—you can contact me at drcharlesbell@gmail.com.

CHAPTER 1

Getting Started with MySQL in the Cloud

The cloud age has been upon us for some time. It is a glorious vision where we no longer need to design, build, and staff enormous rooms full of very expensive computing equipment that needs round-the-clock attention and maintenance by a highly trained trusted staff. The ultimate goal is lower cost and higher capability. This has led to a rapid growth in cloud solutions and cloud providers.[1]

While cloud services have been around, only recently have cloud services become full featured and sophisticated enough to support real-world use cases. One such use case is having your data storage needs hosted by a cloud service.

In this case, we want to use MySQL for all of our database needs, but we don't want to build and maintain our own hardware and software. Rather, we want to be able to concentrate on building our applications and meeting the needs of our customers without worrying about the database system.

This is what the Oracle Cloud Infrastructure and the MySQL Database Service are designed to do – to free you to concentrate on your business by providing a fully managed MySQL Database Service.

MySQL has long been considered the world's most popular open source database and consistently ranked second in the world ranking of database systems with only its owner (Oracle) ranking above it. The justification for such accolades includes proven reliability, high performance, and ease of use. MySQL is known to power the world's most used websites including Facebook, YouTube, and booking.com. As you may surmise, MySQL enjoys a robust and vast ecosystem as well as the backing of Oracle, the world's leading database company.

---

[1] See the whitepaper, "Guide to MySQL Database Service in Oracle Cloud" (www.oracle.com/a/ocom/docs/mysql/guide-to-mysql-in-oracle-cloud-wp.pdf) for more details about the rapid growth of cloud computing.

© Charles Bell 2023

C. Bell, *MySQL Database Service Revealed*, https://doi.org/10.1007/978-1-4842-8945-7_1

1

In recent years, MySQL Bastion Service has permitted organizations to grow their infrastructure to meet their business goals while keeping costs low and productivity high. That trend continues as MySQL moves to the cloud. In fact, organizations can now innovate and integrate their solutions even faster now that the routine management of MySQL is provided for them in OCI.

In this chapter, we will learn what the Oracle Cloud Infrastructure and MySQL Database Service are and how we can use them. While this book isn't a tutorial on cloud computing or the Oracle Cloud Infrastructure, we need to understand the basic concepts of cloud computing and the Oracle Cloud Infrastructure so that we can take advantage of the MySQL Database Service.

Overview

In recent years, MySQL has been offered by various cloud providers promising better experiences with MySQL. While some have succeeded in offering MySQL in various forms for cloud customers, there hasn't been an offering that encapsulated the best that MySQL has to offer in a fully managed package. That is, until now.

Oracle has added MySQL to its long and impressive list of services in its Oracle Cloud Infrastructure (OCI). In this section, we will see a high-level overview of cloud computing, Oracle Cloud Infrastructure, and MySQL Database Service.

What Is Cloud Computing?

It is unlikely to find an information technology manager or engineer who hasn't heard of cloud computing by now. Indeed, the term "cloud" is pandered about so much that we've come to think of it as a marketing term and some of us just ignore it as a result. Others have heard many good things among the hype and want to learn more. If you fall into this category, the following will help set the stage for our journey. If you already use OCI, feel free to skip ahead to the MySQL Database Service section.

Cloud services have grown considerably since the early days when cloud simply meant the use of virtual machines to host servers that customers can use to build and run their own services. As cloud services grew, more components were added such as virtual networking and similar infrastructure components often as "elastic" devices that broke the bonds of conventional computing.

For example, elastic technologies permitted the separation of networking allowing you to create an IP address that can be assigned to a server and later reused for other resources. Not only did this permit separation of the IP or networking from the server, but it also meant you could reduce retooling or reconfiguring of your applications should you need to replace a failed server with another.

Since these early days, cloud computing has become more sophisticated and now includes characteristics or technologies that include the following examples:

- *On-Demand Resources*: You can create, deploy, use, and destroy resources at will

- *Networking Resources*: Virtualized networking components

- *Resource Pooling*: Ability to consume resources from a pool of like components/virtualized resources

- *Elasticity Among Components*: Connecting separate components together and mix-and-matching resources

In addition to the resource characteristics, cloud systems have evolved to include three primary forms or models of cloud services. The primary difference among these models is level of control or depth that the customer (enterprise) can interact with the resources. The following briefly describes each from the perspective of the cloud service provider:

- *Software as a Service (SaaS)*: Software is delivered as a managed service typically as components that run on virtualized servers and accessed via web applications. Virtualized hardware components to support the SaaS application are fully managed and often hidden from the customer. Some example SaaS solutions include DocuSign, Dropbox, and Microsoft Office 365 (online).

- *Infrastructure as a Service (IaaS)*: Components and resources are provided for the customer to build their own infrastructure from virtualized components. These components may be fully managed. For example, database systems are considered IaaS components where the supporting virtualized components are managed, but the databases and data are managed and owned by the customer. Some example IaaS solutions include Rackspace, Google Compute Engine, and Digital Ocean.

- *Platform as a Service (PaaS)*: This provides a framework for customers to create customized applications. Typically, the customer manages the platform components with the cloud provider managing the underlying support components. Some example PaaS solutions include Google App Engine, Heroku, and OpenShift.

Figure 1-1 presents a graphical view of the three models plus the traditional on-prem model for developing applications. Notice the management responsibility changes among the models.

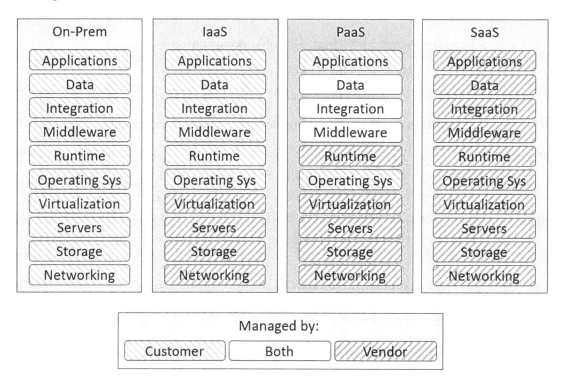

Figure 1-1. *Management Responsibilities Among On-Prem, IaaS, PaaS, and SaaS*

However, these models can be intermixed and often one model is used to provide resources from other models. For example, in this book, we will be focused on the MySQL Database Service, which is a PaaS component in the Oracle Cloud Infrastructure – an IaaS service. Thus, the MySQL Database Service is built on top of the Oracle Cloud Infrastructure.

Why Move to the Cloud?

There are many reasons an organization would want to move their infrastructure components to the cloud. We have already read where we can save money and increase agility in our development of products and how cloud services allow for more automation. Let's dive into these a bit deeper.

Improved Agility

This is perhaps the biggest organizational benefit of using cloud services. Having the ability to react quickly to your business and market changes makes organization stronger and more successful in keeping up (and ahead) of the competition. Why is that?

Consider for a moment the time, resources, and funds required for standing up a new project. Specifically, consider the information technology resources you need to support the development and later deployment of the project. Most organizations would have to rely on their information technology departments to research, acquire, install, and configure the hardware and software before you can fully get development underway. Depending on the complexity and uniqueness of the components, you could spend months tooling your infrastructure.

However, with cloud systems, you can skip all of the length budgeting, ordering, installation, and similar processes and jump directly to creating those resources with a few clicks of a mouse in a web console for a cloud service. By moving critical and often new resources to the cloud, you gain the following potential benefits:

- *Agility*: Take advantage of opportunities and changing priorities

- *Rapid Deployment*: Deploy resources in hours versus days or months

- *Adaptability*: Respond quickly to market changes and verisimilitudes of technology

- *Streamline Processes*: Remove the burden of lengthy procurement processes

- *Reduce IT Investment*: Reduce the overhead of owning and maintaining your own hardware by reducing capital investment and human resources

- *Improved Delivery*: Develop and deliver solutions quickly

Automation

It is no secret that installing, configuring, tuning, and maintaining your own resources such as database systems can be time consuming and require careful, ongoing monitoring. For most on-prem installations, this requires not only the burden of procurement, but also the need for highly skilled engineers and technicians. This only intensifies when the number of resources start growing. For example, the human resources for managing a couple of database systems may be minimal, but when the number of systems increases, the complexity of the technology puts a higher demand on the human resources often requiring a larger staff and training for existing staff.

Cloud systems cut these costs dramatically when you use managed services. For example, a fully managed database service means you no longer need human resources to tune and monitor the database system – the majority of that is done for you through automation built into the cloud services platform.

This frees organizations to turn their resources to managing their solutions and in doing so free up time for development operations (DevOps) that often include automation for configuring, deploying, and maintaining the organization solutions, which is a more direct investment in the end product of your development than the hardware and supporting software and can lead to faster delivery and higher profit margins.

As you can see, the cloud has many intriguing benefits, and the Oracle Cloud Infrastructure is built to exceed these benefits. Let's learn more about the Oracle Cloud Infrastructure.

What Is the Oracle Cloud Infrastructure?

The Oracle Cloud Infrastructure, hence, OCI, is positioned to transform your cloud experience by allowing you to adapt the OCI resources to your unique business needs and meet the demands of your innovations. The OCI is a cloud platform that is autonomous, scalable, and built especially for a vast range of enterprise workloads from basic cloud systems with key components residing in OCI to native cloud infrastructures. Better yet, with OCI, you get to control and manage your resources including security and monitoring as if they were part of your on-premises (also called on-prem) infrastructure laboratories.

The key IaaS components you will be interacting with and building your cloud-based infrastructure include the following:

- *Compute*: You can choose from a wide range of compute devices (think server hardware and operating system as a virtual unit) from those that require a small amount of computational power, memory to those that require more computational power including processing cores and larger memories. You also have the option to choose a bare metal compute resource that ensures you have greater isolation, higher performance, and consistency. These form the basis for your applications and middleware software services that you build yourself.

- *Storage*: Like compute, you can choose a wide range of cloud-based storage for use with your compute resources. You can choose from network file, object, network block, flash, archive, database backup, data transfer, and even a software storage gateway. With so many choices, you are sure to find the storage mechanisms that you can best employ for your solutions.

- *Network*: You can choose private, secure networking with virtual private networking (VPN), setup subnets, scale load balancing, and much more. The virtual cloud networking resources allow you to create highly available, secure network solutions that can replace existing expensive on-prem hardware. With the elasticity features, you won't need to rewrite or reconfigure your software every time you make network-wide changes. For example, if the networking addresses do not change when you replace or upgrade your compute or storage resources, you won't need excessive downtime to reconfigure.

- *Edge*: The OCI also has resources to provide network edge services such as domain name service (DNS).

- *Containers*: The OCI also provides production and enterprise-grade resources to run container-based solutions in a high-performance, highly available manner.

- *Database*: Aside from the expected host of Oracle database resources, the OCI also provides the PaaS MySQL database solution. The MySQL Database Service is your one-stop resource for building and integrating your solutions with a database server as a key component. We'll learn more about the MySQL Database Service in the next section.

While this list is a high-level view of the core resources and capabilities of OCI, there is much more to offer and many more ways you can leverage OCI to solve your cloud computing needs. Figure 1-2 shows a summary of the categories of features and capabilities of OCI.

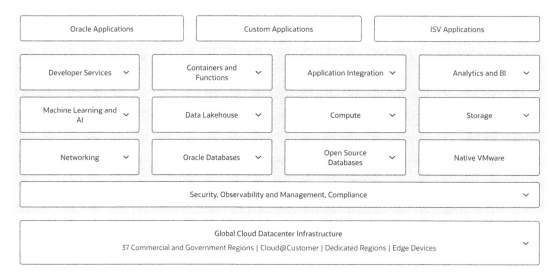

Figure 1-2. *OCI Capabilities and Features (Courtesy of oracle.com)*

Tip   For more information about OCI, visit `www.oracle.com/cloud/`. There you will see Figure 1-2 which contains links to more information about each category and feature.

OCI provides a web-based console that allows you to create, configure, and destroy resources. This is likely to be your default access mechanism. You will be presented with the OCI console once you log into your OCI account.

We will learn more about OCI in the next chapter including how to set up your account as we explore how to set up our first MySQL Database Service.

What Is the MySQL Database Service?

The MySQL Database Service, hence, MDS, is a fully managed OCI resource that runs as a native service. That is, it is built into the OCI core components and therefore fully integrated into the OCI architecture. MDS continues to be developed, managed, and supported by the same MySQL engineering team at Oracle. Better still, MDS is compatible with on-prem MySQL installations, which means you do not need to alter your applications to migrate from on-prem MySQL to MDS.

Simply put, MDS is MySQL. It isn't a hybrid of components bundled together to look and feel like MySQL. While the MySQL version used with MDS is the Enterprise Edition, you do not have to purchase a license to use MDS. In many ways, you're using MySQL just like you would if you used the open source community edition. The difference is you're getting all of the enterprise features and paying only a small, nominal fee to use it!

With MDS, you get all of the features, maturity, reliability, and performance you would if you were running MySQL on-prem. The difference is OCI permits the automation of maintenance tasks such as upgrades, backup, database and operating system patching, and so on. You are freed from that burden allowing you to focus exclusively on managing your data, schema designs, and access policies. Thus, you spend less money and yet still gain the benefits from using MySQL as your database server.

Indeed, MDS in OCI enables the following benefits:

- *Rapid Provisioning*: Create MySQL instances using preconfigured settings optimized for production deployments

- *Automation*: Configuration, upgrades, patching, etc., are all fully automated

- *Customization*: Tailor your MDS resources by selecting from a list of configurations that pair computational power, memory, and storage sizes, which allows you to limit your costs for those resources – pay for only what you need

- *Secure Storage*: Choose cost-effective storage solutions that range from high-performance attached solid-state disks (SSD) to reliable, high-performance block volumes, and cost-effective archival

- *Fast Networking*: Create a virtual cloud network configured to meet your privacy needs

- *Monitoring*: Use monitoring to optimize your applications and respond quickly to events that require changes for optimal performance

- *Fewer Resources*: Migrating to MDS permits you to recruit new and train human resources for tasks and skills that are vital to your business

We will see more details about most of these as we learn more about MDS and OCI.

MDS in OCI

Now that we know a bit more about OCI, we should discuss some of the constraints and terminology as well as OCI mechanisms that are required for using MDS. We won't talk about how to set up and connect to MDS yet. We'll cover that in the next chapter. Rather, the following are some of the things you should be familiar with to prepare you for using MDS. If you already use OCI, some of these will be familiar.

Region Availability

A region in OCI is a localized geographic area typically servicing the area with OCI data centers in the region. MDS is available in most regions but may not be available in new regions immediately as they are deployed. Check with your Oracle account liaison to ensure MDS is available in your region.

Required Identity and Access Management Policy

Access to OCI services is governed by another OCI resource called Identity and Access Management (IAM), which is used for all authentication and authorization including access via the console, SDK or CLI, and REST API. In order to use MDS, your OCI administrator will need to set up IAM to permit access to MDS resources.

Data Security

MDS uses encryption to protect your data. Under the hood, MDS uses a storage mechanism called a block volume, which is always encrypted. MDS also supports encryption between MDS and clients using Transport Layer Security (TLS). By default, MDS applications attempt to connect using encryption.

MDS and Audit Service

MDS integrates with the OCI Audit Service to allow you to perform auditing on your database servers for access and other goals.

MDS Versions and Storage Engines

MDS is built with MySQL Enterprise Edition version 8.0 and uses the InnoDB Storage Engine exclusively. MySQL Enterprise Edition offers a host of enterprise-grade features including auditing, external authentication modules to easily integrate MySQL with security infrastructures via Pluggable Authentication Modules ("PAM") or native Windows services, transparent data encryption (TDE), enhanced encryption and other cryptographic features, and firewall features to against cyber security threats.

Shape

MDS is configured to choose from a list of configurations for the compute resource that describes the size of the compute, memory, and storage. These are called shapes. When you provision (create) an MDS, you choose from a list of shapes that best meets your needs.

Tip   For more information about MDS, visit the online document `https://docs.oracle.com/en-us/iaas/mysql-database/doc/overview-mysql-database-service.html`.

DB System

An MDS DB System (sometimes called dbSystem) is a logical unit or container for the MySQL server instance. Its primary purpose is to facilitate provisioning, backup, restore, monitoring, termination, etc., for the MDS. The DB System container consists of these components. Except for the intersection with the user interface (such as the OCI console), this list should be considered informational since you cannot interact directly with some of the components:

- *Compute*: Also called the compute instance, it is an OCI compute resource configured with a shape selected at creation.

- *Operating System*: The operating system, while considered separate from the compute, which is a virtual machine, is predefined with Oracle Enterprise Linux.

- *MySQL Server Enterprise Edition*: An MDS is configured with latest release of version 8.0 in the MySQL product line.

- *Virtual Network Interface Card (VNIC)*: Attaches the DB System to a subnet of the Virtual Cloud Network (VCN).

- *Network-Attached Block Storage*: MDS uses the high-performance options for all block storage. Depending on the size of the storage in the shape chosen, the storage may consist of multiple block volumes in a group setup for high-performance access.

While this list may seem like a lot to configure and set up, the DB System container is optimized for rapid deployment (creation and provisioning) of the components. In fact, the operating system and MySQL are preconfigured as a special image that is loaded when an MDS is configured.

Tip   For a complete description of a DB System including all of the details about how MySQL is configured, see `https://docs.oracle.com/en-us/iaas/mysql-database/doc/db-systems.html`.

MySQL HeatWave

One of the biggest and most exciting features of MDS is actually a separate product. MySQL HeatWave is built on MDS. HeatWave provides a high-performance in-memory analytical processing engine that has been optimized to run on OCI.

You run HeatWave using your data stored in MDS without requiring expensive data migrations, intermediary systems, or any change to the application. Your applications can connect to and interact with HeatWave using the normal MySQL communication protocols (think same application). Like MDS itself, all of the typical administrative and maintenance operations are automated. You can also manage your HeatWave instances using the same OCI Web Console, REST API, CLI, or DevOps tools.

While all that sounds great, the most important aspect of HeatWave is your queries can achieve orders of magnitude acceleration over the MySQL database permitting you to form complex and fast online transaction processing and online analytical processing operations using the same database storage as your applications. We'll learn more about HeatWave in Chapter 8.

To help us understand how we may leverage MDS in your infrastructure, let's look at the use cases for MDS.

Use Cases

There are many use cases for MDS. Indeed, most use cases you already know for MySQL are applicable to MDS. However, there are a few unique to MDS in OCI. The following lists a few of the more significant use cases:

- *Migrate Workloads*: You can move your most intensive or even all of your MySQL workloads to OCI allowing you to free up resources and focus on the more important goals of your business.

- *Develop Cloud Applications*: You can improve and grow your applications into cloud-native MySQL-based applications more quickly and eliminate many of the burdens in developing infrastructure from the ground up.

- *Deployment Flexibility*: Since MDS is completely compatible with on-prem MySQL, you have flexibility in deploying some or all of your MySQL servers to OCI.

- *SaaS Applications*: Since MySQL is the database of choice for many SaaS products, you can build and scale your SaaS applications to OCI.

However, there are some limitations to what you can do with MDS in OCI.

Limitations

While we expect to be able to use all MySQL features in MDS, there are some that are unsupported either because they are not applicable to a cloud environment, have not been adapted for use in OCI, or they need additional features for use in OCI. The following are currently unsupported in MDS:

- Authentication plugin

- Modification of system tables

- Binary log access

- Error logging to the system log

- Group replication plugin

- InnoDB tablespace encryption

- Password strength plugin

- Setting global variables

- Persisted system variables

- Replication filters

- Semi-synchronous replication

- Transportable tablespace

If you are currently planning to use one or more of these MySQL features, check the online DB System documentation for more details before you try to use them. You may also want to see https://docs.oracle.com/en-us/iaas/mysql-database/doc/db-systems.html#GUID-DAF5136C-C602-434E-8EBB-E1AFA57F0BB7 for a complete list of the limitations in MDS including limitations on existing features.

Cloud Services Cost Expectations

One of the most attractive aspects of using cloud services for infrastructure components such as IaaS components is cost. Not only will you save the cost of having to host a physical information technology laboratory complete with cooling and security measures, you also do not have to invest in additional human resources to operate and maintain the hardware and server.

However, you must take care when planning your database systems. Oracle has many different configurations you can use such as selecting the shape (size of the compute object), which defines the CPU processing power as well as memory and disk size. Naturally, the larger (more powerful) shapes will cost more than the smaller shapes.

Fees for using cloud services vary among vendors, but all base the cost on hourly rates for consumable processing (such as virtual compute platforms) and in some cases cost per unit (such as disk or other storage devices). In addition, you may incur costs for data transfer rates when you interact with the database system (for uploading data, exporting, networking, etc.). The combination of those costs over time will determine your savings.

Let's explore a simple hypothetical example. We will keep it simple and calculate only the cost of the database service. Let us use a fictitious cloud service that charges $0.05/hour for the compute service and $0.025 per GB per day for storage. That seems really cheap, yes? Let's do some math. For a single day, we will incur a compute cost of $36.00 (30 days times 24 hours times $0.05) and if we use 10 Gb of disk storage per day, we add $0.25 (10 Gb times $0.025) giving us a total of $36.25 per month. Clearly, that is a lot cheaper than the physical and human resources you would need to maintain your own MySQL server!

While this example is pure fiction and wildly inaccurate,[2] it should give you the perspective of how cloud services are billed and how your bill can add up over a month. But it need not be a complete surprise because you can create an OCI account and experiment with the resources available. In fact, if you follow the tutorial in the next chapter to create your own account with OCI, you can see how these fees are generated and billed against the sign-up credit Oracle grants to new accounts. That is, you will be given a credit in dollars that you can use to explore OCI resources. Once that credit has been used up, you will be billed for the services you use each month.

Regardless, be sure to do your homework and work with an account representative at Oracle to set your expectations for your monthly billing liabilities.

Tip   For more accurate pricing for MDS, contact your Oracle sales representative to discuss your needs and set expectations for cost.

---

[2] This fictional example does not accurately portray Oracle's cost structure for MDS. Please consult Oracle sales for accurate pricing information.

Summary

Cloud Services are a part of everyday life for most system architects, infrastructure planners, and information technology experts alike. Leveraging the cloud to meet critical business needs for capacity, growth, and innovation is the key to the future for most businesses.

In this chapter, we discovered the benefits of using cloud services, a brief introduction to the Oracle Cloud Infrastructure, and how using OCI can make your business more agile with fewer resources and less dependence on often complex procurement, installation, configuration, and maintenance of critical infrastructure components.

We also took a brief look at the MySQL Database Service including a survey of its benefits over on-prem MySQL installations as well as the features you can employ to migrate your MySQL applications to OCI.

In addition to the benefits of the MySQL Database Service, we also got a glimpse at the OCI terminology and the major MySQL resources available including the MySQL DB System and HeatWave. We will continue to explore these features and more throughout the book.

In the next chapter, we will take a closer look at the Oracle Cloud Infrastructure including a brief tour of the services available, how to get your account set up, and most importantly how to deploy your first MySQL DB System.

CHAPTER 2

Oracle Cloud Infrastructure

Thus far, we have learned a little about cloud computing and have learned that Oracle Cloud Infrastructure is a powerful service that offers a host of tools you can use to move your critical infrastructure components to the cloud. OCI contains infrastructure as a service (IaaS) resources for you to leverage to build and grow your business.

Recall, the MySQL Database Service (MDS) is one of those IaaS resources and indeed the focus of this book. Since MDS is built entirely on OCI, we must learn more about OCI in order to understand not only the nomenclature of OCI but also the core components with which we will be working. For example, while a database system (DB System) is fully managed, knowing the OCI resources involved can help you understand how best to configure a DB System for your uses.

In this chapter, we will learn what the Oracle Cloud Infrastructure is and take a tour of some of its features. We will also see how to get started with a special free account that you can use to learn how to use OCI.

A Brief Tour of Services

OCI is a robust IaaS public cloud service platform that offers computational, storage, and advanced networking capabilities. Among its many features are also some platform as a service (PaaS) tools for businesses such as fully managed Oracle Autonomous Database as well as container services and other PaaS tools.

A detailed tour or tutorial on OCI services will consume many pages and even a library of books to describe every nuance of every service. Rather than attempt to squash a tutorial into a few pages, we will focus only on those OCI services that make up your normal activity when working with MDS.

© Charles Bell 2023
C. Bell, *MySQL Database Service Revealed*, https://doi.org/10.1007/978-1-4842-8945-7_2

Tip   See the online OCI User Guide (`https://docs.oracle.com/en-us/iaas/pdf/ug/OCI_User_Guide.pdf`) for more in-depth coverage of OCI and its services including tutorials on some of the major core features.

However, before we jump into our tour of the core services, let's review some terminology.

Terminology

There are a number of terms and concepts you will encounter when getting started with OCI. Some are rather easy to figure out while others can sometimes lead to confusion or misunderstanding for beginners. The following is a short list of key terms you will encounter when learning OCI. As you will see once you become proficient with OCI, this is list not complete, but it is a good place to start. The terms are presented roughly in order that you may encounter them when starting with OCI for the first time. Some terms and concepts use common abbreviations, which are also listed.

Tip   For more information about concepts and terminologies, see the *Key Concepts and Terminology* section at `https://docs.oracle.com/en-us/iaas/Content/GSG/Concepts/concepts.htm`.

Virtualization

Let's begin with what virtualization means with respect to cloud services. This may be the hardest concept for beginners to master since some feel nothing is "real" in the cloud.

Simply, virtualization simply means a service, feature, or even hardware has been represented as an independent entity. In most cases, this means the object or resource in question is indeed running as a process or in some form as software in a vast computing framework.

For example, a compute resource (think server) can be running as a virtual machine on a hypervisor stack. In other cases, it could mean a conceptual, managed concept such as a virtual network that is presented to the user (you) as if it were a physical network.

Further, some virtual resources are simply parts of other virtual resources and not intended to be used individually. For example, a block storage device is typically connected to a compute resource and accessed via the operating system (or platform service) running on top of the operating system.

Tenancy

A tenancy is how Oracle groups all of the resources for a particular customer (user). When you sign up for OCI, you will be given a tenancy for your account. All of your resources, billing, etc., will be associated with your tenancy. Resources in your tenancy cannot interact with resources in other tenancies (without additional resources configured to grant access) and you can administer only those resources that reside in your tenancy.

Compartments

Compartments are another level of organization for your tenancy. You can create compartments to contain a collection of related resources. Access to resources in a compartment is defined by user groups to which you give specific permissions. Thus, a compartment is a virtual or logical group (not a physical grouping). Interestingly, when you work with the OCI Cloud Console, you can use the compartment to filter the resources for viewing.

A tenancy can be thought as the "root" compartment for your cloud resources and, once you create a compartment, any resources created will require you to select the compartment where the resource will reside.

Tip   To keep things simple for beginners, it is recommended that you wait to create multiple compartments once you have become accustomed to using OCI. Adding the compartments and their security profiles can make the learning curve steeper and error prone.

When you create a compartment, it is associated with your tenancy. You can create multiple compartments as your need arises. Each compartment is controlled via access policies specific to that compartment allowing you to restrict access to user groups ensuring they can access only those resources they need. Thus, when you work with multiple compartments, some thought must be taken to plan how you are going to grant (or restrict) access to the compartmental resources for your users.

Security Zone

Each compartment has a security zone or security zone profile. When a compartment is created and resources added, OCI will validate all operations against those resources using the security zone policies. If the operation is restricted (the validation fails), the operation is rejected. We will learn more about security in the next section when we see a walk-through of setting up a free trial OCI account.

OCI Resource Allocation

You may be wondering where all of these OCI resources are housed or even how they are organized. OCI resources are organized in both physical and logical groupings. OCI resources may be physically located or distributed in one or more local data centers called regions, which have one or more physical layouts (geographically isolated hardware, power, cooling, etc.) called availability domains, and then into physically adjacent (same server rack) groupings called fault domains. The following attempt to explain how resources are within OCI:

- *Region*: A localized geographical area comprised of one or more data centers. Within each region, the resources are allocated to one or more availability domains, which allow for additional organization. All resources are either region-specific, for example, virtual networking, or are availability-specific such as storage and compute resources.

- *Availability Domain (AD)*: A geographically isolated (from other availability domains), fault-tolerant physical grouping of resources. Availability domain isolation allows for reduced risk of failures by permitting you to distribute your resources among availability domains. Note that some resources must be created within the same availability domain. For example, if you create a compute resource and want to attach storage, the storage resources must be in the same availability domain as the compute resource.

- *Fault Domain (FD)*: A grouping of hardware within an availability domain. Fault domains permit you to distribute your instances so that the instances are not on the same hardware within an availability domain. This permits protection against a hardware failure affecting one fault domain (the chances of the same or similar event affecting multiple fault domains are remote), the outage does not affect resources in the other fault domains. Thus, if you want high availability among your resources, you will want to allocate your resources across the availability domains and within each availability domain across fault domains.

- *Realm*: A (logical) collection of regions. Realms are isolated from one another. Your tenancy would exist in a single realm and be able to access regions within that realm. OCI currently offers several commercial and government realms.

Figure 2-1 presents a visual guide to how regions, availability domains, and fault domains are arranged logically. As you can see, we can distribute resources across regions, within a region across availability domains, and within an availability domain, across fault domains. Each layer adds a significant level of isolation against hardware or outside influences that cause failures.

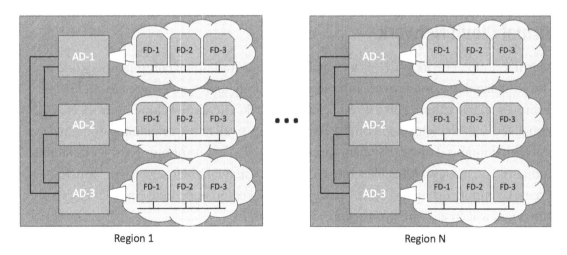

Figure 2-1. *Regions, Availability, and Fault Domains*

Notice we have a region, region 1, that contains three availability domains (typically abbreviated as AD-n), which each have three fault domains (typically abbreviated FD-n). Oracle currently supports regions throughout the world with more being added regularly. Figure 2-2 shows the current status of OCI regions taken from `https://oracle.com/cloud/architecture-and-regions`.

△ Commercial

☐ Commercial planned

■ Government

Figure 2-2. *OCI Regions (Courtesy of oracle.com)*

Virtual Cloud Network

A virtual cloud network (VCN) is a virtualization of a traditional computer network. The virtualization extends to creating subnets, routing tables, gateways, etc. All of your resources will be running on a virtual cloud network. The virtual cloud network is associated with a single region but has connectivity to all of the availability domains and fault domains. Further, for each subnet you can span one or more of the availability domains. You must set up at least one virtual cloud network before you can launch (create) compute instances. Thus, creating a virtual cloud network is one of the first things you will create when you set up your account.

Oracle Cloud Identifier (OCID)

Every resource in OCI has an Oracle Cloud Identifier. It is a unique string of characters that identifies a resource in OCI. The Oracle Cloud Identifier is required for almost every operation you want to execute on a resource when accessing it via the command line interface (CLI), REST API, or a developer API via code. The following shows the format for the OCID:

```
ocid1.<RESOURCE TYPE>.<REALM>.[REGION][.FUTURE USE].<UNIQUE ID>
```

The following shows an example of an OCID for a MySQL Database Service DB System. Other OCI resources will use a similar format but typically the preamble shows the type of resource the OCID references:

```
ocid1.mysqldbsystem.oc1.iad.aaaaaaaapuif...sbg5z7sy5imjtlclhbxwbjmrq
```

Compute

Also called a compute instance, is a compute host running in OCI. In other words, it is a server that you can use to run software, install your own applications, etc. A compute instance can be a virtual machine or a bare metal host. The size or virtualized hardware capabilities of a compute instance are governed by a logical grouping of CPU size, number of cores, performance, and memory settings called a shape. The configuration of the server (operating system, etc.) is governed by a template called an image.

Virtual Machine

A virtual machine is a software implementation of an abstract set of hardware running on a large system host (called a hypervisor server) that allocates virtualized memory, CPU, and sometimes disk for a server. You may have encountered virtual machines when using your own server or PC. Virtual machines in OCI are similar but are much more complex because they can be tailored to performance and capacity using shapes.

Bare Metal Host

When performance or isolation is paramount, OCI provides a small set of physical (or "bare metal") machines. These run directly on hardware bypassing the hypervisor and do not use virtualized memory, CPU, etc. (but may be connected to virtualized resources). Oracle Cloud Infrastructure provides you control of the physical host ("bare metal") machine. When you use a bare metal host, you are the only tenant using the physical CPU, memory, and network interface card (NIC). You can use it as you would any other compute instance and appears no different than a compute instance using a virtual machine.

Shapes

A shape is a set of configuration items that defines the number of CPU cores, size of memory, and in some cases the disk space for a compute instance. This allows you to "tune" your compute instance to meet your needs. For example, if you do not need a lot of memory, you can choose a "smaller" shape and therefore save some money when you incur costs.

Images

An image is a template of a virtualized disk that defines the operating system and default installed software. When you create a compute instance, you can select the image you want to use. For example, you can select an image preinstalled with Oracle Linux. You can also create an image from one of your configured compute instances so you can deploy a new compute instance of the same configuration saving you the setup and configuration time. Cool!

A WORD ABOUT THE WORD INSTANCE

The word instance is one of those overused terms in cloud computing. In OCI parlance, it is not correct to refer to a compute instance as simply "instance." This is because there are other resources that are considered instances.

For example, in MySQL parlance, "instance" can mean a running MySQL server application (MySQL running on a server platform), or in MySQL Database Services, a DB System can be referred to as a DB System instance. Thus, you should always qualify what you mean by "instance": a compute instance, MySQL instance, or DB System instance.

Provisioning

This is one of those terms you will encounter once you start creating resources. Provisioning in this case means the set of operations required by OCI to create the resource including its subcomponents as well as configure the resource for use. For example, provisioning a new compute instance includes, at a high level, allocating a virtual machine, installing the operating system and base software via an image, and configuring the compute instance for your region, availability domain, etc. You may see this term when working with OCI resources as state or status.

Tip   You may encounter in the documentation and blogs some of these terms and concepts are presented as acronyms or simply abbreviated. Be sure to refer to the documentation dictionary section to confirm the meaning of terms and acronyms you may not be familiar with so to avoid confusion.

Next, let's discuss the major interfaces you can use to interact with OCI.

OCI User Interfaces

OCI provides several mechanisms you can use to interact with OCI resources. More specifically, there are several user interfaces you can use to create, manage, and destroy your OCI resources. These include the web-based OCI Cloud user interface called the Oracle Cloud Console (or simply cloud console), a command-line tool called the OCI Command Line Interface (CLI), and, for developers, programmable interfaces including a Representational State Transfer (REST) application programming interface (API) interface[1] as well as language-specific APIs to allow you to work with OCI directly from code. There is even a cloud-based terminal application called the Cloud Shell. We will look at the web-based cloud console interface in this chapter saving the CLI, REST, and developer APIs for Chapter 9.

Note   The CLI, REST, and APIs require setup and configuration on your PC. We will walk through those steps in Chapter 9.

The OCI Cloud Console is the most used mechanism of working with OCI resources. It is easy to use, easy to navigate, and doesn't require any special software to use. While some of the menus can see a bit long, there is a consistency across the resource and detail pages that makes it all feel completely seamless. Once you've spent some time with the cloud console, you may find yourself using it as your go-to tool when working with OCI.

---

[1] https://restfulapi.net/

To reach the OCI Cloud Console, navigate to `https://cloud.oracle.com`. Once you login, you will see the cloud console. The key points or features of the interface you should learn first are the menu button in the top-left, the search box in the center, the helpful quick tips and tutorials in the center, and your account information on the right. Depending on the type of account you created, once the account is created and active, the console can show you your expenses so far in the billing cycle. That helps you keep track of your spending. This information is not currently shown for the free trial accounts. Figure 2-3 shows an example of the OCI Cloud Console, hence OCI console.

Note   Many of the images in this chapter show UUIDs or other data specific to my personal account. Those data are masked for security. When you visit the same pages in your own account, you will see such values. You should treat all OCIDs as private data unless you are sharing them specifically among your trusted users.

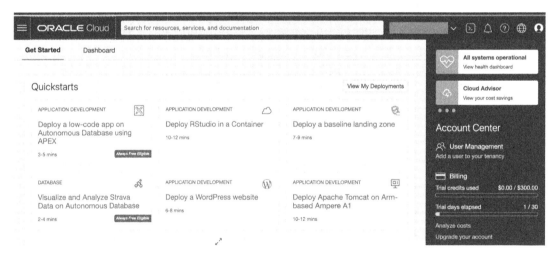

Figure 2-3. *OCI Cloud Console*

Note   Oracle makes minor changes to the OCI console weekly. Some of the images presented may differ slightly in the future, but the methods and mechanisms are largely unchanged. For example, a dialog may have a new field for you to complete or the fields may be reorganized for better viewing.

There is one other feature you may be interested in after you have learned how to use OCI. If you look in the upper-right corner of the cloud console, you will see a symbol that looks like a prompt. This opens the OCI Cloud Shell that includes the command-line interface (CLI) which you can use to manage your resources. Click on that button and the cloud shell will be created. Interestingly, it is created as a resource itself which can save state from one use to another. Figure 2-4 shows the OCI Cloud Console.

Figure 2-4. *The OCI Cloud Shell*

To learn more about OCI Cloud Shell, type *help* in the console or see the online documentation at `https://docs.oracle.com/en-us/iaas/Content/API/Concepts/cloudshellintro.htm`. We will learn more about the CLI in the next section.

You can also get help with OCI from the cloud console by clicking on the question mark in the upper right corner or clicking on any of the quick start links/buttons to learn about specific resources. You may want to start with clicking the question mark symbol and selecting the *Using the Console* topic to learn more about the cloud console.

Now we are ready to begin our tour with a look at the core services you will encounter when working with OCI.

Core Services

Thus far in our exploration of OCI, we've encountered things like virtual networks, compute instances, storage, and access concepts. These resources are managed and provided by a cloud service (sometimes called a cloud capability), which is devoted to that type of resource. The mechanisms with which you use to create, manage, and destroy those resources are largely hidden from view and involve a set of often intensive automation processes. For example, when you create a compute instance, several automation mechanisms and other routines (called workflows) are initiated to complete the provisioning of the resources.

These concepts are considered the very core of the services available in OCI. Since they are each a service provided by OCI, we refer to the capability as a service and the individual resources by their object name. For example, the compute service is used to create a compute instance.

The following lists the core services provided by OCI. We will see more about each in a later section:

- Networking Services

- Compute Services

- Storage Services

- Identity and Access Management Services

These core services in OCI are used to build and provide more complex services and resources. In fact, every complex resource in OCI is typically built using one or more of these core services. For example, the MySQL Database Service is built on top of compute, networking, storage, and identity and access management services. Other examples include container orchestration, additional managed services, serverless computer, and many more.

Let's look at the core services in more detail.

Networking Services

Perhaps the most important core service is the networking services. Like other resources, networking services are virtualized. This means the traditional hardware/software components such as networks, subnets, routing, gateways, and similar building blocks of traditional, hardware-based networks are presented as resources that you can create and use with other resources to permit network connectivity.

This virtual networking component concept is sometimes called software-defined networking (SDN). Thus, cloud-based resources connect to these virtual networking components are also SDN-enabled infrastructure that lets you create and terminate your virtual cloud networks (VCNs), organize them into subnets, and use them with your compute instances and other cloud resources. OCI networking resources include the following. We will only touch on the high-level concepts in this section and more details when we see a tutorial on creating networking resources:

- Virtual cloud networks and their subnets

- Reserved public IP addresses

- Security lists and security rules

- Gateways

- Route tables and rules

- Load balancers

- DNS zones

- Web Application Firewall (WAF) policies

Tip   For more information about the OCI networking services and resources, see https://docs.oracle.com/en-us/iaas/Content/Network/Concepts/landing.htm#top.

When working with OCI networking, you typically start with creating a virtual cloud network (VNC) and assigning a range of private internet protocol (IP) addresses for use in the network. You can create multiple VCNs and can configure them to be accessible via the Internet (or not), as well as cloud-specific (isolated) and inter-connected networks. You can also organize your VCNs into subnets; a logical subdivision of the networking addresses. Subnets in this case are the same concept as hardware networking subnets.

When you create resources that require network connections such as compute instances must be assigned to one or more subnets through a cloud resource called a virtual network interface card (vNIC). A vNIC attached to a public subnet can have a public IP address assigned which permits access from the Internet.

Interestingly, OCI uses a pool of public IP addresses assigned dynamically. When a vNIC requests a public IP address, it is assigned from the pool. When the resource is terminated, the public IP address is returned to the pool. This is another example of the elasticity of cloud services. However, if you need a permanent public IP address, you can request a reserved public IP address that is allocated to your cloud account (there may be a fee involved too).

You can also create a security list that stores rules for adding a layer of a software firewall to block or permit access to your resources. It works like a port and address filter permitting only those connects that meet the security permission lists.

Similarly, you can create route rules, which are used to control VCN outbound communication to permit packets to be moved to the next stop (hop) in the network. Routing rules are associated with gateway resources.

The hard work for networking in the cloud is the same as hardware-based networking. You must carefully choose the resources you need along with selecting the correct set of rules to make it all work correctly to permit only the desired traffic to and from the subnets. Fortunately, OCI provides a wizard we can use to automate some of the more common configurations.

Compute Services

Compute services are those resources that represent computing hardware such as servers that run applications or services. Recall, we use the term compute instance to refer to a provisioned compute resource.

When you provision a compute instance, you can choose from a wide variety of options including the type of machine (bare metal, virtual machine, etc.) as well as a set of performance settings (called a shape) that lets you tailor the compute instance to your capacity and performance needs.

Storage Services

These services are the disk and data storage resources provided by OCI. You have several choices of data storage resources that you can use to tailor to your data workload. These include resources with characteristics such as persistent/non-persistent, data type, performance of read/write input/output operations per second (IOPS), throughput, durability, connectivity, storage interface protocol, capacity, and more.

Like compute instances, you have many options you can use to tailor your storage to your business needs. The following sections briefly describe the more common choices you have for storage in OCI.

Block Volume

A virtualized hard disk. Block volumes are disks that provide persistent storage for compute instances. They are, like most resources, virtual meaning you can detach and reattach them (using another virtual resource called block volume attachment) among different compute instances (one compute instance at a time) with no loss of data.

Block volumes are used the same way you would a hard drive on your PC. You simply read and write data from/to the disk or install your applications as well. You can choose from a boot volume, which is used by compute instances where the image is written (think operating system), or block volume which is used for data. Block volumes are persistent and durable. You can choose from basic, balanced, and high-performance varieties that define performance characteristics.

Local NVMe

A virtualized memory drive (like an SSD). Like block volumes, these can be attached as block storage but is nonpersistent and nondurable. These are used mainly for applications that require high-performance local storage without the need for long-term storage.

File Storage

A distributed file system that you can attach to a compute instance and use as if it were a local drive. Commonly used as a shared file system storage and file storage is persistent and highly durable.

Object Storage

Unlike block volumes, object storage is a different architecture designed to store data as objects. Thus, storage is optimized for object-level access rather than individual file access like block volumes, so you would not use object storage to read/write your data files.

Data objects are stored in buckets, which is a special container you create to place your data objects. Each bucket can contain an unlimited number of data objects. However, data objects can be of any type up to 50 GB in size.

You can choose between two tiers: standard object storage, which is life and accessible (sometimes called hot), or archive storage, which is archived when not used (sometimes called cold) and must be made available when you want to use it.

Object storage is also not something you would attach directly to a compute instance. Rather, you use object storage to copy data to object store. Use cases for object storage include backing up data, sharing files, and unstructured data storage such as logs.

Identity and Access Management Services

Identity and Access Management (IAM) services are those resources that you use to control access to your OCI resources, which make these core services one of the more complicated and yet vital for building your OCI-based infrastructure. You can create users and groups as well as apply access policies.

The most used concept is called a principal (sometimes called an instance principal), which is a resource used to apply to IAM users and compute instances to permit access or interactions with OCI resources. The operations and actions that can be performed by an authenticated principal is called authorization.

Users and groups are what you would expect where users have a name, password, API signing key, and one or more authentication tokens. Access is granted to users and groups by using policy resources that allow a user or group to access a specific compartment in a tenancy with any restrictions or conditions.

For example, when a user wants to access an OCI resource, the user (or application/service) must be part of a group, which should have a policy with permissions in the same compartment and tenancy.

Now that we've had a brief introduction to OCI core services, let's learn how we can set up our OCI account and create our first OCI resources.

Setting Up Your Account

Getting started with OCI is really easy. In fact, Oracle allows you to create a free account that you can use to learn how to work with OCI. While the free account has a few limits on the size or complexity of resources you can create, Oracle gives each free account a $300.00 credit for signing up. This means you can use resources to try them out with the cost deducted from the initial credit. Once that amount is depleted, you will begin to incur charges. Thus, you must supply a valid credit card when creating the account.

A free tier account also has access to certain always free services such as the following:

- Two Oracle Autonomous Databases with tools like Application Express (APEC) and Oracle SQL Developer

- Two OCI compute instances (VMs); Block, Object, and Archive Storage; Load Balancer and data egress; Monitoring and Notification services

As mentioned, the free account is limited to the following:

- Up to eight compute instances across all available services

- Up to 5 TB of storage

You can upgrade your account at the end of the 30 days to a pay-as-you-go account. If you created paid resources that you want to keep beyond the 30 days, you will need to upgrade your account.

Caution   Any resources provisioned with your credit allowance are reclaimed by Oracle after the 30-day period expires unless you upgrade your account.

You can upgrade to a paid account at any. Simply click the *Upgrade your account* link in the panel on the right side of the cloud console page. You will continue to have ownership and access to your cloud resources after upgrading your account.

Always Free Resources

All OCI accounts (including pay-as-you-go) can create resources that are identified as "always free." They are denoted by a label that reads, *Always Free*, in the cloud. Some of these resources may be limited to certain configurations. For example, compute instances that are always free are those that are provisioned as a virtual machine. Similarly, an Oracle Autonomous Database, and the networking, load balancing, and storage resources needed to support the applications that you want to build may also be free for sample applications or to perform prototyping.

See the OCI documentation (`https://docs.oracle.com/en-us/iaas/Content/ FreeTier/freetier_topic-Always_Free_Resources.htm#resources`) for more details about which resources are always free.

There is one more concept we should discuss that relates to all accounts but is more restrictive for the free tier account.

Service Usage and Limits

Service usage and limits are put in place to limit how many of certain resources you can create in your account. These may be applied to your tenancy or across your compartments.

You can find your tenancy's limits by clicking on the cloud console menu then select *Governance and Administration* then *Limits, Quotas, and Usage*. This gives you a long list of service limits, but you can filter by service, scope, resource name, or compartment.

For example, if you look at the block volume service, you will see limits for number of backups, free backups, and free storage in GBs. Figure 2-5 shows an example of these limits in the cloud console.

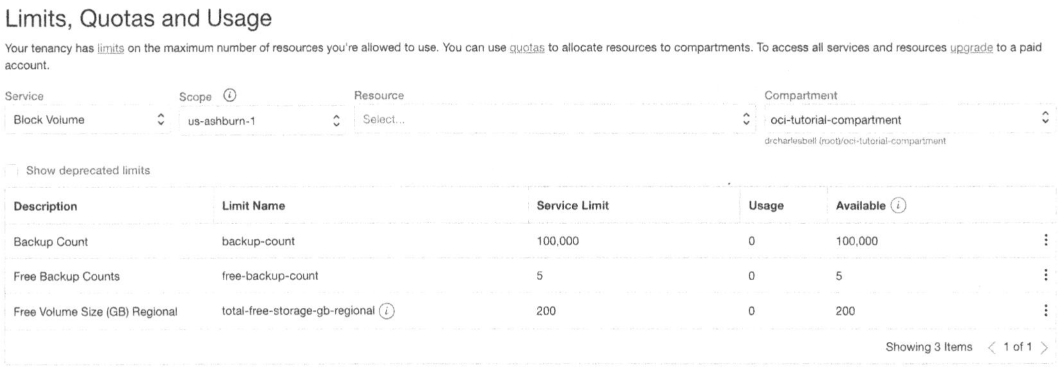

Limits, Quotas and Usage

Your tenancy has limits on the maximum number of resources you're allowed to use. You can use quotas to allocate resources to compartments. To access all services and resources upgrade to a paid account.

Service	Scope ⓘ	Resource		Compartment	
Block Volume ⌄	us-ashburn-1 ⌄	Select...		oci-tutorial-compartment	⌄
				drcharlesbell (root)/oci-tutorial-compartment	

☐ Show deprecated limits

Description	Limit Name	Service Limit	Usage	Available ⓘ	
Backup Count	backup-count	100,000	0	100,000	⋮
Free Backup Counts	free-backup-count	5	0	5	⋮
Free Volume Size (GB) Regional	total-free-storage-gb-regional ⓘ	200	0	200	⋮

Showing 3 Items ⟨ 1 of 1 ⟩

Figure 2-5. *Service Limits Example*

With that mind, let's see how we can create our OCI account and take a small tour of some of the basic resources you may want to use. Interestingly, the resources in the tutorial are some of the components used to build a database system resource in the MySQL Database Service.

Navigate to `https://cloud.oracle.com/`. Click *Sign Up* under "Not an Oracle Cloud customer yet?" on the left. Figure 2-6 shows the initial landing page.

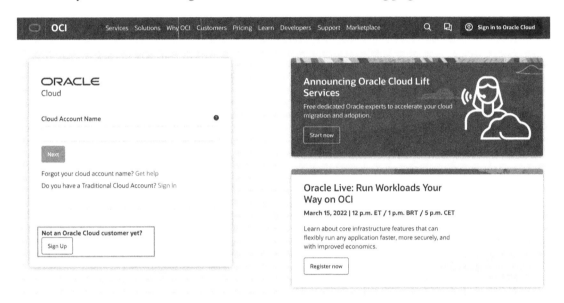

Figure 2-6. *Oracle Cloud Landing Page*

This will open a new browser where you can create your Oracle cloud account. Figure 2-7 shows the required information you will need to enter. Notice it defaults to the free tier account.

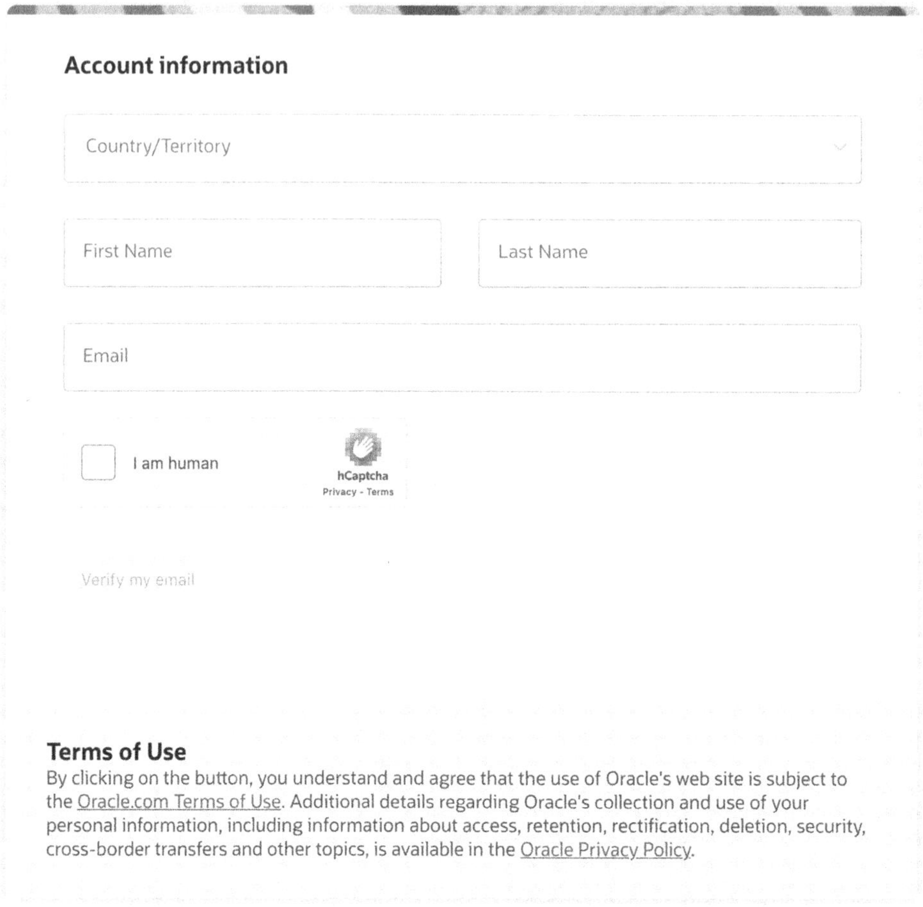

Account information

Country/Territory

First Name

Last Name

Email

☐ I am human

hCaptcha
Privacy - Terms

Verify my email

Terms of Use
By clicking on the button, you understand and agree that the use of Oracle's web site is subject to the Oracle.com Terms of Use. Additional details regarding Oracle's collection and use of your personal information, including information about access, retention, rectification, deletion, security, cross-border transfers and other topics, is available in the Oracle Privacy Policy.

Figure 2-7. *New Account Information (Part 1)*

You will need to choose the country or region where you live, enter your first and last name, successfully meet the captcha challenge, then click *Verify my email*. You should also read the terms of use shown at the bottom of the dialog.

Once you click the button, you will get an email and in the email will be a link (button named *Verify email*) for you to click to complete the account creation process. If you are following along, go ahead and open your email and click the link/button. You will then be returned to the login creation page and the dialog will change to allow you to set your password, company name, cloud account name, and your home region as shown in Figure 2-8.

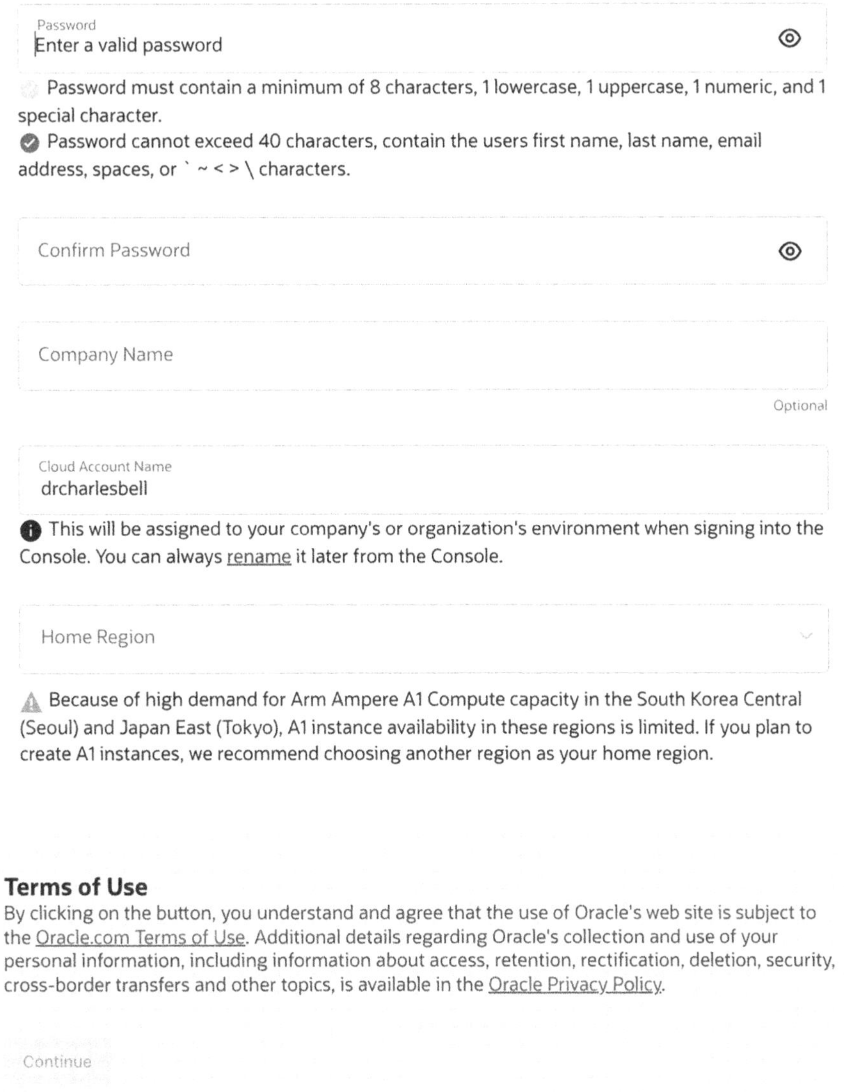

Password

Enter a valid password   ◎

  Password must contain a minimum of 8 characters, 1 lowercase, 1 uppercase, 1 numeric, and 1
special character.
  ✔ Password cannot exceed 40 characters, contain the users first name, last name, email
address, spaces, or ` ~ < > \ characters.

Confirm Password   ◎

Company Name

                                                                                  Optional

Cloud Account Name

drcharlesbell

  ℹ This will be assigned to your company's or organization's environment when signing into the
Console. You can always rename it later from the Console.

Home Region   ⌄

  ⚠ Because of high demand for Arm Ampere A1 Compute capacity in the South Korea Central
(Seoul) and Japan East (Tokyo), A1 instance availability in these regions is limited. If you plan to
create A1 instances, we recommend choosing another region as your home region.

Terms of Use
By clicking on the button, you understand and agree that the use of Oracle's web site is subject to
the Oracle.com Terms of Use. Additional details regarding Oracle's collection and use of your
personal information, including information about access, retention, rectification, deletion, security,
cross-border transfers and other topics, is available in the Oracle Privacy Policy.

Continue

Figure 2-8. *New Account Information (Part 2)*

Your home region is the geographical data center group closest to where you live. It
is important to choose the closest to help reduce potentially longer latency across the
Internet. When you have entered the information, click *Continue* at the bottom. Once
again, you should read the terms of use statement above the button.

Once you click the button, you will be presented with another dialog asking for your
mailing address and phone number as shown in Figure 2-9.

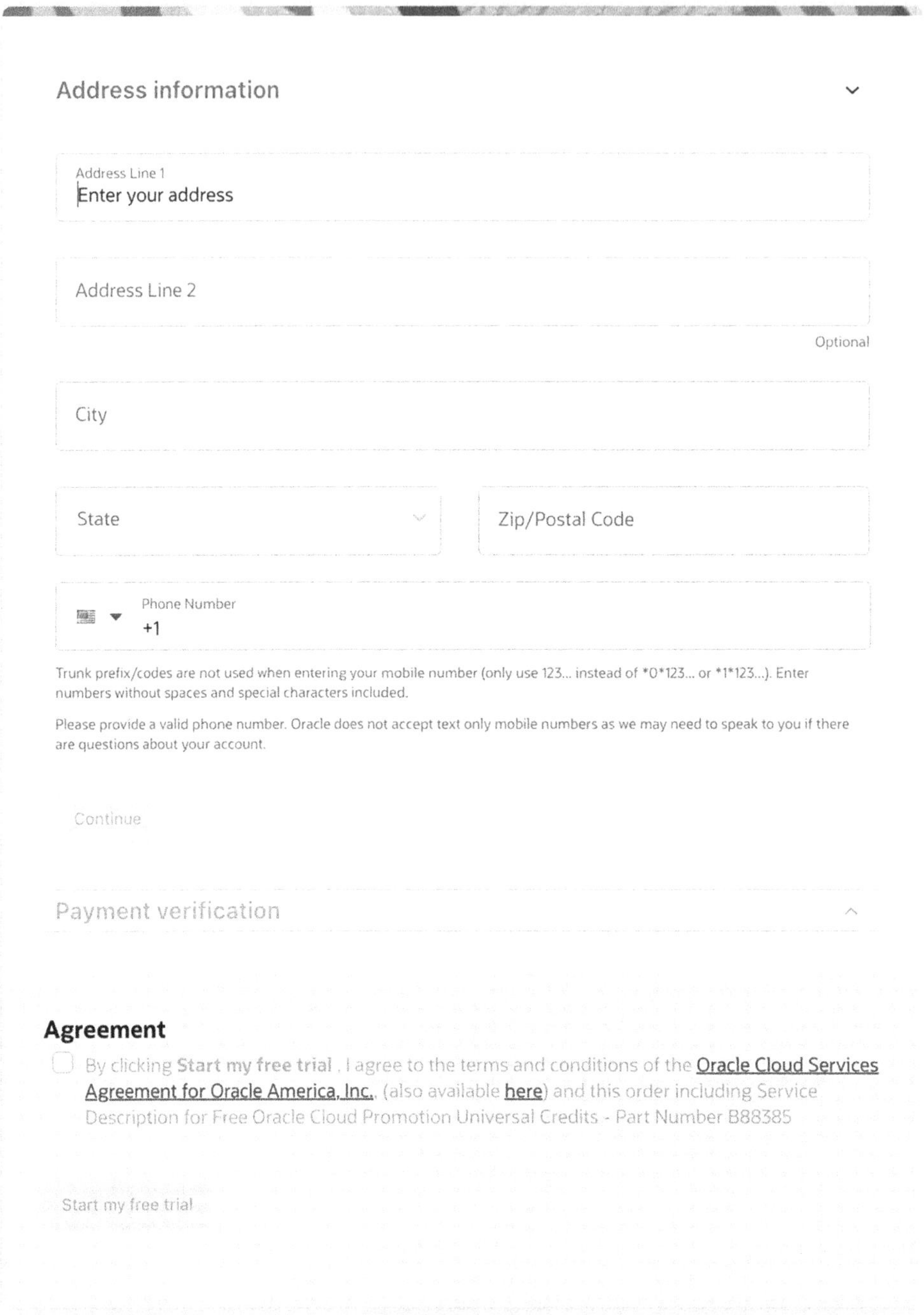

Figure 2-9. *New Account Information (Part 3)*

Once you have entered your personal information, click *Continue* to move to the payment information section as shown in Figure 2-10. To add your payment preference, click the *Add payment verification method* button and follow the prompts.

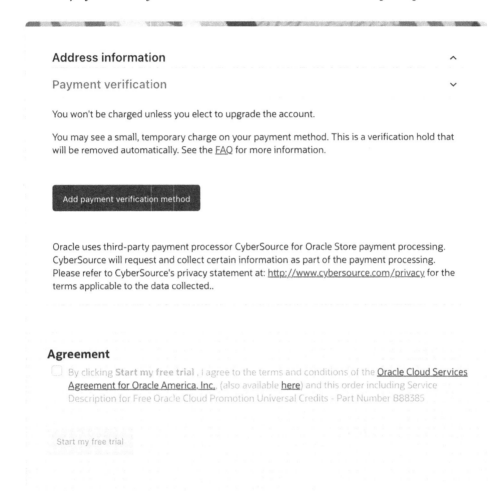

Figure 2-10. *New Account Information (Part 4)*

Once you've entered your payment information and it has been validated, you will return to the dialog. To complete your account creation, tick the *Agreement* checkbox (after reading the agreement), then click *Start my free trial* as shown in Figure 2-11.

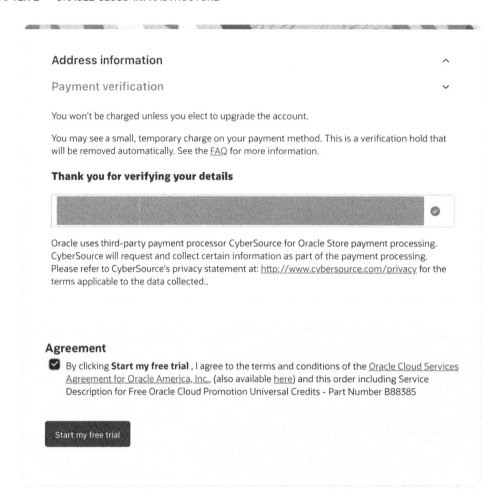

Figure 2-11. *New Account Information (Part 5)*

At this point, your new account is being provisioned. You may receive a message that the process will take some time as shown in Figure 2-12. This is normal. Notice Oracle provides a link for you to learn more about OCI while you wait. That's nice. You will be notified via email when your account is ready.

Thank you for signing up for Oracle Cloud

We are creating your account, which may take up to 15 minutes. Check your email for further instructions.

While you wait, you can read about Oracle Cloud Infrastructure.

Figure 2-12. *Account Creation Message*

Once your account is created and you click the link in the email to login, you will be sent to the OCI login page (your username is your email address) and once logged in, you may see a short questionnaire. Once you get past that, will see the OCI start page. You may see a notice that additional account setup tasks are being run in the background as shown in Figure 2-13.

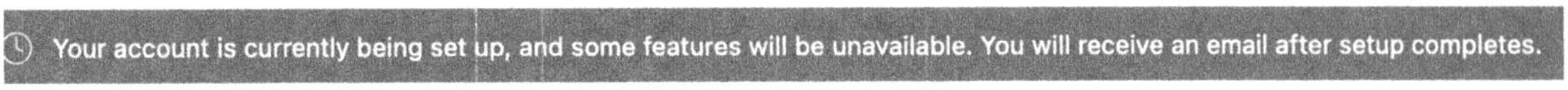

Your account is currently being set up, and some features will be unavailable. You will receive an email after setup completes.

Figure 2-13. *New Account Start Notice*

At this point, you're all set to start working with OCI! However, recall we mentioned each account has its own tenancy. Your tenancy name is the first part of your email address that you used when you signed up. For example, if you used `mynamehere@wesayso.com`, your tenancy name would be `mynamehere`. Keep this in mind as we work through the example in the tutorial.

Let's take a quick tutorial of how to create our very first OCI resources.

OCI Tutorial

In this tutorial, we are going to create our first resources in OCI. The objective is to create a compute instance where we can login and experiment using it. We will see how to navigate the OCI Cloud Console (web interface) to create the resources needed to make the compute instance operational, which includes adding a block storage device to our compute instance, which will reveal some of the things going on in the background when you create a MySQL Database Service DB System. We will see how to do that in Chapter 4.

For now, let's get started provisioning new OCI resources. There are a couple of things we should do first. The following lists the resources we will create in order:

- Create a new Compartment

- Create the Virtual Cloud Network

- Create the Compute Instance

- Add Block Storage to the Compute Instance

- Terminate the Resources

The tutorial is written to allow you to follow along and create the same resources in your own OCI account. If you have not created your own OCI account, you should do that now.

Create a New Compartment

The first thing you should do is to create a new compartment to organize your resources. While it is not required, using compartments can make organizing your resources for different projects, customers, or experiments much easier. Not only that, but with the added security you can assign to users and groups, you can ensure users access only those resources you permit.

We will use the Oracle Cloud Console sidebar menu, which you can access via the menu button in the upper-left corner of the console. Each of the entries in the menu and submenus will take you to a different dialog from which you can view and manage resources of that category/group. To open the compartment page, open the sidebar menu, select *Identity & Security*, and then *Compartments* as shown in Figure 2-14.

Figure 2-14. *Compartments (Main Menu)*

This will open the Compartment page as shown in Figure 2-15. Like most resource pages, you will see a list of your current resources in the center and a menu on the left that lets you manipulate the resources. Each resource page is a little different, but you will become familiar with the layout over time. However, notice the filters section. This allows you to filter the view by different groups such as state or in other resources the compartment.

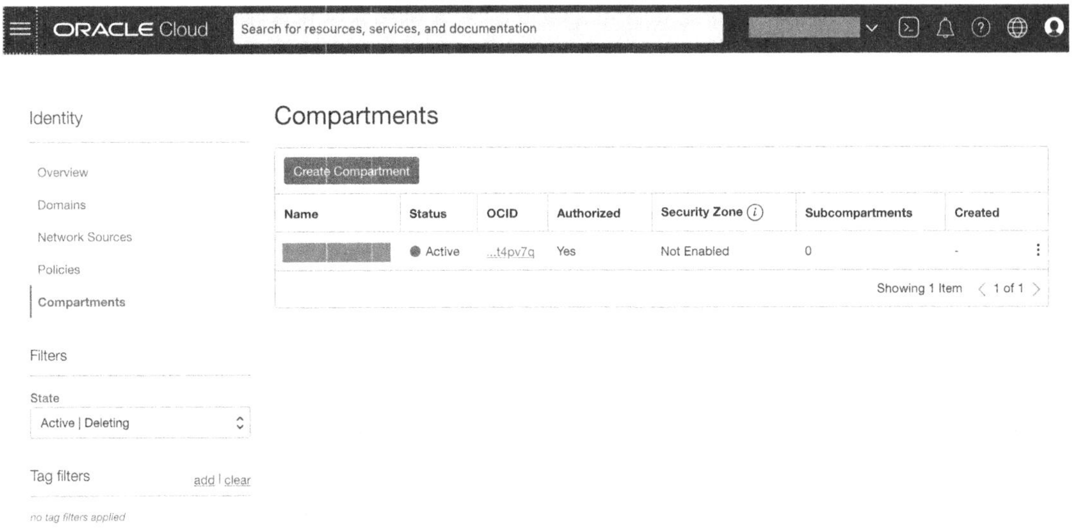

Figure 2-15. *Components Page*

To create a new compartment, click the *Create Compartment* button. This will open the create component dialog. Here, we give the compartment a name. Try to use something that has some meaning for the use. For example, if you are creating a compartment for a particular project or customer, you may want to include something in the name to associate it. For our testing purposes, we will name the compartment `mysql-tutorial-compartment`. Go ahead and fill out the dialog with the name and whatever description you want. Leave the other fields at the default as shown in Figure 2-16.

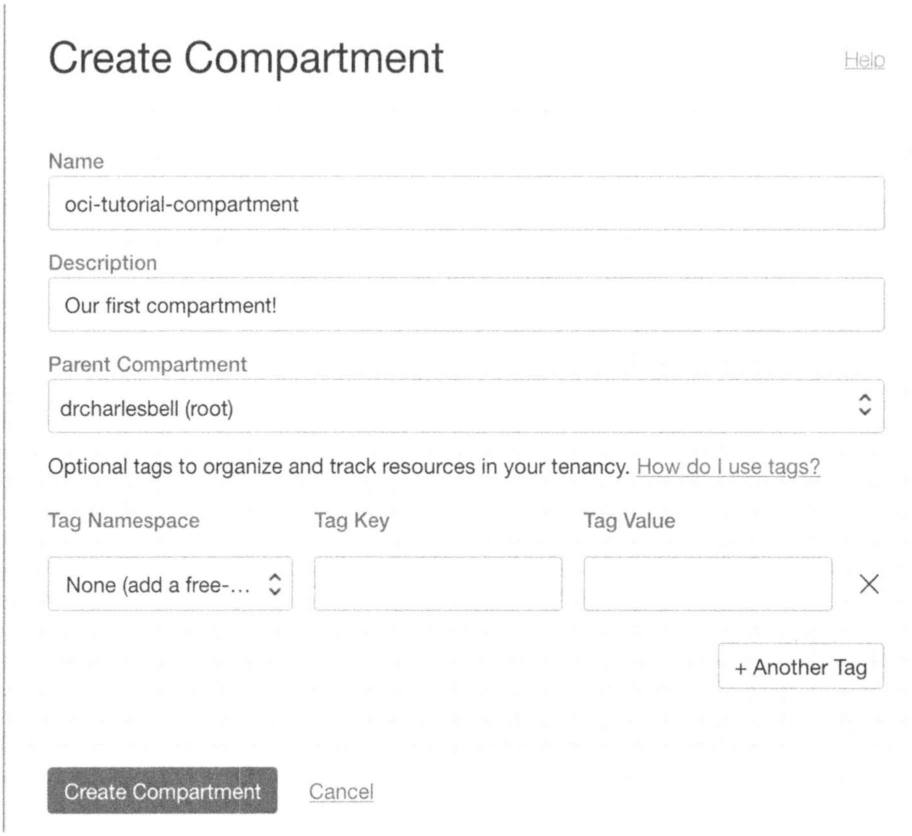

Create Compartment

Help

Name

oci-tutorial-compartment

Description

Our first compartment!

Parent Compartment

drcharlesbell (root)

Optional tags to organize and track resources in your tenancy. How do I use tags?

Tag Namespace   Tag Key   Tag Value

None (add a free-... ⌄   ✕

+ Another Tag

Create Compartment   Cancel

Figure 2-16. *Create Component Dialog*

Notice there is a space to add tags. Tags are what they sound like – labels you can use to add to resources to make them easier to sort or locate. While it is discouraged to use tags to store perishable information, you could use tags to store critical accounting information if you'd like.

When you are ready to create the compartment, click the *Create Component* button. Once the compartment is provisioned (it only takes a few seconds), you will see it listed in the compartments dialog as shown in Figure 2-17.

Compartments

Name	Status	OCID	Authorized	Security Zone ⓘ	Subcompartments	Created	
▓▓▓▓▓▓▓	● Active	...t4pv7q	Yes	Not Enabled	1	-	⋮
oci-tutorial-compartment	● Active	...wys7pa	Yes	Not Enabled	0	Fri, Mar 11, 2022, 19:40:29 UTC	⋮

Showing 2 Items ‹ 1 of 1 ›

Figure 2-17. *List of Compartments*

Notice we see both the root and the new compartment. Recall from the discussion of compartments, all accounts have that root account. This is what makes creating a compartment optional – you already have one (root)[2]. Clearly, if you want any form of organization you will need to use compartments.

Caution   Once you start creating resources, your account will begin to incur charges. Due to the $300 credit when you signed up, you won't see any charges on your credit card for some time but be aware all resources you create except for those labeled "always free" or "free tier" will incur charges against your initial credit. When that runs out, your credit card will be billed.

If you want to see the compartment page for the new compartment, you can click on the link (the underlined name in the list). This will open the compartment detail page as shown in Figure 2-18.

---

[2]Who puts everything in the root? I've seen numerous PC hard drives with everything in the root folder. Most of those eventually failed or had access issues. While the risks of placing everything in the root compartment isn't as bad as that of the root folder in a PC, it is still a good idea to plan some level of organization with compartments.

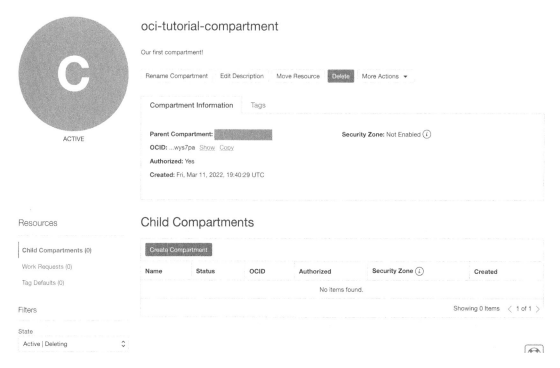

Figure 2-18. *The oci-tutorial-compartment Detail Page*

Notice you can manage the resource on its detail page including deleting it. Also, notice the bottom of the detail page has another list for child compartments. Yes, you can create a hierarchy of compartments! Just open the detail page for the compartment and create new compartments using the *Create Compartment* button above the child list.

Now that we have a compartment, we can start creating resources to place in it. The next step is to create a VCN.

Create the Virtual Cloud Network

Next, we will need a virtual cloud network (VCN) to connect to our compute instance so we can access it. Rather than attempt to configure the VCN manually, we will be using the VCN wizard which greatly simplifies the work needed. In this case, we will create a VCN that has Internet access so that we can place a compute instance in the network and access it.

Begin by clicking on the cloud console menu button (upper-left corner) then select *Networking* then *Virtual Cloud Networks* as shown in Figure 2-19. This will open the main page for VCNs.

Search
Networking
Home
Compute
Storage
Networking
Oracle Database
Databases
Overview
Virtual Cloud Networks
Load Balancers
Network Visualizer
Inter-Region Latency

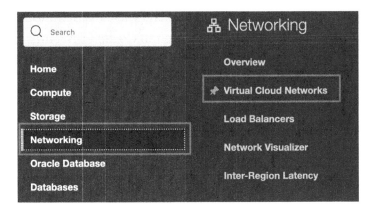

Figure 2-19. *Virtual Cloud Networks (Main Menu)*

On the VCN page, you will need to select the compartment using the filter control on the left as shown in Figure 2-20. Select the `oci-tutorial-compartment` that we created earlier.

List Scope
Compartment
Search compartments
oci-tutorial-compartment

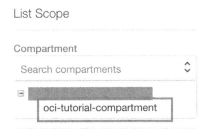

Figure 2-20. *Set List Scope (VCN Page)*

Once you've set the compartment, the display will change to show a list of all the VCNs in that compartment. Currently, it will show an empty list. To start the VCN wizard, click the Start VCN Wizard button as shown in Figure 2-21.

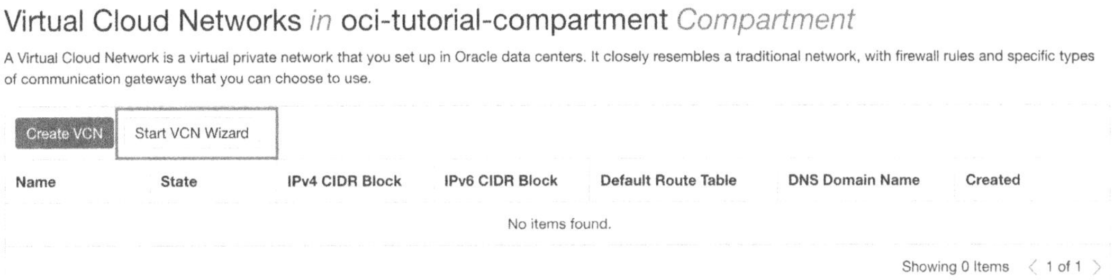

Virtual Cloud Networks in oci-tutorial-compartment Compartment
A Virtual Cloud Network is a virtual private network that you set up in Oracle data centers. It closely resembles a traditional network, with firewall rules and specific types of communication gateways that you can choose to use.
Create VCN
Start VCN Wizard
Name
State
IPv4 CIDR Block
IPv6 CIDR Block
Default Route Table
DNS Domain Name
Created
No items found.
Showing 0 Items
1 of 1

Figure 2-21. *VCN Network List (oci-tutorial-compartment)*

Once you click the button, the wizard opens, and you can enter the information needed. In this case, we will want to select the option *Create VCN with Internet Connectivity* as shown in Figure 2-22. Once selected, click the *Start VCN Wizard* button as shown.

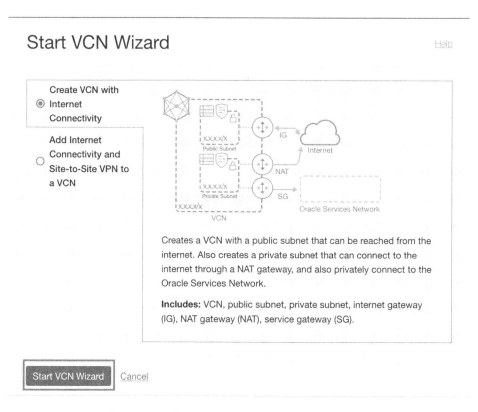

Figure 2-22. Start VCN Wizard

This will trigger a check in OCI to ensure the VCN is permitted, and you can create it. You may see a banner in the wizard indicating such. When the page opens, we will need to supply a name for the VCN and ensure the correct compartment is selected. If you are following along, use `oci-tutorial-vcn` for the VCN name then click *Next* as shown in Figure 2-23. Leave the default values in the *Configure VCN and Subnets* section.

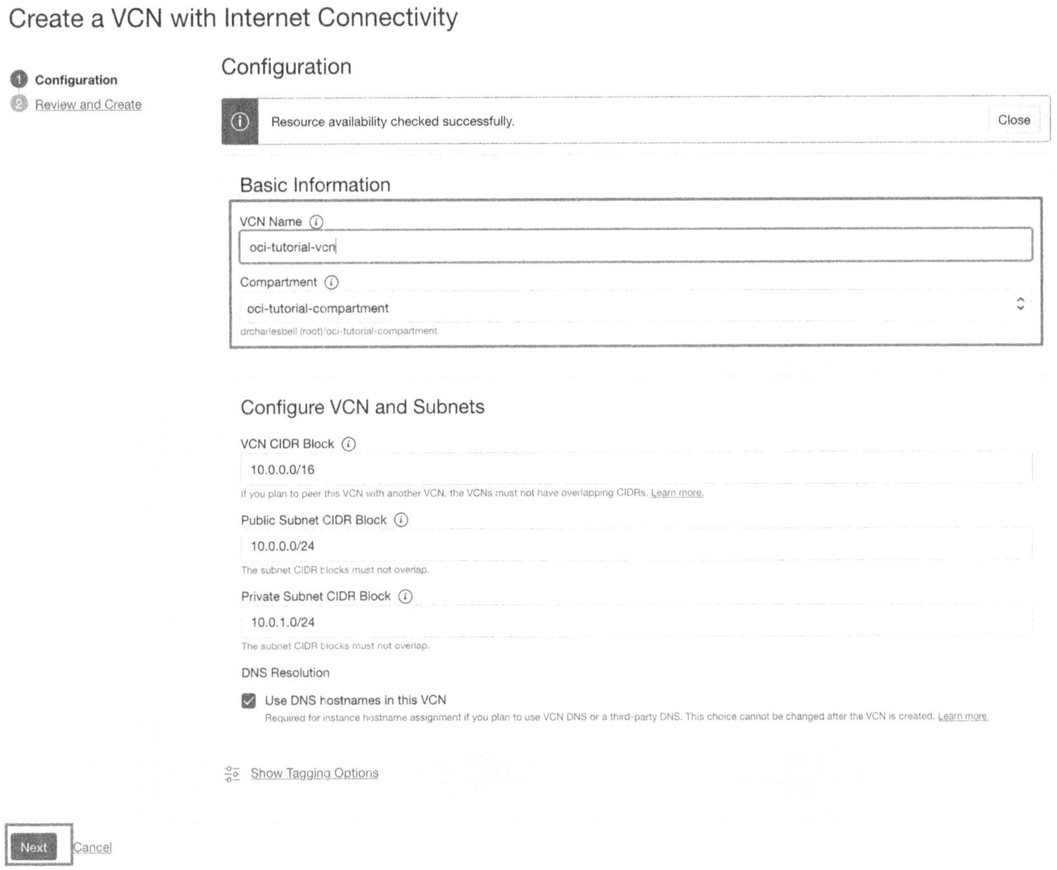

Create a VCN with Internet Connectivity

① **Configuration**
② Review and Create

Configuration

ⓘ   Resource availability checked successfully.   Close

Basic Information

VCN Name ⓘ

oci-tutorial-vcn

Compartment ⓘ

oci-tutorial-compartment   ⌄

drcharlesbell (root)/oci-tutorial-compartment

Configure VCN and Subnets

VCN CIDR Block ⓘ

10.0.0.0/16

If you plan to peer this VCN with another VCN, the VCNs must not have overlapping CIDRs. Learn more.

Public Subnet CIDR Block ⓘ

10.0.0.0/24

The subnet CIDR blocks must not overlap.

Private Subnet CIDR Block ⓘ

10.0.1.0/24

The subnet CIDR blocks must not overlap.

DNS Resolution

☑ Use DNS hostnames in this VCN

Required for instance hostname assignment if you plan to use VCN DNS or a third-party DNS. This choice cannot be changed after the VCN is created. Learn more.

⚬⚬ Show Tagging Options

Next   Cancel

Figure 2-23. *Create VCN with Internet Connectivity – Basic Information*

On the next page, we are given a summary of the VCN parameters most have come from the wizard. Take a moment and look it over. Notice we have a public subnet as well as a private subnet. We will see how to make this work with our compute instance in a later section. Click the *Create* button when ready as shown in Figure 2-24.

Create a VCN with Internet Connectivity

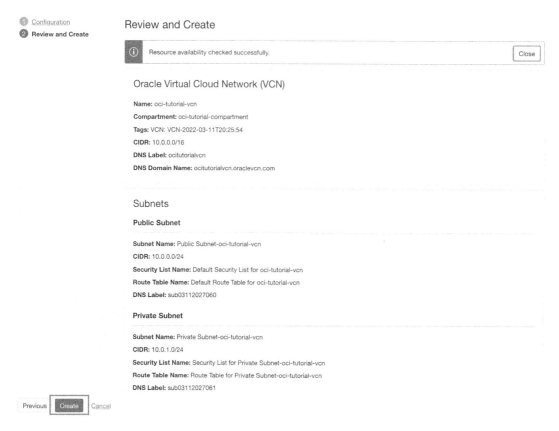

Figure 2-24. *Review and Create VCN*

At this point, a dialog will appear informing you of the progress of the provisioning. Since we are using the wizard, it is natural to think this is a single resource, but it is not. There are several resources being provisioned and configured for you to include the VCN, its subnets, gateways for Internet and private subnet access, routing tables and security lists for the gateways, and more. Figure 2-25 shows the dialog once all resources are provisioned and ready.

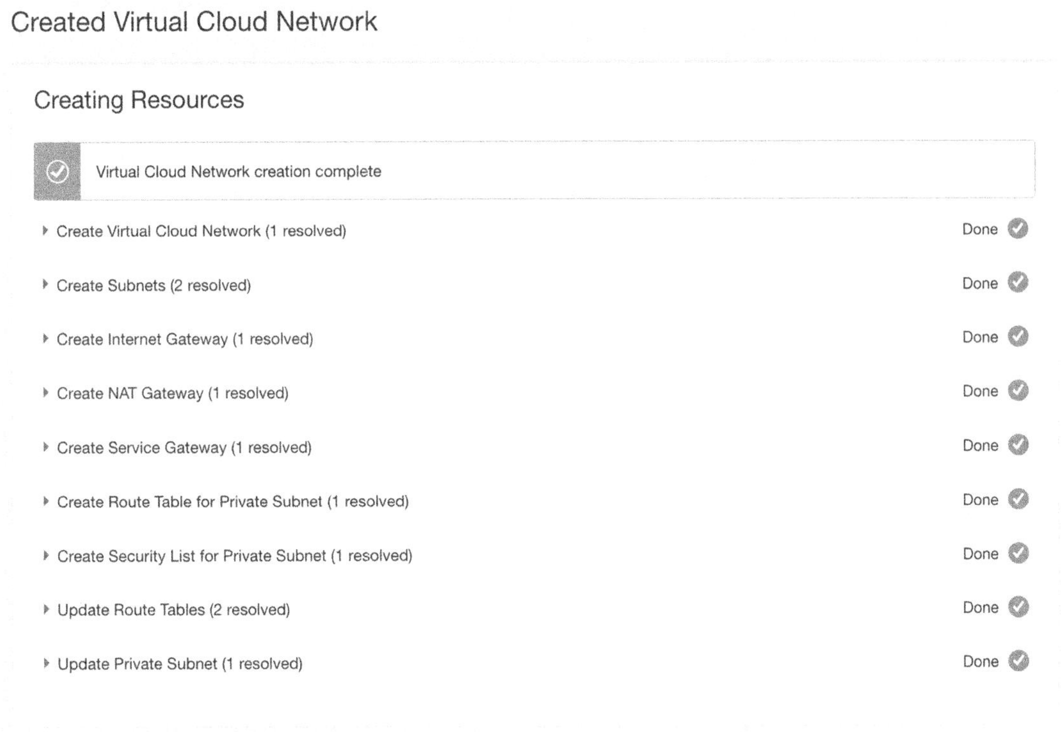

Created Virtual Cloud Network

Creating Resources

⊘ Virtual Cloud Network creation complete	
▸ Create Virtual Cloud Network (1 resolved)	Done ✓
▸ Create Subnets (2 resolved)	Done ✓
▸ Create Internet Gateway (1 resolved)	Done ✓
▸ Create NAT Gateway (1 resolved)	Done ✓
▸ Create Service Gateway (1 resolved)	Done ✓
▸ Create Route Table for Private Subnet (1 resolved)	Done ✓
▸ Create Security List for Private Subnet (1 resolved)	Done ✓
▸ Update Route Tables (2 resolved)	Done ✓
▸ Update Private Subnet (1 resolved)	Done ✓

Figure 2-25. *Provisioning the VCN*

Once the VCN is created, you can close the dialog and then click the *View Virtual Cloud Network* button at the bottom to navigate to the VCN page as shown in Figure 2-26. Here we see the VCN with both of its subnets ready. Cool!

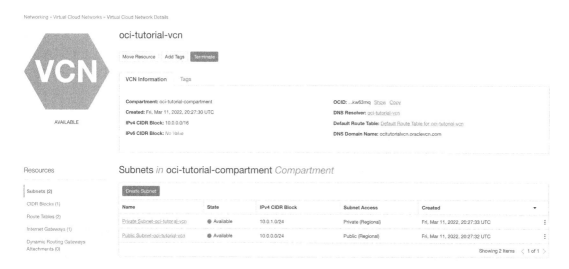

Figure 2-26. *VCN Detail Page*

Now that we have our VCN, we're ready to create the compute instance.

Create the Compute Instance

For this tutorial, we will create a simple compute instance using the smallest shape since we don't need it for more than a demonstration. We will use the default values, which happen to be an always free compute instance. To get started, open the cloud console main menu and select Compute | Instances as shown in Figure 2-27.

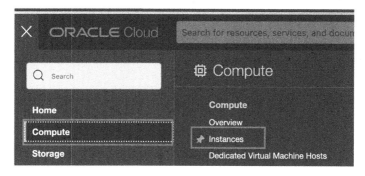

Figure 2-27. *Compute Instances (Main Menu)*

On the Compute page, you will need to select the compartment using the filter control on the left as shown in Figure 2-28. Select the `oci-tutorial-compartment` that we created earlier.

Figure 2-28. *Set List Scope (Compute Page)*

Next, click the *Create instance* button in the instances list as shown in Figure 2-29. This will launch the create instance dialog.

Figure 2-29. *Compute Instances List (oci-tutorial-compartment)*

The create instance dialog is a long form. Let's go through it a portion at a time.

The first portion we will examine includes entries for the name, selecting the compartment, placement (availability domain), and the image and shape. Once again, we will use the defaults for the *Placement* and *Image and shape* entries. If you are curious what selections are available, you can click the *Edit* link in each section.

If you are following along, change the name to oci-tutorial-instance-1 as shown in Figure 2-30. You may see the name of the compute instance generated for you and may be in the form like instance-20220312-1956. You should also verify the correct compartment (oci-tutorial-compartment) is selected and then scroll.

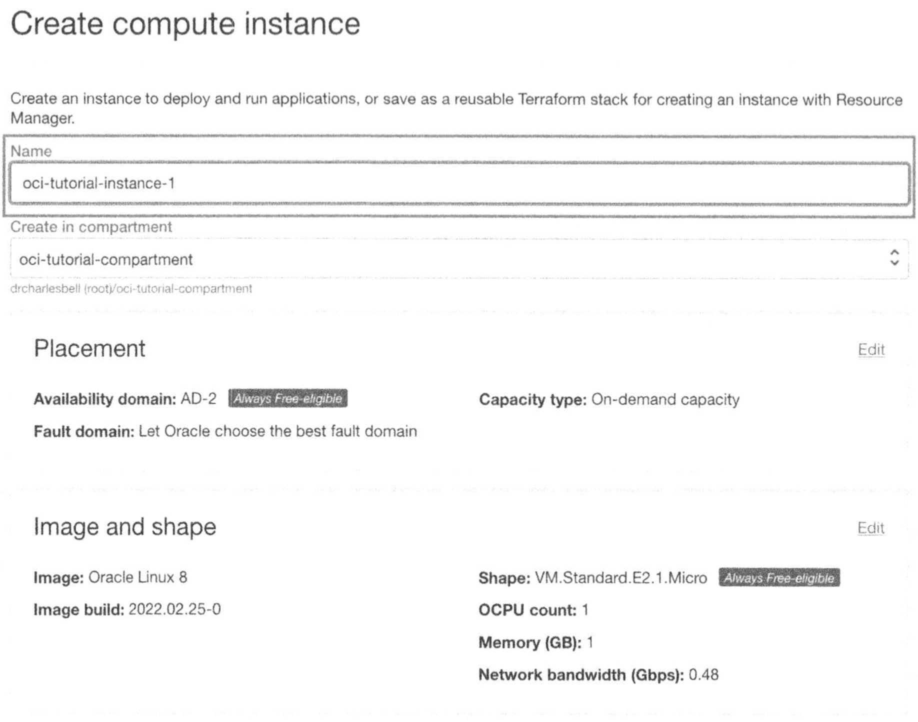

Create compute instance

Create an instance to deploy and run applications, or save as a reusable Terraform stack for creating an instance with Resource Manager.

Name

oci-tutorial-instance-1

Create in compartment

oci-tutorial-compartment

drcharlesbell (root)/oci-tutorial-compartment

Placement   Edit

Availability domain: AD-2   `Always Free-eligible`   **Capacity type:** On-demand capacity

Fault domain: Let Oracle choose the best fault domain

Image and shape   Edit

Image: Oracle Linux 8   **Shape:** VM.Standard.E2.1.Micro   `Always Free-eligible`

Image build: 2022.02.25-0   **OCPU count:** 1

                                                   Memory (GB): 1

                                                   Network bandwidth (Gbps): 0.48

Figure 2-30. *Create Compute Instance (Part 1)*

The next portion is the *Networking* and *Add SSH Keys* sections. Here, we see OCI has once again chosen the VCN resource we created (it is the only one in the compartment). If you are curious about what networking options are available, you can click the *Edit* button. However, for the tutorial, the defaults are acceptable.

The *Add SSH Keys* section is important because OCI will generate an SSH key pair for you. You will need to use these keys in order to be able to login to the compute instance.

To download the private key, click the *Save Private Key* button to save the private key to your PC as shown in Figure 2-31.

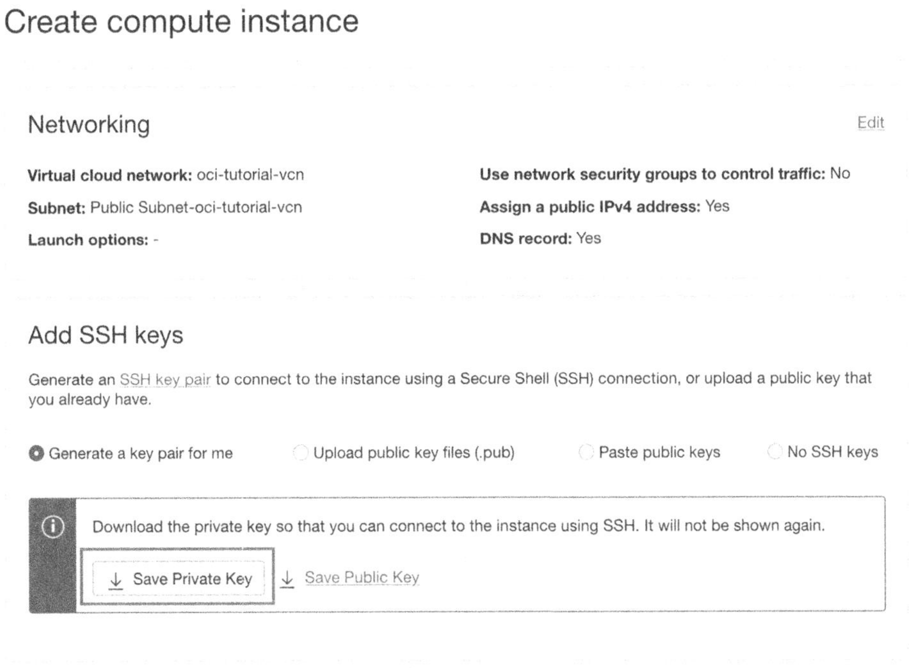

Create compute instance

Networking

Edit

Virtual cloud network: oci-tutorial-vcn

Subnet: Public Subnet-oci-tutorial-vcn

Launch options: -

Use network security groups to control traffic: No

Assign a public IPv4 address: Yes

DNS record: Yes

Add SSH keys

Generate an SSH key pair to connect to the instance using a Secure Shell (SSH) connection, or upload a public key that you already have.

- ● Generate a key pair for me
- ○ Upload public key files (.pub)
- ○ Paste public keys
- ○ No SSH keys

ⓘ Download the private key so that you can connect to the instance using SSH. It will not be shown again.

↓ Save Private Key   ↓ Save Public Key

Figure 2-31. *Create Compute Instance (Part 2)*

You will need to place it in your SSH key directory (folder). For example, on macOS or Linux, you can save the files in `~/.ssh`. However, you can place the file anywhere you want so long as the permissions are set correctly as demonstrated below.

```
% mkdir ~/.ssh
% mv ~/Downloads/ssh-key-2022-03-13.key ~/.ssh/.
% chmod 400 ~/.ssh/ssh-key-2022-03-13.key
```

The next portion defines the *Boot volume* parameters including setting a custom size and specifying encryption. We will use the default, but you can explore the other options with the links provided. When you are ready, click the *Create* button as shown in Figure 2-32.

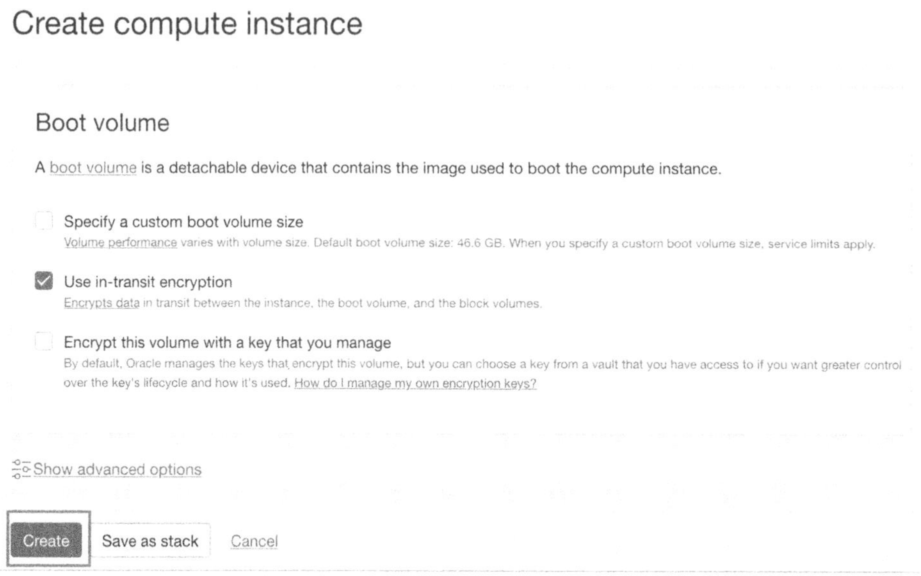

Create compute instance

Boot volume

A boot volume is a detachable device that contains the image used to boot the compute instance.

☐ Specify a custom boot volume size
Volume performance varies with volume size. Default boot volume size: 46.6 GB. When you specify a custom boot volume size, service limits apply.

☑ Use in-transit encryption
Encrypts data in transit between the instance, the boot volume, and the block volumes.

☐ Encrypt this volume with a key that you manage
By default, Oracle manages the keys that encrypt this volume, but you can choose a key from a vault that you have access to if you want greater control over the key's lifecycle and how it's used. How do I manage my own encryption keys?

Show advanced options

[Create] Save as stack Cancel

Figure 2-32. *Create Compute Instance (Part 3)*

Now the compute instance will be provisioned. The detail page for the compute instance will be opened and the status will be shown as PROVISIONING with an orange background. This can take a while so you may not see any changes to the status right away. When the compute instance is provisioned and started, the status will change to RUNNING with a green background as shown in Figure 2-33. Take a moment and scan through the data presented. You will see a number of important values including the *Public IP address* and the OCID. We will use the *Public IP address* to login to the compute instance via a secure shell host (SSH) session.

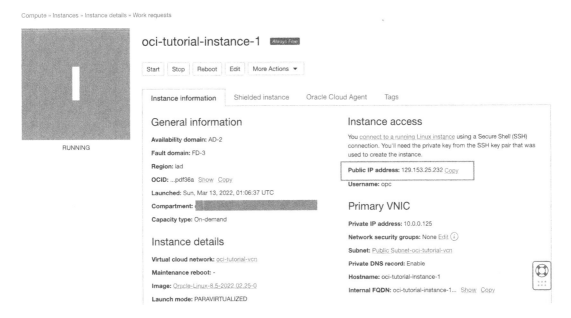

Figure 2-33. *Compute Instance Details Page*

If you do not have an SSH client installed on your PC, you will need to do so before connecting to your compute instance. An encrypted SSH session is required. An SSH client is installed by default for macOS and most Linux distributions. See your platform documentation for how to install an SSH client.

Sadly, Windows does not come with an SSH client. Fortunately, there are several varieties available as third-party applications. One of the popular options is called PuTTY, which is actually a general terminal session application. The SSH feature in PuTTY is very easy to use. What I like most about PuTTY is it is open source software and therefore free to download and use.

You can download PuTTY from `www.putty.org`. The download is not an installation package (`.msi`), rather, it is simply the PuTTY executable (`putty.exe`). Simply download the file and place it in a folder that is in your path environment variable. You can also put it in your documents folder and simply execute it from there or by referencing the folder.

Returning to the compute instance details page, if you scroll down, you will see the Work requests section, which shows the workflows that have been or are executing on the compute instance. The workflow that we want to ensure is complete is the Create instance workflow, which should have a state of Succeeded as shown in Figure 2-34.

Work requests

A work request is an activity log that tracks each step in an asynchronous operation. Use work requests to monitor the progress of long-running operations.

Operation	State	% Complete	Accepted	Started	Finished
Create instance	● Succeeded	100	Sun, Mar 13, 2022, 01:06:37 UTC	Sun, Mar 13, 2022, 01:06:38 UTC	Sun, Mar 13, 2022, 01:0

Showing 1 Item ‹ 1 of 1 ›

Figure 2-34. *Compute Instance Work Requests List*

Once you see the workflow has succeeded, we're ready to connect to the instance with a terminal. To do so, simply use the following command. Here we see we are using the `ssh` utility and the `-i` parameter with a path to the private SSH key we downloaded previously. Next, we supply the username and the public IP address we found on the compute instance details page. The default username is `opc`:

```
ssh -i <path_to_private_ssk_key> opc@<PublicIPAddress>
```

Let's see the command in action. We will use the key we downloaded earlier that we copied to the `.ssh` folder of our user account and the public IP address from Figure 2-33 (`129.153.25.232`). Listing 2-1 shows the command in action. You may be asked to add the IP address to your hosts file as shown. Once the connection succeeds, we execute a simple `ls -lsa` to show the contents of the user directory on the compute instance.

Listing 2-1. Connecting to the Compute Instance with SSH

```
% ssh -i ~/.ssh/ssh-key-2022-03-13.key opc@129.153.25.232
The authenticity of host '129.153.25.232 (129.153.25.232)' can't be
established.
...
Are you sure you want to continue connecting (yes/no/[fingerprint])? yes
Warning: Permanently added '129.153.25.232' (ED25519) to the list of
known hosts.
Activate the web console with: systemctl enable --now cockpit.socket

[opc@oci-tutorial-instance-1 ~]$ ls -lsa
total 12
0 drwx------. 3 opc  opc   74 Mar 13 01:08 .
0 drwxr-xr-x. 3 root root  17 Mar 13 01:08 ..
```

```
4 -rw-r--r--. 1 opc  opc    18 Oct 10 01:59 .bash_logout
4 -rw-r--r--. 1 opc  opc   141 Oct 10 01:59 .bash_profile
4 -rw-r--r--. 1 opc  opc   376 Oct 10 01:59 .bashrc
0 drwx------. 2 opc  opc    29 Mar 13 01:08 .ssh
[opc@oci-tutorial-instance-1 ~]$ exit
```

To close the connection, simply use the exit command. Once that is done, we've demonstrated we can successfully connect to and use the compute instance. Now, let's add block storage to our compute instance.

Add Block Storage to the Compute Instance

Since the default boot volume is 50 GB, it is likely too small for storing any large applications or even data. After all, the boot volume is intended to be used to store system applications and the like rather than user applications. Fortunately, we can add a block volume easily to the compute instance for our application and data purposes.

The process to add a block volume is a bit more complicated than a simple click-through interface like we've seen thus far. Briefly, we will need to perform the following operations:

- Create a block volume
- Attach the block volume to the compute instance
- Connect the block volume on the compute instance
- Format and mount the block volume on the compute instance

To create a block volume, open the cloud console menu and select *Storage* then *Block Volumes* as shown in Figure 2-35. However, this time, right-click on the *Block Volumes* label and open the selection in a new tab. We will need to see both the compute instance detail and block volume pages.

ORACLE Cloud
Search for resources, services, and
Search
Home
Compute
Storage
Networking
Storage
Block Storage
Block Volumes
Block Volume Backups
Block Volume Replicas
Volume Groups

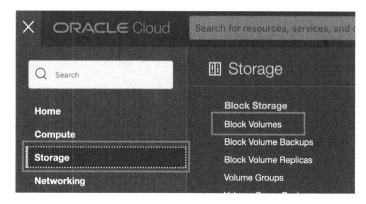

***Figure 2-35.** Block Volumes (Main Menu)*

On the Block Volumes page, you will need to select the compartment using the filter control on the left as shown in Figure 2-36. Select the `oci-tutorial-compartment` that we created earlier.

List Scope
Compartment
oci-tutorial-compartment
drcharlesbell (root)/oci-tutorial-compartment

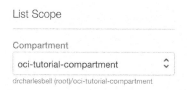

***Figure 2-36.** Set List Scope (Block Volumes Page)*

Next, click the *Create Block Volume* button in the instances list as shown in Figure 2-37. This will launch the create instance dialog.

Block Volumes in oci-tutorial-compartment Compartment
Block volumes provide high-performance network storage to support a broad range of I/O intensive workloads. Learn more
Create Block Volume
Name
State
Size
Target Volume Performance
Auto-tune
Auto-tuned Performance
Cross Region Replication
Availability Domain
Backup Policy
Created
No items
Showing 0 Items
1 of 1

***Figure 2-37.** Block Volumes List (oci-tutorial-compartment)*

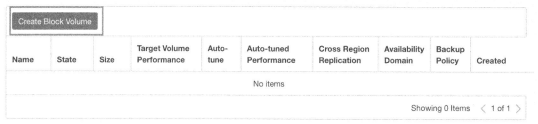

When you click the *Create Block Volume* button, you will see the create block volume dialog. At the top of the form is an entry for the block volume name. If you are following along, use `oci-tutorial-block-volume-1` as the name. You should also see the `oci-tutorial-compartment` selected for the compartment.

Below that is an area to select the availability domain. This is where things can go wrong. If you select an availability domain different from your compute instance, you will not be able to attach the block volume to your compute instance.

Go back to the compute instance detail page and look for the availability domain located beneath the *General Information* label. Be sure to note which availability domain is used and select the same availability domain in the create block volume dialog. In this tutorial, we used the `AD-2` availability domain (it may be spelled differently depending on what region you are in).

You can leave the size of the block volume the default (50 GB).

When you are ready, click the *Create Block Volume* button as shown in Figure 2-38.

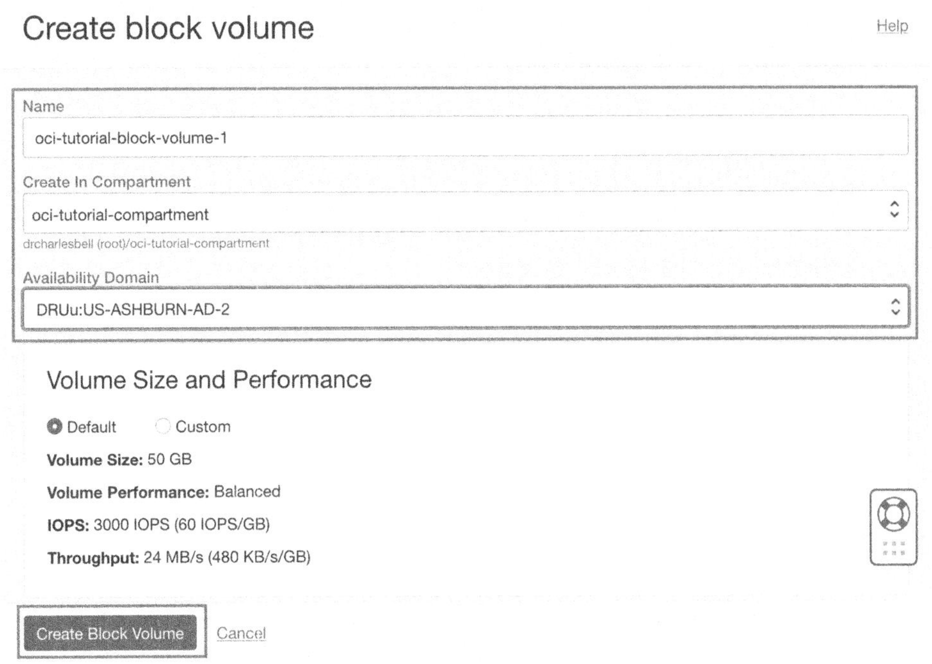

Create block volume   Help

Name

oci-tutorial-block-volume-1

Create In Compartment

oci-tutorial-compartment

drcharlesbell (root)/oci-tutorial-compartment

Availability Domain

DRUu:US-ASHBURN-AD-2

Volume Size and Performance

● Default   ○ Custom

Volume Size: 50 GB

Volume Performance: Balanced

IOPS: 3000 IOPS (60 IOPS/GB)

Throughput: 24 MB/s (480 KB/s/GB)

Create Block Volume   Cancel

Figure 2-38. *Create Block Volume Dialog*

Like the compute instance, you will be directed to the block volume detail page where you can watch the block volume being provisioned. When it is ready, the state will change to `AVAILABLE` with a green background as shown in Figure 2-39.

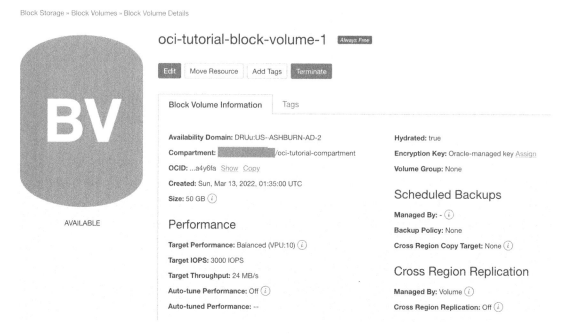

Block Storage » Block Volumes » Block Volume Details

Figure 2-39. *Block Volume Details Page*

Now, navigate back to your compute instance dialog. If you did not open the compute instance in a separate tab, use the cloud console menu to select *Compute | Instances* and click on the instance we created (`oci-tutorial-instance-1`) to see its detail page. Notice it is marked as *Always Free*.

To attach the block volume to the compute instance, look for the *Attached block volumes* item in the *Resources* menu item on the left side of the compute instance details page and click it as shown in Figure 2-40.

Figure 2-40. *Resources Menu (Compute Instance Detail)*

This will show the Attached Block Volumes list where we will start the attachment process. However, there is one piece of information we need. We will need the OCID for the block volume we just created. This is needed because the attach block volume dialog may not populate the list of block volumes available immediately (it should be given time). That is, you can either select a block volume from a list or specify the OCID. We will use the select OCI option in this example.

To locate the block volume OCID, open the block volumes detail page (tab) and locate the OCID on the *Block Volume Information* tab as shown in Figure 2-41. You can copy the OCID from the block volume detail page and click the *Copy* link next to the OCID.

Figure 2-41. *Locating the OCID on the Block Volume Details Page*

Now we can return to the compute instance detail page and locate the *Attach block volume* button in the *Attached block volumes* list as shown in Figure 2-42. Click the button once you have copied the OCID of the block volume.

Figure 2-42. *Attached Block Volumes List (Compute Instance Detail Page)*

Select *Enter volume OCID* and paste the OCID into the box. For the *Device path*, choose `/dev/oracleoci/oraclevdb` as shown in Figure 2-43. Leave the other sections with their default values. When ready, click the *Attach* button.

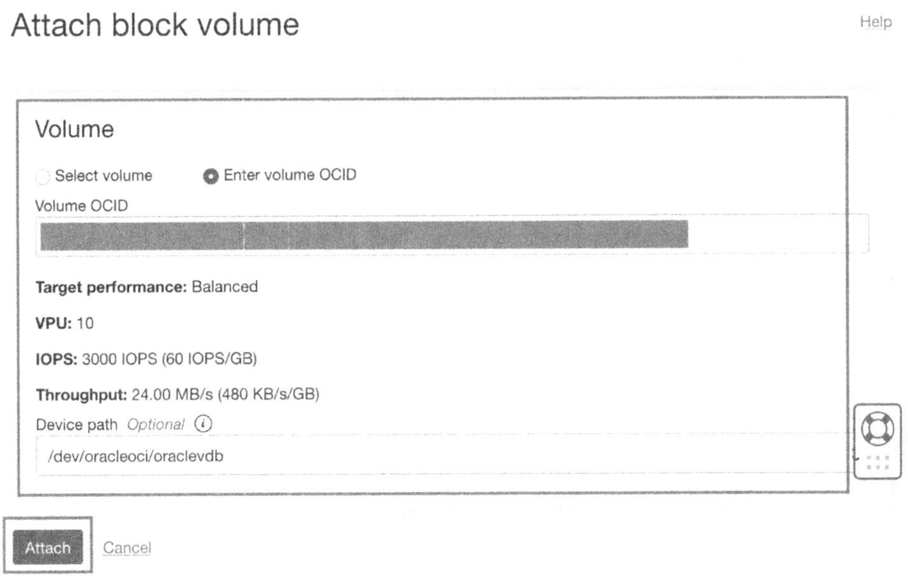

Attach block volume   Help

> **Volume**
>
> ○ Select volume   ● Enter volume OCID
> Volume OCID
>
> ▓▓
>
> **Target performance:** Balanced
>
> **VPU:** 10
>
> **IOPS:** 3000 IOPS (60 IOPS/GB)
>
> **Throughput:** 24.00 MB/s (480 KB/s/GB)
>
> Device path *Optional* ⓘ
>
> /dev/oracleoci/oraclevdb

[Attach] Cancel

Figure 2-43. *Attach Block Volume Dialog*

This process will create another OCI resource called a block volume attachment. You will not see this resource, but it is object used by OCI to associate a block volume with a compute instance. It is important to understand the attachment is like any other resource in OCI; it is a virtual object and in this case a device used to accomplish a goal of associating a block volume with a compute instance.

Once you click the *Attach* button, you may see a dialog reminding you to run a set of iSCSI commands to connect the block volume to the operating system on the compute instance. We will see how to do this once the attachment process completes.

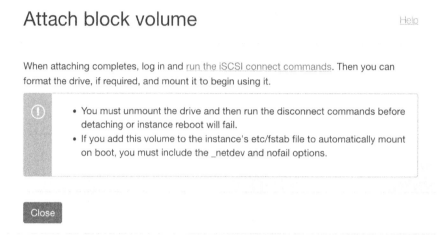

Attach block volume   Help

When attaching completes, log in and run the iSCSI connect commands. Then you can
format the drive, if required, and mount it to begin using it.

> ⊙ • You must unmount the drive and then run the disconnect commands before
>   detaching or instance reboot will fail.
>   • If you add this volume to the instance's etc/fstab file to automatically mount
>   on boot, you must include the _netdev and nofail options.

Close

Figure 2-44. *Run iSCSI Commands Reminder*

Once the attachment process is complete, the block volume will appear in the
Attached block volumes list.

Recall, we were told to run some iSCSI commands on the compute instance. We
can get the commands we need to run from the *Attached block volumes* by clicking on
the special menu (indicate with three vertical dots) and choosing *iSCSI commands &
information* as shown in Figure 2-45

Figure 2-45. *Getting the iSCSI Information (Compute Instance Details)*

This will open a new dialog that shows the commands you need to run as shown in
Figure 2-46.

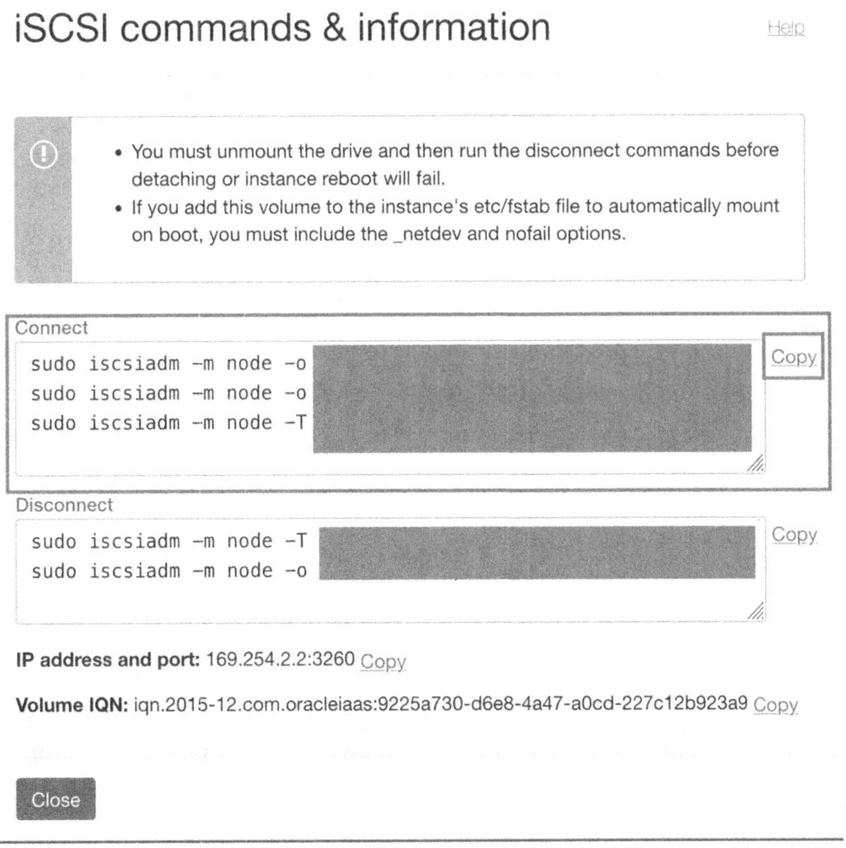

iSCSI commands & information

Help

- You must unmount the drive and then run the disconnect commands before detaching or instance reboot will fail.
- If you add this volume to the instance's etc/fstab file to automatically mount on boot, you must include the _netdev and nofail options.

Connect

```
sudo iscsiadm -m node -o
sudo iscsiadm -m node -o
sudo iscsiadm -m node -T
```

Copy

Disconnect

```
sudo iscsiadm -m node -T
sudo iscsiadm -m node -o
```

Copy

IP address and port: 169.254.2.2:3260 Copy

Volume IQN: iqn.2015-12.com.oracleiaas:9225a730-d6e8-4a47-a0cd-227c12b923a9 Copy

Close

Figure 2-46. *iSCSI Information Dialog*

You will find a section for *Connect* and another for *Disconnect* that have the exact commands you need for connecting and disconnecting the block volume on the compute instance. We won't cover the parameters of the commands in this chapter. Rather, we will simply copy the three commands in the *Connect* section and run them on the compute instance.

If you closed your SSH connection from the previous section, open a new one and paste the commands into the terminal as shown below:

```
$ sudo iscsiadm -m node -o new -T iqn.2015-12.com.oracleiaas:UUID -p
169.254.2.2:3260
New iSCSI node [tcp:[hw=,ip=,net_if=,iscsi_if=default] 169.254.2.2,3260,-1
iqn.2015-12.com.oracleiaas:UUID] added
```

```
$ sudo iscsiadm -m node -o update -T iqn.2015-12.com.oracleiaas:UUID -n
node.startup -v automatic
$ sudo iscsiadm -m node -T iqn.2015-12.com.oracleiaas:UUID -p
169.254.2.2:3260 -l
Logging in to [iface: default, target: iqn.2015-12.com.oracleiaas:UUID,
portal: 169.254.2.2,3260]
Login to [iface: default, target: iqn.2015-12.com.oracleiaas:UUID, portal:
169.254.2.2,3260] successful.
```

Next, we need to know the device associated with the attached block volume. We can find that by issuing the following command in the SSH terminal session:

```
$ ls -lsa /dev/oracleoci
total 0
0 drwxr-xr-x.  2 root root  140 Mar 13 02:27 .
0 drwxr-xr-x. 21 root root 3320 Mar 13 02:27 ..
0 lrwxrwxrwx.  1 root root    6 Mar 13 02:25 oraclevda -> ../sda
0 lrwxrwxrwx.  1 root root    7 Mar 13 02:25 oraclevda1 -> ../sda1
0 lrwxrwxrwx.  1 root root    7 Mar 13 02:25 oraclevda2 -> ../sda2
0 lrwxrwxrwx.  1 root root    7 Mar 13 02:25 oraclevda3 -> ../sda3
0 lrwxrwxrwx.  1 root root    6 Mar 13 02:27 oraclevdb -> ../sdb
```

Note   The example commands in this section are only one of several ways to format and mount the drive. Use whatever mechanism you'd like that works with Oracle Linux to complete the drive mapping.

Here we see the device used is /dev/sdb. We can now use fdisk to create a partition as shown below. Be sure to use sudo as shown. The commands we will use are shown in bold.

```
$ sudo fdisk /dev/sdb
Command (m for help): n
Partition type
   p   primary (0 primary, 0 extended, 4 free)
   e   extended (container for logical partitions)
Select (default p): p
```

```
Using default response p.
Partition number (1-4, default 1):
First sector (2048-104857599, default 2048):
Last sector, +sectors or +size{K,M,G,T,P} (2048-104857599, default
104857599):

Created a new partition 1 of type 'Linux' and of size 50 GiB.
Command (m for help): w
The partition table has been altered.
Calling ioctl() to re-read partition table.
Syncing disks.
```

Next, we format the drive with the xfs file system as shown below:

```
$ sudo mkfs.xfs /dev/sdb -f
meta-data=/dev/sdb                  isize=512    agcount=4,
                                                 agsize=3276800 blks
         =                          sectsz=4096  attr=2, projid32bit=1
         =                          crc=1        finobt=1, sparse=1, rmapbt=0
         =                          reflink=1
data     =                          bsize=4096   blocks=13107200, imaxpct=25
         =                          sunit=0      swidth=0 blks
naming   =version 2                 bsize=4096   ascii-ci=0, ftype=1
log      =internal log              bsize=4096   blocks=6400, version=2
         =                          sectsz=4096  sunit=1 blks, lazy-count=1
realtime =none                      extsz=4096   blocks=0, rtextents=0
```

Finally, we can create a mount point and mount the drive as shown below:

```
$ sudo mkdir /mnt/data
$ sudo mount /dev/sdb /mnt/data
$ ls -lsa /mnt/data
total 0
0 drwxr-xr-x. 2 root root  6 Mar 13 02:43 .
0 drwxr-xr-x. 3 root root 18 Mar 13 02:35 ..
```

And now we can use the drive to store applications and data.

PERSISTENT MOUNT

If you plan to use the compute instance with an attached block volume for more than experimentation or more than a single session, you will want to make the mapping permanent. To do so, you will need to edit the /etc/fstab file. To do so, you will need the UUID for the block volume. You can find the UUID using the sudo blkid command. Once you have the UUID, add the following line to the /etc/fstab file then run sudo mount -a to check the mapping:

UUID=<UUID_FOUND> /mnt/data xfs defaults,_netdev,nofail 0 2

Once that is done, the drive will be mapped on boot.

That's it! Our tutorial is complete. If you are following along, feel free to explore the compute instance and block volume or create additional compute instances or block volumes as additional practice.

The next step in the tutorial once you are done experimenting is to terminate the resources we don't want to persist.

Terminate the Resources

This step is optional, but if you are experimenting with OCI resources, it is something you will not want to forget to do. Remember, any resources you create that aren't part of the "always free" category/promotion will incur charges on your account. You don't want to pay for things if you aren't going to use them.

This is one of the first lessons most people will learn about the cloud; unlike on-prem hardware that, when powered off, don't cost you anything beyond the original investment (however complex that may be), most cloud resources are always billable. Some notable exceptions are resources that can be stopped. For example, the cost of a stopped compute instance is different from one that is active (running). Conversely, block storage incurs costs whether you are using it or not.

We can minimize our costs by simply terminating (deleting) the resources we no longer need. In this case, we will take a more extreme step and terminate all of the resources we created in the tutorial that incurs costs or simply aren't needed. In this tutorial, we only need to terminate the compute instance and block volume. Fortunately, terminating these high-level resources will also terminate the ancillary resources such as the block volume attachment:

> There are several ways to terminate resources. The easiest to use is navigating directly to the resource details page and filter the view to show those you want to terminate (delete) and then use the *Terminate* button or *Other Actions | Terminate* menu.
>
> Let's start with the compute instance. We'll start from the main cloud console page. From there, open the main menu and select *Compute* then *Instances*. In the Compute Instances list, we can click on the name of the compute instance (shown as a hyperlink) to open the compute instance details page. From there, we click the *Other actions* menu near the top and then select *Terminate* as shown in Figure 2-47.

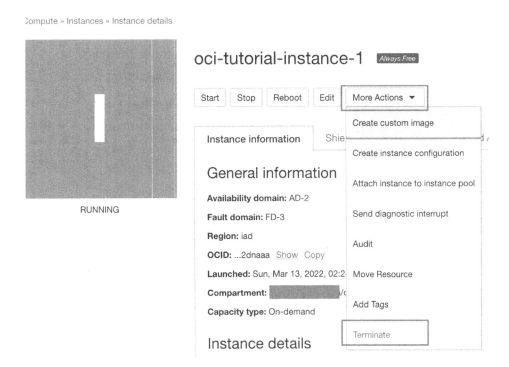

Figure 2-47. *Terminate Compute Instance (Compute Instance Details Page)*

When you click the button, you will see a popup message asking if you also want to delete the boot volume permanently. In this case, we do, and we should tick the *Permanently delete the attached boot volume* tick box as shown in Figure 2-48. When ready, click the *Terminate instance* button.

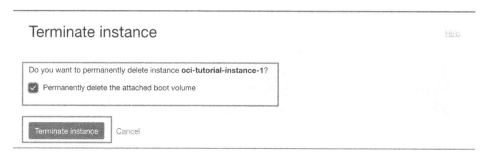

Figure 2-48. *Permanently Deleting the Attached Boot Volume*

Notice the use of the term, attached, in the message. As you may surmise, this means a boot volume is attached like a block volume. While they are connected in the same manner, there is a boot volume attachment resource object behind the scenes.

It is also interesting to note that this means it is possible to use a single boot volume from one compute instance to another. For example, if you need a larger shape, you can terminate the one compute instance saving the boot volume for use in another, larger shape-based compute instance. Cool.

Once you click the Terminate instance button, the status will change to TERMINATING and the icon will change to orange. Once it is terminated, the status will change to TERMINATED and the icon grey. Be sure to wait until this happens before proceeding because the compute instance needs to be in a terminated state for before we can terminate the block volume.

Once the compute instance has terminated, you can navigate to the block volume details page by clicking on the cloud console menu and select *Storage* then *Block Volumes*. You can then click on the block volume name (shown as a hyperlink) to open the block volumes detail page. From there, we can click on the Terminate button to terminate the block volume as shown in Figure 2-49.

Figure 2-49. *Terminate Block Volume (Block Volume Details Page)*

You will be prompted to confirm the termination. Click the Terminate button again to terminate the block volume as shown in Figure 2-50.

Figure 2-50. *Terminate Block Volume Dialog*

Like the compute instance, the state will change to TERMINATING and the icon will change to orange. Once it is terminated, the status will change to TERMINATED and the icon grey. You can now close the tabs in your web browser.

That's it for our tutorial! We've seen how easy it is to get started creating OCI resources including compartments, VCNs, compute instances, and block storage devices.

Be sure to logout of your account if you are following along with the tutorial. You can do so by clicking on the account icon in the top-right of the cloud console and select *Sign Out* as shown in Figure 2-51.

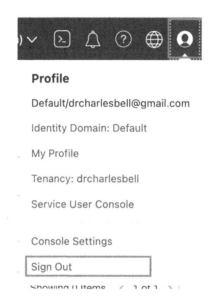

Figure 2-51. *Sign Out of the Cloud Console*

Summary

The Oracle Cloud Infrastructure is a vast set of cloud infrastructure that provides dozens of services for you to build your own cloud solutions. We have the basic, core services such as networking and compute services for creating servers, advanced managed services such as database systems, and even platform-level services such as container orchestration. Even though we've learned more about these concepts and features, we are only scratching the surface of the capabilities provided by OCI.

We have also learned how virtualization and automation are the key tools used to make OCI easy for you to create (provision), manage, and destroy resources. This simple set of use cases can be accomplished in minutes with virtual computing that would take hours or days to do with physical hardware.

In this chapter, we learned more about OCI including terminology used, the user interfaces available for working with OCI, as well as explanations of the core services in OCI. Finally, we saw a short tutorial on how to set up our OCI trial account and create our very first OCI resources.

In the next chapter, we will take a few moments and learn more about MySQL including a short tutorial on how to get started using MySQL. As you will see, it is a robust, full-featured database management system that is easy to use.

CHAPTER 3

A Brief Tutorial of MySQL

Perhaps you've never used a database system before or maybe you've used one as a user but have never had any need to set up one from scratch. Or perhaps you've decided to discover what all the fuss is about database systems in general.

In this chapter, I present a short introduction to MySQL in the general SQL interface sense (traditional MySQL). Not only will you see how MySQL 8 is used to create and use databases, but you will also be introduced to some of the basics of the SQL interface, which is necessary and indeed required to fully integrate a MySQL server in your infrastructure.

We will also take a brief look at the MySQL Shell and how you can use that to connect to and work with MySQL via both a SQL and NoSQL interface for both applications and interactive sessions.

We will conclude the chapter with a brief look at how to connect your applications to MySQL servers to work with the databases you create.

Let's begin with a brief foray into what MySQL is and what it can do for us. We will start with installing MySQL on our local PC for experimentation.

Note While this book presents the MySQL Database Service in the Oracle Cloud Infrastructure, much of the information in this chapter can be used with any MySQL server.

Getting Started

MySQL is the world's most popular open source database system for many excellent reasons. First, it is open source, which means anyone can use it for a wide variety of tasks for free. Best of all, MySQL is included in many platform repositories, making it easy to get and install. If your platform doesn't include MySQL in the repository (such as aptitude), you can download it from the MySQL website (`http://dev.mysql.com`).

© Charles Bell 2023
C. Bell, *MySQL Database Service Revealed*, https://doi.org/10.1007/978-1-4842-8945-7_3

Oracle Corporation owns MySQL. Oracle obtained MySQL through an acquisition of Sun Microsystems, which acquired MySQL from its original owners, MySQL AB. Despite fears to the contrary, Oracle has shown excellent stewardship of MySQL by continuing to invest in the evolution and development of new features as well as faithfully maintaining its open source heritage. Although Oracle also offers commercial licenses of MySQL – just as its prior owners did in the past – MySQL is still open source and available to everyone.

IS OPEN SOURCE REALLY FREE?

Open source software grew from a conscious resistance to the corporate-property mindset. Richard Stallman is credited as the father of the free software movement who pioneered a licensing mechanism to help protect ownership of software and yet make the use of the software and so some degree its revision free to all. The goal was to reestablish a cooperating community of developers cooperating with a single imperative – to guarantee freedom rather than restrict it.

This ultimately led to the invention of some cleverly worded (read legally binding) licensing agreements that permit the code to be copied and modified without restriction, stating that derivative works (the modified copies) must be distributed under the same license as the original version without any additional restrictions. One such license (created by Stallman) is called the GNU Public License (GPL). This is the license that is used by Oracle to license MySQL and as such it is indeed free for anyone to use.

However, GPL and similar licenses are intended to guarantee freedom to use, modify, and distribute; most never intended "free" to mean "no cost" or "free to a good home." To counter this misconception, the Open Source Initiative (OSI) formed and later adopted and promoted the phrase open source to describe the freedoms guaranteed by the GPL license. For more information about open source software and the GPL, visit `www.opensource.org`.

MySQL runs as a background process (or as a foreground process if you launch it from the command line) on your system. Like most database systems, MySQL supports Structured Query Language (SQL). You can use SQL to create databases and objects (using data definition language [DDL]), write or change data (using data manipulation language [DML]), and execute various commands for managing the server.

There are two mechanisms for connecting to MySQL. You can use an application like the MySQL Shell or MySQL Workbench, or you can use the older MySQL client. Let's look at both options.

Connecting with MySQL Shell

The MySQL Shell is a new and exciting addition to the MySQL portfolio. The MySQL Shell represents the first modern and advanced client for connecting to and interacting with MySQL. The shell can be used as a scripting environment for developing new tools and applications for working with data. While it does support an SQL mode, its main purpose is to permit access to data with the JavaScript and Python languages. That's right, you can write JavaScript and Python scripts and execute them within the shell interactively or as a batch. Cool!

Note   I use the term "shell" to refer to features or objects supported by the MySQL Shell. I use "MySQL Shell" to refer to the product itself.

The MySQL Shell is designed to use the new X Protocol for communicating with the server via the X Plugin. However, the shell can also connect to the server using the older protocol albeit with limited features in the scripting modes. What this means is, the shell allows you to work with both relational (SQL), JSON documents (NoSQL), or both.

The NoSQL interface is based on an application programming interface called the X DevAPI (https://dev.mysql.com/doc/x-devapi-userguide/en/). Administrative operations are supported by another API called the AdminAPI. See the online documentation for more information about these APIs if you plan to use the shell for development work (https://dev.mysql.com/doc/mysql-shell/8.0/en/).

Oracle provides the MySQL Shell as a free download from the MySQL download website (https://dev.mysql.com/downloads/shell/). You can download the specific release for your platform (e.g., Windows, macOS, Linux) and install it using the normal mechanisms for your platform. Once installed, you can launch it via the menu system for your platform or by entering mysqlsh on a command line. Figure 3-1 shows an example of launching MySQL Shell. Notice the nifty prompt that displays the MySQL logo, connection information, and mode. Nice!

```
MySQL Shell 8.0.28

Copyright (c) 2016, 2022, Oracle and/or its affiliates.
Oracle is a registered trademark of Oracle Corporation and/or its affiliates.
Other names may be trademarks of their respective owners.

Type '\help' or '\?' for help; '\quit' to exit.
 MySQL  Py >
```

Figure 3-1. *The MySQL Shell*

The following sections present the major features of the shell at a high level. We will not explore every detail of every feature or option, rather, this section provides a broad overview so that you can get started quickly and, more importantly, learn enough about the shell so that you can follow along with the examples in this book.

For more information about the MySQL Shell, see the section entitled, "MySQL Shell User Guide" in the online MySQL reference manual.

Features

The MySQL Shell has many features including support for traditional SQL command processing, script prototyping, and even support for customizing the shell. The following lists some of the major features of the shell. Most of the features can be controlled via command line options or with special shell commands. We take a deeper look at some of the more critical features in later sections:

- *Logging*: You can create a log of your session for later analysis or to keep a record of messages. You can set the level of detail with the --log-level option ranging from 1 (nothing logged) to 8 (max debug).

- *Output Formats*: The shell supports three format options; table (--table), which is the traditional grid format you're used to from the old client, tabbed, which presents information using tabs for spacing and is used for batch execution, and JSON (--json), which formats the JSON documents in an easier to read manner. These are command-line options you specify when launching the shell.

- *Interactive Code Execution*: The default mode for using the shell is an interactive mode, which works like a traditional client where you enter a command and get a response.

- *Batch Code Execution*: If you want to run your script without the interactive session, you can use the shell to run the script in batch mode. However, the output is limited to non-formatted output (but can be overridden with the `--interactive` option).

- *Scripting Languages*: The shell supports both JavaScript and Python although you can use only one at a time.

- *Sessions*: Sessions are essentially connections to servers. The shell allows you to store and remove sessions. We will see more about sessions in a later section.

- *Startup Scripts*: You can define a script to execute when the shell starts. You can write the script in either JavaScript or Python.

- *Command History and Command Completion*: The shell saves the commands you enter allowing you to recalling them using the up and down arrow keys. The shell also provides code completion for known keywords, API functions, and SQL keywords.

- *Global Variables*: The shell provides a few global variables you can access when in interactive mode. These include the following:

  - `session`: global session object if established

  - `db`: schema if established via a connection

  - `dba`: the AdminAPI object for working with the InnoDB Cluster

  - `shell`: general purpose functions for using the shell

  - `util`: utility functions for working with servers

- *Customize the Prompt*: You can also change the default prompt by updating a configuration file named `~/.mysqlsh/prompt.json` using a special format or by defining an environment variable named `MYSQLSH_PROMPT_THEME`. See the MySQL Shell Reference manual for more details about changing the prompt.

- *Auto Completion*: Starting in 8.0.4, the shell permits users to press the *TAB* key to auto-complete keywords in SQL mode and the major classes and methods in JavaScript and Python modes.

- *Extensions*: You can define extensions in the form of reports and extension objects. Reports and extension objects can be created using JavaScript or Python.

- *Utilities*: The shell also provides several utilities that you may find helpful including the following. You access them via an API call as demonstrated.

  - *Upgrade Checker*: Used to verify whether MySQL server instances are ready for upgrade (e.g., `util.checkForServerUpgrade()`).

  - *JSON Import*: Import JSON documents to a MySQL Server collection or table (e.g., `util.importJSON()`).

  - *Parallel Table Import*: Splits up a single data file and uses multiple threads to load the chunks into a MySQL table.

- *Shell Commands*: Like the original MySQL client, there are some special commands that control the application itself rather than interact with data. To execute a shell command, issue the command with a slash (\). For example, `\help` prints the help for all of the shell commands.

- *Options*: The shell can be launched using several startup options that control the mode, connection, behavior, and more. Common options include the mode (SQL, JavaScript, or Python) and connection parameters. For a complete list of options, execute the shell with the `--help` option with `mysqlsh -- help`.

As you can see, there is a long list of features for the MySQL Shell. See the online reference manual for a complete list of features.

Let's look at the two most important to those getting started working with MySQL: modes and how to connect.

Modes Supported

The shell supports three modes (also called language support or simply the active language); SQL, JavaScript, and Python. Recall we can initiate any one of these modes by using a shell command. You can switch modes (languages) as often as you want without disconnection each time. The following lists the three modes and how to switch to each:

- `\sql`: Switch to the SQL language

- `\js`: Switch to the JavaScript language (default mode)

- `\py`: Switch to the Python language

You can also issue these commands as startup by using `--` instead of `\` (`--sql`, `--js`, `--py`).

Making Connections

Making connections in the shell is one area that may take some getting used to doing differently than the original MySQL client (`mysql`). You can use a specially formatted URI string or connect to a server using individual options by name (like the old client). SSL connections are also supported. Connections can be made via startup options, shell commands, and in scripts. However, all connections are expected to use a password. Thus, unless you state otherwise, the shell will prompt for a password if one is not given.

Note   If you want to use a connection without a password (not recommended), you must use the `--password` option or, if using an URI, include an extra colon to take the place of the password.

Rather than discuss all the available ways to connect and all the options to do so, the following presents one example of each method of making a connection in the following sections.

Using a URI

A URI in the case of a MySQL Shell connection is a special string coded using the following format: `<dbuser>[:<dbpassword>]@host[:port][/schema/]`, where `<>` indicates string values for the various parameters. Notice the password, port, and schema are optional but the user and host are required. Schema in this case is the default schema (database) that you want to use when connecting.

Note   The default port for the X Protocol is 33060.

To connect to a server using a URI on the command line when starting the shell, specify it with the --uri option as follows:

```
$ mysqlsh --uri root:secret@localhost:33060
```

The shell assumes all connections require a password and will prompt for a password if one is not provided. Listing 3-1 shows the same connection above made without the password. Notice how the shell prompts for the password.

Listing 3-1. Connecting with a URI

```
$ mysqlsh --uri root@localhost:33060/world_x
Please provide the password for 'root@localhost:33060':
Save password for 'root@localhost:33060'? [Y]es/[N]o/Ne[v]er
(default No): Y
MySQL Shell 8.0.28

Copyright (c) 2016, 2022, Oracle and/or its affiliates.
Oracle is a registered trademark of Oracle Corporation and/or its
affiliates.
Other names may be trademarks of their respective owners.

Type '\help' or '\?' for help; '\quit' to exit.
Creating a session to 'root@localhost:33060/world_x'
Fetching schema names for autocompletion... Press ^C to stop.
Your MySQL connection id is 8 (X protocol)
Server version: 8.0.23 MySQL Community Server - GPL
Default schema `world_x` accessible through db.
 MySQL  localhost:33060+ ssl  world_x  JS >
```

Notice I also specified the default schema (world_x) with the /schema option in the URI.

Tip   The world_x database is a sample database you can download from
https://dev.mysql.com/doc/index-other.html.

Using Individual Options

You can also specify connections on the shell command line using individual options such as specifying the user, host, port, etc. See the online reference manual for a complete list of connection options (https://dev.mysql.com/doc/mysql-shell/8.0/en/mysql-shell-connections.html). Listing 3-2 shows how to connect to a MySQL server using individual options.

Listing 3-2. Connecting Using Individual Options

```
$ mysqlsh --user root --host localhost --port 33060 --schema world_x --
py --mx
MySQL Shell 8.0.28

Copyright (c) 2016, 2022, Oracle and/or its affiliates.
Oracle is a registered trademark of Oracle Corporation and/or its
affiliates.
Other names may be trademarks of their respective owners.

Type '\help' or '\?' for help; '\quit' to exit.
Creating an X protocol session to 'root@localhost:33060/world_x'
Fetching schema names for autocompletion... Press ^C to stop.
Your MySQL connection id is 9 (X protocol)
Server version: 8.0.23 MySQL Community Server - GPL
Default schema `world_x` accessible through db.
 MySQL  localhost:33060+ ssl  world_x  Py >
```

Notice I changed the mode (language) to Python with the --py option.

Using SSL Connections

You can also create SSL connections for secure connections to your servers. To use SSL, you must configure your server to use SSL. To use SSL on the same machine where MySQL is running, you can use the --ssl-mode=REQUIRED option. You can also specify the SSL options as shown in the online reference manual (https://dev.mysql.com/doc/mysql-shell/8.0/en/mysql-shell-connections.html). You can specify them on the command line using the command line options or as an extension to the \connect shell command. The following shows how to connect to a server using SSL and command line options.

```
$ mysqlsh -uroot -h127.0.0.1 --port=33060 --ssl-mode=REQUIRED
```

> **Tip** See the section "Using Encrypted Connections" in the MySQL Shell reference manual for more details about encrypted connections.

The MySQL Shell is a huge leap forward in technology for MySQL clients. Not only is it designed to work with SQL in MySQL in a smarter way, it is also designed to enable prototyping of JavaScript and Python. You can work with any language you want and switch between them easily without having to restart the application or drop the connection. How cool is that?

Now, let's look at the older application for connecting to MySQL servers.

Connecting with the MySQL Client

While the MySQL Shell has been around for a few years and has many features including scripting and development capabilities, there is another client that has been around in MySQL for decades. It is an application named mysql, which enables you to connect to and run SQL commands on the server. Interestingly, this MySQL client was originally named the MySQL monitor but has long since been called simply the "MySQL client," terminal monitor, or even the MySQL command window.

You can only get the mysql client if you install the MySQL server (on Windows or macOS) or one of the package components. For example, on Linux, you can install only the client package, which will give you the client as well. We will save installation of the client to a later section where we install MySQL on our local PC.

NEW DEFAULT AUTHENTICATION

Prior to MySQL version 8.0.4, the default authentication mechanism used an authentication plugin called the mysql_native_password plugin, which used the SHA1 algorithm. This mechanism was fast and did not require an encrypted connection. However, since NIST has suggested organization stop using the SHA1 algorithm, Oracle has changed the default authentication plugin in MySQL version 8.0.4 to the cachin_sha2_password plugin.

If you would like to learn more about the changes including why Oracle made the change and the advantages for users, see https://mysqlserverteam.com/mysql-8-0-4-new-default-authentication-plugin-caching_sha2_password/.

To connect to the server using the MySQL client (mysql), you must specify a user account and the server to which you want to connect. If you are connecting to a server on the same machine, you can omit the server information (host and port) since they default to localhost on port 3306. The user is specified using the --user (or -u) option. You can specify the password for the user on the command, but the more secure practice is to specify --password (or -p), and the client with prompt you for the password. If you do specify the password on the command line, you will be prompted with a warning encouraging you to not use that practice.

Using the mysql client on the same machine without the --host (or -h) and --port option does not use a network connection. If you want to connect using a network connection or want to connect using a different port, you must use the loopback address. For example, to connect to a server running on port 3307 on the same machine, use the command mysql -uroot -p –h127.0.0.1 --port=3306. Listing 3-3 shows an example of connecting (and disconnecting) to a MySQL server with the mysql client.

Listing 3-3. Connecting with the mysql Client

```
$ mysql -uroot -p -h 127.0.0.1 --port=3306
Enter password:
Welcome to the MySQL monitor.  Commands end with ; or \g.
Your MySQL connection id is 15
Server version: 8.0.23 MySQL Community Server - GPL

Copyright (c) 2000, 2021, Oracle and/or its affiliates.

Oracle is a registered trademark of Oracle Corporation and/or its
affiliates. Other names may be trademarks of their respective
owners.

Type 'help;' or '\h' for help. Type '\c' to clear the current input
statement.

mysql> quit
Bye
```

Basic SQL Commands

Now that we've seen how to connect to MySQL, let's take a brief look at some of the more popular SQL commands you will likely use by way of a short example. We will discuss the commands in more detail in a later section. Listing 3-4 shows examples of several SQL commands in action using the mysql client.

Tip   To see a list of the commands available in the client, type help; and press *Enter* at the prompt.

Listing 3-4.   Example SQL Commands Using the mysql Client

```
$ mysql -uroot -p -h 127.0.0.1 --port=3306
Enter password:
Welcome to the MySQL monitor.  Commands end with ; or \g.
Your MySQL connection id is 15
Server version: 8.0.23 MySQL Community Server - GPL

Copyright (c) 2000, 2021, Oracle and/or its affiliates.

Oracle is a registered trademark of Oracle Corporation and/or its
affiliates. Other names may be trademarks of their respective
owners.

Type 'help;' or '\h' for help. Type '\c' to clear the current input
statement.

mysql> CREATE DATABASE greenhouse;
Query OK, 1 row affected (0.00 sec)

mysql> CREATE TABLE greenhouse.plants (plant_name char(50), sensor_value
int, sensor_event timestamp);
Query OK, 0 rows affected (0.02 sec)

mysql> INSERT INTO greenhouse.plants VALUES ('living room', 23, NULL);
Query OK, 1 row affected (0.01 sec)
```

```
mysql> SELECT * FROM greenhouse.plants;
+-------------+--------------+--------------+
| plant_name  | sensor_value | sensor_event |
+-------------+--------------+--------------+
| living room |           23 | NULL         |
+-------------+--------------+--------------+
1 row in set (0.00 sec)

mysql> SET @@global.server_id = 106;
Query OK, 0 rows affected (0.00 sec)

mysql> quit
Bye
```

In this example, you see data definition language[1] (DDL) in the form of the CREATE DATABASE and CREATE TABLE statements, data manipulation language[2] (DML) in the form of the INSERT and SELECT statements, and a simple administrative command to set a global server variable.

Next you see the creation of a database and a table to store the data, the addition of a row in the table, and finally the retrieval of the data in the table. Notice how I used capital letters for SQL command keywords. This is a common practice and helps make the SQL commands easier to read and easier to find user-supplied options or data.

Tip   You can exit the MySQL client by typing the command quit. On Linux and Unix systems, you can press Ctrl+D to exit the client.

A great many commands are available in MySQL. Fortunately, you need to master only a few of the more common ones. The following are the commands you will use most often. The portions enclosed in <> indicate user-supplied components of the command, and [...] indicates that additional options are needed:

- CREATE DATABASE <database_name>: Creates a database

- USE <database>: Sets the default database (not an SQL command)

---

[1]https://en.wikipedia.org/wiki/Data_definition_language
[2]https://en.wikipedia.org/wiki/Data_manipulation_language

- `CREATE TABLE <table_name> [...]`: Creates a table or structure to store data

- `INSERT INTO <table_name> [...]`: Adds data to a table

- `UPDATE [...]`: Changes one or more values for a specific row

- `DELETE FROM <table_name> [...]`: Removes data from a table

- `SELECT [...]`: Retrieves data (rows) from the table

- `SHOW [...]`: Shows a list of the objects

Note   You must terminate each command with a semicolon (;) or \G.

Although this list is only a short introduction and nothing like a complete syntax guide, there is an excellent online reference manual that explains every command (and much more) in greater detail. You should refer to the online reference manual whenever you have a question about anything in MySQL. You can find it at `http://dev.mysql.com/doc/`.

One of the more interesting commands shown allows you to see a list of objects. For example, you can see the databases with `SHOW DATABASES`, a list of tables (once you change to a database) with `SHOW TABLES`, and even the permissions for users with `SHOW GRANTS`. I find myself using these commands quite frequently.

If you are thinking that there is a lot more to MySQL than a few simple commands, you are correct. Despite its ease of use and fast startup time, MySQL is a full-fledged relational database management system (RDBMS). There is much more to it than you've seen here. For more information about MySQL, including all the advanced features, see the reference manual.

How to Get and Install MySQL

The MySQL server is available for a variety of platforms including most Linux and Unix platforms, Mac OS X, and Windows. It is available as a community download (open source) or as a licensed product (enterprise edition). You can download the community editions directly from Oracle or you can download enterprise editions through your Oracle account. For the purposes of this chapter, we will use the community edition.

To download community releases of MySQL 8, visit `www.mysql.com/downloads/` and scroll down and click *MySQL Community (GPL) Downloads*, then click *MySQL*

Community Server. The page will automatically detect your operating system. If you want to download for another platform, you can select it from the drop-down list.

The download page will list several files for download. Depending on your platform, you may see several options including compressed files, source code, and installation packages. Most will choose the installation package for installation on a laptop or desktop computer. Figure 3-2 shows an example of the various download options for macOS platforms.

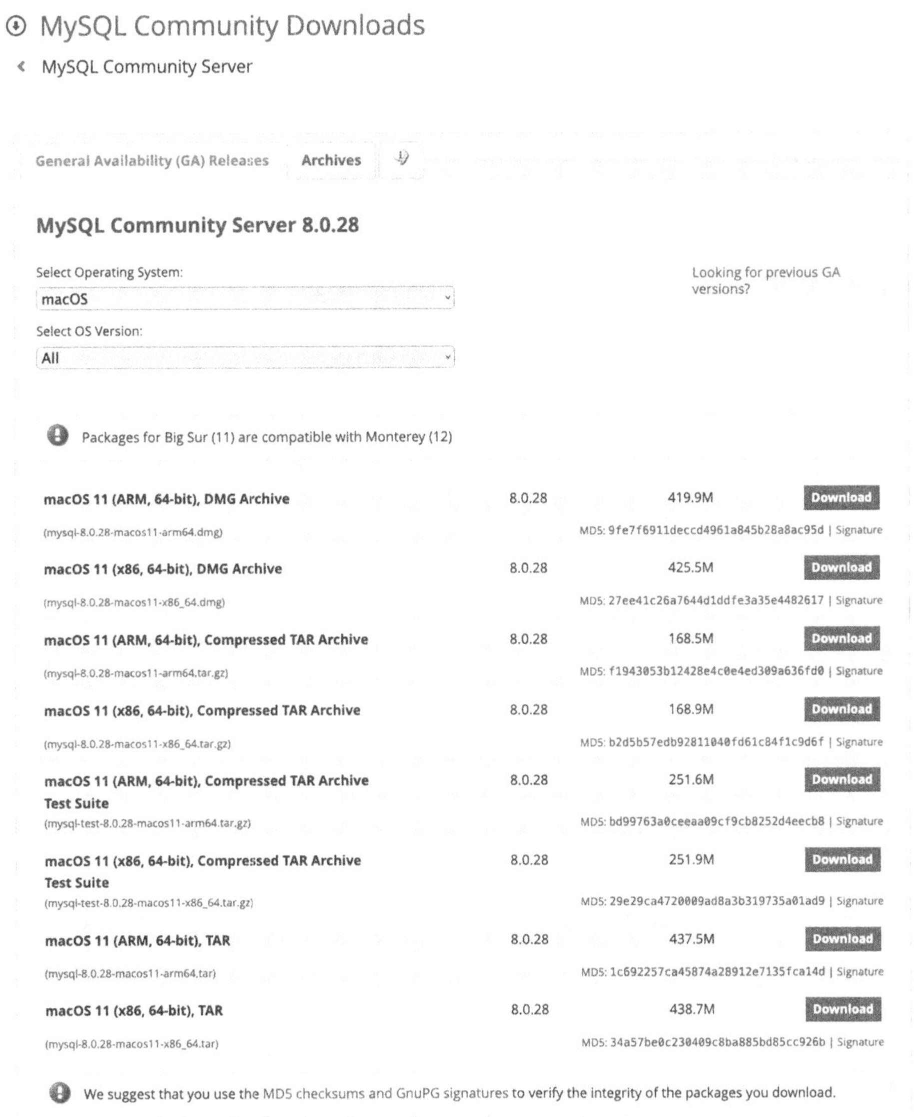

⊙ **MySQL Community Downloads**

‹ MySQL Community Server

General Availability (GA) Releases   **Archives** ⬇

MySQL Community Server 8.0.28

Select Operating System:
macOS

Select OS Version:
All

Looking for previous GA versions?

ⓘ Packages for Big Sur (11) are compatible with Monterey (12)

macOS 11 (ARM, 64-bit), DMG Archive (mysql-8.0.28-macos11-arm64.dmg)	8.0.28	419.9M MD5: 9fe7f6911deccd4961a845b28a8ac95d | Signature	Download
macOS 11 (x86, 64-bit), DMG Archive (mysql-8.0.28-macos11-x86_64.dmg)	8.0.28	425.5M MD5: 27ee41c26a7644d1ddfe3a35e4482617 | Signature	Download
macOS 11 (ARM, 64-bit), Compressed TAR Archive (mysql-8.0.28-macos11-arm64.tar.gz)	8.0.28	168.5M MD5: f1943053b12428e4c0e4ed309a636fd0 | Signature	Download
macOS 11 (x86, 64-bit), Compressed TAR Archive (mysql-8.0.28-macos11-x86_64.tar.gz)	8.0.28	168.9M MD5: b2d5b57edb92811040fd61c84f1c9d6f | Signature	Download
macOS 11 (ARM, 64-bit), Compressed TAR Archive Test Suite (mysql-test-8.0.28-macos11-arm64.tar.gz)	8.0.28	251.6M MD5: bd99763a0ceeaa09cf9cb8252d4eecb8 | Signature	Download
macOS 11 (x86, 64-bit), Compressed TAR Archive Test Suite (mysql-test-8.0.28-macos11-x86_64.tar.gz)	8.0.28	251.9M MD5: 29e29ca4720009ad8a3b319735a01ad9 | Signature	Download
macOS 11 (ARM, 64-bit), TAR (mysql-8.0.28-macos11-arm64.tar)	8.0.28	437.5M MD5: 1c692257ca45874a28912e7135fca14d | Signature	Download
macOS 11 (x86, 64-bit), TAR (mysql-8.0.28-macos11-x86_64.tar)	8.0.28	438.7M MD5: 34a57be0c230409c8ba885bd85cc926b | Signature	Download

ⓘ We suggest that you use the MD5 checksums and GnuPG signatures to verify the integrity of the packages you download.

Figure 3-2. *Download Page for macOS*

One of the most popular platforms is Microsoft Windows. Oracle has provided a special installation packaging for Windows named the Windows Installer. This package includes all the MySQL products available under the community license including MySQL Server, Workbench, Utilities, and all of the available connectors (program libraries for connecting to MySQL). This makes installing on Windows a one-stop, one-installation affair. Figure 3-3 shows the download page for the Windows installer.

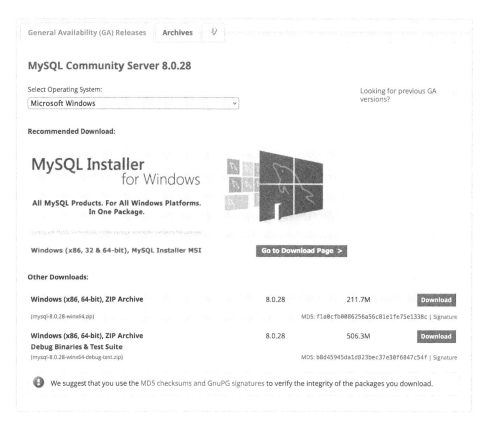

Figure 3-3. *Download Page for Windows Installer*

We see these below the Windows Installer download link in the image. You can choose either the Windows Installer 32- or 64-bit installation. Note that the package may be nothing more than a `.zip` file containing the server code. In this case, you may need to either run the server from the unzipped folder or do a local, manual install.

If you want to follow along with the examples in this chapter, you should consider installing MySQL on your PC or another PC on your local network. While you will not have to do any installation or configuration when using MDS, we can learn a bit about MySQL by installing it locally so we can use it at our leisure without incurring costs.

Installing MySQL is very easy and takes only a few minutes once you've downloaded the correct packages for your platform. Simply install the server and any subcomponents as you would for any other software for your platform. If you need step-by-step instructions, you can refer to the online reference manual (`https://dev.mysql.com/doc/refman/8.0/en/installing.html`).

For our experimental purposes, you can install MySQL with the default settings. More specifically, as a standard installation. You can always reinstall it if you want to install it preconfigured for a different environment. During the install, you may be asked to provide a password for the root user. Be sure to use best practices for choosing a password.

Ok, now that we have the MySQL 8 server installed, we can begin configuring the server for use. You will not need to do any of these operations when using MDS, but it is always good to know more about how MySQL is configured and how access is granted to user accounts.

Configuring and Managing Access to MySQL

Now that you have MySQL installed locally, let's briefly discuss how to configure MySQL and how to grant access to the server (and databases) to others as well as how to set up the X Plugin (the key component to enable the Document Store). We begin with a look at the configuration file used to define the behavior and configure options in MySQL.

Configuration Files

The primary way to configure startup options and variables in MySQL is accomplished using a text file named `my.cnf` (or `my.ini` on Windows). This file is normally located on Posix systems in the `/etc` folder. For example, on macOS, the file is named `/etc/my.cnf`. Listing 3-5 shows the first few dozen lines from a typical MySQL configuration file.

Listing 3-5. MySQL Configuration File Excerpt

```
# Example MySQL config file for small systems.
# The following options will be passed to all MySQL clients
[client]
port            = 3306
socket          = /tmp/mysql.sock

# Here follows entries for some specific programs
```

```
# The MySQL server
[mysqld]
port            = 3306
socket          = /tmp/mysql.sock
skip-external-locking
key_buffer_size = 16K
max_allowed_packet = 1M
table_open_cache = 4
sort_buffer_size = 64K
read_buffer_size = 256K
read_rnd_buffer_size = 256K
net_buffer_length = 2K
thread_stack = 1024K
...
innodb_log_file_size = 5M
innodb_log_buffer_size = 8M
innodb_flush_log_at_trx_commit = 1
innodb_lock_wait_timeout = 50
innodb_log_files_in_group = 2
slow-query-log
general-log
...
```

Notice we have settings grouped by section defined using square brackets [ ]. For example, we see a section named [client], which is used to define options for any MySQL client that reads the configuration file. Similarly, we see a section named [mysqld], which applies to the server process (because the executable is named mysqld). Notice also we see settings for basic options like port, socket, etc. However, we can also use the configuration file to set options for InnoDB, replication, and more.

I recommend locating and browsing the configuration file for your installation so that you can see the options and their values. If you encounter a situation where you need to change an option – say to test the effect or perhaps to experiment – you can use the SET command to change values either as a global setting (affects all connections) or a session setting (applies only to the current connection).

However, if you change a global setting that is also in the configuration file, the value (state) will remain only until the server is rebooted. Thus, if you want to keep global changes, you should consider placing them in the configuration file.

Conversely, setting a value at the session level could be beneficial for a limited time or may be something you want to do only for a specific task. For example, the following turns off the binary log, executes one or more SQL commands, and then turns the binary log back on. This is a simple but profound example of how to perform actions on a server participating in replication without having the actions affect other servers:

```
SET sql_log_bin=0;
<SOME SQL STATEMENTS>
SET sql_log_bin=1;
```

For more information about the configuration file and how to use it to configure MySQL 8 including using multiple option files and where the files exist on each platform, see the section entitled, "Using Option Files" in the online reference manual (`http://dev.mysql.com/doc/refman/8.0/en/`).

Creating Users and Granting Access

There are two additional administrative operations you need to understand before working with MySQL: creating user accounts and granting access to databases. You must first issue a `CREATE USER` command followed by one or more `GRANT` commands. For example, the following shows the creation of a user named `hvac_user1` and grants the user access to the database `room_temp`:

```
CREATE USER 'hvac_user1'@'%' IDENTIFIED BY 'secret';
GRANT SELECT, INSERT, UPDATE ON room_temp.* TO 'hvac_user1'@'%';
```

The first command creates the user named `hvac_user1`, but the name also has an @ followed by another string. This second string is the host name of the machine with which the user is associated. That is, each user in MySQL has both a username and a host name, in the form `user@host`, to uniquely identify them. That means the user and host `hvac_user1@10.0.1.16` and the user and host `hvac_user1@10.0.1.17` are not the same. However, the % symbol can be used as a wildcard to associate the user with any host. The `IDENTIFIED BY` clause sets the password for the user.

A NOTE ABOUT SECURITY

It is always a good idea to create a user for your application that does not have full access to the MySQL system. This is so you can minimize any accidental changes and also to prevent exploitation. For example, it is recommended that you create a user with access only to those databases where you store (or retrieve) data.

Also be careful about using the wildcard % for the host. Although it makes it easier to create a single user and let the user access the database server from any host, it also makes it much easier for someone bent on malice to access your server (once they discover the password).

The second command allows access to databases. There are many privileges that you can give a user. The example shows the most likely set that you would want to give a user of a sensor network database: read (SELECT), add data (INSERT), and change data (UPDATE). See the online reference manual for more about security and account access privileges.

The command also specifies a database and objects to which to grant the privilege. Thus, it is possible to give a user read (SELECT) privileges to some tables and write (INSERT, UPDATE) privileges to other tables. This example gives the user access to all objects (tables, views, and so on) in the room_temp database.

Basic SQL Commands

If you have never used a database system, learning and mastering the system requires training, experience, and a good deal of perseverance. Chief among the knowledge needed to become proficient is how to use the common SQL commands and concepts. This section completes the primer on MySQL by introducing the most common MySQL commands and concepts as a foundation for learning how to use the Document Store.

Note   Rather than replicate the reference manual, this section introduces the commands and concepts at a high level. If you decide to use any of the commands or concepts, please refer to the online reference manual for additional details, complete command syntax, and additional examples.

This section reviews the most common SQL and MySQL-specific commands that you will need to know to get the most out of your MySQL server databases. While you have already seen some of these in action, this section provides additional information to help you use them.

One important rule to understand is user-supplied variable names are case sensitive and obey case sensitivity of the host platform. Check the online reference manual for your platform to see how case sensitivity affects user-supplied variables.

Note   Most of the example queries in this section are taken from an Internet of Things (IoT) application where data is recorded from one or more sensors and devices. Regardless, the examples represent typical ways we interact with MySQL via SQL statements.

Creating Databases and Tables

The most basic commands you will need to learn, and master are the CREATE DATABASE and CREATE TABLE commands. Recall that database servers such as MySQL allow you to create any number of databases that you can add tables and store data in a logical manner.

To create a database, use CREATE DATABASE followed by a name for the database. If you are using the MySQL client, you must use the USE command to switch to a specific database. The client focus is the latest database specified either at startup (on the command line) or via the USE command.

You can override this by referencing the database name first. For example, SELECT * FROM db1.table1 will execute regardless of the default database set. However, leaving off the database name will cause the mysql client to use the default database. The following shows two commands to create and change the focus of the database:

```
mysql> CREATE DATABASE greenhouse;
mysql> USE greenhouse;
```

Tip   If you want to see all the databases on the server, use the SHOW DATABASES command.

Creating a table requires the, yes, CREATE TABLE command. This command has many options allowing you to specify not only the columns and their data types but also additional options such as indexes, foreign keys, and so on. An index can also be created using the CREATE INDEX command (see the following code). The following shows how to create a simple table for storing plant sensor data like what may be used for monitoring a personal greenhouse:

```
CREATE TABLE `greenhouse`.`plants` (
  `plant_name` char(30) NOT NULL,
  `sensor_value` float DEFAULT NULL,
  `sensor_event` timestamp NOT NULL DEFAULT CURRENT_TIMESTAMP ON UPDATE
  CURRENT_TIMESTAMP,
  `sensor_level` char(5) DEFAULT NULL,
  PRIMARY KEY `plant_name` (`plant_name`)
) ENGINE=InnoDB DEFAULT CHARSET=latin1;
```

Notice here that I specified the table name (plants) and four columns (plant_name, sensor_value, sensor_event, and sensor_level). I used several data types. For plant_name, I used a character field with a maximum of 30 characters, a floating-point data type for sensor_value, a timestamp value for sensor_event, and another character field for sensor_level of five characters.

The TIMESTAMP data type is of particular use any time you want to record the date and time of an event or action. For example, it is often helpful to know when a sensor value is read. By adding a TIMESTAMP column to the table, you do not need to calculate, read, or otherwise format a date and time when the value is inserted into the database table.

Notice also that I specified that the plant_name column be defined as a key, which creates an index. In this case, it is also the primary key. The PRIMARY KEY phrase tells the server to ensure there exists one and only one row in the table that matches the value of the column. You can specify several columns to be used in the primary key by repeating the keyword. Note that all primary key columns must not permit nulls (NOT NULL).

If you cannot determine a set of columns that uniquely identify a row (and you want such a behavior – some favor tables without this restriction, but a good DBA would not), you can use an artificial data type option for integer fields called AUTO INCREMENT. When used on a column (must be the first column), the server automatically increases this value for each row inserted. In this way, it creates a default primary key. For more information about auto increment columns, see the online reference manual.

Best practices suggest using a primary key on a character field to be suboptimal in some situations such as tables with large values for each column or many unique values. This can make searching and indexing slower. In this case, you could use an auto increment field to artificially add a primary key that is smaller in size (but somewhat more cryptic).

There are far more data types available than those shown in the previous example. You should review the online reference manual for a complete list of data types. See the section "*Data Types.*" If you want to know the layout or "schema" of a table, use the SHOW CREATE TABLE command.

Tip   Like databases, you can also get a list of all the tables in the database with the SHOW TABLES command.

Searching for Data

The most used basic command you need to know is the command to return the data from the table (also called a result set or rows). To do this, you use the SELECT statement. This SQL statement is the workhorse for a database system. All queries for data will be executed with this command. As such, we will spend a bit more time looking at the various clauses (parts) that can be used starting with the column list.

Note   While we examine SELECT statements first, if you want to try these out on your system, be sure to run the INSERT statements in the following section first.

The SELECT statement allows you to specify which columns you want to choose from the data. The list appears as the first part of the statement. The second part is the FROM clause, which specifies the table(s) you want to retrieve rows from.

Note   The FROM clause can be used to join tables with the JOIN operator. You will see a simple example of a join in a later section.

The order that you specify the columns determines the order shown in the result set. If you want all of the columns, use an asterisk (*) instead. Listing 3-6 demonstrates three statements that generate the same result sets. That is, the same rows will be displayed in the output of each. In fact, I am using a table with only four rows for simplicity.

Listing 3-6. Example SELECT Statements

```
mysql> SELECT plant_name, sensor_value, sensor_event, sensor_level FROM
greenhouse.plants;
+--------------------+--------------+---------------------+--------------+
| plant_name         | sensor_value | sensor_event        | sensor_level |
+--------------------+--------------+---------------------+--------------+
| fern in den        |       0.2319 | 2015-09-23 21:04:35 | NULL         |
| fern on deck       |         0.43 | 2015-09-23 21:11:45 | NULL         |
| flowers in bedroom1 |       0.301 | 2015-09-23 21:11:45 | NULL         |
| weird plant in kitchen |    0.677 | 2015-09-23 21:11:45 | NULL         |
+--------------------+--------------+---------------------+--------------+
4 rows in set (0.00 sec)

mysql> SELECT * FROM greenhouse.plants;
+--------------------+--------------+---------------------+--------------+
| plant_name         | sensor_value | sensor_event        | sensor_level |
+--------------------+--------------+---------------------+--------------+
| fern in den        |       0.2319 | 2015-09-23 21:04:35 | NULL         |
| fern on deck       |         0.43 | 2015-09-23 21:11:45 | NULL         |
| flowers in bedroom1 |       0.301 | 2015-09-23 21:11:45 | NULL         |
| weird plant in kitchen |    0.677 | 2015-09-23 21:11:45 | NULL         |
+--------------------+--------------+---------------------+--------------+
4 rows in set (0.00 sec)

mysql> SELECT sensor_value, plant_name, sensor_level, sensor_event FROM
greenhouse.plants;
+--------------+--------------------+--------------+---------------------+
| sensor_value | plant_name         | sensor_level | sensor_event        |
+--------------+--------------------+--------------+---------------------+
```

```
|        0.2319 | fern in den         | NULL      | 2015-09-23 21:04:35 |
|          0.43 | fern on deck        | NULL      | 2015-09-23 21:11:45 |
|         0.301 | flowers in bedroom1 | NULL      |          23 21:11:45 |
|         0.677 | weird plant in kitchen | NULL   | 2015-09-23 21:11:45 |
+--------------+------------------------+---------+---------------------+
4 rows in set (0.00 sec)
```

Notice that the first two statements result in the same rows as well as the same columns in the same order, but the third statement, while it generates the same rows, displays the columns in a different order.

You can also use functions in the column list to perform calculations and similar operations. One special example is using the COUNT() function to determine the number of rows in the result set, as shown here. See the online reference manual for more examples of functions supplied by MySQL:

```
SELECT COUNT(*) FROM greenhouse.plants;
```

The next clause in the SELECT statement is the WHERE clause. This is where you specify the conditions you want to use to restrict the number of rows in the result set. That is, only those rows that match the conditions. The conditions are based on the columns and can be quite complex. That is, you can specify conditions based on calculations, results from a join, and more. But most conditions will be simple equalities or inequalities on one or more columns in order to answer a question. For example, suppose you wanted to see the plants where the sensor value read is less than 0.40. In this case, we issue the following query and receive the results. Notice I specified only two columns: the plant name and the value read from sensor:

```
mysql> SELECT plant_name, sensor_value FROM greenhouse.plants WHERE sensor_
value < 0.40;
+---------------------+--------------+
| plant_name          | sensor_value |
+---------------------+--------------+
| fern in den         |       0.2319 |
| flowers in bedroom1 |        0.301 |
+---------------------+--------------+
2 rows in set (0.01 sec)
```

There are additional clauses you can use including the GROUP BY clause, which is used for grouping rows for aggregation or counting, and the ORDER BY clause, which is used to order the result set. Let's take a quick look at each starting with aggregation.

Suppose you wanted to average the sensor values read in the table for each sensor. In this case, we have a table that contains sensor readings over time for a variety of sensors. While the example contains only four rows (and thus may not be statistically informative), the example demonstrates the concept of aggregation quite plainly, as shown in Listing 3-7. Notice what we receive is simply the average of the four sensor values read.

Listing 3-7. GROUP BY Example

```
mysql> SELECT plant_name, sensor_value FROM greenhouse.plants WHERE plant_
name = 'fern on deck';
+--------------+--------------+
| plant_name   | sensor_value |
+--------------+--------------+
| fern on deck |         0.43 |
| fern on deck |         0.51 |
| fern on deck |        0.477 |
| fern on deck |         0.73 |
+--------------+--------------+
4 rows in set (0.00 sec)

mysql> SELECT plant_name, AVG(sensor_value) AS avg_value FROM greenhouse.
plants WHERE plant_name = 'fern on deck' GROUP BY plant_name;
+--------------+-------------------+
| plant_name   | avg_value         |
+--------------+-------------------+
| fern on deck | 0.536750003695488 |
+--------------+-------------------+
1 row in set (0.00 sec)
```

Notice I specified the average function, AVG(), in the column list and passed in the name of the column I wanted to average. There are many such functions available in MySQL to perform some powerful calculations. Clearly, this is another example of how much power exists in the database server that would require many more resources on a typical lightweight sensor or aggregator node in the network.

Notice also that I renamed the column with the average with the AS keyword. You can use this to rename any column specified, which changes the name in the result set, as you can see in the listing.

Another use of the GROUP BY clause is counting. In this case, we replaced AVG() with COUNT() and received the number of rows matching the WHERE clause. More specifically, we want to know how many sensor values were stored for each plant.

```
mysql> SELECT plant_name, COUNT(sensor_value) as num_values FROM
greenhouse.plants GROUP BY plant_name;
+------------------------+------------+
| plant_name             | num_values |
+------------------------+------------+
| fern in den            |          1 |
| fern on deck           |          4 |
| flowers in bedroom1    |          1 |
| weird plant in kitchen |          1 |
+------------------------+------------+
4 rows in set (0.00 sec)
```

Now let's say we want to see the results of our result set ordered by sensor value. We will use the same query that selected the rows for the fern on the deck, but we order the rows by sensor value in ascending and descending order using the ORDER BY clause. Listing 3-8 shows the results of each option.

Listing 3-8. ORDER BY Examples

```
mysql> SELECT plant_name, sensor_value FROM greenhouse.plants WHERE plant_
name = 'fern on deck' ORDER BY sensor_value ASC;
+--------------+--------------+
| plant_name   | sensor_value |
+--------------+--------------+
| fern on deck |         0.43 |
| fern on deck |        0.477 |
| fern on deck |         0.51 |
| fern on deck |         0.73 |
+--------------+--------------+
4 rows in set (0.00 sec)
```

```
mysql> SELECT plant_name, sensor_value FROM greenhouse.plants WHERE plant_
name = 'fern on deck' ORDER BY sensor_value DESC;
+--------------+--------------+
| plant_name   | sensor_value |
+--------------+--------------+
| fern on deck |         0.73 |
| fern on deck |         0.51 |
| fern on deck |        0.477 |
| fern on deck |         0.43 |
+--------------+--------------+
4 rows in set (0.00 sec)
```

As I mentioned, there is a lot more to the SELECT statement than shown here, but what we have seen here will get you very far, especially when working with data typical of most small to medium-sized database solutions.

Creating Data

Now that you have a database and tables created, you will want to load or insert data into the tables. You can do so using the INSERT INTO statement. Here we specify the table and the data for the row. The following shows a simple example:

```
INSERT INTO greenhouse.plants (plant_name, sensor_value) VALUES ('fern in
den', 0.2319);
```

In this example, I am inserting data for one of my plants by specifying the name and value. What about the other columns, you wonder? In this case, the other columns include a timestamp column, which will be filled in by the database server. All other columns (just the one) will be set to NULL, which means no value is available, the value is missing, the value is not zero, or the value is empty.

Notice I specified the columns before the data for the row. This is necessary whenever you want to insert data for fewer columns than what the table contains. More specifically, leaving the column list off means you must supply data (or NULL) for all columns in the table. Also, the order of the columns listed can be different from the order they are defined in the table. Leaving the column list off will result in the ordering of the column data based on how they appear in the table.

You can also insert several rows using the same command by using a comma-separated list of the row values, as shown here:

```
INSERT INTO greenhouse.plants (plant_name, sensor_value) VALUES ('flowers
in bedroom1', 0.301), ('weird plant in kitchen', 0.677), ('fern on
deck', 0.430);
```

Here I've inserted several rows with the same command. Note that this is just a shorthand mechanism and, except for automatic commits, no different than issuing separate commands.

Updating Data

There are times when you want to change or update data. You may have a case where you need to change the value of one or more columns, replace the values for several rows, or correct formatting or even scale of numerical data. To update data, we use the UPDATE command. You can update a particular column, update a set of columns, perform calculations on one or more columns, and more.

What may be more likely is you or your users will want to rename an object in your database. For example, suppose we determine the plant on the deck is not actually a fern but was an exotic flowering plant. In this case, we want to change all rows that have a plant name of "fern on deck" to "flowers on deck." The following command performs the change:

```
UPDATE greenhouse.plants SET plant_name = 'flowers on deck' WHERE plant_
name = 'fern on deck';
```

Notice the key operator here is the SET operator. This tells the database to assign a new value to the column(s) specified. You can list more than one set operation in the command.

Notice I used a WHERE clause here to restrict the UPDATE to a particular set of rows. This is the same WHERE clause as you saw in the SELECT statement, and it does the same thing; it allows you to specify conditions that restrict the rows affected. If you do not use the WHERE clause, the updates will apply to all rows.

Caution   Don't forget the WHERE clause! Issuing an UPDATE command without a WHERE clause will affect all rows in the table!

Deleting Data

Sometimes you end up with data in a table that needs to be removed. Maybe you used test data and want to get rid of the fake rows, or perhaps you want to compact or purge your tables or want to eliminate rows that no longer apply. To remove rows, use the DELETE FROM command.

Let's look at an example. Suppose you have a plant-monitoring solution under development, and you've discovered that one of your sensors or sensor nodes are reading values that are too low, because of a coding, wiring, or calibration error. In this case, we want to remove all rows with a sensor value less than 0.20. The following command does this:

```
DELETE FROM plants WHERE sensor_value < 0.20;
```

Caution   Don't forget the WHERE clause! Issuing a DELETE FROM command without a WHERE clause will permanently delete all rows in the table!

Notice I used a WHERE clause here. That is, a conditional statement to limit the rows acted upon. You can use whatever columns or conditions you want; just be sure you have the correct ones! I like to use the same WHERE clause in a SELECT statement first. For example, I would issue the following first to check that I am about to delete the rows I want and only those rows. Notice it is the same WHERE clause:

```
SELECT * FROM plants WHERE sensor_value < 0.20;
```

Using Indexes

Tables are created without the use of any ordering. That is, tables are unordered. While it is true MySQL will return the data in the same order each time, there is no implied (or reliable) ordering unless you create an index. The ordering I am referring to here is not like you think when sorting (that's possible with the ORDER BY clause in the SELECT statement).

Rather, indexes are mappings that the server uses to read the data when queries are executed. For example, if you had no index on a table and wanted to select all rows with a value greater than a certain value for a column, the server will have to read all rows to find all the matches. However, if we added an index on that column, the server would have to read only those rows that match the criteria.

I should note that there are several forms of indexes. What I am referring to here is a clustered index where the value for column in the index is stored in the index, allowing the server to read the index only and not the rows to do the test for the criteria.

To create an index, you can either specify the index in the CREATE TABLE statement or issue a CREATE INDEX command. The following shows a simple example:

```
CREATE INDEX plant_name ON plants (plant_name);
```

This command adds an index on the plant_name column. Observe how this affects the table:

```
CREATE TABLE `plants` (
  `plant_name` char(30) NOT NULL,
  `sensor_value` float DEFAULT NULL,
  `sensor_event` timestamp NOT NULL DEFAULT CURRENT_TIMESTAMP ON UPDATE
  CURRENT_TIMESTAMP,
  `sensor_level` char(5) DEFAULT NULL,
  PRIMARY KEY (`plant_name`),
  KEY `plant_name` (`plant_name`)
) ENGINE=InnoDB DEFAULT CHARSET=latin1
```

Indexes created like this do not affect the uniqueness of the rows in the table, in other words, making sure there exists one and only one row that can be accessed by a specific value of a specific column (or columns). What I am referring to is the concept of a primary key (or primary index), which is a special option used in the creation of the table as described earlier.

Views

Views are logical mappings of results of one or more tables. They can be referenced as if they were tables in queries, making them a powerful tool for creating subsets of data to work with. You create a view with CREATE VIEW and give it a name similar to a table. The following shows a simple example where we create a test view to read values from a table. In this case, we limit the size of the view (number of rows), but you could use a wide variety of conditions for your views, including combining data from different tables:

```
CREATE VIEW test_plants AS SELECT * FROM plants LIMIT 5;
```

Views are not normally encountered in small or medium-sized database solutions, but I include them to make you aware of them in case you decide to do additional analysis and want to organize the data into smaller groups for easier reading.

Triggers

Another advanced concept (and associated SQL command) is the use of an event-driven mechanism that is "triggered" when data is changed. That is, you can create a short set of SQL commands (a procedure) that will execute when data is inserted or changed.

There are several events or conditions under which the trigger will execute. You can set up a trigger either before or after an update, insert, or delete action. A trigger is associated with a single table and has as its body a special construct that allows you to act on the rows affected. The following shows a simple example:

```
DELIMITER //
CREATE TRIGGER set_level BEFORE INSERT ON plants FOR EACH ROW
BEGIN
  IF NEW.sensor_value < 0.40 THEN
    SET NEW.sensor_level = 'LOW';
  ELSEIF NEW.sensor_value < 0.70 THEN
    SET NEW.sensor_level = 'OK';
  ELSE
    SET NEW.sensor_level = 'HIGH';
  END IF;
END //
DELIMITER ;
```

This trigger will execute before each insert into the table. As you can see in the compound statement (BEGIN...END), we set a column called sensor_level to LOW, OK, or HIGH depending on the value of the sensor_value. To see this in action, consider the following command. The FOR EACH ROW syntax allows the trigger to act on all rows in the transaction:

```
INSERT INTO plants (plant_name, sensor_value) VALUES ('plant1', 0.5544);
```

Since the value we supplied is less than the middle value (0.70), we expect the trigger to fill in the `sensor_level` column for us. The following shows this indeed is what happened when the trigger fired:

```
+------------+--------------+---------------------+--------------+
| plant_name | sensor_value | sensor_event        | sensor_level |
+------------+--------------+---------------------+--------------+
| plant1     |       0.5544 | 2015-09-23 20:00:15 | OK           |
+------------+--------------+---------------------+--------------+
1 row in set (0.00 sec)
```

This demonstrates an interesting and powerful way you can create derived columns with the power of the database server and save the processing power and code in your applications. I encourage you to consider this and similar powerful concepts for leveraging the power of the database server.

Simple Joins

One of the most powerful concepts of database systems is the ability to make relationships (hence the name relational) among the data. That is, data in one table can reference data in another (or several tables). The most simplistic form of this is called a master-detail relationship where a row in one table references or is related to one or more rows in another.

A common (and classic) example of a master-detail relationship is from an order-tracking system where we have one table containing the data for an order and another table containing the line items for the order. Thus, we store the order information such as customer number and shipping information once and combine or "join" the tables when we retrieve the order proper.

Let's look at an example from the sample database named world. You can find this database on the MySQL website (`http://dev.mysql.com/doc/index-other.html`). Feel free to download it and any other sample database. They all demonstrate various designs of database systems. You will also find it handy to practice querying the data as it contains more than a few, simple rows.

Note   If you want to run the following examples, you need to install the world database as described in the documentation for the example (`http://dev.mysql.com/doc/world-setup/en/world-setup-installation.html`).

Listing 3-9 shows an example of a simple join. There is a lot going on here, so take a moment to examine the parts of the SELECT statement, especially how I specified the JOIN clause. You can ignore the LIMIT option because that simply limits the number of rows in the result set.

Listing 3-9. Simple JOIN Example

```
mysql> USE world;
mysql> SELECT Name, Continent, Language FROM Country JOIN CountryLanguage
ON Country.Code = CountryLanguage.CountryCode LIMIT 10;
+-------------+---------------+------------+
| Name        | Continent     | Language   |
+-------------+---------------+------------+
| Aruba       | North America | Dutch      |
| Aruba       | North America | English    |
| Aruba       | North America | Papiamento |
| Aruba       | North America | Spanish    |
| Afghanistan | Asia          | Balochi    |
| Afghanistan | Asia          | Dari       |
| Afghanistan | Asia          | Pashto     |
| Afghanistan | Asia          | Turkmenian |
| Afghanistan | Asia          | Uzbek      |
| Angola      | Africa        | Ambo       |
+-------------+---------------+------------+
10 rows in set (0.00 sec)
```

Here I used a JOIN clause that takes two tables specified such that the first table is joined to the second table using a specific column and its values (the ON specifies the match). What the database server does is read each row from the tables and returns only those rows where the value in the columns specified a match. Any rows in one table that are not in the other are not returned.

Tip   You can retrieve those rows with different joins. See the online reference manual at `https://dev.mysql.com/doc/refman/8.0/en/join.html` for more information about the types of joins possible including the inner and outer joins for more details.

Notice also that I included only a few columns. In this case, I specified the country name and continent from the Country table and the language column from the CountryLanguage table. If the column names were not unique (the same column appears in each table), I would have to specify them by table name such as Country. Name. In fact, it is considered good practice to always qualify the columns in this manner.

There is one interesting anomaly in this example that I feel important to point out. In fact, some would consider it a design flaw. Notice in the JOIN clause I specified the table and column for each table. This is normal and correct but notice the column name does not match in both tables. While this really doesn't matter, and creates only a bit of extra typing, some DBAs would consider this erroneous and would have a desire to make the common column name the same in both tables.

Another use for a join is to retrieve common, archival, or lookup data. For example, suppose you had a table that stored details about things that do not change (or rarely change) such as cities associated with ZIP codes or names associated with identification numbers (e.g., SSN). You could store this information in a separate table and join the data on a common column (and values) whenever you needed. In this case, that common column can be used as a foreign key, which is another advanced concept.

Foreign keys are used to maintain data integrity (i.e., if you have data in one table that relates to another table, but the relationship needs to be consistent). For example, if you wanted to make sure when you delete the master row that all of the detail rows are also deleted, you could declare a foreign key in the master table to a column (or columns) to the detail table. See the online reference manual for more information about foreign keys.

This discussion on joins touches only the very basics. Indeed, joins are arguably one of the most difficult and often confused areas in database systems. If you find you want to use joins to combine several tables or extend data so that data is provided from several tables (outer joins), you should spend some time with an in-depth study of database concepts such as Clare Churcher's book *Beginning Database Design* (Apress, 2012).

Stored Routines

There are many more concepts and commands available in MySQL, but two that may be of interest are PROCEDURE and FUNCTION, sometimes called stored routines. I introduce these concepts here so that if you want to explore them, you understand how they are used at a high level.

Suppose you need to run several commands to change data. That is, you need to do some complex changes based on calculations. For these types of operations, MySQL provides the concept of a stored procedure. The stored procedure allows you to execute a compound statement (a series of SQL commands) whenever the procedure is called. Stored procedures are sometimes considered an advanced technique used mainly for periodic maintenance, but they can be handy in even the more simplistic situations.

For example, suppose you want to develop your own database application that uses SQL, but since you are developing it, you need to periodically start over and want to clear out all the data first. If you had only one table, a stored procedure would not help much, but suppose you have several tables spread over several databases (not unusual for larger databases). In this case, a stored procedure may be helpful.

When entering commands with compound statements in the MySQL client, you need to change the delimiter (the semicolon) temporarily so that the semicolon at the end of the line does not terminate the command entry. For example, use `DELIMITER //` before writing the command with a compound statement, use `//` to end the command, and change the delimiter back with `DELIMITER ;`. This is only when using the client.

Since stored procedures can be quite complicated, if you decide to use them, read the "*CREATE PROCEDURE and CREATE FUNCTION Syntax*" section of the online reference manual before trying to develop your own. There is more to creating stored procedures than described in this section.

Now suppose you want to execute a compound statement and return a result – you want to use it as a function. You can use functions to fill in data by performing calculations, data transformation, or simple translations. Functions therefore can be used to provide values to populate column values, provide aggregation, provide date operations, and more.

You have already seen a couple of functions (`COUNT`, `AVG`). These are considered built-in functions, and there is an entire section devoted to them in the online reference manual. However, you can also create your own functions. For example, you may want to create a function to perform some data normalization on your data. More specifically, suppose you have a sensor that produces a value in a specific range, but depending on that value and another value from a different sensor or lookup table, you want to add, subtract, average, and so on, the value to correct it. You could write a function to do this and call it in a trigger to populate the value for a calculation column.

WHAT ABOUT CHANGING OBJECTS?

You may be wondering what you do when you need to modify a table, procedure, trigger, and so on. Rest easy, you do not have to start over from scratch! MySQL provides an ALTER command for each object. That is, there is an ALTER TABLE, ALTER PROCEDURE, and so on. See the online reference manual section entitled "Data Definition Statements" for more information about each ALTER command.

Now that we have learned what the basic SQL commands are and how to use them, let's look at how we can connect our applications to MySQL.

Connecting Applications

You have already seen how to connect to the MySQL server with the MySQL client and MySQL Shell. These tools are interactive tools where we can execute queries, but it isn't helpful for saving data from our applications or other users. What we need is something called a connector. A connector is a programming module designed to permit our scripts or programs to send data to the database server. Connectors also allow us to query the database server to get data from the server.

I will cover two primary connectors you are likely to encounter when developing your own applications. I present each as a tutorial that you can use to follow. I begin with a connector for use with Python scripts (Connector/Python) and then present a connector for use in writing simplified Java (Connector/J). But first, let's see what connectors are available for our applications.

MySQL Database Connectors

There are many database connectors for MySQL. Oracle supplies a number of database connectors for a variety of languages. Table 3-1 shows the current database connectors available for download from `http://dev.mysql.com/downloads/`.

Table 3-1. *MySQL Connectors*

Connector	Description	Download URL
C API (libmysqlclient)	A client library for C development	`https://dev.mysql.com/downloads/c-api/`
Connector/C++	Standardized C++ applications	`https://dev.mysql.com/downloads/connector/cpp/`
Connector/J	Java applications	`https://dev.mysql.com/downloads/connector/j/`
Connector/Net	Windows .Net platforms	`https://dev.mysql.com/downloads/connector/net/`
Connector/Node.js	Node.js applications	`https://dev.mysql.com/downloads/connector/nodejs/`
Connector/ODBC	Generalized ODBC applications	`https://dev.mysql.com/downloads/connector/odbc/`
Connector/Python	Python applications	`https://dev.mysql.com/downloads/connector/python/`
MySQL native driver for PHP (mysqlnd)	PHP 5.3 or newer connector	`https://dev.mysql.com/downloads/connector/php-mysqlnd/`

As you can see, there is a connector for just about any programming language you are likely to encounter. You can find documentation for each of the connectors above at `https://dev.mysql.com/doc/connectors/en/`.

Sample Database

If you'd like to follow along with the examples, you will need to set up the sample database. If you have MySQL installed, you can use the MySQL Shell or client to execute the following queries:

```
-- A database for storing plant soil moisture and ambient temperature
CREATE DATABASE plant_monitoring;
USE plant_monitoring;
```

```
-- This table stores information about a plant.
CREATE TABLE plant_monitoring.plants (
  id int NOT NULL AUTO_INCREMENT,
  name char(50) DEFAULT NULL,
  location char(30) DEFAULT NULL,
  climate enum ('inside','outside') DEFAULT 'inside',
  PRIMARY KEY (`id`)
) ENGINE=InnoDB DEFAULT CHARSET=latin1;
```

We will be inserting data as part of the examples. If you want to run both examples and run the insert example more than once, be sure to empty the table with the following query:

```
DELETE FROM plant_monitoring.plants;
```

Now let's take a look at two examples starting with Connector/Python.

Example Connector: Connector/Python

The connector for Python from Oracle is a full-featured connector that provides connectivity to the MySQL database server for Python applications and scripts. Connector/Python features support for all current MySQL server releases. It is written to provide automatic data type conversion between Python and MySQL, making building queries and deciphering results easy. It also has support for compression, permits connections via SSL, and supports all MySQL SQL commands.

Connector/Python must be installed on the PC where you will run your code in the same manner any Python library that you may use. Using Connector/Python in your Python scripts consists of importing the base module, initiating a connection, and executing queries with a cursor.

Before we jump into how we can use Connector/Python to write some MySQL database–enabled applications, let's talk about how to get and install Connector/Python.

PYTHON? ISN'T THAT A SNAKE?

The Python programming language is a high-level language designed to be as close to like reading English as possible while being simple, easy to learn, and powerful. Pythonistas will tell you the designers have indeed met these goals.

If you have never used Python or you would like to know more about it, the following are few good books that introduce the language. A host of resources are also available on the Internet, including the Python documentation pages at `www.python.org/doc/`:

- *Programming the Raspberry Pi* by Simon Monk (McGraw-Hill, 2013)

- *Beginning Python from Novice to Professional*, 2nd Edition, by Magnus Lie Hetland (Apress, 2008)

- *Python Cookbook* by David Beazley and Brian K. Jones (O'Reilly Media, 2013)

Interestingly, Python was named after the British comedy troupe Monty Python and not the reptile. As you learn Python, you may encounter campy references to Monty Python episodes. Having a fondness for Monty Python, I find these references entertaining. Of course, your mileage may vary.

Installing Connector/Python

Downloading is the same process as you discovered for the server. You can download Connector/Python from Oracle's MySQL website (`http://dev.mysql.com/downloads/connector/python/`). The page will automatically detect your platform and show the available downloads for your platform. You may see several choices. Be sure to choose the one that matches your configuration.

Since most platforms come with Python installed, you may not need to do anything to prepare your system; just download the installer and install it. However, the preferred method of installation is to use the Python package manager (from PyPi) to get and install the connector with the command `pip install`. The following demonstrates how to install Connector/Python using `pip`:

```
% pip3 install mysql-connector-python
Collecting mysql-connector-python
  Downloading mysql_connector_python-8.0.28-py2.py3-none-any.whl (342 kB)
```

```
|                                                                      |
|                              | 342 kB 198 kB/s
Collecting protobuf>=3.0.0
  Downloading protobuf-3.19.3-cp310-cp310-macosx_10_9_universal2.whl
  (1.0 MB)
        |                                                              |
|                             | 1.0 MB 544 kB/s
Installing collected packages: protobuf, mysql-connector-python
Successfully installed mysql-connector-python-8.0.28 protobuf-3.19.3
```

Notice the pip installer command. The command pip3 is used in this example because the PC has both Python 2.X and 3.X installed and we want to ensure we install it for the Python 3.X installation.

Note   You should install Python 3.7 or later.

Also notice any prerequisites required for the package being installed are also automatically downloaded and installed. As you can see, using pip is much easier than downloading and installing packages separately.

Tip   See the online reference manual for specific notes about installing on some platforms (http://dev.mysql.com/doc/connector-python/en/connector-python-installation.html).

Checking the Installation

Once Connector/Python is installed, you can verify it is working with the following short example. Begin by entering the command python (or python3 if you want to ensure you are using the Python 3.X installation). This will open an interactive prompt that permits you to enter one line of Python code at a time and execute it; it's a Python command-line interpreter and useful in testing small snippets of code. Just enter the following lines as shown in the example:

```
% python3
```

```
Python 3.10.2 (v3.10.2:a58ebcc701, Jan 13 2022, 14:50:16) [Clang 13.0.0
(clang-1300.0.29.30)] on darwin
Type "help", "copyright", "credits" or "license" for more information.
>>> import mysql.connector
>>> print(mysql.connector.__version__)
8.0.28
>>>
>>> quit()
```

What you should see is the version of Connector/Python printed. If you see any errors about not finding the connector, be sure to check your installation to ensure it worked. Once you can successfully access Connector/Python, you're ready to move on to some example scripts.

Python scripts (applications) are saved using a file name and extension like <something>.py and executed from the command line as follows. We will use this method to execute the following examples. Thus, for each example, you should open a file in a text editor, enter the code as shown, save the file, and then run the script from the command line:

```
$ python3 my_script.py
```

If you have and are familiar with a Python integrated development environment (IDE), you can use that instead of creating a file with a text editor and executing it via the command line. Examples of good Python IDEs include Thonny (https://thonny.org/) and PyCharm (www.jetbrains.com/pycharm/download). Both are available for Windows, macOS, and Linux.

Thonny is a free, basic IDE and therefore very easy to use but limited in features whereas PyCharm is available in a community and enterprise editions supporting a host of features for enterprise-wide Python development.

Example 1: Connecting to MySQL

Let's start with a simple example where we connect to the MySQL server and get a list of databases. We will name this example mysql_connector.py.

In this case, we start by importing the Connector/Python connector class and then to keep things tidy, we use a dictionary to store the connection information. Once we have the dictionary for the connection, we call the connect() method to connect to the server.

Next, we open a new cursor and get an instance of the cursor class with the `cursor()` method of the connection class. With the cursor class, we can then call the `execute()` method passing in a SQL statement and once executed, fetch the rows returned and print out the first column in each row. Finally, we close both the cursor and connection to tidy things up. Listing 3-10 shows the complete code for this example. As you will see, it is very easy to follow.

Caution   Be sure to change the user and password to match your installation.

Listing 3-10. MySQL Connect and Query Example

```python
"""mysql_connect.py"""
#
# MySQL Database Service
#
# Chapter 03 - MySQL Connect
#
# This script demonstrates the basics for using the MySQL Connector/
Python to
# connect to a MySQL server and issue a simple query and print the results.
#
# Dr. Charles Bell
#
# Import libraries
import mysql.connector
# Connection parameters dictionary
server = {
    'user': 'root',
    'password': 'SECRET',
    'host': '127.0.0.1',
    'database': 'plant_monitoring',
}
# Connect to the server
cnx = mysql.connector.connect(**server)
# Create a cursor
```

```
cur = cnx.cursor()
# Execute a query
cur.execute("SHOW DATABASES")
# Fetch and print the results
rows = cur.fetchall()
for row in rows:
    print(row[0]) # Print first column only
# Close the cursor and connection
cur.close()
cnx.close()
```

Once you have to code entered, you can execute it to see the results as shown below:

Tip   Be sure your MySQL server is running, and you provide the correct password and hostname for the server in the dictionary.

```
% python3 ./mysql_connect.py
animals
greenhouse
information_schema
mysql
performance_schema
plant_monitoring
sakila
sys
world
world_x
```

Depending on what sample databases or other databases you have installed or created, your results may be different, but you should see the plant_monitoring, mysql, information_schema, and performance_schema at a minimum.

If you encounter errors like the one below, be sure to check your credentials in the dictionary to ensure you are using the correct hostname (or IP address), port, user, and password.

```
Error: 1045 (28000): Access denied for user 'root'@'localhost' (using
password: YES)
```

Now let's look at how to insert data.

Example 2: Inserting Data

Now let's see how we can insert some data in a table. We will name this example code `mysql_insert.py`.

In this case, we simply want to read data from a file and insert it into a table. We will use the same code as the previous example to connect to the server and use a cursor to execute a query. The difference is we will use a file to read in sample data in a comma-separated value format (`.csv`). It is a common format used in a variety of applications.

For each row in the file, we decode the fields then form an `INSERT` command using the data in the columns. Once again, we will use the `execute()` method of the cursor class to execute the query to insert the data. Since there are no results, we don't fetch anything. However, after we finish inserting the rows, we must call the `commit()` method for the cursor class to commit the changes. Listing 3-11 shows the complete code for the example. Take a moment to read through it for clarity.

Listing 3-11. MySQL Insert Data Example

```
"""mysql_insert.py"""
#
# MySQL Database Service
#
# Chapter 03 - MySQL Insert
#
# This script demonstrates the basics for using the MySQL Connector/
Python to
# connect to a MySQL server and insert data into a table.
#
# Dr. Charles Bell
#
# Import libraries
import mysql.connector
# Query
INSERT_SQL = "INSERT INTO plant_monitoring.plants (name, location, climate)
VALUES ("
# Connection parameters dictionary
server = {
```

```
  'user': 'root',
  'password': 'SECRET',
  'host': '127.0.0.1',
  'database': 'plant_monitoring',
}
# Connect to the server
cnx = mysql.connector.connect(**server)
# Create a cursor
cur = cnx.cursor()
# Read rows from a file for inserting into plant_monitor table
with open("plants_data.txt", encoding='UTF-8') as data_file:
    data = data_file.readlines()
# Now insert the data in the table
for row in data:
    cols = row.strip('\n').split(",") # comma-separated row
    INSERT = f"{INSERT_SQL}'{cols[0]}','{cols[1]}',{cols[2]})"
    print(INSERT)
    cur.execute(INSERT)
# We must commit the changes
cnx.commit()
# Close the cursor and connection
cur.close()
cnx.close()
```

The file we are reading has only a few rows and is a mockup of the plant-monitoring system example. The following shows the file contents. Note that I labeled it `plants_data.txt`. If you change the file name, be sure to change the code accordingly:

```
Jerusalem Cherry,deck,2
Moses in the Cradle,patio,2
Peace Lilly,porch,1
Thanksgiving Cactus,porch,1
African Violet,porch,1
```

To run the script, issue the following command from the folder where you stored the file. Be sure to put the data file in the same folder first. I show the results of running the script:

```
% python3 ./mysql_insert.py
INSERT INTO plant_monitoring.plants (name, location, climate) VALUES
('Jerusalem Cherry','deck',2)
INSERT INTO plant_monitoring.plants (name, location, climate) VALUES
('Moses in the Cradle','patio',2)
INSERT INTO plant_monitoring.plants (name, location, climate) VALUES
('Peace Lilly','porch',1)
INSERT INTO plant_monitoring.plants (name, location, climate) VALUES
('Thanksgiving Cactus','porch',1)
INSERT INTO plant_monitoring.plants (name, location, climate) VALUES
('African Violet','porch',1)
```

Now let's check our table. If we started with an empty table, we should see the following if we execute the SELECT for the plants table. Notice we use the MySQL Shell passing the query to execute and formatting the output as a table:

```
% mysqlsh -uroot -p --sql -e "SELECT * FROM plant_monitoring.
plants" --table
+----+---------------------+----------+---------+
| id | name                | location | climate |
+----+---------------------+----------+---------+
| 11 | Jerusalem Cherry    | deck     | outside |
| 12 | Moses in the Cradle | patio    | outside |
| 13 | Peace Lilly         | porch    | inside  |
| 14 | Thanksgiving Cactus | porch    | inside  |
| 15 | African Violet      | porch    | inside  |
+----+---------------------+----------+---------+
```

You can do much more with the connector than shown here. You should read the online reference manual (https://dev.mysql.com/doc/connector-python/en/) for more information and examples of how to use the connector to meet your application needs.

Now, let's look at a Connector/J example. We will use the same examples only implemented in Java.

Example Connector: Connector/J

The connector for Java from Oracle is a full-featured connector that provides connectivity to the MySQL database server for Java applications. Connector/J features support for all current MySQL server releases. It is a full-featured connector with all of the necessary features for creating secure connections and supports all MySQL SQL commands.

Connector/J must be installed on the PC where you will run your code in the same manner any Java library that you may use. Using Connector/J in your applications consists of importing the base module, initiating a connection, and executing queries with a cursor.

To keep things simple, we will be using a simplistic form of Java programming to write and execute the examples. More specifically, we will use a simple text editor to create the code files and the Java Development Kit (JDK) to compile the code (`javac`) and execute (`java`). If you have experience with more robust Java IDEs, you can use those instead.

Note   The Java Runtime Environment (JRE) is not the same as the JDK. You will have to install the JDK even if you have the JRE installed.

Naturally, to use Connector/J, you will need to ensure you have the latest version of the Java Runtime Environment installed on your PC. Most PCs have the JDK installed. However, if you want to check, simply issue `javac --version` in a terminal. If you get an error that the command cannot be found, visit `www.oracle.com/java/technologies/downloads/` to learn how to download and install JDK on your PC.

Note   You should use JDK version 8.0 or later.

Before we jump into how we can use Connector/J to write some MySQL database–enabled applications, let's talk about how to get and install Connector/J.

Installing Connector/J

Downloading is the same process as you discovered for the server. You can download Connector/J from Oracle's MySQL website (`http://dev.mysql.com/downloads/connector/j/`). The page will automatically detect your platform and show the available downloads for your platform. You may see several choices. Be sure to choose the one that matches your configuration. Note, however, there is no installation package for macOS. If you do not see your platform in the list, you can download using the *Platform Independent* operating system option.

In this demonstration, we will use the *Platform Independent* option. We do this to demonstrate how you can use this option and use classes from an installation directory (folder) rather than install it on the system. You may want to do this if you are working on a system used for Java development as to not disrupt your IDE or Java installation.

Simply choose the *Platform Independent* operating system option from the download page and download either the .zip or .tar.gz file. Once downloaded, copy the file to your project directory and unzip it. For example, if you had a folder named `../Ch03/java` to store the examples in this section, you can unzip the file in that directory. This will result in a folder in the same path named `../Ch03/java/ mysql-connector-java-8.0.28` (or similar if you download a newer version of the connector).

To access the classes in that folder, we will need to set the `CLASSPATH` as follows so that the classes can be found. This is a temporary setting that is only active for the terminal session opened and will not affect your Java installation. Just remember to execute this command once before you run the examples in this section.

```
% cd ../Ch03/java
% export CLASSPATH=./mysql-connector-java-8.0.28/mysql-connector-java-8.0.28.jar:$CLASSPATH
```

Tip See the online reference manual for specific notes about installing on some platforms (`https://dev.mysql.com/doc/connector-j/8.0/en/connector-j-installing.html`).

Checking the Installation

Once Connector/J is installed, you can verify it is working with the following short example. We will create a new code file named `MySQLTest.java` with a class of the same name.

Connector/J works with the Java database connectivity (JDBC) libraries. As such, rather than supply individual parameters for the connection, we build a universal resource locator[3] (URL) that corresponds to the JDBC standard.

The following shows a mockup format for the database connection URL syntax for MySQL Connector/J:

```
jdbc:mysql://[host][,failoverhost...]
    [:port]/[database]
    [?propertyName1][=propertyValue1]
    [&propertyName2][=propertyValue2]...
```

- `host`: the host name of the MySQL server. The default value is 127.0.0.1.

- `port`: the port number of the MySQL server. The default value is 3306.

- `database`: name of the default database for the connection.

- `failoverhost`: hostname of a standby database server. MySQL Connector/J supports failover when a connection fails. See the online reference for more details.

- `propertyNameN = propertyValueN`: one or more ampersand-separated list of properties (optional)

Tip   For a complete tutorial on JDBC, see Oracle's JDBC tutorial website `https://docs.oracle.com/javase/tutorial/jdbc/basics/index.html`.

Thus, to connect to our local MySQL server using the localhost and default port for MySQL, the URL will be as follows:

```
"jdbc:mysql://localhost:3306/plant_monitoring?useSSL=false";
```

Notice we left off the user and password. To make the connection to the server, we will use the Java `DriverManager` class to get the connection. We supply those as additional parameters when we call the `getConnection()` method of the `DriverManager` class.

---

[3] URLS are only one form of passing connection information to JDBC. See the online documentation for other options.

Now that we understand how to make the connection, let's look at an example Java application that is designed to test if the Connector/J is installed. In this example, we attempt a connection using a user account that does not exist. We do this to ensure we will get the MySQL access denied error message. If it succeeds without that specific error, we know something else is wrong (it should not succeed). Conversely, if the connection generates a different error, we know that Connector/J is either not installed (not found on the CLASSPATH) or something else is wrong. Either way, we print the message for the exception so the user can determine a course of action to fix the issue.

We place this logic inside the main() method. If Connector/J is installed, you should see an error message stating the user (not_a_user) cannot connect. Once again, any other error means either the URL path is invalid, or Connector/J is not installed. Listing 3-12 shows the completed code.

Listing 3-12. Test Connector/J Example

```
//
//  MySQL Database Service
//
// Chapter 03 - MySQL Test Connector/J
//
// This example tests installation of Connector/J by attempting to connect
// to a MySQL server. Be sure to get the URL statement connect before
// compiling and running the test.
//
// Dr. Charles Bell
//
// Imports
import java.sql.Connection;
import java.sql.DriverManager;
import java.sql.SQLException;

// Class
public class MySQLTest {
    public static void main(String[] args) {
        // Connection parameters
        String url = "jdbc:mysql://localhost:3306/"
                    + "plant_monitoring?useSSL=false";
```

```
        String user = "not_a_user";
        String password = "SECRET";
        // Attempt connection
        try (Connection con = DriverManager.getConnection(url, user,
             password)) {
            System.out.println("ERROR: Should not connect with "
                               "'not_a_user'!");
        } catch (SQLException ex) {
            // Test to see if access denied error (expected).
            if (ex.getMessage().contains("Access denied")) {
                System.out.println("Success!");
            } else {
                // If Connector/J is not installed, print message.
                System.out.println("Connector/J is missing.");
                System.out.println(ex.getMessage());
            }
        }
    }
}
```

Once you have the code saved in a file named MySQLTest.java, go ahead and compile and run it with the following commands. If Connector/J is not installed, you should see the error message depicted:

```
% javac MySQLTest.java
% java MySQLTest
Connector/J is missing.
No suitable driver found for jdbc:mysql://localhost:3306/plant_
monitoring?useSSL=false
```

If you installed Connector/J in a local folder, you could set the CLASSPATH as described above and run the code again. This time, you should see a success message like the following:

```
% export CLASSPATH=./mysql-connector-java-8.0.28/mysql-connector-
java-8.0.28.jar:$CLASSPATH
% java MySQLTest
Success!
```

Once you confirm Connector/J is installed and working, you are ready for the examples.

Example 1: Connecting to MySQL

Let's start with a simple example where we connect to the MySQL server and get a list of databases. We will name this example MySQLConnect.java.

The logic of the code follows the same as the MySQLTest.java above, except this time we will make the connection, request a statement class, and execute the query in a single block We then loop through the rows returned and print the first column of the result set. Listing 3-13 shows the complete code for this example. As you will see, it is very easy to follow:

Listing 3-13. MySQL Connect and Query Example

```
//
//  MySQL Database Service
//
// Chapter 03 - MySQL Connect
//
// This example attempts to connect to a MySQL server, execute a query
// then print the first column of the result set.
//
// Dr. Charles Bell
//
// Imports
import java.sql.Connection;
import java.sql.DriverManager;
import java.sql.ResultSet;
import java.sql.SQLException;
import java.sql.Statement;
import java.util.logging.Level;
import java.util.logging.Logger;

public class MySQLConnect {
```

```
    public static void main(String[] args) {
        // Connection parameters
        String url = "jdbc:mysql://localhost:3306/"
                        + "plant_monitoring?useSSL=false";
        String user = "root";
        String password = "SECRET";
        String query = "SHOW DATABASES";
        // Attempt the connection and execute a query then print
        the results
        try (Connection con = DriverManager.getConnection(url, user,
        password);
            Statement st = con.createStatement();
            ResultSet rs = st.executeQuery(query)) {
            while (rs.next()) {
                System.out.println(rs.getString(1));
            }
        } catch (SQLException ex) {
            Logger lgr = Logger.getLogger(MySQLConnect.class.getName());
            lgr.log(Level.SEVERE, ex.getMessage(), ex);
        }
    }
}
```

Once you have to code entered, you can compile and execute it to see the results as shown below:

Tip   Be sure your MySQL server is running, and you provide the correct password and hostname for the server in the dictionary.

```
% javac MySQLConnect.java
% java MySQLConnect
animals
greenhouse
information_schema
```

```
mysql
performance_schema
plant_monitoring
sakila
sys
world
world_x
```

Depending on what sample databases or other databases you have installed or created, your results may be different, but you should see the `plant_monitoring`, `mysql`, `information_schema`, and `performance_schema` at a minimum.

If you encounter errors like the one below, be sure to check your credentials in the dictionary to ensure you are using the correct hostname (or IP address), port, user, and password.

```
Error: 1045 (28000): Access denied for user 'root'@'localhost' (using
password: YES)
```

Now let's look at how to insert data.

Example 2: Inserting Data

Now let's see how we can insert some data in a table. We will name this example code `mysql_insert.py`.

In this case, we simply want to read data from a file and insert it into a table. We will use the same code as the previous example to connect to the server and execute a query. The difference is we will use a file to read in sample data in a comma-separated value format (`.csv`). It is a common format used in a variety of applications.

For each row in the file, we decode the fields then form an `INSERT` command using the data in the columns. Once again, we will use the `execute()` method of the cursor class to execute the query to insert the data. Since there are no results, we don't fetch anything. However, after we finish inserting the rows, we must call the `commit()` method for the cursor class to commit the changes. Listing 3-14 shows the complete code for the example. Take a moment to read through it for clarity.

Listing 3-14. MySQL Insert Data Example

```
//
//  MySQL Database Service
//
// Chapter 03 - MySQL Insert
//
// This example attempts to connect to a MySQL server, read rows
   from a file
// and insert data into a table.
//
// Dr. Charles Bell
//
// Imports
import java.io.File;
import java.sql.Connection;
import java.sql.DriverManager;
import java.sql.SQLException;
import java.sql.Statement;
import java.util.logging.Level;
import java.util.logging.Logger;
import java.util.Scanner;

public class MySQLInsert {

    public static void main(String[] args) {
        String url = "jdbc:mysql://localhost:3306/plant_
        monitoring?useSSL=false";
        String user = "root";
        String password = "SECRET";

        try (Connection con = DriverManager.getConnection(url, user,
        password);
                Statement st = con.createStatement()) {
            // Open the file and read all rows inserting them.
            try {
                File myObj = new File("plants_data.txt");
```

```java
            Scanner myReader = new Scanner(myObj);
            while (myReader.hasNextLine()) {
                String data = myReader.nextLine();
                String cols[] = data.split(",");
                String sql = "INSERT INTO plant_monitoring.plants
                (name, "
                            + "location, climate) VALUES ('" + cols[0]
                            + "','" + cols[1] + "'," + cols[2] + ");";
                System.out.println(sql);
                st.executeUpdate(sql);
            }
            myReader.close();
        } catch (Exception e) {
            System.out.println("An error occurred.");
            e.printStackTrace();
        }
    } catch (SQLException ex) {
        Logger lgr = Logger.getLogger(MySQLInsert.class.getName());
        lgr.log(Level.SEVERE, ex.getMessage(), ex);
    }
  }
}
```

The file we are reading has only a few rows and is a mockup of the plant-monitoring system example. The following shows the file contents. Note that I labeled it plants_ data.txt. If you change the file name, be sure to change the code accordingly:

```
Jerusalem Cherry,deck,2
Moses in the Cradle,patio,2
Peace Lilly,porch,1
Thanksgiving Cactus,porch,1
African Violet,porch,1
```

Recall if you want to run this example after having run the Python example above or if you want to rerun the examples, you should run the following command between executions to empty the table:

```
% mysqlsh -uroot -p --sql -e "DELETE FROM plant_monitoring.plants" --table
```

To compile and execute the code, issue the following commands from the folder where you stored the file. Be sure to put the data file in the same folder first. I show the results of running the code:

```
% javac MySQLInsert.java
% java MySQLInsert
INSERT INTO plant_monitoring.plants (name, location, climate) VALUES
('Jerusalem Cherry','deck',2);
INSERT INTO plant_monitoring.plants (name, location, climate) VALUES
('Moses in the Cradle','patio',2);
INSERT INTO plant_monitoring.plants (name, location, climate) VALUES
('Peace Lilly','porch',1);
INSERT INTO plant_monitoring.plants (name, location, climate) VALUES
('Thanksgiving Cactus','porch',1);
INSERT INTO plant_monitoring.plants (name, location, climate) VALUES
('African Violet','porch',1);
```

Now let's check our table. If we started with an empty table, we should see the following if we execute the SELECT for the plants table. Notice we use the MySQL Shell passing the query to execute and formatting the output as a table:

```
% mysqlsh -uroot -p --sql -e "SELECT * FROM plant_monitoring.
plants" --table
+----+---------------------+----------+---------+
| id | name                | location | climate |
+----+---------------------+----------+---------+
| 11 | Jerusalem Cherry    | deck     | outside |
| 12 | Moses in the Cradle | patio    | outside |
| 13 | Peace Lilly         | porch    | inside  |
| 14 | Thanksgiving Cactus | porch    | inside  |
| 15 | African Violet      | porch    | inside  |
+----+---------------------+----------+---------+
```

Once again, these examples only give you the very basics of using the connector. You can do much more with the connector than shown here. You should read the online reference manual (https://dev.mysql.com/doc/connector-j/8.0/en/) for more information and examples of how to use the connector to meet your application needs.

Summary

The MySQL database server is a powerful tool. Given its unique placement in the market as the database server for the Internet, it is not surprising that web developers (as well as many startup and similar Internet properties) have chosen MySQL for their solutions. Not only is the server robust and easy to use, but it is also available as a free community license that you can use to keep your initial investment within budget.

In this chapter, you discovered some of the power of using the MySQL database server in its traditional role using the SQL interface; how to issue commands for creating databases and tables for storing data as well as commands for retrieving that data, and even how to connect your applications to MySQL for storing data. While this chapter presents only a small primer on MySQL, you learned how to get started by practicing with your own installation of MySQL, which will pay dividends when employing the MySQL Database Service in a production environment.

In the next chapter, we will take a deeper look into the MySQL Database Service including how to get started creating and using your first database system (called a dbSystem in MDS).

CHAPTER 4

MySQL Database Service

If you are new to MySQL and read through the last chapter, you are now familiar enough with MySQL to appreciate its power and simplicity. However, if you are a long-term MySQL user and you've built your own MySQL servers into your infrastructure, chances are you are well aware of the effort needed to manage your MySQL servers. What the world has needed for some time is a fully managed cloud-based MySQL service that runs in a secure environment with the backing of a cloud vendor that provides real-time management of the service to ensure your database needs are fully fulfilled and reliable. That day has come, and it is the MySQL Database Service running on the Oracle Cloud Infrastructure owned and managed by Oracle.

And now that we understand more about the Oracle Cloud Infrastructure (OCI) and MySQL, we can move on to learning how to use and work with MySQL in OCI, which is named the MySQL Database Service, hence MDS. Within that service is a resource called a database system, hence DB System. This is the OCI resource that provides the managed MySQL server for your use.

Recall from Chapter 1 that the DB System is built on top of existing OCI resources including a compute instance and block storage. However, there are more components used and managed behind the scenes.

This fully managed service provides a number of advantages for you including not having to set up hardware, install the operating system, install MySQL, configure everything to work nicely, etc., initially and then, later on, you won't have to worry about updates or upgrades to the base operating system or even MySQL – all those tasks are taken care of by automation within OCI and overseen by the MySQL engineering branch themselves. Sweet!

© Charles Bell 2023
C. Bell, *MySQL Database Service Revealed*, https://doi.org/10.1007/978-1-4842-8945-7_4

MANAGED MYSQL RESPONSIBILITIES

The word, managed, is used to describe how MySQL is operated in OCI. While this includes things we've discussed such as setup, configuration, and upgrades, what else is included and what exactly is the customer versus Oracle's responsibility?

Oracle is responsible for ensuring backup and recovery mechanisms are available and, if requested, automated backups are executed on schedule, MySQL version patching and upgrades, operating system patches and upgrades, monitoring the system for anomalies and responding to urgent issues, and ensuring your DB Systems execute in a secure environment. The customer is responsible for modeling, designing, and maintaining any schemas (databases) created, query design and optimization, and data access and retention policies.

Thus, maintenance tasks to keep the MySQL server running successfully are the realm of Oracle's responsibility while the data and access to it are the responsibility of the customer.

In this chapter, we will return to our OCI account and learn how to set up and use an MDS database system. We will take a short tour of the MDS service and a DB System via the cloud console so that we fully understand what all of the things are on the page. Thus, we're going to dive a bit deeper! Let's get started.

Getting Started

If you have been following along with the OCI and MySQL tutorials in Chapters 2 and 3, you should have an OCI account setup and be familiar with the terminology and SQL commands commonly used in MySQL. If you haven't worked through at least the OCI tutorial in Chapter 2, you may want to review that chapter first.

There are several prerequisites you must have in place before you can begin deploying your first DB System. The following steps summarize those things we will need to set up in our OCI account:

1. You must have a Virtual Cloud Network (VCN) in which to place your MySQL resources.

2. You must create a user group and add at least one user to the group.

3. You must create a policy that allows the group certain privileges to work with MDS and DB Systems

If you do not have all of these conditions, you may not be able to deploy a DB System. Interestingly, OCI produces a banner at the top of the MDS resource page as shown in Figure 4-1.

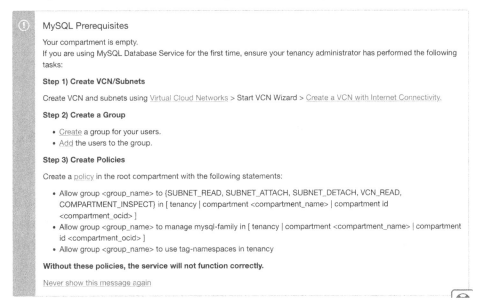

Figure 4-1. *First-Time MDS Use Banner*

Notice it outlines all three steps along with the privileges you will need to grant via a policy on the root compartment. Also, notice at the bottom of the banner is a link to turn off the notice. It is recommended you don't turn off the banner until after your first successful DB System deployment.

Let's go through all three steps and see a demonstration of how to satisfy each. Be sure to first login to your OCI account by visiting `cloud.oracle.com`.

Note   We will omit images showing menu selections and similar mundane operations going forward as we've had enough practice on those in Chapter 2.

Step 1: Create a VCN

Since we have already created a VCN (`oci-tutorial-vcn`) in Chapter 2, we will use that one. If you'd like to create another, you can do so. Similarly, if you terminated the VCN, you would need to recreate it. Just follow the demonstration in Chapter 2 and create a VCN with the same settings (using a different name). In short, you will need to open the main menu in the cloud console then choose *Networks* then *Virtual Cloud Networks* then click the *Start VCN Wizard* button to being the process.

Step 2: Create a Group

This next step is something we have seen. In OCI, you can create users and groups to place users in for the purposes of setting security policies. OCI requires you to create a group and user for use with MDS.

In this tutorial, we will create a sample group with a single user. We will name the group `mysql-users` and the user `mysqladmin`. Names are not overly important, but it is nice to give them some name that at least hints at their intended use. There are two steps involved. First, we will create the group, then we will add the user to the group.

Create a Group

Groups are created in domains. There is no direct cloud console menu to take you directly to the groups' resource page, rather, to create a group, you must first open the resource page for your current (default) domain. To do so, open the main menu in the cloud console, then select *Identity & Security* then click *Domains*. You will see the Domains resource page as shown in Figure 4-2.

Figure 4-2. Domains Resource Page

To open the domain details page, simply select the Default label as shown. On the Default domain details page in the Identity menu on the left, click *Groups* as shown in Figure 4-3.

Figure 4-3. Default Domain Details Page

At this point, we will see the list of groups for the domain. At the top of the list, click the *Create Group* button to start the process to create a group as shown in Figure 4-4.

Groups *in* Default *Domain*

Figure 4-4. *Groups List (Default Domain)*

On the Create Group dialog, we will want to enter the following information at a minimum:

- *Name*: Choose a unique name for the group. The name must be between 1 and 100 characters.

- *Description*: Enter a description that communicates how the group will be used.

- *Tags* (optional): You can assign one or more short text strings to a resource. You should not store critical information or confidential information.

Tip   Names in OCI are permitted to contain the following characters: lowercase letters a-z, uppercase letters A-Z, 0-9, period (.), dash (-), and underscore (_). Spaces are not allowed.

If you are following along, we will use mysql-users for the group name and "Users who use MySQL DB Systems" for the description as shown in Figure 4-5. We will not use tags.

Note   You can use your root user account if you do not want to create a user at this time. Simply add the root user to the group by ticking the root user account when you create the group.

When you are ready to create the group, click the *Create* button as shown.

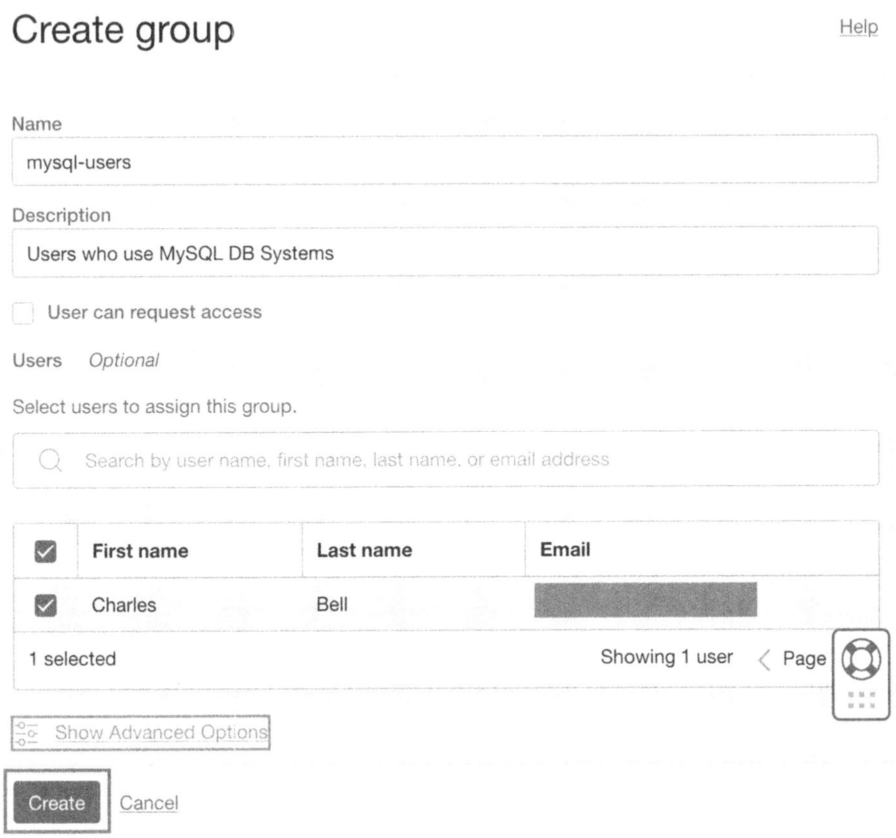

Create group

Help

Name

mysql-users

Description

Users who use MySQL DB Systems

☐ User can request access

Users   *Optional*

Select users to assign this group.

🔍 Search by user name, first name, last name, or email address

☑	First name	Last name	Email
☑	Charles	Bell	

1 selected   Showing 1 user   ‹ Page

⚙ Show Advanced Options

[Create] Cancel

Figure 4-5. *Create Group Dialog*

It only takes a few moments for the group creation. When complete, you will be directed to the Group details page as shown in Figure 4-6. You can edit the group and change parameters using the *Edit group* button. You can also use the *Delete* button (a rare departure from "terminate" used elsewhere in the interface) to delete the group.

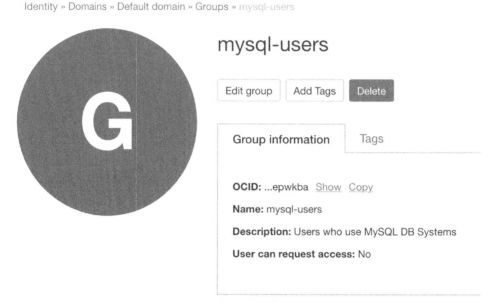

Identity » Domains » Default domain » Groups » mysql-users

mysql-users

Edit group   Add Tags   Delete

Group information   Tags

OCID: ...epwkba Show Copy
Name: mysql-users
Description: Users who use MySQL DB Systems
User can request access: No

Figure 4-6. *Group Details Page*

Now that we have our group, we can create a user and add them to the group. This may be an optional step if you decided to add your root user to the group.

Create and Add a User to the Group

It is good practice to create new users even if you are the only one using your OCI account so that you can test how users interact with your resources. Not only does this ensure your users can execute applications or use resources you create, but it also ensures your security policies are defined correctly.

In this section, we will create a new user and add that user to the group. You will need to enter a name and username as well as a valid email address. The email address is among the required information because OCI will email the user a link to set the user account password very similar to how your root account was notified.

To create the user, you will need to navigate back to the Default domain details page. Recall, you can reach this page by using the cloud console menu selecting *Identity & Security* then click *Domains* and on the Domains resource page select the *Default* domain. Refer to the sections above for more details.

Once you are back to the Default domain details page, click the *Users* entry in the menu on the left and then click the *Create user* button in the Users lists as shown in Figure 4-7.

Figure 4-7. *Users List (Default Domain Details Page)*

Next, we will be creating a new user with the name Joe User and a valid email address. The dialog is designed to allow you to use the email address for the username, but you can also use a custom username. To do so, untick the *Use the email address as username* checkbox to allow you to enter joeuser as the username. Be sure to check to make sure the email you entered is a valid email address. Hint: you can use your own email address there if you'd like. This is why we changed the login to use a username instead of the email address. Smart. Figure 4-8 shows the create user dialog with the data entered.

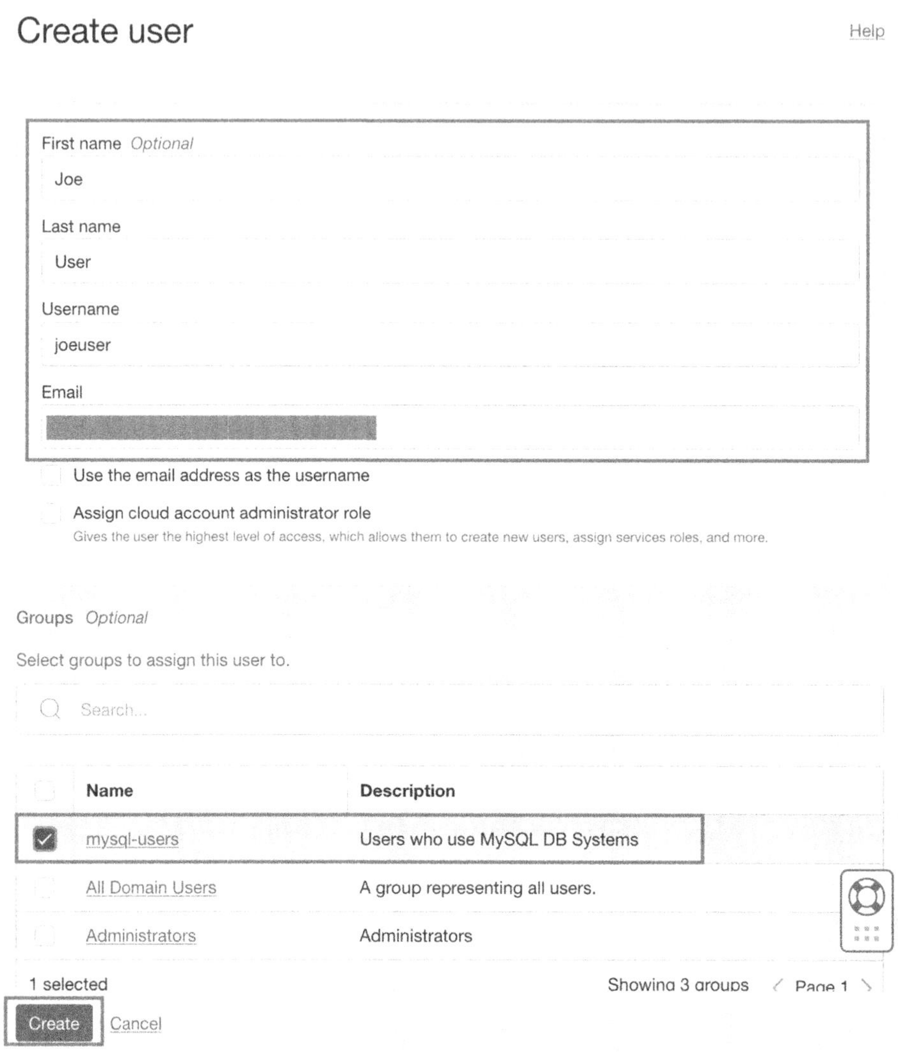

Create user

First name *Optional*

Joe

Last name

User

Username

joeuser

Email

[ ] Use the email address as the username

[ ] Assign cloud account administrator role
Gives the user the highest level of access, which allows them to create new users, assign services roles, and more.

Groups *Optional*

Select groups to assign this user to.

Q Search...

	Name	Description
☑	mysql-users	Users who use MySQL DB Systems
	All Domain Users	A group representing all users.
	Administrators	Administrators

1 selected   Showing 3 groups ‹ Page 1 ›

[Create] Cancel

Figure 4-8.   *Create User Dialog*

Notice we can also add the user to a group in the same step! Here, we simply select the group we created earlier (`mysql-users`) as shown. When ready, click the *Create* button to create the user. An email will be sent to the email address you provided allowing you to set the password for the new user. If you are currently logged in with your root account, you will have to logout of that account before the password set/reset will work.

Note   To login as the user when you attempt to create a MySQL DB System, you will need to logout of your root account and back in with your new user account.

Now that we have the group created and a new user, we only need to grant certain privileges to the group using a security policy.

Step 3: Create Policies

Finally, we will need a security policy that grants certain permissions to the group so that users can access and use MySQL resources. There are several ways to do this including using the cloud console interface to build the specific commands we need, or we can enter the commands manually. We will use the manual option in this example.

To satisfy the requirements for MDS, we need to assign the following to the group:

- `SUBNET_READ, SUBNET_ATTACH, SUBNET_DETACH, VCN_READ, COMPARTMENT_INSPECT`: To allow the group to work with subnets and VCNs

- `manage mysql-family`: To allow the group to manage MySQL resources

- `use tag-namespaces`: To allow the group to use tag-namespaces in the tenancy

We will be using the `Allow` permission statement to grant these privileges, which permits you to apply the privileges to either the tenancy itself or a specific compartment. Since we will be using the `oci-tutorial-compartment`, we will use that value in the statements. However, the last privilege is applied to the tenancy.

Let's see how we can do this. To create a security policy, click on the cloud console main menu, select *Identity & Security* then click *Policies*. This will open the Policies resource page as shown in Figure 4-9. To create a new policy, click the *Create Policy* button as shown.

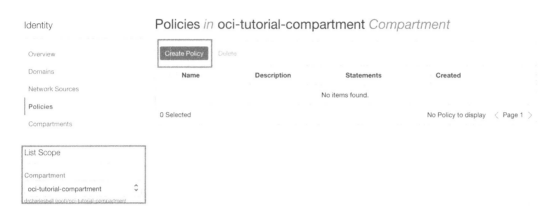

Figure 4-9. *Policies Resource Page*

Security policies are created in the root compartment. You may have the oci-tutorial-compartment selected in the List Scope, but that is Ok. We can select the compartment in the next page.

The information we need to provide when creating the policy includes the following. If you are following along, example entries are shown for each data item:

- Name: A name for the policy. Use mysql-users-policy.

- Description: A short description of what the policy provides. Use Allow users to access MySQL DB Systems.

- Compartment: Be sure to select your root compartment.

We also need to supply the policy statements as we discussed above. The format of the statements we need was provided for us in the banner OCI presented earlier. In this case, the following are the suggested policy statements. Notice the use of [..|..]. This indicates we have a choice of parameters to use. We will use the compartment_name option where applicable (we remove the other options and the brackets). The statements are artificially formatted for reading:

```
Allow group <group_name> to
  {SUBNET_READ, SUBNET_ATTACH, SUBNET_DETACH, VCN_READ, COMPARTMENT_
  INSPECT}
  in [
    tenancy |
    compartment <compartment_name> |
    compartment id <compartment_ocid>
  ]

Allow group <group_name> to manage mysql-family in [
  tenancy |
  compartment <compartment_name> |
  compartment id <compartment_ocid>
]

Allow group <group_name> to use tag-namespaces in tenancy
```

We can use these to substitute the `<group_name>` with `mysql-users` and the `<compartment_name>` with `oci-tutorial-compartment` as shown below once again formatted for easier reading:

```
Allow group mysql-users to
  {SUBNET_READ, SUBNET_ATTACH, SUBNET_DETACH, VCN_READ, COMPARTMENT_
  INSPECT}
  in compartment oci-tutorial-compartment

Allow group mysql-users to manage mysql-family
  in compartment oci-tutorial-compartment

Allow group mysql-users to use tag-namespaces in tenancy
```

To add these to the Create Policy dialog, you will have to click the switch *Shown manual editor* to allow you to get a text box to paste the statements.

Figure 4-10 shows the Create Policy dialog with the data entered. Be sure to double-check everything including selecting your root compartment and then click the *Create* button to create the policy.

Create Policy

Name

mysql-users-policy

No spaces. Only letters, numerals, hyphens, periods, or underscores.

Description

Allow users to access MySQL DB Systems

Compartment

▓▓▓▓▓ (root)

Policy Builder   Show manual editor 🔘

```
Allow group mysql-users to {SUBNET_READ, SUBNET_ATTACH, SUBNET_DETACH, VCN_READ, COMPARTMENT_INSPECT} in
compartment oci-tutorial-compartment
Allow group mysql-users to manage mysql-family in compartment oci-tutorial-compartment
Allow group mysql-users to use tag-namespaces in tenancy
|
```

Example: Allow group [group_name] to [verb] [resource-type] in compartment [compartment_name] where [condition]

Create   Cancel   ⬜ Create Another Policy

Figure 4-10. *Create Policy Dialog*

Caution   If you do not select your root compartment, you may receive a red banner at the bottom of the dialog with a somewhat cryptic error stating the compartment doesn't exist. If this happens, double-check your compartment selection and try the create again.

When the policy is created, you will be directed to the Policies Detail page as shown in Figure 4-11. Notice you can edit the policy with the *Edit Policy* button or delete it with the *Delete* button.

Figure 4-11. *Policies Detail Page*

Ok, now that we have all three prerequisites completed, it's time to take a tour of MDS and learn how to create our first DB System.

A Tour of MDS

Now is the point in the book where most are eager to see in action – using MDS in OCI. We will start off with a simple example to explore the nuances of creating and getting to know about DB Systems before we move on to the more advanced features of MDS.

One thing that may not be clear for some is the difference between MDS and a DB System. MDS is an OCI platform as a service (PaaS), and a DB System is one of the resources available in the service. The MySQL service menu is shown in the cloud console menu as shown in Figure 4-12. As MDS continues to mature, you may see additional resources appear under the MySQL menu.

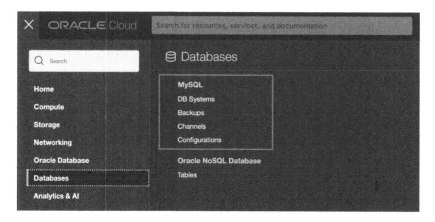

Figure 4-12. *MySQL Service Menu (Cloud Console)*

Notice we see there are four resources under the MySQL menu. The following briefly summarizes them:

- *DB Systems*: Fully managed MySQL server resources

- *Backups*: Backups taken of the DB Systems

- *Channels*: A replication resource consisting of inbound or outbound replication channels. Inbound channels permit asynchronous replication between a MySQL source and a DB System. Outbound channels permit asynchronous replication of a DB System database to a MySQL replica.

- *Configurations*: A collection of user, system, initialization, or service-specific variables that define the operation of the DB System. List includes many predefined configurations, but you may create your own.

We will see all of the features of MDS in the coming chapters. For now, let's see a tutorial for creating out very first DB System.

Note   If you have not followed along with satisfying the prerequisites for creating a DB System, go back and do those steps first.

Creating Your First DB System

At this point, we should have our OCI account setup as well as a virtual cloud network (oci-tutorial-vcn), a compartment resource (oci-tutorial-compartment), a new user (joeuser), a group (mysql-users) to which the user is assigned, and a policy (mysql-users-policy) to allow users to create and use MDS resources. If you don't have all of those, be sure to review the previous sections for more details.

There are a lot of things to learn and a few steps to creating a DB System. It is rather easy once you learn how, but unlike previous tutorials which walked you through the minimal steps, this tutorial will proceed step-by-step and learn more about what is available to us on each of the OCI cloud console pages. So, this tutorial may take some time to get through, but it will be worth it to learn about what you can do with a DB System.

Open the DB Systems Resource Page

We will be using the MySQL menu from the cloud console to create a DB System. Simply open the cloud console menu, select *Databases*, and then click on *DB Systems* under the *MySQL* menu. This will open the DB Systems resource page as shown in Figure 4-13.

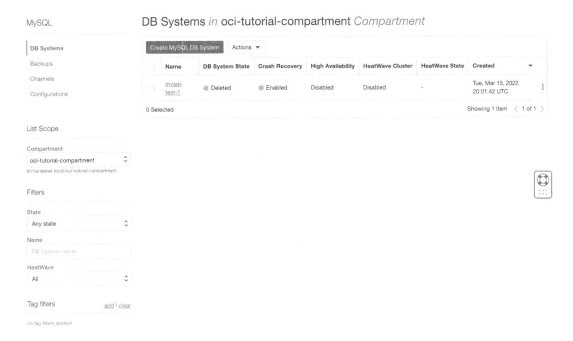

Figure 4-13. *DB Systems Resource Page*

We see to the right a list of the DB Systems (*DB Systems in …*) we have created and their states including the DB System, Crash Recovery, High Availability, and HeatWave states as well as the date and time when the resource was created.

Notice the buttons above the *DB Systems in…* list. We have a *Create DB System* button and an *Action* drop-down menu. On the *Action* drop-down menu, you can execute an operation on any of the DB Systems that are selected in the list. These include the following:

- *Stop*: Stop the DB System

- *Start*: Start the DB System

- *Restart*: Stop then start the DB System

- *Create a Manual Backup*: Create a backup of the DB System

- *Apply Tags*: Apply one or more tags to the resources

- *Delete*: Delete (terminate) the DB System

As you can see, this is a powerful menu and quite a shortcut for working with multiple DB Systems. Fortunately, the *Action* drop-down menu is a common feature among the OCI cloud console resource page lists. The actions may differ, but the concept is the same.

Notice also that there is one DB System here that has been terminated (*Deleted*). A DB System that has been terminated will remain on the list for a few days until all resources have been purged (e.g., the block volumes are not immediately destroyed).

On the left side of the page, we see the *MySQL* menu repeated. We can use that to navigate among the MySQL resources by clicking the label we want to see. Below that on the left is the *List Scope* list that we've seen before where we can choose the compartment to filter the DB Systems list.

At the bottom left is a special *Filters* section where we can filter the list even further by selecting a specific state, name, or even selecting among HeatWave entries (we will see more about HeatWave in Chapter 8).

Finally at the bottom is a Tag filter where, if we used tags, we could further filter the list to show only those DB Systems that have those tags.

These three filtering mechanisms are common among all OCI cloud console pages that provide a list. Some resources may have differing filter selections, but all resource pages allow you to filter the list. Nice.

Create a DB System

Let's go ahead and create a DB System. The dialog to create a DB System is long, so we will present a portion at a time. The information we will need to provide includes the following:

- *Name*: A name for the DB System.

- *Description* (optional): Provides a description for your own use to explain the DB System such as why it was created, to which projects it is allocated, etc. You should avoid any confidential data in the description.

- *Type of DB System*: You can choose from a standalone (no high availability), High Availability enabled, and a HeatWave DB System. We will learn more about the high availability features in Chapter 7 and HeatWave in Chapter 8.

- *Administrator*: You will need to specify the MySQL admin user account and password.

- *Networking*: You will need to select the VCN and subnet for the DB System.

- *Availability Domain* (placement): Choose the availability domain.

- *Hardware*: Choose the shape and size of the data storage (block volume).

- *Backup Plan*: You have the option to turn on automatic backups.

We will walk-through all of these data and show how to complete each for a standalone DB System without automatic backups placed in the `oci-tutorial-compartment`. From the *DB Systems in…* list on the DB Systems resource page, click the *Create DB System* button to create a DB System.

Tip   Notice in the create dialog there are several underlined phrases. These are links to the documentation that you can use to explore more of the details. You should consider taking time to explore these in order to become more familiar with the details of a DB System.

We will examine portions of the dialog from top-to-bottom. You can scroll down to see the other sections of the create DB System dialog. Figure 4-14 shows the first portion that requests the compartment, name, and description. Be sure to select the `oci-tutorial-compartment` in the *Create in compartment* dropdown list and use the name `mysql-test-1`. You can fill in the description if you'd like.

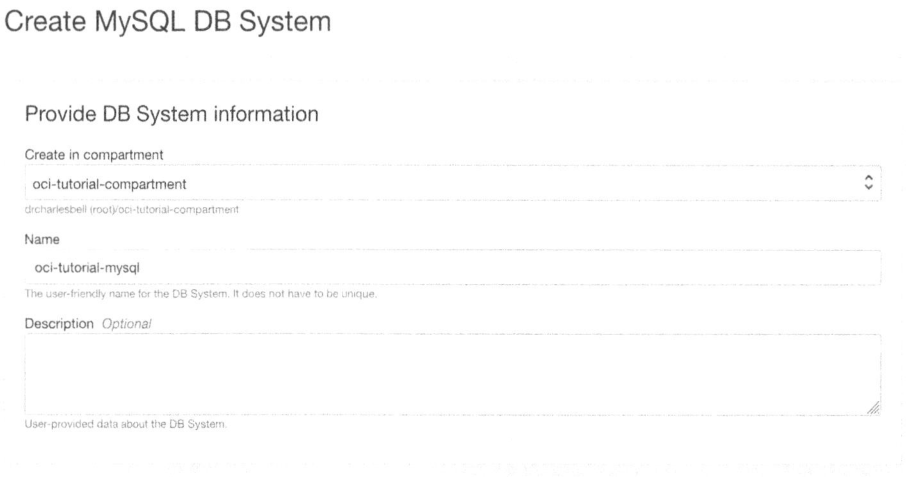

Create MySQL DB System

Provide DB System information

Create in compartment

oci-tutorial-compartment

drcharlesbell (root)/oci-tutorial-compartment

Name

oci-tutorial-mysql

The user-friendly name for the DB System. It does not have to be unique.

Description *Optional*

User-provided data about the DB System.

Figure 4-14. *Create DB System (Part 1)*

Scroll down to the next portion, which requests the type of DB System, and the MySQL administrator credentials. Select the *Standalone* option for the DB System type and use `mysql_admin` for the username and provide a password. Be sure to follow the password restrictions and enter the password a second time to verify. Figure 4-15 shows the portion with the data selected and entered.

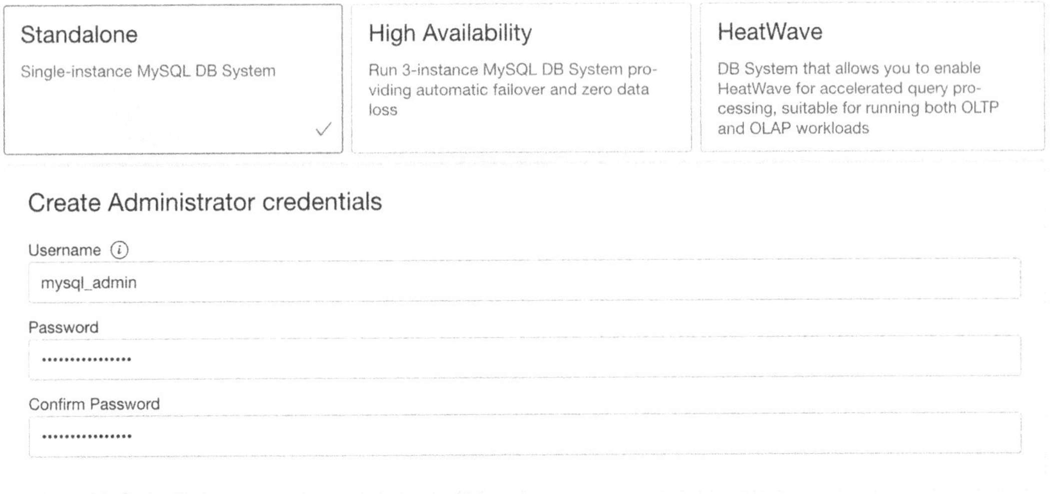

Standalone	High Availability	HeatWave
Single-instance MySQL DB System	Run 3-instance MySQL DB System providing automatic failover and zero data loss	DB System that allows you to enable HeatWave for accelerated query processing, suitable for running both OLTP and OLAP workloads
✓		

Create Administrator credentials

Username ⓘ

mysql_admin

Password

••••••••••••••••

Confirm Password

••••••••••••••••

Figure 4-15. *Create DB System (Part 2)*

Once that information is added, scroll down to the next portion, which is the *Configure networking* section as shown in Figure 4-16. Here, we want to ensure the oci-tutorial-vcn is selected in the *Virtual Cloud Networking in oci-tutorial-compartment* list and the Private Subnet oci-tutorial-vcn (Regional) entry is selected in the *Subnet in oci-tutorial-compartment* list. If you do not see these entries, you can change the compartment using the Change Compartment link.

Configure networking   Collapse

The VCN and subnet where the DB System endpoint will be attached. The DB System endpoint uses a private IP address and is not directly accessible from the internet. How do I connect to a DB System? If you do not have a VCN, create a VCN.

Virtual Cloud Network in **oci-tutorial-compartment**   (Change Compartment)

oci-tutorial-vcn	⌄

Subnet in **oci-tutorial-compartment**   (Change Compartment)

Private Subnet-oci-tutorial-vcn (Regional)	⌄

Figure 4-16. *Create DB System (Part 3)*

Once you have verified those entries, scroll down to the next section, which is the placement of availability domain. Here, it doesn't matter which availability domain you choose, but since we've been using *AD-2* thus far, go ahead and select it as shown in Figure 4-17.

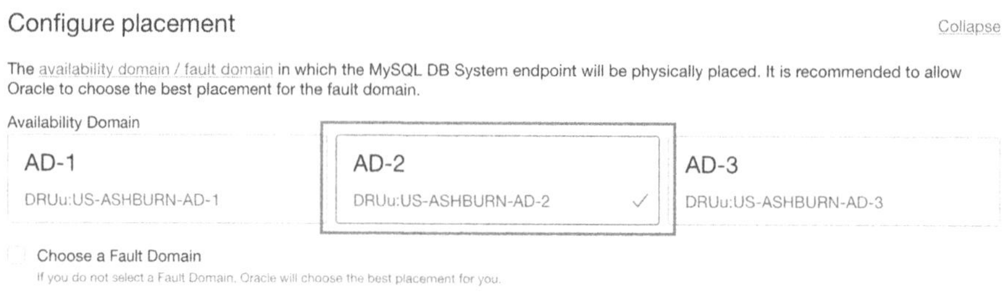

Figure 4-17. *Create DB System (Part 4)*

Once the AD-2 is selected, scroll down to the next section, which is the *Configure hardware* section. Here, we have the option of changing the shape and changing the size of the data storage as shown in Figure 4-18. Since we are creating a DB System as an exercise, we will use the defaults as shown. In this case, it is a small VM shape with 8 GB of RAM and a 50 GB block storage attached for data. As you can surmise, the process of creating and provisioning the DB System includes provisioning the block volume, attaching, connecting, and mounting the block volume to a folder.

Figure 4-18. *Create DB System (Part 5)*

Scroll down to the next section, which allows you to choose automatic backups by selecting a backup plan. A backup plan is simply the frequency of the backup including the type. We will learn more about backups in Chapter 5. For now, we can turn off the backup feature as shown in Figure 4-18. We do not need backups since we will not be creating any data or configuring the database for any retention purposes. When you have confirmed the data entered, click the Create button to create the DB System. This will direct you to the DB Systems detail page.

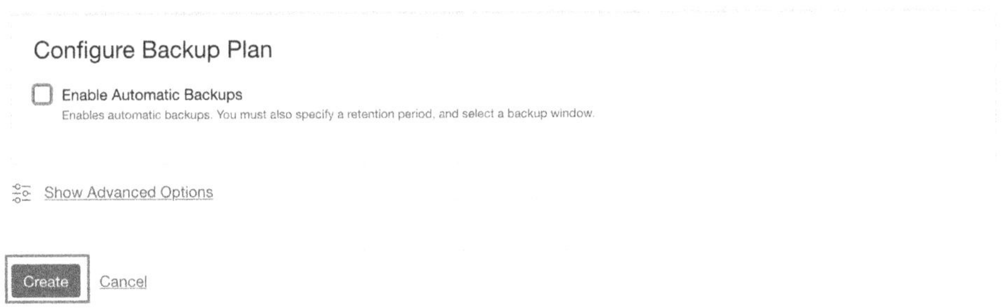

Figure 4-19. *Create DB System (Part 6)*

Once you click the button, the DB System create, set up, and provisioning processes will start and the `Create DB System` work request (also called a workflow) will commence. This can take a while so do not be alarmed if nothing happens right away or you think it may be stuck. Like we saw with other resources, once you start the create, you will be directed to the resource detail page. In this case, you should see the DB System details page similar to Figure 4-20. Notice the DB System is still in the `CREATING` state.

Figure 4-20. *DB System Details Page (Creating)*

You can check on the status of the initial workflow to provision the DB System by scrolling down to the *Resources* menu then click *Work Requests* to view the *Work Requests* section as shown in Figure 4-21. Here, we can see all work requests (workflows) that have been run or are running. As you can see, the initial workflow is still running and may stay that way for some time.

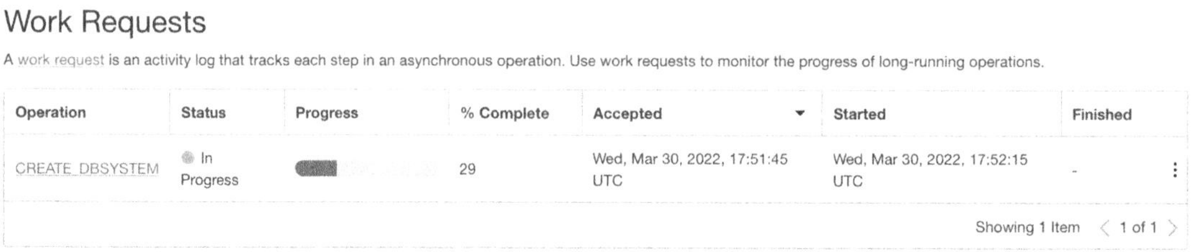

Work Requests

A work request is an activity log that tracks each step in an asynchronous operation. Use work requests to monitor the progress of long-running operations.

Operation	Status	Progress	% Complete	Accepted ▼	Started	Finished
CREATE_DBSYSTEM	● In Progress	▬▬	29	Wed, Mar 30, 2022, 17:51:45 UTC	Wed, Mar 30, 2022, 17:52:15 UTC	-

Showing 1 Item ⟨ 1 of 1 ⟩

Figure 4-21. *DB System Details Page (Work Requests List)*

Once the workflow is done, the icon for the DB System will turn green, the status will change to ACTIVE, and the workflow will show complete. The process can take some minutes to complete. Let's learn more about the DB System details page.

DB System Details Page

This is a good opportunity to look at the DB System details page more closely. Figure 4-22 shows a map of the various sections we will explore. You have seen some of these in other resource pages, so the layout should not be a surprise. We won't go through every detail of every portion, rather, we will spend some time learning what each does and what data is available to you.

Figure 4-22. *DB System Details Page (Feature Map)*

There are three areas identified in the figure. These include the following. We will look at each in more detail in the following sections. The number in the list corresponds to the numbered dot in the figure:

1.   Status and Buttons

2.   Resource Menu

3.   DB System Information and Tags

Status and Buttons

The status and buttons section of the details page is like any other OCI resource detail page. That is, on the left is an icon depicting the state of the resource by color and state value written below the icon. To the right of the icon is a set of buttons for the common operations on a DB System as shown in Figure 4-23.

Figure 4-23. *Status and Buttons, Action Menu*

There are several states that the DB System can have. Table 4-1 shows a list of the states along with the color of the icon.

Table 4-1. *DB System States and Icon Colors*

Icon Color	State	Description
Grey	INACTIVE	The DB System is powered off by the stop or reboot action in the Console or API.
Red	DELETED	The DB System is deleted and is no longer available.
	FAILED	An error condition prevented the creation or continued operation of the DB System.
Yellow	CREATING	The DB System is reserving resources, booting, and creating the initial database. Provisioning can take several minutes. You cannot use the system yet.
	UPDATING	The DB System is starting, stopping, restarting, or updating a replication channel associated with the DB System.
	DELETING	The DB System is being deleted by the terminate action in the Console or API.
Green	ACTIVE	The DB System is successfully created.

The buttons are for operations that include the following:

- *Edit*: Change name and description for the DB System for an active DB System. You can change the shape for an inactive DB System.

- *Start*: Start a stopped or inactive DB System. Note that this button is greyed out (inoperative) for an active DB System.

- *Stop*: Stop an active DB System.

- *Restart*: Stop then start a DB System.

- *More Actions*: Perform resource-specific actions on the DB System.

If you are following along in this tutorial and want to stop and come back later to finish the chapter, you may want to stop the DB System so that you do not incur any costs for execution. You will still incur costs for having an inactive DB System, but not as much as if it were active. To stop the DB System, click the *Stop* button and optionally change the stop type. You will be prompted for a fast, slow, etc. options but you should choose the default. Once the DB System is stopped, its icon will change to yellow and the status INACTIVE will be displayed.

The *More Actions* menu contains the following operations. Some of these operations may be available (repeated) on the various resource panes as defined in the next section. For example, you can create a new backup while viewing the list of existing backups.

We won't cover all of these operations in this chapter saving the explanations for later chapters. We will cover backup operations in Chapter 5, high availability options in Chapter 7, and HeatWave in Chapter 8:

- *Edit Backup Plan*: Enable or disable automatic backups.

- *Create Manual Backup*: Create a backup of the DB System.

- *Enable High Availability*: Change a standalone DB System to a high availability enabled DB System.

- *Disable Crash Recovery*: Enable or disable crash recovery. Disabling crash recovery can improve performance but will also turn off automatic backups. Use wisely.

- *Add HeatWave Cluster*: Add another cluster to the HeatWave configuration (valid only for DB Systems with HeatWave enabled).

- *Create Channel*: Create a replication channel for use in accepting replication data from another source. See Chapter 7 for more details on this advanced topic.

- *Update Storage Size*: Change the storage size of the MySQL data.

- *Edit MySQL Version*: If the DB System is running a lower (older) version of MySQL than what is available in OCI, you have the option of updating the DB System to use the latest version of MySQL.

- *Add Tags*: Add one or more user-defined tags that are displayed in the *Tags* tab.

- *Delete*: Terminate the DB System and delete all resources for it.

Next, let's look at the *Resource* menu and its selections.

Resource Menu

The resource menu is used to change the bottom portion (pane) of the details page to one of several resource views as shown in Figure 4-24. Some views contain a filter section for filtering the view. The resources available for viewing and interacting with include metrics, replication endpoints, HeatWave clusters, backups, channels, and work requests. We will see an example of each of these in the following sections:

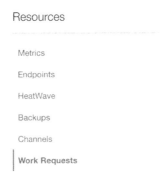

Figure 4-24. *Resources Menu*

Metrics

One of the most powerful tools in diagnosing performance and related issues are the metrics you gather from the system. MySQL includes a long list of things you can monitor from the performance schema views and elsewhere in MySQL. However, most of that information is managed by OCI. Fortunately, you can still see graphical representation of many of those performance metrics as well as important OCI-related performance metrics for a DB System.

When you click on *Metrics* in the menu, you will see a grid of various metric counters displayed as shown in Figure 4-25. These include metrics for connections, statements, CPU, memory, network latency, disk utilization, and backups.

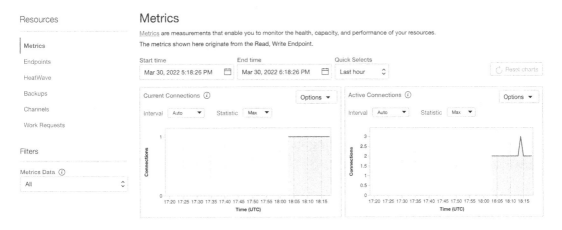

Figure 4-25. *Metrics Resource Pane (DB System)*

Notice the metrics resource pane has a filter to the left that you can use to show all metrics or limit the view to either the DB System or backups.

As you become more familiar with DB Systems and start using them in production environments, you may want to visit this resource pane to learn how your DB Systems are performing over time.

Endpoints

Endpoints are connection points for DB Systems. You can use them for advanced replication operations as we will see in Chapter 7, or for connecting to MySQL from another process or system.

When you click on *Endpoints* in the menu, you will see a list of the endpoints you have created as shown in Figure 4-26. The list will display the hostname for the endpoint, its status, IP address, MySQL ports, and the modes of operation. Notice the only entry in the endpoints list for our tutorial DB System is the IP address to which you can use to connect to MySQL from the VCN. We will see how to use this endpoint in the next section.

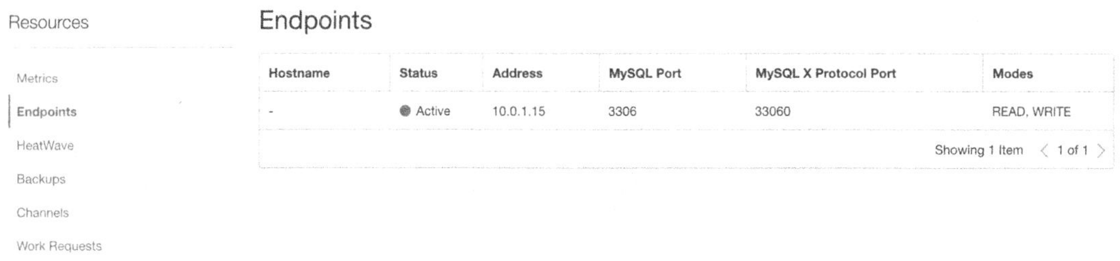

Resources	Endpoints					
	Hostname	Status	Address	MySQL Port	MySQL X Protocol Port	Modes
Metrics						
Endpoints	-	● Active	10.0.1.15	3306	33060	READ, WRITE
HeatWave						Showing 1 Item ⟨ 1 of 1 ⟩
Backups						
Channels						
Work Requests						

Figure 4-26. *Endpoints Resource Pane (DB System)*

HeatWave

The HeatWave resource pane is used to display information about the clusters in the HeatWave configuration. When you click on *HeatWave* in the menu, you will see a list of the clusters created. Since we have not enabled HeatWave when we created the DB System, we will see a message stating such as shown in Figure 4-27. We will cover HeatWave in more detail in Chapter 8.

Figure 4-27. *HeatWave Resource Pane (DB System)*

Backups

Backups are special entities in OCI that include a backup of all of the data as well as the MySQL configuration. Like a backup for your PC, you can use a backup to restore the DB System to the state at the time of the backup. Backups are an essential tool in maintaining integrity of your data. We will cover backups in more detail in Chapter 5.

When you click on *Backups* in the menu, you will see a list of the backups available for the DB System. The list will display the name, state (status), creation type (full, incremental), retention days, size, and the date it was created as shown in Figure 4-28. Notice this resource pane includes a filter that lets you filter the list (scope) by compartment.

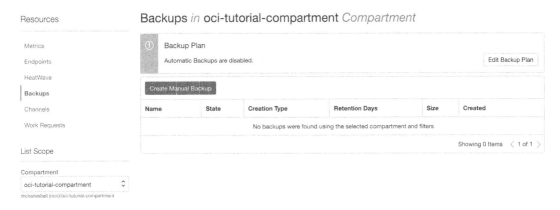

Figure 4-28. *Backups Resource Pane (DB System)*

Channels

Channels are used in replication to permit data from/to other systems (including DB Systems). We will learn more about channels in Chapter 7.

When you click on *Channels* in the menu, you will see a list of the channels associated with the DB System to include the name, source, target, state (status), details, whether it is enabled, and date it was created.

Figure 4-29. *Channels Resource Pane (DB System)*

Work Requests

Recall from our earlier look at when we created the DB System, a work request (workflow) is an OCI internal process or processes that are run to execute some operation on the DB System. These can include backups, editing (updating) the DB System, stopping, restarting, etc.

When you click on *Work Requests* in the menu, you will see a list of the work requests appear in the pane to the right as shown in Figure 4-30. This will include all past work requests and any that are currently active. The list shows the operation (work request name), status, progress bar, % complete, when the work request was accepted by OCI, date when it started, and the date when it finished.

Resources	Work Requests						
Metrics	A work request is an activity log that tracks each step in an asynchronous operation. Use work requests to monitor the progress of long-running operations.						
Endpoints	Operation	Status	Progress	% Complete	Accepted ▾	Started	Finished
HeatWave	CREATE DBSYSTEM	● Succeeded		100	Wed, Mar 30, 2022, 17:51:45 UTC	Wed, Mar 30, 2022, 17:52:15 UTC	Wed, Mar 30, 2022, 18:00:13 UTC ⋮
Backups							
Channels						Showing 1 Item ‹ 1 of 1 ›	
Work Requests							

Figure 4-30. *Work Requests Resource Pane (DB System)*

If there are work requests listed, you can act on the context menu (the three vertically stacked dots to the right of the row) to manipulate the work request to view the details.

Now, let's look at the DB System information shown in the center of the details page.

MySQL DB System Information and Tags

There are two tabs in the center of the DB System details page; one for the DB System *Information* that shows critical metadata for working with the DB System, and *Tags* that shows the tags or labels created for the DB System including system-generated and user-defined tags. Let's look at each of these tabs.

DB System Information Tab

The large area in the center of the details page contains a host of important information. The details are broken into several sections described below. Included in the description are key values or parameters that you may need to use for certain operations. Figure 4-31 shows an excerpt of the tutorial DB System for you to use in locating the information described in the list.

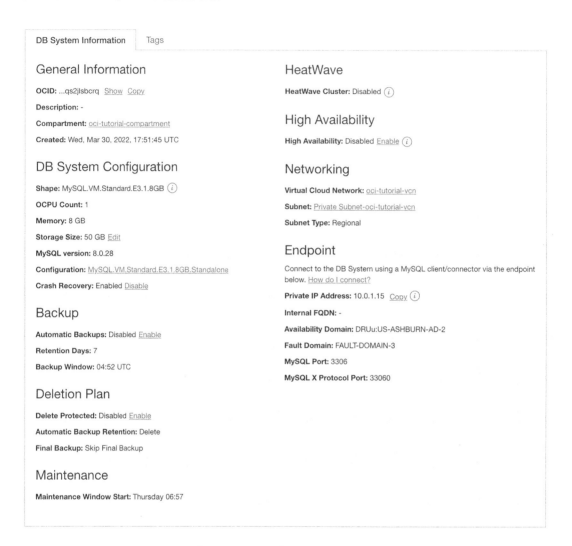

Figure 4-31. *DB System Information Tab*

The DB System Information tab displays the following information by section. Notice there are some data presented as a link. These can be used to navigate to the details page for that resource or object or as shortcuts to run common operations. Nice.

- *General Information*: Displays the OCID with a link to copy it to your clipboard, description (that you provided when you created the DB System), compartment where the DB System resides, and the date created. The OCID is the most important piece of information in this section as you may need to use it for certain advanced operations and features.

- *DB System Configuration*: Displays information about the DB System including its shape, memory and storage size, MySQL version and configuration, and if crash recover is enabled. The edit link next to the storage size is a shortcut to changing the storage size of the DB System.

- *Backup*: Displays whether automatic backups are enabled, the retention (in days) of backups, and the window for running automatic backups. The enable/disable links are shortcuts for enabling or disabling automatic backups.

- *Deletion Plan*: Displays the deletion plan for the DB System including if it is enabled, the retention time for automatic backups, and the state of the final backup. The enable/disable links are shortcuts for enabling or disabling the deletion plan.

- *Maintenance*: Displays the start of the next maintenance cycle for MDS. This is the time when automatic upgrades and updates will occur. You can use it to time or delay critical operations to ensure your applications run smoothly.

- *HeatWave*: Displays information about HeatWave clusters. See Chapter 8 for more details.

- *High Availability*: Displays information about the high availability configuration. See Chapter 7 for more details.

- *Networking*: Displays the VCN, subnet, and subnet type where the DB System is connected. You may need to refer to this information for connecting services.

- *Endpoint*: Displays the private IP address the DB System is using on the VCN, a fully qualified domain name (FQDN), availability domain, fault domain, and the MySQL ports configured along with a helpful link to the documentation on how to connect to a DB System. We will explore that topic in the next section. The critical information you will need to use from this section includes the Private IP address (use the copy link to copy it to your clipboard). It may also be helpful to see the availability domain and fault domain at-a-glance when planning connections and other features.

Tags Tab

Next are the tabs section of the interface as shown in Figure 4-32. Here, we will see all of the tags for the DB System to include any OCI-generated as well as user-defined tags. Notice we have two OCI-generated tags and a single user-defined tag. You can switch between these lists by clicking on the *Defined Tags* or *Free-form Tags* labels.

You can create a user-defined tag by using the *More Actions* menu and selecting *Add Tags*. Note that tag names do not permit spaces or any character that cannot be printed (ASCII).

Notice in the figure we see a small pencil icon next to the tag. If the pencil icon is enabled (not greyed out), you can click on it to edit the tag.

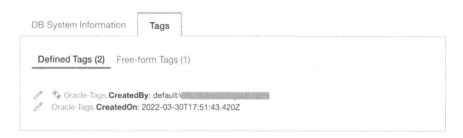

Figure 4-32. *DB System Tags Tab*

Now, let's look at the most common operations for the DB System; stopping and starting.

Tip   See `https://docs.oracle.com/en-us/iaas/mysql-database/doc/managing-db-system.html` for more details on the resources and operations available on the DB System Details page.

Stopping and Starting the DB System

If you recall from the *More Actions* menu discussed earlier, you can stop and start a DB System. If you are not using or won't be planning to use the DB System for some time, it may be a good idea to stop it. Stopping the DB System will reduce the cost burden against your account. You will still be billed a small amount since you have allocated billable resources, but you won't be billed for an idle compute instance. If you plan to follow along with the next section, you do not need to stop the DB System. However, if you plan to come back to it later, you should stop the DB System and start it again when you are ready to continue the tutorial.

To stop a DB System, you can use the *More Actions* button menu to select *Stop*. Similarly, to start a stopped DB System, you can use the Action button menu and select *Start*. Both operations take a while to complete but the status of the DB System will change accordingly, and you can watch the work requests list to check its progress.

Now that we have our DB System created, you may be wondering how we can connect to it like we did with our MySQL server that we installed on our PC in Chapter 4. As you will see, there are several mechanisms we can use depending on our requirements.

Connecting to Your DB System

Connecting to your MySQL DB System is not like a MySQL server you've installed on your PC or in your local network. Recall, a DB System is created in a VCN and, more specifically, in a private subnet. This means the DB System is only reachable by a machine that is also attached to or has access to the private subnet. So, you cannot connect to your DB System directly from your PC without some additional steps. In fact, there are several mechanisms you can use to connect to your DB System. We will learn about these mechanisms in this section.

Note   Preparing your connection method may take some time as you work through the steps. If you created a DB System in the last section and following along with this tutorial, you can leave the DB System running. However, if you want to read through this section and come back to it later, you should stop your DB System to reduce the cost and start it when you are ready to connect.

Connection Mechanisms

The connection mechanisms for connecting to your DB System include the following. A short overview is included for each. As you will see, some are very easy to set up while others are more complex. Fortunately, there are enough options to meet just about any need. There may be other, more advanced mechanisms, but these are the ones most commonly seen in the demos and documentation.

In all cases, the tool you use to connect to MySQL includes the normal tools such as a MySQL client such as the older `mysql` client, MySQL Shell, or MySQL Workbench. See `https://docs.oracle.com/en-us/iaas/mysql-database/doc/connecting-db-system.html` for more information about the tools you can use to connect to a DB System:

- *Compute Instance*: Use a compute instance in the VCN in the public subnet. Connection is made by logging into the compute instance and then running one of the MySQL clients to connect to the DB System. This mimics how an application server would likely be used to host your application and communicate with the DB System.

- *Bastion Session*: Use a Bastion Service, an OCI resource, provides restricted and time-limited access to target resources that do not have public endpoints. You can permit authorized users to connect from specific IP addresses to targeted resources using SSH using one of several options. For example, you can create a port-forwarding session (also known as an SSH tunnel) and use that via a Bastion Session to connect a MySQL client to your DB System.

- *VPN Connection*: Use either site-to-site VPN, FastConnect (an OCI resource)[1], or OpenVPN Access Server[2] to bridge your local network with your OCI VCN. For more information, visit the OCI documentation (`https://docs.oracle.com/en-us/iaas/Content/home.htm`) and use the table of contents menu to navigate to *Data Management | MySQL Database | Networking Setup | VPN Connection* for more details.

- *OpenVPN Access Server*: Configure OpenVPN Access Server to connect your local network to your VCN. For more information, visit the OCI documentation (`https://docs.oracle.com/en-us/iaas/Content/home.htm`) and use the table of contents menu to navigate to *Data Management | MySQL Database | Networking Setup | OpenVPN Access Server* for more details.

---

[1] `https://www.oracle.com/cloud/networking/fastconnect/`
[2] `https://openvpn.net/access-server/`

Tip   For more information about networking and DB Systems, see the Networking Setup documentation at `https://docs.oracle.com/en-us/iaas/mysql-database/doc/networking-setup-mysql-db-systems.html`.

Let's look at a couple of these options to complete our tutorial on DB Systems. We will see how to use a Compute Instance and create a Bastion Session to connect a MySQL client on our PC to our DB System.

Connecting via a Compute Instance

This mechanism is the easiest to use and it offers the fastest method for experimentation with or learning about MDS and DB Systems. In this case, we simply create a Compute Instance and place it in the same compartment as the DB System. We will place it in the public subnet of the same VCN where the DB System resides.

Tip   If you skipped the tutorial in Chapter 2, you may want to go back to the tutorial to see the steps needed to create a Compute Instance.

If you have created a Compute Instance in Chapter 2 and still have it available, you can use it to connect to your DB System provided it is in the same VCN and in the public subnet. We will summarize the steps in case you need to create a new Compute Instance.

Create a Compute Instance

The steps to create a compute instance are summarized below. Refer to Chapter 2 if you need to revisit the tutorial to learn more about each step in the process. Values used for entry or selection are shown in parenthesis:

1. Open the cloud console main menu select *Compute | Instances* then click *Create instance* button.

2. Give the instance a name (`connection-instance`).

3. Verify the correct compartment (`oci-tutorial-compartment`). Select the correct compartment from the list.

4. Verify the correct VCN is chosen (`oci-tutorial-vcn`). Click the *Edit* button to change the VCN.

5. Click on the *Save Private Key* button to download the private key.

6. (optional) Copy the private key to your `~/.ssh` folder and change the file permissions (e.g., `chmod 400 ~/.ssh/ssh-key-2022-04-01.key`).

7. Click the Create button.

Finally, wait for the compute instance to provision and status set to `ACTIVE`. Recall, you can track the progress of the work request to create the compute instance (`Create instance`) on the *Work Requests* pane on the compute instance details page.

Modify the VCN – Create an Ingress Rule for the Private Subnet

There is one thing we need to do for our VCN. We need to create an ingress rule on the private subnet to allow connections from the public subnet. In this case, to allow the new compute instance on the public subnet of the VCN to the DB System on the private subnet of the VCN. This is not done for us when we ran the VCN setup wizard earlier, but it is easy to do.

Start by navigating to the VCN by clicking the cloud console main menu then select *Networking* | *Virtual Cloud Networks*. Next, click on your VCN (`oci-tutorial-vcn`).

On the VCN details page, click on the *Subnets* entry in the *Resources* menu on the left then click on the private subnet (`Private Subnet-oci-tutorial-vcn`) as shown in Figure 4-33. Alternatively, you can click on the context menu to the right of the private subnet and choose *View Details*.

Resources	Subnets *in* oci-tutorial-compartment *Compartment*					
Subnets (2)	Create Subnet					
CIDR Blocks (1)	Name	State	IPv4 CIDR Block	IPv6 CIDR Block	Subnet Access	Created
Route Tables (2)	Private Subnet-oci-tutorial-vcn	● Available	10.0.1.0/24	-	Private (Regional)	Fri, Mar 11, 2022, 20:27:33 UTC
Internet Gateways (1)						
Dynamic Routing Gateways Attachments (0)	Public Subnet-oci-tutorial-vcn	● Available	10.0.0.0/24	-	Public (Regional)	Fri, Mar 11, 2022, 20:27:32 UTC

Figure 4-33. *Selecting the Private Subnet (VCN)*

Next, we need to create the ingress rule. On the private subnet details page, click on the *Security Lists* entry in the *Resources* menu on the left then click on the security list as shown in Figure 4-34. Alternatively, you can click on the context menu to the right of the private subnet and choose *View Details*.

Figure 4-34. *Select Security List (Private Subnet)*

Next, under the Ingress Rules list, click the *Add Ingress Rules* button as shown in Figure 4-35.

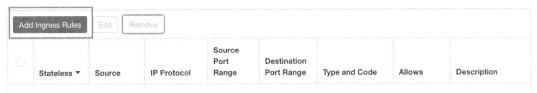

Figure 4-35. *Adding an Ingress Rule (Private Subnet Security List)*

A dialog will open where you can fill in the data. At a minimum, we need to enter the CIDR (`10.0.0.0/16`), the destination ports (`3306, 33060`), and (optionally) a description (`MySQL Ingress Rule`). Once you have the data entered, you can click the *Add Ingress Rules* button as shown in Figure 4-36. Notice you can add additional ingress rules in this dialog by clicking the + *Another Ingress Rule* button.

Figure 4-36. *Creating an Ingress Rule for MySQL*

This will create a pathway for our compute instance, which resides on the public subnet of our VCN to communicate with the DB System, which resides on the private subnet of our VCN but only through ports 3306 and 33060. Now we are ready to proceed.

Note   You need only add the ingress rule for MySQL once. It remains in place until you remove it.

Connect to the Compute Instance

Now that we have a compute instance running and it is in the same VCN as our DB System with a public IP address, we can connect to it from our PC. You will need the public IP address for the compute instance as found on the Compute Instance details page in the *Instance Information* tab (in the center of the page) under the header *Instance access* as shown in Figure 4-37.

Instance access

You connect to a running Linux instance using a Secure Shell (SSH) connection. You'll need the private key from the SSH key pair that was used to create the instance.

Public IP address: 129.158.195.169 Copy

Username: opc

Figure 4-37. *Locating the Public IP Address (Compute Instance)*

Recall, we can connect to the compute instance from our PC by using the public IP address and the SSH key we downloaded earlier. You can click on the *Copy* link to copy the public IP address and paste it into the following command to connect via SSH as shown. Also, the opc user is the default user created for compute instances:

```
ssh -i ~/.ssh/ssh-key-2022-04-01.key opc@129.158.195.169
```

If you placed the downloaded SSH key in a different location, be sure to change it in the command shown in bold. Once you enter the command, you will be connected to your compute instance as shown in Listing 4-1.

Listing 4-1. Connecting to a Compute Instance (From Your PC)

```
% ssh -i ~/.ssh/ssh-key-2022-04-01.key opc@129.158.195.169
The authenticity of host '129.158.195.169 (129.158.195.169)' can't be
established.
...
This key is not known by any other names
Are you sure you want to continue connecting (yes/no/[fingerprint])? yes
Warning: Permanently added '129.158.195.169' (ED25519) to the list of
known hosts.
Activate the web console with: systemctl enable --now cockpit.socket

[opc@connection-instance ~]$
```

Once you connect to the compute instance, we can now connect to the DB System from the compute instance.

Connect to the DB System

We are using the compute instance we created as a gateway to the DB System. Once you are logged into the compute instance, you can connect to the MySQL instance running on the DB System. We can use either the MySQL client (`mysql`) or MySQL Shell (`mysqlsh`).

However, you have to install these packages on the compute instance first. The commands to do so are shown below. Note that you are using the `sudo` command since you will need elevated privileges to connect and the `opc` user account has permission to use `sudo`. Also, when you install these packages, you may see one or more dependent packages installed:

```
$ sudo yum install mysql-shell
$ sudo yum install mysql
```

You can install these separately or install both with the following command:

```
$ sudo yum install mysql-shell mysql
```

Listing 4-2 shows an excerpt of installing the MySQL Shell. Installing the MySQL client (or both) will generate similar output with potentially other packages included.

Listing 4-2. Installing the MySQL Shell (Compute Instance)

```
$ sudo yum install mysql-shell
Ksplice for Oracle Linux 8
(x86_64)                                    6.4 MB/s | 779 kB     00:00
MySQL 8.0 for Oracle Linux 8
(x86_64)                                    6.5 MB/s | 2.2 MB     00:00
MySQL 8.0 Tools Community for Oracle
Linux 8 (x86_64)                            2.0 MB/s | 249 kB     00:00
MySQL 8.0 Connectors Community for Oracle
Linux 8 (x86_64)                            166 kB/s |  20 kB     00:00
Oracle Software for OCI users on Oracle
Linux 8 (x86_64)                             32 MB/s |  29 MB     00:00
Oracle Linux 8 BaseOS Latest
(x86_64)                                     29 MB/s |  43 MB     00:01
```

```
Oracle Linux 8 Application Stream
(x86_64)                                      22 MB/s | 32 MB      00:01
Oracle Linux 8 Addons
(x86_64)                                      10 MB/s | 2.9 MB     00:00
Latest Unbreakable Enterprise Kernel
Release 6 for Oracle Linux 8 (x86_64          21 MB/s | 41 MB      00:02
Dependencies resolved.
...
Install  4 Packages
Total download size: 27 M
Installed size: 137 M
Is this ok [y/N]: Y
...
Installed:
  mysql-shell-8.0.28-1.el8.x86_64
  python39-libs-3.9.6-2.module+el8.5.0+20364+c7fe1181.x86_64
  python39-pip-wheel-20.2.4-6.module+el8.5.0+20364+c7fe1181.noarch
  python39-setuptools-wheel-50.3.2-4.module+el8.5.0+20364+c7fe1181.noarch
Complete!
```

Once the client(s) are installed, you can connect to your MySQL instance using the MySQL admin user and password you provided when you created the DB System along with the private IP address from the DB System details page. Recall, this information is shown in the DB System Information (in the center of the page) under the DDD heading as shown in Figure 4-38. You can use the *Copy* link to copy the IP address.

Figure 4-38. *Locating the Private IP Address (DB System)*

Now we're ready to connect. The following command shows the correct options (just one possible combination) for using the MySQL Shell to connect to our DB System. The options are similar for the MySQL client (remove the `--sql` option as it applies only to MySQL Shell):

```
$ mysqlsh --sql -umysql_admin -p -h 10.0.1.15 --port=33060
```

Alternatively, you can use an URI that combines the username, host, and port with the following command:

```
$ mysqlsh --sql mysql_admin@10.0.1.15:33060
```

Caution   If you stopped your DB System earlier, be sure to start it and wait for it to become active before proceeding.

Listing 4-3 shows a demonstration of using the command to connect to MySQL from the compute instance.

Listing 4-3. Connecting to MySQL on the DB System (Compute Instance)

```
[opc@connection-instance ~]$ mysqlsh --sql mysql_admin@10.0.1.73:33060
Please provide the password for 'mysql_admin@10.0.1.73:33060':
****************
Save password for 'mysql_admin@10.0.1.73:33060'? [Y]es/[N]o/Ne[v]er
(default No): y
MySQL Shell 8.0.28

Copyright (c) 2016, 2022, Oracle and/or its affiliates.
Oracle is a registered trademark of Oracle Corporation and/or its
affiliates.
Other names may be trademarks of their respective owners.

Type '\help' or '\?' for help; '\quit' to exit.
Creating a session to 'mysql_admin@10.0.1.73:33060'
Fetching schema names for autocompletion... Press ^C to stop.
Your MySQL connection id is 21 (X protocol)
Server version: 8.0.28-u2-cloud MySQL Enterprise - Cloud
No default schema selected; type \use <schema> to set one.
```

```
MySQL  10.0.1.73:33060+ ssl  SQL > SHOW DATABASES;
+--------------------+
| Database           |
+--------------------+
| information_schema |
| mysql              |
| performance_schema |
| sys                |
+--------------------+
4 rows in set (0.0009 sec)
 MySQL  10.0.1.73:33060+ ssl  SQL > \q
Bye!
```

If you see something similar to the listing, congratulations! You have just connected to your first DB System. Go ahead and run some sample SQL statements if you want to play around with it.

WAIT, IT DOESN'T WORK!

If you were not able to connect, go back and be sure your compute instance is in the same availability domain, on the same VCN (in the public subnet), and that you have added the correct ingress rule to the VCN private subnet as described above.

Another common issue is forgetting the MySQL admin username and password. While writing it down is a very poor practice, you should ensure you are using the username and password you supplied when you created the DB System. There is no easy way to change that password, so worst case may require you to delete the current DB System and create another one with the same data and ensure you are recording the username and password for the MySQL admin user.

That's it! Pretty easy to set up and use, yes? Once again, this is very similar to how you would typically build an application in OCI. You would have the application server or the forward facing, public connection point on the public subnet of your VCN and your data resources on the private subnet protecting your vital investment with good security practices.

Now, let's see how we can connect to our DB System directly from our PC.

Connecting Using a Bastion Session

Bastion is an OCI service that provides restricted and time-limited connections via SSH to resources that do not have public endpoints. Once the connection is made, users can interact with the target resource by using any software or protocol supported by SSH. Connections are made using a session object on a Bastion resource using an SSH Client or SSH Tunnel to connect to a resource on a private subnet. For example, you can use a MySQL client (that supports SSH) to connect to a DB System. Let's learn more about the terminology used in Bastion before we see a demonstration.

Note   Bastions are associated with a single VCN. They cannot be moved from one VCN to another.

Bastion Terminology

The following summarizes key terminology used in the Bastion Service:

- *Bastion*: An OCI service that provides a secure, public access to target resources. These resources are those you cannot access from outside the VCN because they are placed in a private subnet in the VCN. The Bastion Service (sometimes an instance is simply called a bastion) is placed in the public subnet of the VCN. Clients are identified using a CIDR allow list to specify the address or address range you will permit to connect to a specific resource or range of resources in the private subnet.

- *Session*: A session is used to provide access to users via an SSH private key that matches the public SSH key pair. The SSH key pair is recorded in the session when it is created. A session therefore can be considered an active connection via the Bastion Service.

- *Target Resource*: A resource in the private subnet of the VCN to which you want to connect.

- *Target Host*: A specific type of target resource that supports SSH connections such as compute instances.

Session Types

Bastion has two types of sessions that are designed for connecting to a certain type of target resource. The session types include the following:

- *Managed SSH*: Allows SSH access to a compute instance executing Linux, running an OpenSSH server, and the Oracle Cloud Agent with the Bastion plugin enabled.

- *SSH Port Forwarding*: Also known as SSH tunneling. Does not require either an OpenSSH server or the Oracle Cloud Agent to be running on the target resource. Creates a secure connection between a specific port on the client to a specific port on the target resource. The tunnel supports most TCP protocols including Remote Desktop Protocol (RDP), Oracle Net Services, and MySQL.

A bastion can be accessed via any of the normal clients used to communicate with OCI resources that also support SSH. For example, you can use the cloud console, CLI, or the OCI APIs.

Tip   To learn more about Bastion, see `https://docs.oracle.com/en-us/iaas/Content/Bastion/Concepts/bastionoverview.htm`.

In this tutorial, we will use a port-forwarding option and a Bastion Session to connect to our DB System using our PC.

Prerequisites

Before we begin, we will need the following pieces of information. We will see how (and where) to find this information as we proceed:

- Private IP Address of the DB System

- VCN and Subnet

- Classless Inter-Domain Routing (CIDR) for the IP Address of the client (e.g., PC)

- Maximum session time (time you want to allow the connection to remain open)

- SSH Key Pair

- Ingress Rule on the Private Subnet of the VCN

Clearly, you will need to have a running (or one that you can start) DB System, the VCN it is connected to, and the subnet. If you do not have a DB System that you can use, go back and create one before proceeding.

We must also have an ingress rule for our private subnet to allow the MySQL ports 3306 and 33060 to pass from the public subnet. If you skipped the previous example, return to the section entitled *Modify the VCN – Create an Ingress Rule for the Private Subnet* and create the ingress rule before continuing.

Create a Bastion Service

Now let's create our Bastion Service. Using the cloud console main menu, choose *Identity & Security | Bastion* (you may need to scroll down a bit) and then click the *Create Bastion* button as shown in Figure 4-39. Make sure you have the correct compartment selected.

Bastions *in* oci-tutorial-compartment *Compartment*

Bastions let you create and manage sessions that provide authenticated users with ephemeral, timebound access to resources in the tenancy. Bastions establish secure bridge connections from preconfigured IP addresses to supported target hosts that do not have a public IP address, such as compute instances running an OpenSSH server or autonomous transaction processing databases that support SSH tunneling to an arbitrary port.

Name	State	Bastion type	Created
		No items found.	

Create bastion

Showing 0 Items ⟨ 1 of 1 ⟩

Figure 4-39. *Creating a New Bastion Service (Bastion Main Page)*

This will open a new dialog where you will be creating a new Bastion Service running on our VCN. First, name the bastion MySQL Bastion. Note that the name for a bastion cannot have spaces, underscores, or dashes (it will remind you). Next, select the oci-tutorial-vcn and the Public Subnet-oci-tutorial-vcn from the dropdown boxes. Recall, we want to create a bridge from the public subnet to the private subnet so the bastion must reside on the public subnet. Next, we will also use a CIDR of 0.0.0.0/0 (enter the string then press *ENTER* to accept it in the box), which is very open (allows all IP addresses), but you may want to modify that to restrict access for production uses.

Figure 4-40 shows the dialog with the same data. When you have verified the entered data is correct, click the *Create bastion* button.

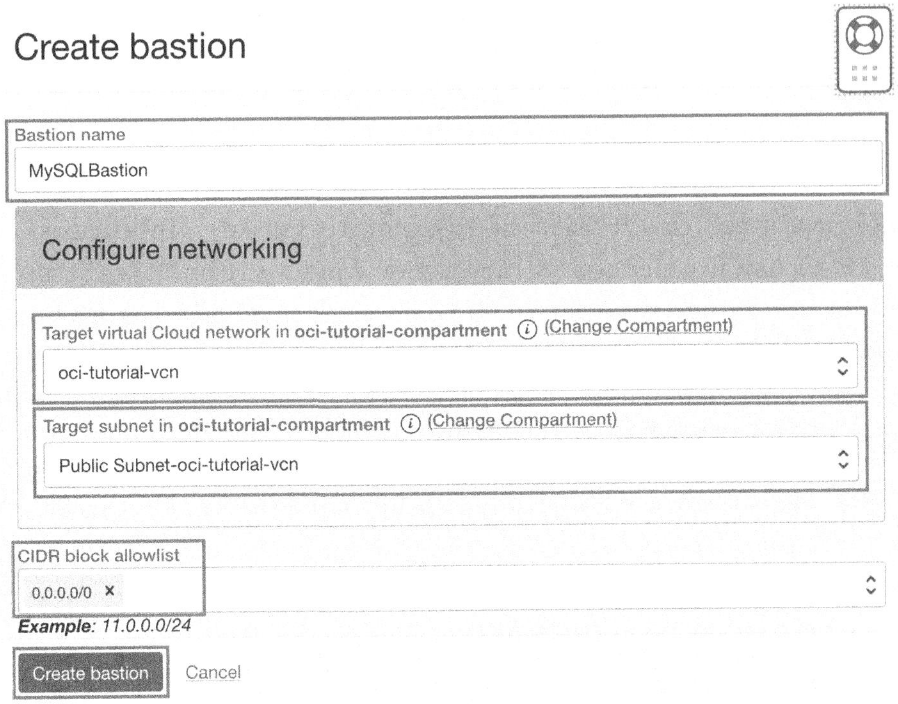

Create bastion

Bastion name

MySQLBastion

Configure networking

Target virtual Cloud network in **oci-tutorial-compartment** ⓘ (Change Compartment)

oci-tutorial-vcn

Target subnet in **oci-tutorial-compartment** ⓘ (Change Compartment)

Public Subnet-oci-tutorial-vcn

CIDR block allowlist

0.0.0.0/0 ✕

Example: 11.0.0.0/24

Create bastion   Cancel

Figure 4-40. *Creating a Bastion Service (Dialog)*

You should wait for the bastion to be created and provisioned before proceeding.

Create a SSH Key Pair

We will need an SSH key pair to use with the bastion. Go ahead and create one now on your PC. Listing 4-4 shows an example of creating the key pair in the `~/.ssh` folder assigning permissions to the private key. Notice the name used is `bastion_rsa`, but you can use whatever you'd like just don't overwrite any existing key pairs.

Listing 4-4. Generating a SSH Key Pair

```
% ssh-keygen -t rsa
Generating public/private rsa key pair.
Enter file in which to save the key (/Users/XXXX/.ssh/id_rsa): /Users/
XXXX/.ssh/bastion_rsa
```

```
. . .
The key fingerprint is:
SHA256:NGrshx+714+XXXXXXXXXXXXXXXXXXXXXXXXU YYYYYYYY.local
The key's randomart image is:
+---[RSA 3072]----+
. . .
+----[SHA256]-----+
```

See www.howtogeek.com/762863/how-to-generate-ssh-keys-in-windows-10-and-windows-11/ for how to generate a SSH key pair on Windows 10 or 11. See https://docs.oracle.com/en-us/iaas/Content/API/Concepts/apisigningkey.htm#two for how to create an API signing key on macOS and Linux.

Create a Port-Forwarding Session

Now that we have what we need to create a port-forwarding session (also called an SSH tunnel), navigate to the Bastion details page by clicking on the newly created bastion in the list (MySQLBastion) as shown in Figure 4-41. Alternatively, you can use the context menu to the right and choose *View Details*.

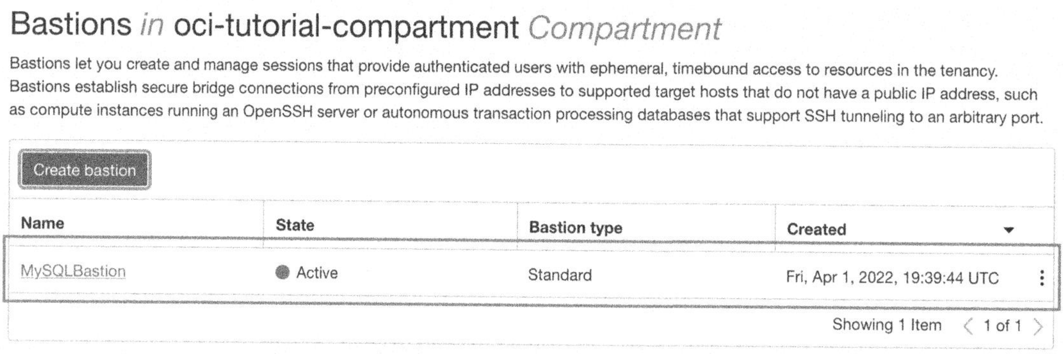

Figure 4-41. *Select the New Bastion Service*

On the bastion details page under the *Sessions* section, click the *Create session* button as shown in Figure 4-42.

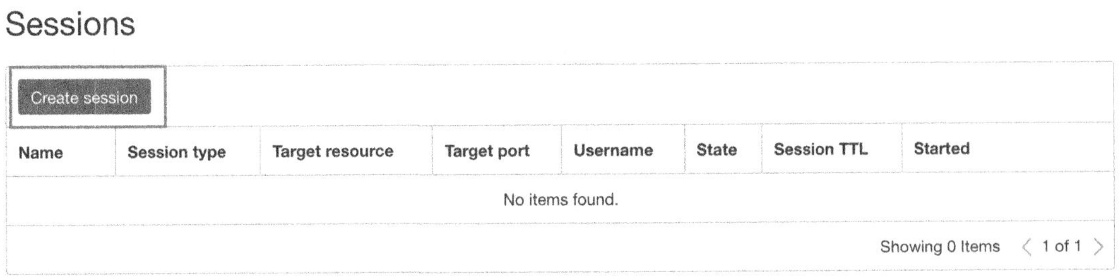

Sessions

Name	Session type	Target resource	Target port	Username	State	Session TTL	Started

Create session

No items found.

Showing 0 Items   〈 1 of 1 〉

Figure 4-42. *Create Session (Bastion Details Page)*

This will open a dialog where we will create a port forwarding session. In the dialog, select the SSH port forwarding session in the *Session Type* drop-down, (optionally) name the session MySQLSession, enter opc in the *Username* text box, the Private IP address of the DB System (e.g., 10.0.1.73), and the port we want to open (e.g., 33060) as shown in Figure 4-43.

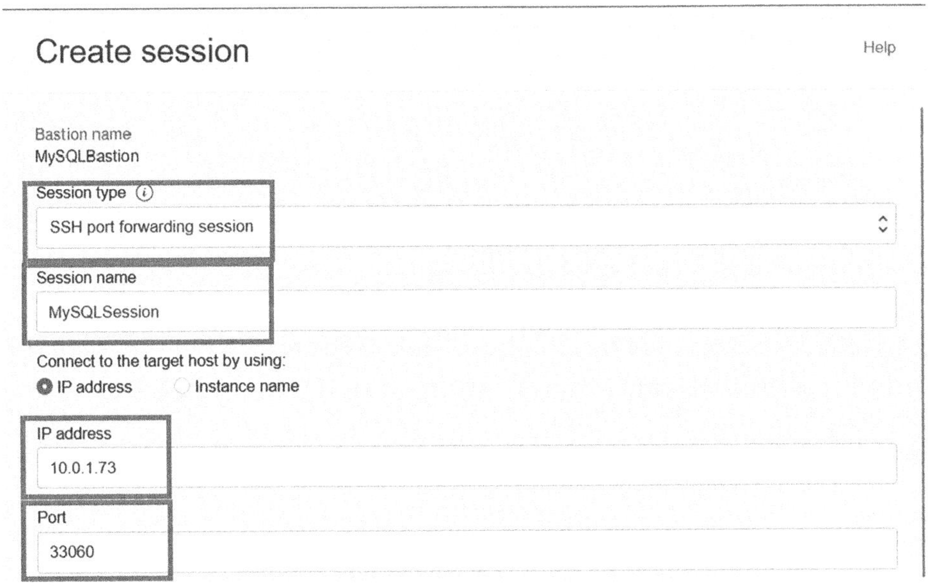

Create session

Help

Bastion name
MySQLBastion

Session type ⓘ

SSH port forwarding session

Session name

MySQLSession

Connect to the target host by using:
◉ IP address   ○ Instance name

IP address

10.0.1.73

Port

33060

Figure 4-43. *Creating a Port Forwarding Session (Part 1)*

We use the opc user because it is the default user for systems like Bastion and Compute instances. The port you specify will be the port used to create the tunnel. You can choose whatever valid port you want. If you have MySQL installed on your PC, you may want to choose another port to use.

As you scroll down in the dialog, you will see the next section where we will need to upload the public key from the key pair we generated. To do so, click the *Browse* link and select the public key we created earlier (e.g., `bastion_rda.pub`) as shown in Figure 4-44. When you've verified the information entered is correct, you can click the *Create session* button.

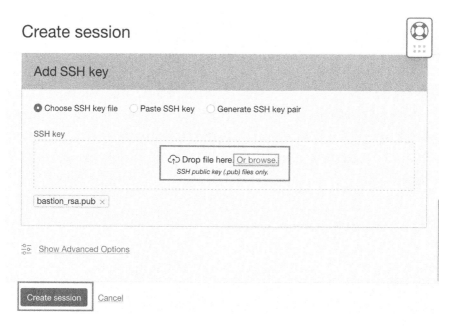

Figure 4-44. *Creating a Port Forwarding Session (Part 2)*

You may need to wait a moment for the session to be created, but when it is, it will show in the list of sessions with a status of `Active` as shown in Figure 4-45.

Sessions

Create session								
Name	**Session type**	**Target resource**	**Target port**	**Username**	**State**	**Session TTL**	**Started** ▼	
MySQLSession	Port forwarding	10.0.1.73	33060	-	● Active	3 hours, 00 minutes	Sat, Apr 2, 2022, 23:41:18 UTC	⋮
							Showing 1 Item 〈 1 of 1 〉	

Figure 4-45. *Sessions List in Bastion*

Notice the column Session TTL. This is the timeout (called time-to-live) for the SSH session. It represents a maximum limit for the time the session can be used. The default is 30 minutes (or 1800 seconds). You can set this when you create the session by clicking on *Advanced Options* in the create session dialog and changing the *Maximum session tine-to-live* value (and, optionally, the units) as shown in Figure 4-46.

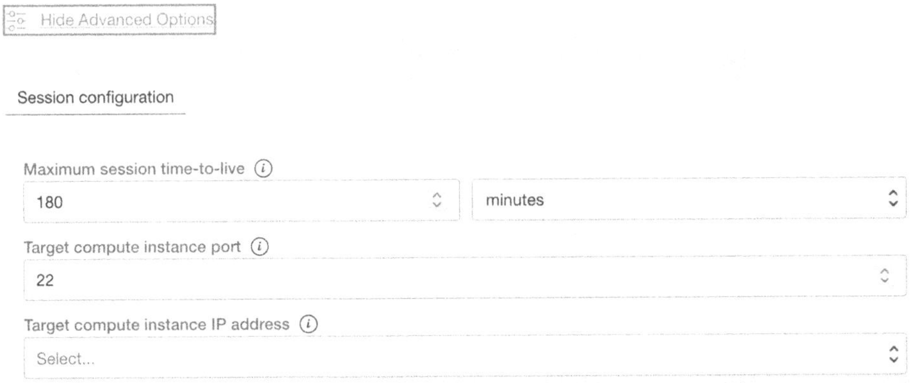

Figure 4-46. *Setting Session TTL*

You can now use it to connect your PC to your DB System.

Connect from Your PC

Now that we have the port forwarding session, we can open the tunnel. The command we need to use is a little complex, but fortunately OCI makes it easy for us by making a sample command that includes a special OCID that you can use to access the bastion port forwarding session. Simply click on the context menu in the *Sessions* list on the Bastion details page to open the context menu then choose *View SSH Command* as shown in Figure 4-47.

Figure 4-47. *Sessions Context Menu*

This will open a dialog as shown in Figure 4-48 that displays the command. Click the *Copy* label to copy that command and then close the dialog by clicking the *Close* button.

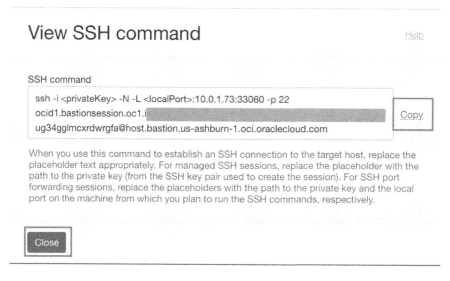

Figure 4-48. *View SSH Command Dialog (Session)*

We will need to edit it before we can use it. Specifically, we will need to add the SSH key path (`~/.ssh/bastion_rsa`) we created earlier and supply the port we used in the port forwarding session (33060), and the power we want to use on the DB System (33060) as shown below. The changes are shown in bold. Finally, we add the & operator to run the command and return to the command line (runs in the background). This is because the port forwarding connection needs to remain open for us to use it:

```
% ssh -i ~/.ssh/bastion_rsa -N -L 33060:10.0.1.73:33060 -p 22 ocid1.
bastionsession.oc1...bfa@host.bastion.us-ashburn-1.oci.oraclecloud.com &
```

If you are following along, go ahead and open a terminal window on your PC and enter the command. You will need to wait until you see the following response before trying to connect to MySQL:

```
Use of the Oracle network and applications is intended solely for Oracle's
authorized users. The use of these resources by Oracle employees and
contractors is subject to company policies, including the Code of Conduct,
Acceptable Use Policy and Information Protection Policy; access may be
monitored and logged, to the extent permitted by law, in accordance with
Oracle policies. Unauthorized use may result in termination of your access,
disciplinary action and/or civil and criminal penalties.
```

Once you get the response from SSH (from OCI), you can connect to MySQL on the DB System with the following command:

```
% mysqlsh --sql mysql_admin@127.0.0.1:33060
```

Notice we are using the MySQL Shell to connect to MySQL on the loopback address (127.0.0.1 or localhost) on port 33060. This will send the communication down the SSH tunnel to the DB System. Listing 4-5 shows a transcript of the connection.

Listing 4-5. Connection to MySQL on DB System via SSH Tunnel

```
% mysqlsh --sql mysql_admin@127.0.0.1:33060
Please provide the password for 'mysql_admin@127.0.0.1:33060':
Save password for 'mysql_admin@127.0.0.1:33060'? [Y]es/[N]o/Ne[v]er
(default No): N
MySQL Shell 8.0.28

Copyright (c) 2016, 2022, Oracle and/or its affiliates.
Oracle is a registered trademark of Oracle Corporation and/or its
affiliates.
Other names may be trademarks of their respective owners.

Type '\help' or '\?' for help; '\quit' to exit.
Creating a session to 'mysql_admin@127.0.0.1:33060'
Fetching schema names for autocompletion... Press ^C to stop.
```

```
Your MySQL connection id is 39 (X protocol)
Server version: 8.0.28-u2-cloud MySQL Enterprise - Cloud
No default schema selected; type \use <schema> to set one.
 MySQL  127.0.0.1:33060+ ssl  SQL > SHOW DATABASES;
+--------------------+
| Database           |
+--------------------+
| information_schema |
| mysql              |
| performance_schema |
| sys                |
+--------------------+
4 rows in set (0.1007 sec)
 MySQL  127.0.0.1:33060+ ssl  SQL > \q
Bye!
```

If you did not get a connection or there was a timeout, you may need to check the Bastion and Session setup. Worst case, you may need to destroy the Bastion and Session and recreate them. You can delete the session by clicking the context menu for the session in the *Sessions List* on the bastion detail page and selecting *Delete session*. You can delete the bastion by clicking on the *Delete bastion* button on the bastion details page.

If the connection opened and you saw similar results to the listing, congratulations! You have successfully connected to your MySQL database server running on your DB System in OCI. You can experiment with MySQL queries as you now have access to the MySQL database system in OCI directly from your PC.

Once you are done with experimenting, be sure to delete any DB Systems, Bastions, Compute Instances, or any other resource that you created in OCI that you do not need. Remember, if you do not want to delete the resources, you can reduce costs by stopping your DB Systems and Compute Instances.

PRACTICING GOOD CLOUD HYGIENE

If you are done experimenting with your DB System and want to continue exploring its features later, be sure to stop the DB System before you log out to minimize charges to your account. If you are going to be away from the tutorials in the book, you may want to consider deleting the DB System and other resources such as the Bastion Service you created to further minimize charges to your account. Remember, anything you leave running that is a billable resource will incur charges to your account. If you are using the trial account, that may not be a problem, but later on when you have a fleet of DB Systems and other OCI resources, leaving things running can add up after a while. Avoid monthly billing shocks by practicing good cloud computing hygiene.

Summary

The MySQL Database Service is a brave, new world for organizations wanting to leverage the power of MySQL – the world's most popular open-source database system – in the cloud. Not only is this possible, but Oracle through its Oracle Cloud Infrastructure has made it easy to create and manage multiple MySQL Database Service DB Systems.

While there are other resources available under the MySQL Database Service, DB Systems represent the core component for any infrastructure that hosts applications that require a database system. The best news is the DB System is a fully featured, managed instance of MySQL that you can tailor to your business needs.

From CPU performance and memory (via shapes) to the size of the data storage, you can configure a host of DB Systems for your immediate needs. And you don't have to spend your hard-earned funds buying hardware and human resources to set up, configure, and tune those servers – all of that is done for you in a manner of minutes! Clearly, DB Systems are the next evolution of the world's leading open-source database system.

In this chapter, we took a tour of the MySQL Database Service focusing on the DB System. We learned how to create a DB System, manage it, and more about the features available that you can use to work with the DB System. We even learned how to connect to the DB System from our PC.

In the next chapter, we will learn more about the backup and restore features of MDS for DB Systems.

CHAPTER 5

Backup and Restore

Now that we understand what the MySQL Database Service (MDS) is and how to create and connect to DB Systems in MDS we are almost ready to start using them in our projects and applications. However, there is one important feature that must be considered before planning integration with MDS and that is how to backup and restore our data.

Professional systems and database administrators know that a good recovery plan needs to be in place before placing any important data on a system and vital to the longevity of the project and the organization. If something goes wrong you must be able to restore the data to some reasonable point where you can recover from the fault and rebuild the data. For many systems, a simple backup and restore mechanism is all that is needed.

In this chapter, we will learn about the backup and restore options available to you in MDS that you can use to protect your data. However, before we jump into the backup and restore operations in MDS, let's learn why it is important to have a plan for recovering your data in MDS.

What Can Go Wrong?

Some may think cloud services are infallible and never go offline. That, sadly, is a myth. Things can happen in many small ways that can affect your ability to access your data. It could be an outage in your Internet provider, a failure of your local hardware, and, yes, failures do occur in cloud services. Fortunately, they are rare, and many steps and much planning go into ensuring the faults are detected early and mitigated by redundancy as well as staff that act quickly to recover.

But let us not forget the one element that can cause the most damage – human error. Whether it is from an accidental delete or and consequences of a poorly planned and executed update to your data, human error is something we must prepare against. Thus,

© Charles Bell 2023
C. Bell, *MySQL Database Service Revealed*, https://doi.org/10.1007/978-1-4842-8945-7_5

backup and restore are still and will continue to be just as important in the cloud and it is on-prem. Furthermore, organizations should incorporate the backup and restore facilities in MDS replacing the current operations that may be in place for backup and restore of on-prem MySQL.

For example, if you use an external application such as MySQL Enterprise Backup (MEB) to backup your on-prem MySQL servers, you will replace that with the DB System backup features in OCI. While the DB System backup does not offer the same options as MEB, DB System backup can still take the place of MEB in your business continuity plan. And, best of all, they are physical backups so you can be assured your data will be backed up and restored quickly and efficiently without space concerns or other issues that logical backups incur.

Similarly, your restore plan can be replaced with the restore feature in DB Systems. However, this is more of a difference with restore. Unlike application like MEB (physical backup) or SQL-based (logical backup) options like `mysqlpump` and `mysqldump`, DB System restore is used to create a new DB System with the data from the restore. More specifically, you cannot restore data onto an existing DB System. The reasons for this are many, but if you think about it, restoring to a new DB System with the same data and configuration means you don't have to destroy the original to roll your data back. You can keep both DB Systems for any recovery analysis you want to conduct.

Tip   See `https://dev.mysql.com/doc/refman/8.0/en/mysqlpump.html` for more information about `mysqlpump` and `https://dev.mysql.com/doc/refman/8.0/en/mysqldump.html` for more information about `mysqldump`.

So, despite the lack of selective backup, selective restore, and restore to an existing DB System, the DB System backup and restore features are robust, efficient, and reliable. As you will see, the automatic backup feature makes protecting your data effortless.

Now that we understand the importance and role of backup and restore in MDS, let's look at the features in more detail.

Note   If you want to follow along in the demonstrations, be sure to have a DB System created and running using parameters similar to those discussed in Chapter 2.

Backup

To better understand DB System backups, let us consider the configuration of a DB System from a high-level point of view. A DB System consists of a compute instance, a boot volume with the operating system and MySQL installed and running, block storage devices for the data (called the data drive or simply data), and a set of configuration parameters for running MySQL.

When a backup is initiated, the block volume service for the data drive(s) is invoked to make a copy of the block volumes (data). The block volume service implements a fast copy that employs a form of logical volume manager (lvm) to make snapshots of the data. So, there is no need to incur any form of wait or blocking or similar disruptions that some backup applications and mechanisms must employ.

The block volume backup is then combined with a copy of the configuration parameters and some additional metadata used to recreate the DB System. The compute instance, boot volume, etc., are not copied or placed into the backup. Rather, the DB System backup has everything it needs to recreate the DB System and your data at the time of the backup.

In this section, we will learn all of the basic operations you can do regarding DB System backups including automatic and manual backups. As you will see, there is a lot of fine-tuning available for setting up backups.

Types of Backups

Backup in DB Systems can be set to occur automatically at preset intervals, manually create a backup at any time, create a final backup, and the OCI operator can make a backup for you should maintenance or corrective actions be required.

DB Systems also support full and incremental backups. Full backups are those that backup all of the data as it exists at the time of backup. Incremental backups include only those changes since the last full backup. Typically, incremental backups are smaller and therefore may occur more frequently. For example, you may want to adopt a plan to run a full backup during low usage each day and incremental backups periodically throughout the day. That way, you can always return your data to within the incremental backup window.

Incremental backups permit you to take backups more frequently since they typically consume less space. This allows you to take a full backup once and then incremental backups throughout a period of time. Should you need to restore, you restore the last full backup then restore the incremental backups taken since.

For example, you may want to adopt a policy to take a full backup during lower usage times, typically at night, then take incremental backups every few hours. Best practices suggest adjusting the frequency to match your data recovery goals. More specifically, the time between incremental backups should be no more than the maximum data loss your organization can safely tolerate. This is because any data changed or added since the last incremental backup may be lost when the full backup and subsequent incremental backups are restored.

Another best practice is utilizing a special feature of MySQL called point-in-time recovery, which is built into MDS. This allows you to set up automated recovery by taking a snapshot of the data every five minutes. Thus, the maximum data loss will be no more than a five-minute period. We will talk more about point-in-time recovery and how you can leverage it to improve data recovery in Chapter 6.

Let's look at each of the backup types in more detail.

Manual Backup

A manual backup is a backup that you, the DB System owner, create via the cloud console or via a REST API call (more on REST API calls in Chapter 9). The retention period for a manual backup can be set from 1 to 365 days. All manual backups are full backups.

You may want to create a manual backup before making major changes to the data, executing any data pruning or conversion scripts, importing large amounts of data, or before a critical moment in your business such as before a large event or new product launch.

Automatic Backup

You can use the automatic backup feature to choose a time to create a backup of the DB System. Unlike manual backups, automatic backups can be retained between 1 and 35 days with a default of 7 days. Note that once you set up an automatic backup retention period, you cannot change it so consider your needs when setting up automatic backups. Interestingly, automatic backups, once configured, will backup a DB System even if it is inactive (e.g., stopped).

Finally, should you delete a DB System, the automatic backups are deleted as well unless you changed the deletion plan in the DB System. Recall, the deletion plan can be set when you create a DB System and can be changed later. One of the settings in the *Deletion Plan* tab is to retain automatic backups. If you tick that, automatic backups are not deleted when the DB System is deleted.

You may want to set up automatic backups so that you can be certain the data is backed up regularly and you don't have to monitor or manage it on a day-to-day basis.

Final Backup

A final backup is a special backup that you can invoke when the DB System is deleted. More specifically, you can set the deletion plan for a DB System to take a final backup before the DB System is deleted. In this case, the backup is taken and once complete, the DB System is deleted. The final backup is always a full backup and can only be set automatically via the Deletion Plan tab for the DB System.

Operator Backup

This form of backup is another special backup that can be invoked by the MDS support team (often referred to as the operator hence the name). This backup is normally taken as a precaution before an operator takes action to correct a problem or in assisting you in solving an issue with your DB System. This type of backup is always a full backup.

Operator backups are deleted automatically and are not part of your billing or service limits. While you can delete operator backups, it is not recommended since you may want to use it if your issue is not resolved, or the DB System cannot be fully recovered.

The MySQL Support team creates this backup to assist in investigating potential issues with your service. These backups are deleted automatically. You can delete these backups too but is not recommended. These backs do not affect your limits.

Backup Details

You can see a list of backups whenever you visit the DB System details page and click on *Backups* in the *Resources* menu on the left. You will then see a list of backups similar to Figure 5-1.

Create Manual Backup						
Name	**State**	**Creation Type**	**Retention Days**	**Size**	**Created**	▼
oci-tutorial-mysql - Backup - Mon, Apr 11, 2022, 18:53:21 UTC	● Active	Manual	2 (Wed, Apr 13, 2022, 18:55:26 UTC)	1 GB	Mon, Apr 11, 2022, 18:55:26 UTC	⋮
					Showing 1 Item ⟨ 1 of 1 ⟩	

Figure 5-1. *Listing Backups with a DB System*

Notice the list shows the name, state, backup (creation) type, retention, size, and date created. If you click on the context menu on the right for each backup, you can see a list of actions you can take on the backup as shown in Figure 5-2.

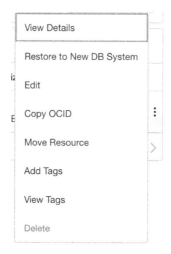

Figure 5-2. *Context Menu (Backup list – DB System Details Page)*

Here we can view the details for the backup, restore to a new DB System, edit the backup (change the name, description, and retention period), copy its OCID, move it to a new location, add or view tags, and delete the backup.

Tip   You can navigate to a list of all your backups by using the cloud console main menu then selecting *Databases | Backups*. You will be able to perform the same operations listed above on each backup in the list.

Let's look at the details page for a backup. The details page for a backup is like most detail pages for OCI resources where critical data is displayed in the center, an icon with the state is to the left, and a Resources menu appears below with tabs for various lists. In this case, a backup has only one entry in the Resources menu; DB System, which displays information about the DB System from which the backup was taken.

Figure 5-3 shows the top portion of the backup details page.

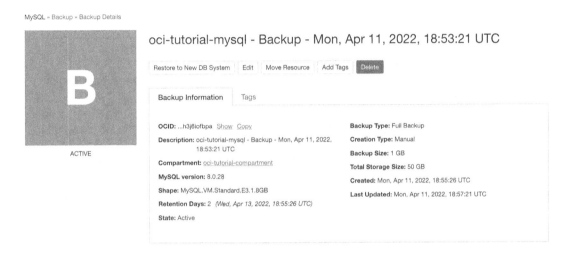

Figure 5-3. *Backup Details Page (Top)*

Notice we have the icon on the left. The icon and state follow the same behavior as other OCI resources changing color for certain states where green is always the `ACTIVE` state. To the right are the name and a series of buttons for common actions. These actions include the following:

- *Restore to New DB System*: Create a new DB System restoring the data from the backup.

- *Edit*: Used to change the backup metadata (name, description, and retention period).

- *Move Resource*: Allows you to move the resource to a new location (compartment).

- *Add Tags*: Used for adding user-defined tags.

- *Delete*: You can delete the backup.

The main information section has two tabs: the *Backup Information* and *Tags*. The backup information includes the OCID, description, compartment, the MySQL version, shape, state, backup type, creation type, size, and creation date. Tags are those tags you or the OCI system set for the backup.

Table 5-1 lists the data in more detail.

Table 5-1. *Backup Information (backup details page)*

Parameter	Description
OCID	The OCID (unique identifier) for the backup.
Description	The description you provided when the backup was taken (for manual backups) or the description generated by OCI.
Compartment	The compartment where the backup was taken. You can click on the link provided to see more details about the compartment
MySQL Version	The version of MySQL running on the DB System when the backup was taken. This could be a critical item to consider if you restore an old backup as DB Systems are constantly upgraded when new MySQL versions are released.
Shape	The shape for the compute instance of the DB System.
Retention Days	The retention period in days for the backup.
State	The current state of the backup.
Backup Type	The type of backup taken; full or incremental.
Creation Type	The backup creation method; manual or automatic.
Backup Size	The backup size in GBs.
Total Storage Size	The data storage size at the time of backup.
Created	The date and time the backup was created.
Last Updated	The date and time the backup was last updated.

The MySQL version and shape are two of the critical components needed when restoring the backup to a new DB System. Here, you can see at-a-glance the general configuration of the DB System.

Figure 5-4 shows the bottom portion of the backup details page.

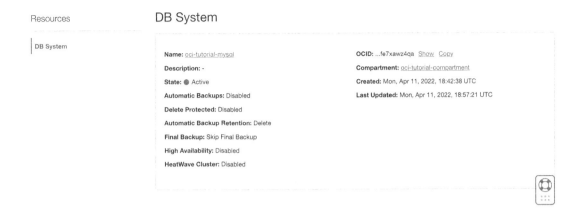

Figure 5-4. *Backup Details Page (Bottom)*

Notice here we see the information about the DB System including its parameters regarding backups, high availability, HeatWave, OCID, compartment, and creation date. Table 5-2 shows the data in more detail.

Table 5-2. *MySQL DB System (backup details page)*

Parameter	Description
Name	The name of the DB System. Presented as a link so you can navigate to the DB System details page.
Description	The description you provided when the DB System was created.
State	The operational state of the DB System.
Automatic Backups	Automatic backup state; enabled or disabled.
High Availability	High availability state; enabled or disabled.
HeatWave Cluster	HeatWave cluster state; enabled or disabled.
OCID	The unique OCID for the DB System. Links are provided for you to show or copy the OCID.
Compartment	The name of the compartment where the DB System resides.
Created	The date and time the DB System was created.
Last Updated	The date and time the DB System was last updated.

Now that we understand the backup types and the type of information you can see with each backup, let's look at how we can take a backup of a DB System. We will see examples of all backup types.

Enable or Disable Automatic Backups

Recall when we created our DB System in Chapter 4, we did not turn on automatic updates. Fortunately, we can turn automatic updates on (enable) or off (disable) at any time.

We simply navigate to the DB System using the cloud console main menu selecting *Databases | DB Systems* and then select the DB System and view its details or use the context menu to the right and select *View Details*. Once you are on the DB System detail page click the *More Actions* button and select *Edit Backup Plan*.

If automatic backups are disabled, you will see a checkbox to enable them. Simply tick the *Enable Automatic Backups* checkbox and then two more options will appear as shown in Figure 5-5.

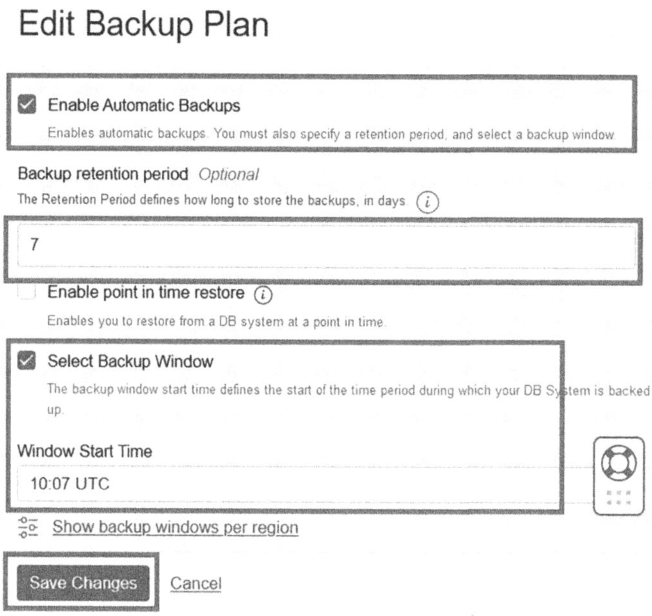

Figure 5-5. *Enabling Automatic Backups*

You will be permitted to change the backup retention (default is 7 days), and you can change the start time for the automatic backup. You must tick the tick box, Select

`Backup Window`, to enable the start window selection. The start window is the time in which the automatic backup can take place.

When you click on the *Window Start Time* box, a dropdown list will appear allowing you to choose a start window from a predefined list of options. Notice the times are in UTC, so be sure to correct for any time zone differences. Note that your automatic backup will be scheduled to start during the 30 minutes following the start time specified. You can also click the *Show backup windows per region* link to view the default backup window specific to your region.

When you are satisfied with your selections, click the *Save Changes* button to enable automatic backups. This may temporarily change the state of the DB System to `UPDATING` and the icon color to yellow.

Note   You can also use the context menu for the DB System in the DB Systems list to choose *Edit Backup Plan* to enable or disable automatic backups.

To disable automatic backups, use the *More Actions* button and select *Edit Backup Plan*. Then, simply untick the *Enable Automatic Backups* checkbox and click the *Save Changes* button to disable automatic backups. This may temporarily change the state of the DB System to `UPDATING` and the icon color to yellow.

Create a Manual Backup

You can create a manual backup of your DB System at a time of your choosing. Recall, a manual backup can be either an increment or full backup and the retention period can be from 1 to 365 days. The manual backup contains a copy of all your data. Once again, it is always a good idea to make a manual backup before any major changes to your data including imports, reorganization, launching a new application, etc. A manual backup taken immediately before these actions will permit you to restore your data to a "known good" state.

A manual backup can be done at any time except during the maintenance cycle where MDS is upgrading your DB System. In fact, MDS may give you a warning if you try to create a backup at a time when it is not advisable or permitted. Fortunately, those times are few and you are unlikely to encounter them.

To create a manual backup, use the cloud console and navigate to your DB System. You can do so by clicking on the main menu and selecting *Databases* then *DB Systems* then click the name of your DB System to see the DB Systems details page.

Once you are on the DB Systems detail page, click on the *Backups* entry in the *Resources* menu then click the *Create Manual Backup* button as shown in Figure 5-6. Alternatively, you can use the *More Actions* button and choose *Create Manual Backup*. Also, instead of navigating to the DB System details page, you can click on the context menu from the DB Systems list and choose *Create Manual Backup*.

	Name	State	Creation Type	Retention Days	Size	Created	
	oci-tutorial-mysql - Backup - Mon, Apr 11, 2022, 18:53:21 UTC	⦿ Deleted	Manual	2 (Wed, Apr 13, 2022, 18:55:26 UTC)	1 GB	Mon, Apr 11, 2022, 18:55:26 UTC	⋮

Metrics *Endpoints* *HeatWave* *Backups* *Channels* *Work Requests* *List Scope*

Backup Plan
Automatic Backups are disabled.
Edit Backup Plan
Create Manual Backup

Showing 1 Item ‹ 1 of 1 ›

Figure 5-6. *Create a Manual Backup (DB System Details Page)*

Once you click the button or launch the manual backup from the context menu, a dialog will open prompting you to provide the following information:

- *Display Name*: Name the backup. MDS will generate a name for you, but if you want to be able to find it quickly or perhaps associate the name with an event or project, you should provide a name. By default, MDS includes the name of the DB System and date and time of the backup.

- *(optional) Description*: You can add a description for the backup. This could contain pertinent information that you cannot (should not) encode in the name[1] such as details that prompted the need for the backup.

- *Configure Backup Type*: Here, you can choose between full or incremental backup. The default is full backup.

- *Configure Retention Period*: You can enter the number of days to retain the backup. You can choose a range from 1 to 365. The backup will be deleted after the number of days has expired. You can also

---

[1] Encoding information in names is never a good practice especially if you must abbreviate terms.

choose a specific date that represents the day the backup retention will expire and therefore be deleted.

- *Navigate to the Backup Details Page After Closing the Dialog*: This tick box redirects you automatically to the backup details page. The box is ticked by default.

Once you have the information entered and validated, click the *Create Manual Backup* button to create the backup. Figure 5-7 shows an example of the *Create Manual Backup* dialog.

Create Manual Backup

ⓘ This will create a backup for the DB System "oci-tutorial-mysql".

Provide basic information for DB System manual backup

Display Name

oci-tutorial-mysql - Test Manual Backup

Description *Optional*

Testing the manual backup feature.

Configure Backup Type

Backup Type
Select backup type. Full Backup creates a complete database backup. Incremental Backup creates a differential backup containing only the changes made since the last backup (full or incremental).

◉ Full Backup   ○ Incremental Backup

Configure Retention Period

Retention Period
Specify the retention period in days or by end date. At the end of the retention period, the backup is deleted.

◉ Select number of days   ○ Select end date

365

⊟ Show Advanced Options

☑ Navigate to the Backup details page after closing the dialog

[Create Manual Backup]   Cancel

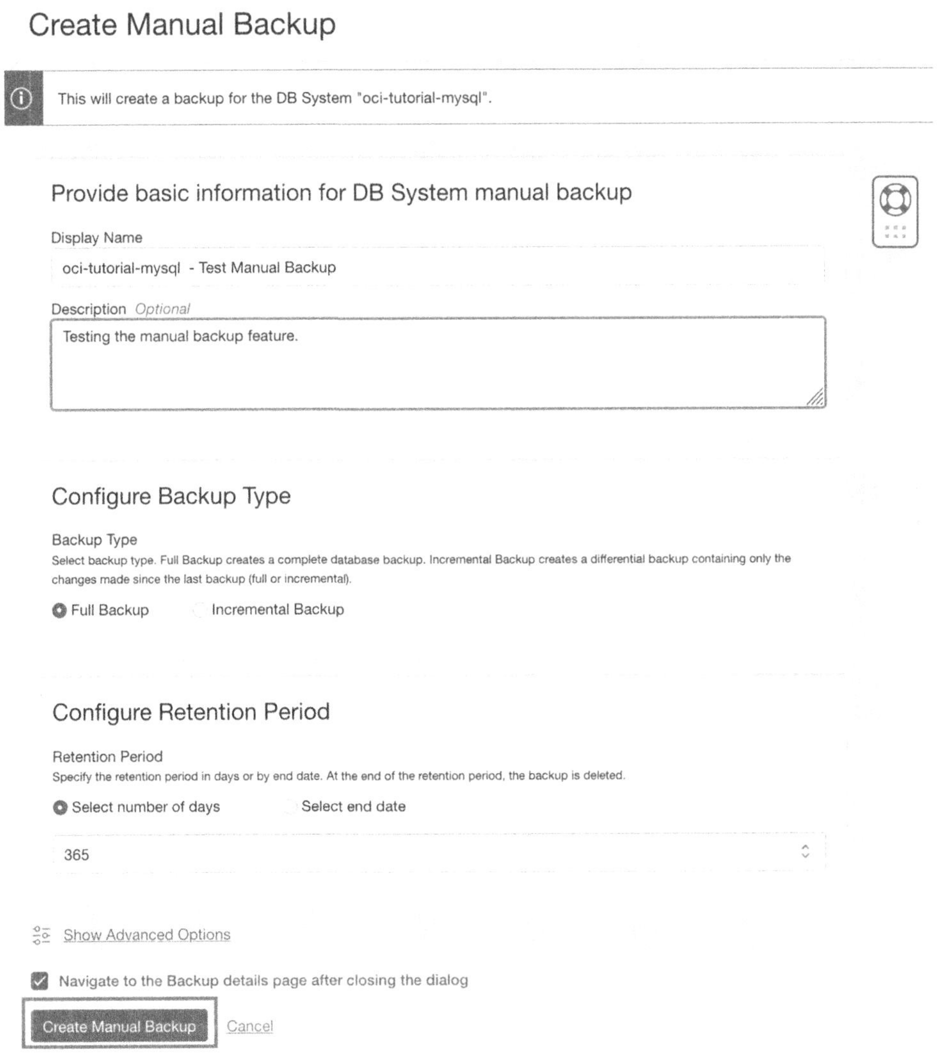

Figure 5-7. *Create Manual Backup Dialog*

> **Tip**   I will stop highlighting all of the entry boxes on dialogs and forms for brevity and highlight the command buttons and other important features.

If you ticked the tick box to show the backup details page, you will be redirected to that page so that you can monitor the backup progress. You can also monitor the backup progress on the *Backups* view from the *Resources* menu on the DB System details page. Figure 5-8 shows the progress of a manual backup as shown in the Backups view on the DB System details page.

Name	State	Creation Type	Retention Days	Size	Created	
oci-tutorial-mysql - Second test	◉ Creating	Manual	1 (Sat, Apr 16, 2022, 19:04:55 UTC)	0 Bytes	Fri, Apr 15, 2022, 19:04:55 UTC	⋮
oci-tutorial-mysql - Test Manual Backup	● Active	Manual	365 (Sat, Apr 15, 2023, 19:03:03 UTC)	1 GB	Fri, Apr 15, 2022, 19:03:03 UTC	⋮
oci-tutorial-mysql - Backup - Mon. Apr 11, 2022, 18:53:21 UTC	◉ Deleted	Manual	2 (Wed, Apr 13, 2022, 18:55:26 UTC)	1 GB	Mon, Apr 11, 2022, 18:55:26 UTC	⋮

Showing 3 Items   ⟨ 1 of 1 ⟩

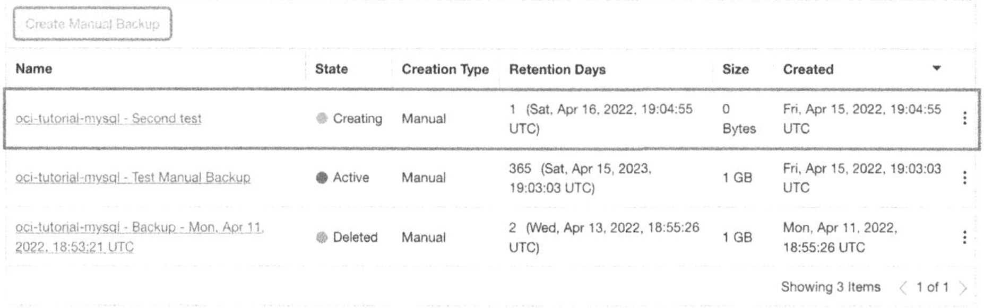

Figure 5-8. *Backup Progress (DB System Details Page)*

> **Note**   The status of the DB System may change briefly to UPDATING when the backup starts.

Edit a Backup

Should you need to edit the name or description of your backup, you can do so using the edit backup feature. To edit a backup from the DB System details page, click on the *Backups* view on the *Resources* menu and click the context menu and choose *Edit* as shown in Figure 5-9.

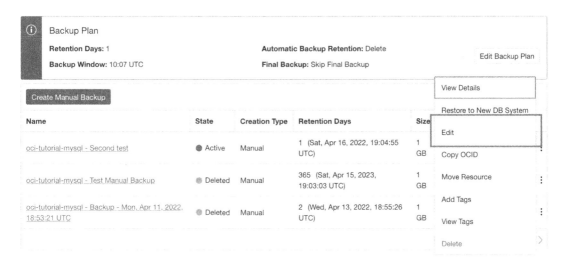

Figure 5-9. *Edit Backup (DB Systems Details Page)*

If you have navigated to the backup details page, you can click on the *Edit* button to edit the backup.

Once you click the button to edit the backup, a dialog will be presented where you can change the following information:

- *Display Name*: You can change the name of the backup. By default, MDS includes the name of the DB System and the date and time of the backup.

- *Description*: You can change the description for the backup.

- *Configure Backup Type*: Here, you can choose between full or incremental backup. The default is full backup.

- *Configure Retention Period*: You can change the number of days to retain the backup. You can also choose a specific date that represents the day the backup retention will expire and therefore be deleted.

Figure 5-10 shows the edit backup dialog.

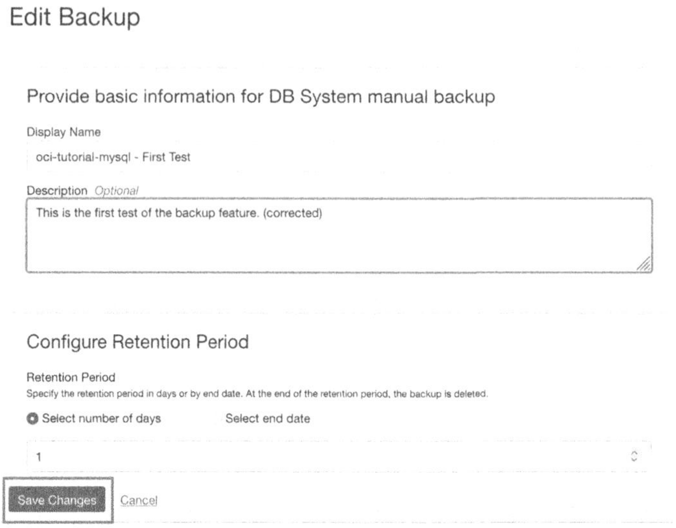

Edit Backup

Provide basic information for DB System manual backup

Display Name

oci-tutorial-mysql - First Test

Description *Optional*

This is the first test of the backup feature. (corrected)

Configure Retention Period

Retention Period
Specify the retention period in days or by end date. At the end of the retention period, the backup is deleted.

◉ Select number of days   Select end date

1

Save Changes   Cancel

Figure 5-10. *Edit Backup Dialog*

Once you have the information corrected, you can click the Save Changes button to save your changes.

Manage Tags

Another mechanism you can use to associate a backup (or any resource in OCI that supports tags) is to add one or more tags to the resource. Tags are short strings that you can add yourself. You may want to add tags for filtering or sorting. For example, you may use a tag to associate a backup with a cost center, event, or project.

You can add tags to your backup at any time. To do so from the DB System details page, click on the *Backups* view on the *Resources* menu and click the context menu and choose *Add Tags* as shown in Figure 5-11.

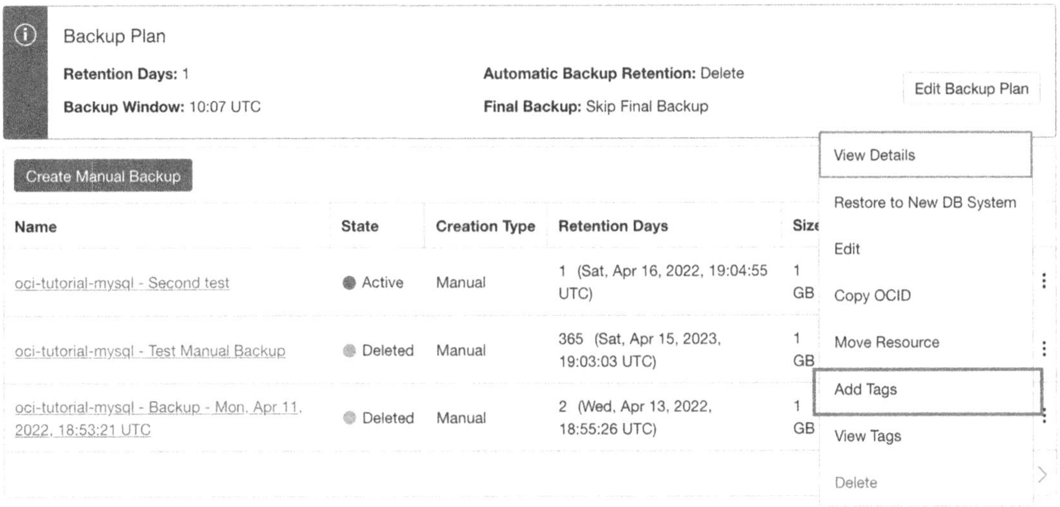

Figure 5-11. *Add Tags (DB Systems Details Page – Backups View)*

If you have navigated to the backup details page, you can click on the *Edit* button to edit the backup.

Once you click the *Add Tags* button, you will see a dialog where you can specify one or more tags to be added to the backup. Figure 5-12 shows an example of adding a single tag. Here, we add a tag named CostCenter with a value of 901. Recall, tags cannot have spaces.

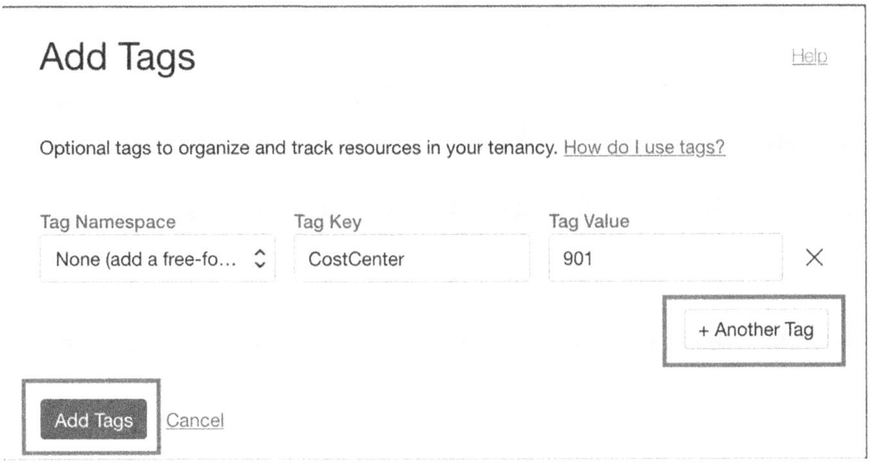

Figure 5-12. *Add Tags Dialog*

If you wanted to add more tags, you can click on the + *Another Tag* button, which will add another set of text boxes for you to specify another tag. When done, you can click the *Add Tags* button to add the tags to your backup.

Recall, you can view the tags associated with your backup by navigating to the backup details page. There, you can select the *Tags* tab and then the *Free-form Tags* view to see tags you've added as shown in Figure 5-13.

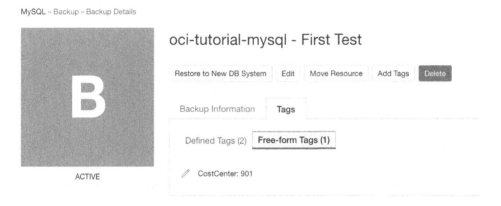

Figure 5-13. *Free-form Tags View (Backup Details Page)*

Delete a Backup

You can delete a backup at any time. If you have created a manual backup or want to prune some of your backup resources by deleting old backups, you can do so easily. The easiest way to delete a set of backups is to use the cloud console main menu and navigate to *Databases | Backups*, which will show all of your MDS backups, as shown in Figure 5-14.

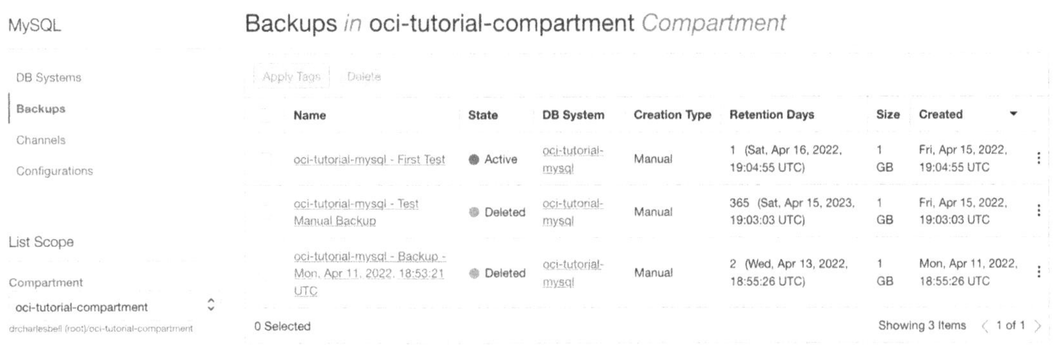

Figure 5-14. *Listing all DB System Backups*

Notice here we see the title of the list is "*Backups in oci-tutorial-compartment*". As you may surmise, the list only shows you the backups from one compartment at a time. This is because backups are contained in the compartment where they are created – much like DB Systems (or any resource that lives at the compartment level).

This list is handy because it allows you to select multiple backups where you can apply one of two operations: adding tags or deleting. The *Apply Tags* button allows you to add one or more tags to all of the backups selected. Similarly, the *Delete* button deletes all of the backups selected.

To delete a single backup, use the context menu on the right and choose *Delete* as shown in Figure 5-15.

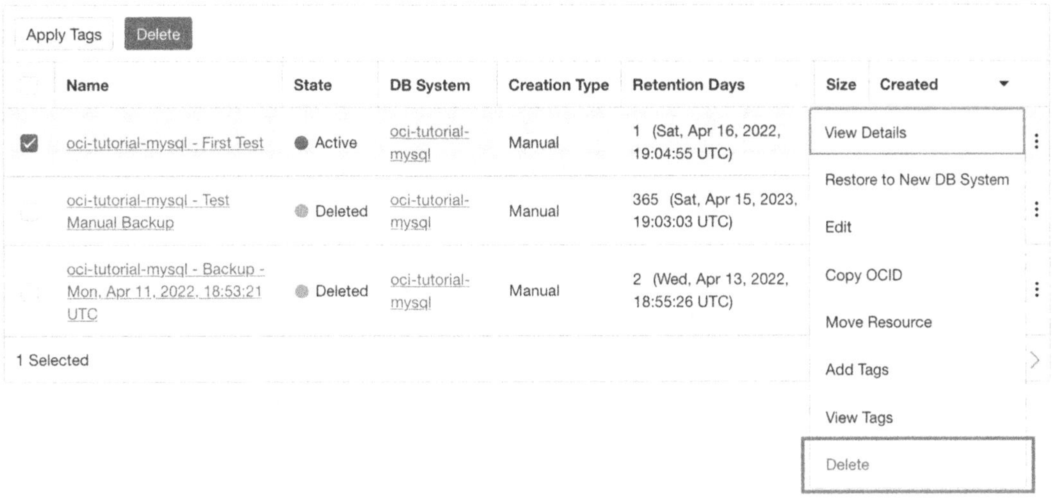

Figure 5-15. *Delete a Backup (MDS Backups List)*

You will be asked to confirm the information as shown in Figure 5-16. Click the *Delete Backup* button to confirm the delete operation. This dialog is shown because deleting a backup renders the backup inaccessible for later use.

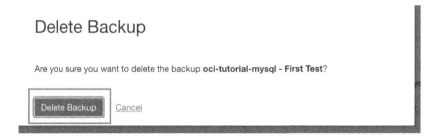

Figure 5-16. *Confirm Backup Delete Dialog*

You can also delete a backup from the backup details page by clicking the *Delete* button. Or, if you are viewing a DB System details page, use the *Backups* view on the *Resources* menu to select the context menu and choose *Delete*.

Move a Backup

Backups are contained within the compartment where they are created. You cannot use a backup in one compartment for, say a restore, in another compartment. You must move the backup to the other compartment before you can use it.

Note   Only active backups can be moved. Backups in any other state cannot be moved to another compartment.

If you are working with more than one compartment, you may need or want to move a backup to a different compartment. For example, you may want to restore the data for a DB System in another compartment perhaps to establish a baseline for a development environment, duplicate the data for other analysis, etc.

Note   The user who initiates the move must have the MYSQL_BACKUP_MOVE permission on the destination compartment. See https://docs.oracle.com/ en-us/iaas/mysql-database/doc/policy-details-mysql-database- service.html for more details.

To move a backup to another compartment, you can navigate to the backup list via the cloud console menu choosing *Databases | Backups* then click the context menu and choose Move Resource as shown in Figure 5-17.

Backups *in* oci-tutorial-compartment *Compartment*

	Name	State	DB System	Creation Type	Retention Days	Size	Created ▼	
	oci-tutorial-mysql - Backup - Fri, Apr 15, 2022, 20:10:30 UTC	● Active	oci-tutorial-mysql	Manual	365 (Sat, Apr 15, 2023, 20:10:34 UTC)	1 Gl	View Details	⋮
	oci-tutorial-mysql - First Test	◉ Deleted	oci-tutorial-mysql	Manual	1 (Sat, Apr 16, 2022, 19:04:55 UTC)	1 Gl	Restore to New DB System Edit	⋮
	oci-tutorial-mysql - Test Manual Backup	◉ Deleted	oci-tutorial-mysql	Manual	365 (Sat, Apr 15, 2023, 19:03:03 UTC)	1 Gl	Copy OCID	⋮
	oci-tutorial-mysql - Backup - Mon, Apr 11, 2022, 18:53:21 UTC	◉ Deleted	oci-tutorial-mysql	Manual	2 (Wed, Apr 13, 2022, 18:55:26 UTC)	1 Gl	Move Resource	⋮

0 Selected

Add Tags
View Tags
Delete

Figure 5-17. *Move Resource (MDS Backups List)*

Once you click Move Resource, you will get a dialog with a single dropdown list where you can choose the compartment to which you want to move the backup. Figure 5-18 shows the dialog.

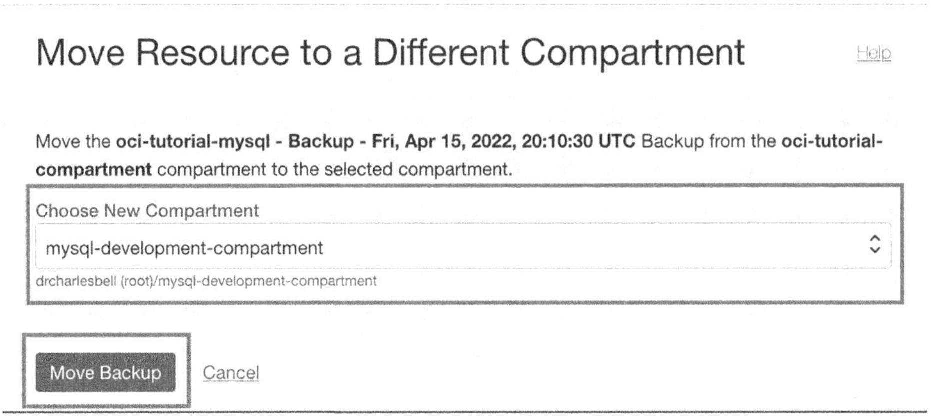

Move Resource to a Different Compartment   Help

Move the **oci-tutorial-mysql - Backup - Fri, Apr 15, 2022, 20:10:30 UTC** Backup from the **oci-tutorial-compartment** compartment to the selected compartment.

Choose New Compartment

mysql-development-compartment ⌄

drcharlesbell (root)/mysql-development-compartment

Move Backup   Cancel

Figure 5-18. *Move Resource Dialog*

Simply choose the destination compartment from the list and click the *Move Backup* button to move the backup. Notice the example shows moving the backup to the `mysql-development` compartment. The operation takes only a few moments and when done, the backup will be removed from the list.

Note   You cannot select the compartment where the backup currently resides.

This is because the MDS backups list uses the compartment as a filter. Since we were looking at the `oci-tutorial-compartment,` but we moved the resource to the `mysql-development` compartment, we have to change the *Compartments* filter to see the backup as demonstrated in Figure 5-19.

Figure 5-19. *Showing Backups in the mysql-development Compartment*

You can now use the backup in the `mysql-development` compartment. You can move backups around any time you need to, but just remember you cannot use them in a compartment unless you move them to that compartment.

Now, let's learn what we can do to restore our data (backups).

Restore

The restore operation in MDS DB Systems is not a separate feature or resource. It is actually a function of the backup resource. This is a slight departure from how other operating system and database backup tools work, so we list the restore operations under their own title for those new to MDS and MDS backups to avoid confusion.

When you restore a backup, you do not restore the data to the same DB System. MDS (and other OCI) resources are designed for and implemented as "create new with" operations. Thus, to restore a backup means you are going to create a new DB System using the data in the backup along with certain configuration metadata stored with the backup. Once you get used to this new procedure, you may find it beneficial in cases where you want to restore a backup for diagnostic purposes where having the current and restored DB System would be advantageous.

Since the restore operation creates a new DB System with the data in the backup, the dialog to create the restore is very similar to the one used to create a new DB System. Thus, some of the details may be very familiar, but we include them for completeness and clarity.

There is just one very important aspect to consider. The new DB System cannot have/use the same IP address as an existing, running DB System. If you want to use the same IP address, you must first delete the existing DB System.

Another thing to consider is the new DB System will retain the administrator credentials from the original DB System, so you will not need to recreate the administrator account and password.

Note   If you want to follow along with this demonstration, be sure to create a manual backup of your existing DB System so that you can have a backup to use for the restore.

To restore a backup, first navigate to the list of DB System backups by using the cloud console main menu then select *Databases | Backups* then click *Restore to New DB System* from the context menu for the backup you want to restore as shown in Figure 5-20. In this case, we see a manual backup taken that we want to restore. The original DB System is still active and running.

Figure 5-20. *Restore to New DB System (DB System Backup List)*

You can also navigate to the backup details page and click the *Restore to New DB System* button as shown in Figure 5-21 to start the restore.

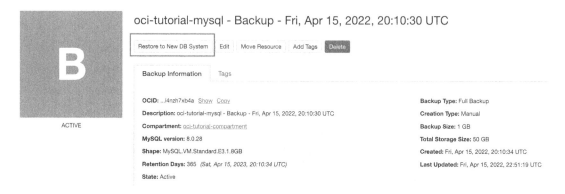

Figure 5-21. *Restore to New DB System (Backup Details Page)*

Once you click the button, the restore to new DB System dialog will appear. The information we will need to provide includes the following:

- *Name*: A name for the DB System.

- *Description* (optional): Provides a description for your own use to explain the DB System such as why it was created, to which projects it is allocated, etc. You should avoid any confidential data in the description.

- *Networking*: You will need to select the VCN and subnet for the DB System.

- *Availability Domain* (placement): Choose the availability domain.

- *Hardware*: Choose the shape and size of the data storage (block volume).

- *Backup Plan*: You have the option to turn on automatic backups.

Since the dialog is quite long and looks very similar to the create new DB System dialog, we will go through the dialog in parts starting from the top. If you are following along with your own restore, you may need to scroll down to see all of the portions of the dialog.

First, we must select the source. Depending on how you initiated the restore, this information may be filled out for you. We must select whether we are restoring from a backup or a point-in-time restore, which is explained in Chapter 6. In this example, we are restoring from a backup so the source is chosen for us. Figure 5-22 shows the source portion of the dialog.

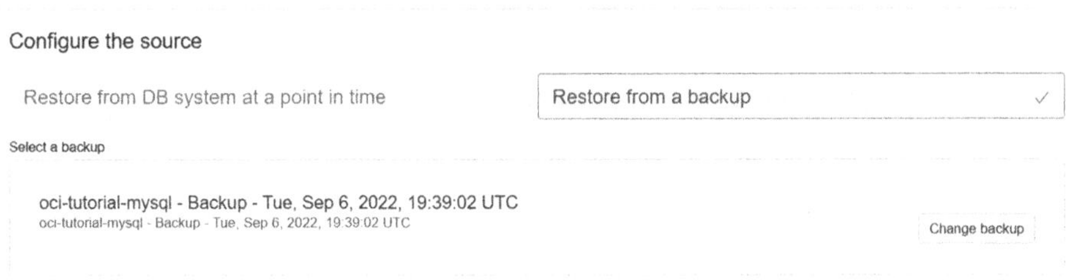

Configure the source

Restore from DB system at a point in time   Restore from a backup   ✓

Select a backup

oci-tutorial-mysql - Backup - Tue, Sep 6, 2022, 19:39:02 UTC
oci-tutorial-mysql - Backup - Tue, Sep 6, 2022, 19:39:02 UTC   Change backup

Figure 5-22. *Restore DB System (Part 1)*

The name section allows you to specify a name for the restored DB System. MDS will provide a default name for you, but you most likely will want to change it. You can also add a description. MDS will provide a description for you that includes the source or origin for the restore including the name of the backup, date and time of the restore, as well as the backup id (the OCID for the backup). Figure 5-23 shows the name section of the dialog.

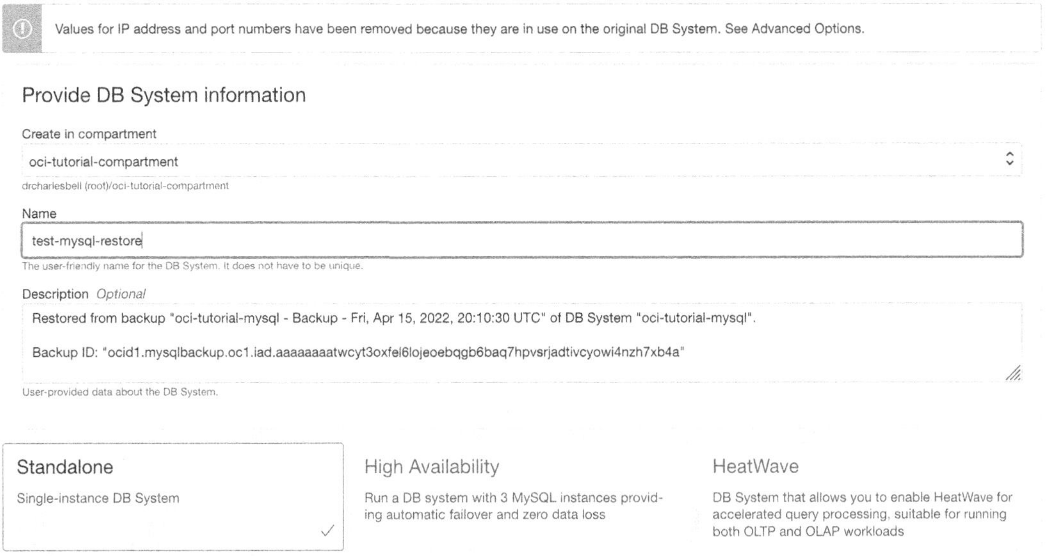

ⓘ   Values for IP address and port numbers have been removed because they are in use on the original DB System. See Advanced Options.

Provide DB System information

Create in compartment

oci-tutorial-compartment   ⌄

drcharlesbell (root)/oci-tutorial-compartment

Name

test-mysql-restore

The user-friendly name for the DB System. It does not have to be unique.

Description *Optional*

Restored from backup "oci-tutorial-mysql - Backup - Fri, Apr 15, 2022, 20:10:30 UTC" of DB System "oci-tutorial-mysql".

Backup ID: "ocid1.mysqlbackup.oc1.iad.aaaaaaaatwcyt3oxfei6lojeoebqgb6baq7hpvsrjadtivcyowi4nzh7xb4a"

User-provided data about the DB System.

Standalone	High Availability	HeatWave
Single-instance DB System	Run a DB system with 3 MySQL instances providing automatic failover and zero data loss	DB System that allows you to enable HeatWave for accelerated query processing, suitable for running both OLTP and OLAP workloads
✓		

Figure 5-23. *Restore DB System (Part 2)*

For this example, we are going to restore one of the manual backups taken of the `oci-tutorial-mysql` DB System and we're restoring it with the name `test-mysql-restore`. Once you enter the information, scroll down to the next section.

In the next section, we must select the compartment where we want to restore the backup, but keep in mind you should restore the backup to a DB System in the same compartment where the backup was taken. We also select the VCN to use and the availability domain. You will notice here MDS has chosen the correct compartment, VCN, and availability domain for you as shown in Figure 5-24.

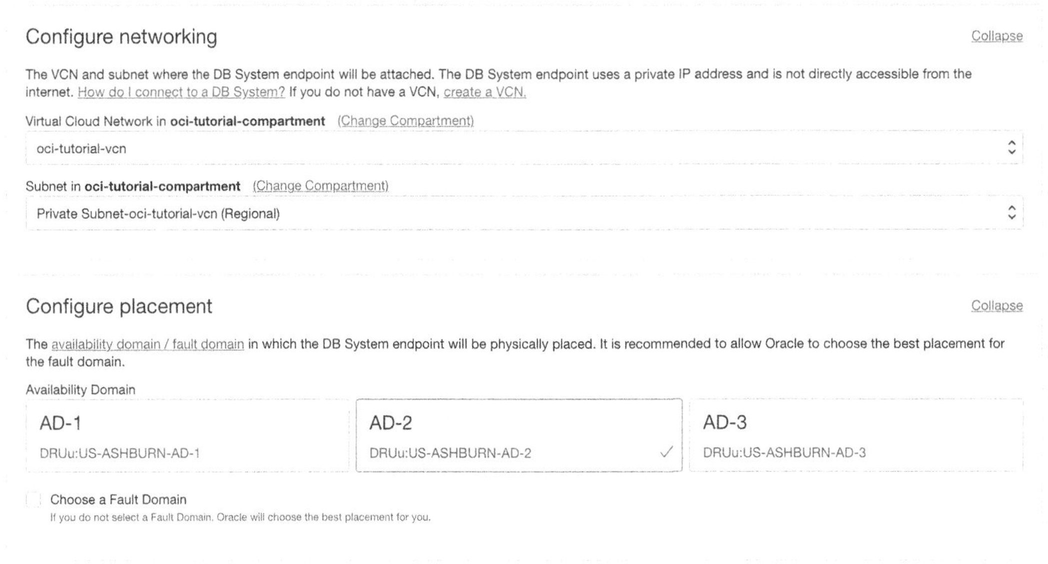

Figure 5-24. *Restore DB System (Part 3)*

If you want to launch the DB System in a compartment other than the current compartment, you can select a different compartment from the list. If you do not select a different compartment, the same compartment where the backup resides is used.

If you are following along with your own account, you should see the `oci-tutorial-vcn` is selected in the *Virtual Cloud Networking in oci-tutorial-compartment* list and the `Private Subnet oci-tutorial-vcn (Regional)` entry is selected in the *Subnet in oci-tutorial-compartment* list and availability domain 2 (*AD-2*) is selected in the *Configure placement* box. Once you inspect the selections, scroll down to the next section, which is the *Configure hardware* section. Here, we have the option of changing the shape and changing the size of the data storage as shown in Figure 5-25.

Configure hardware   Collapse

Select a Shape

MySQL.VM.Standard.E3.1.8GB

CPU Core Count: 1   Change Shape
Memory Size: 8 GB

The shape determines CPU cores and memory allocated to each MySQL instance in a DB System. In multi-instance DB Systems the CPU core count and memory size will be multiplied by the total number of MySQL instances.

Data Storage Size (GB)

50   ⌄

The amount of storage to allocate to the DB System for all data and log files.

Figure 5-25. *Restore DB System (Part 4)*

Since we are creating a new DB System from a backup, we will use the defaults, however you can take this opportunity to change the settings. Just make sure the new size for the data is large enough to store your data.

Caution   If you choose a shape that is smaller than the shape used when the backup was taken, you must ensure the new shape has the correct resources to support your DB System. For example, you must ensure there is sufficient processor and memory allocated to maintain performance expectations and there is enough disk space allocated to restore the data.

Note   You cannot change the type of the DB System when restoring from a backup. For example, if the original DB System was Standalone, your new DB System will also be Standalone.

The next section allows you to choose to enable automatic backups, retention period, and start time as shown in Figure 5-26. This information will be the same as the DB System used for the backup, but you can change the options. If the point-in-time is enabled, you can disable it by checking the tickbox as shown.

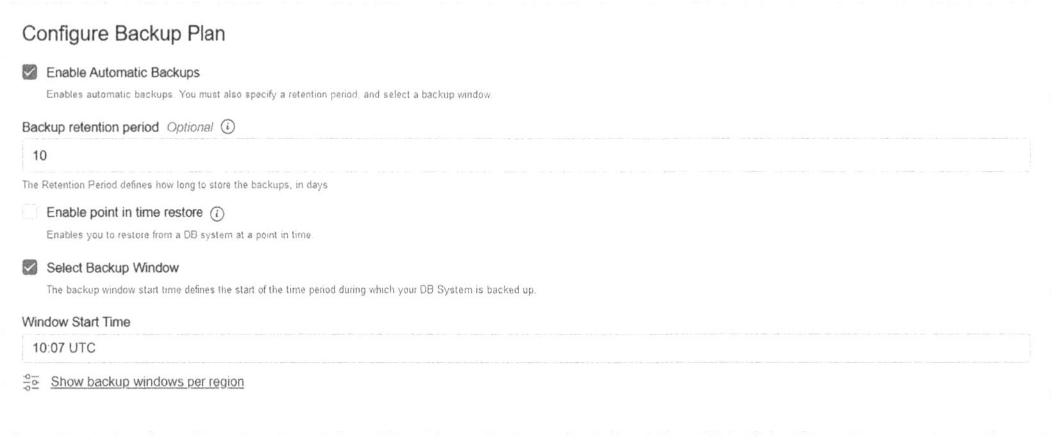

Configure Backup Plan

☑ Enable Automatic Backups
Enables automatic backups. You must also specify a retention period, and select a backup window.

Backup retention period *Optional* ⓘ

10

The Retention Period defines how long to store the backups, in days

☐ Enable point in time restore ⓘ
Enables you to restore from a DB system at a point in time.

☑ Select Backup Window
The backup window start time defines the start of the time period during which your DB System is backed up.

Window Start Time

10:07 UTC

Show backup windows per region

Figure 5-26. Restore DB System (Part 5)

The last section is a summary with several tabs that allow you to change a number of configuration times including the following. Once again, the settings will be the same (by default) as the original DB System used for the backup:

- *Deletion Plan*: Displays the deletion plan for the DB System including whether it is enabled, the retention time for automatic backups, and the state of the final backup. The enable/disable links are shortcuts for enabling or disabling the deletion plan.

- *Configuration*: Displays information about the DB System including its shape, memory and storage size, MySQL version and configuration, and if crash recovery is enabled. The edit link next to the storage size is a shortcut to changing the storage size of the DB System.

- *Crash Recovery*: Enable or disable crash recovery. Disabling crash recovery can improve performance but will also turn off automatic backups. Use wisely.

- *Management*: Displays the MDS maintenance window start time. Be sure to choose a timeframe where your usage is lowest to avoid potential conflicts.

- *Networking*: Displays the hostname, IP address, and MySQL ports. You should not alter these unless you want to customize the endpoint.

- *Tags*: Displays the tags for the DB System. You can also add tags.

Figure 5-27 shows the summary section of the restore backup dialog.

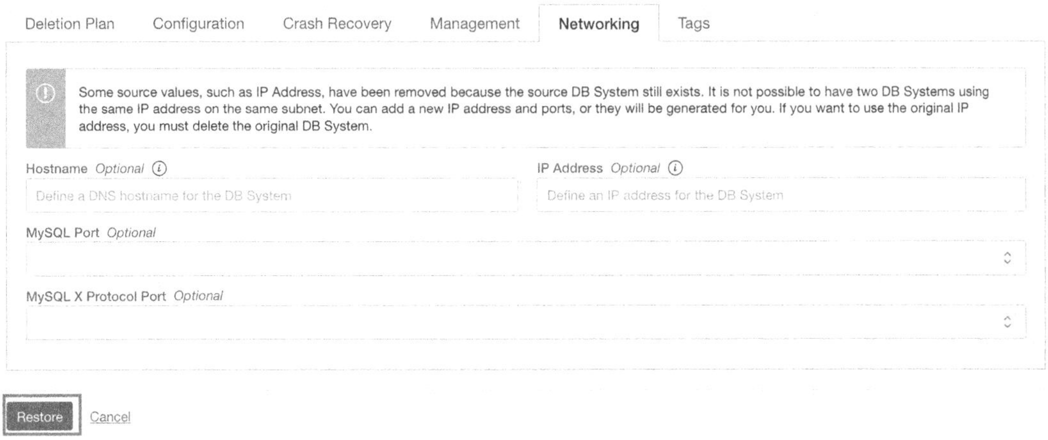

| Deletion Plan | Configuration | Crash Recovery | Management | **Networking** | Tags |

> Some source values, such as IP Address, have been removed because the source DB System still exists. It is not possible to have two DB Systems using the same IP address on the same subnet. You can add a new IP address and ports, or they will be generated for you. If you want to use the original IP address, you must delete the original DB System.

Hostname *Optional* ⓘ

Define a DNS hostname for the DB System

IP Address *Optional* ⓘ

Define an IP address for the DB System

MySQL Port *Optional*

MySQL X Protocol Port *Optional*

[Restore] Cancel

Figure 5-27. *Restore DB System (Part 6)*

Once you've decided on any customizations using these tabs and you're ready to restore the DB System from backup, you can click the *Restore* button.

Once the restore completes, you will see it in the list of DB Systems, and you can now access the new DB System. If you restored a backup for a DB System in use, a new endpoint will be generated so be sure to check the restored DB System details page for details. For example, Figure 5-28 shows the new endpoint on the restored DB System from above.

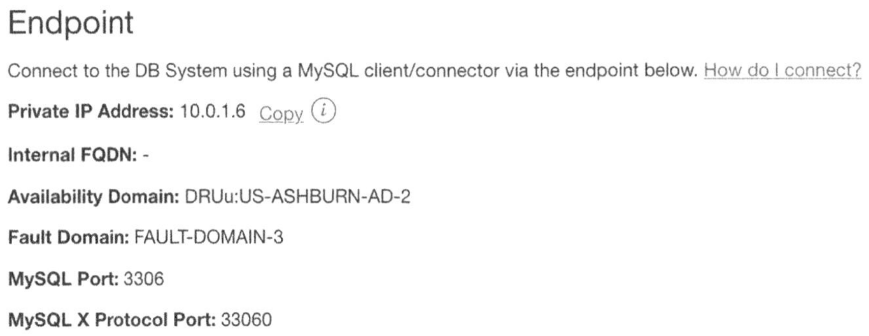

Endpoint

Connect to the DB System using a MySQL client/connector via the endpoint below. How do I connect?

Private IP Address: 10.0.1.6   Copy ⓘ

Internal FQDN: -

Availability Domain: DRUu:US-ASHBURN-AD-2

Fault Domain: FAULT-DOMAIN-3

MySQL Port: 3306

MySQL X Protocol Port: 33060

Figure 5-28. *Restored DB System Details Page (New Endpoint)*

If you followed the tutorial at the beginning of the chapter to create a new DB System, you should see a different endpoint when you navigate to the restored DB System details page.

That concludes our look at the MDS backup and restore operations.

Summary

If you've followed along with the examples in this chapter and created your own DB Systems, backups, and restored DB Systems, you've learned that creating and working with DB Systems is very easy. Once you get the hang of where the operations (buttons) are and the several ways you can access the same function, it becomes rather routine.

And, if you have set up and installed MySQL on your own hardware (or even your PC), chances are you've discovered there is a lot of work needed to configure MySQL. That is, installation is a breeze compared to some other systems, but tuning MySQL can be quite a challenge. Fortunately, MDS makes all of that work a thing of the past.

In this chapter, we learned about MDS backup resources. We learned the details of a backup resource including how to list them. We also learned how to backup our DB Systems including setting up automatic backups as well as how to create manual backups. We learned the differences between incremental and full backups along with when you might want to use each. Finally, we learned how to restore DB Systems using a backup resource.

In the next chapter, we will learn how to enable a new recovery feature named Point-in-Time Recovery; an automated recovery mechanism that can restore your databases to a specific 5-minute time period in the past. Cool.

Point-in-Time Recovery

One of the challenges of backup and recovery is manifested when faced with the task of recovering a database or set of databases to a specific point before a critical event occurs. More specifically, the data is considered valid prior to a specific event that caused inconsistencies or data loss. For example, the event could be the result of operator error, a software defect, or hardware/connectivity issues.

When this happens, systems administrators (or database administrators) must restore the data with the last known good backup. However, if the backup were set up to occur in the middle of the night and the data-altering event occurs during the middle of the day, there could be hours of data changes lost and must be recreated in some manner.

Fortunately, there is a feature in MySQL that you can use to protect yourself against such recovery events. It is named point-in-time recovery (PITR) and is a combination of replication technologies and backup strategies.

In this chapter, we will learn about PITR in the OCI MySQL Database Service (MDS) on a DB System beginning with a brief overview of how PITR works on-prem. This will give you the opportunity to understand PITR in MDS and how to leverage it to your advantage for data recovery.

Overview

Those who have their on-prem MySQL servers have at their disposal a feature in MySQL called binary logs, which record the changes to your data in a special binary format that can be replayed if data recovery is needed. Like physical backups, binary logs are not human readable but unlike physical backups, they must be processed one event (data change) at a time making them cumbersome for use as a recovery mechanism.

The best way to enable binary logging is to place the following line in your my.cnf (or my.ini) configuration file and restart your MySQL server.

© Charles Bell 2023
C. Bell, *MySQL Database Service Revealed*, https://doi.org/10.1007/978-1-4842-8945-7_6

```
log_bin=ON
```

You can also determine if binary logging is enabled by using the following command. Notice the value is ON, which means binary logging is enabled:

```
MySQL  localhost:33060+ ssl  SQL > SHOW VARIABLES LIKE 'log_bin' \G
*************************** 1. row ***************************
Variable_name: log_bin
        Value: ON
1 rows in set (0.0033 sec)
```

You can also turn off binary logging for specific commands or a series of commands with the following, which tells MySQL to skip logging the events. This can be helpful for certain administrative commands or changes to data you do not want to expose to the binary log (or propagate to consumers of the binary logs such as those used in replication):

```
SET sql_log_bin = ON
<EVENTS TO SKIP>
SET sql_log_bin = OFF
```

Interestingly, binary logs are one of the key components in enabling the high availability features in MySQL. We will explore the high availability features in MDS in Chapter 8.

Tip   See https://dev.mysql.com/doc/refman/8.0/en/binary-log.html for more information about the MySQL binary log.

Once binary logging is turned on, your MySQL server is recording each event as it is processed and writes it in the log. The logs are designed so that they can be rotated manually or automatically to reduce file sizes.

When combined with regular backups, you can set up your backup routines to rotate the binary logs immediately before a snapshot of the data. This enables you to begin recording which binary logs have been created since the last backup.

Should an event occur where you need to restore to a time period between the automated backups, you can restore that latest backup and then apply the logs to the point of the event by replaying (executing or applying) the binary logs that were created since the last backup. For those using this mechanism on their on-prem servers, you can use binary logging tools to help locate a precise location to restore your data.

This mechanism, PITR, is available in MDS for DB Systems and is fully automated. You need not worry about binary logs, which backup to restore, or any such details – all of it is handled by the MDS automation mechanisms. In fact, it is so easy to use you merely turn it on and forget about it (until you need to recover your data).

However, automation of complex tasks always results in some level of restriction in order to make it consistent and dependable. The limitation imposed by OCI for MDS PITR is the recovery window. Currently, you can recover your data on your DB System with PITR enabled to any 5-minute time period. Thus, at most you may have to recover manually is 5 minutes of data, which is a small price to pay for automatic recovery of data between backups.

Now that we know a little more about PITR, let's see how to setup our DB Systems.

Setup

You can set up PITR at any time for a DB System by enabling it on the DB System details page. You can also enable PITR when you create a DB System. The feature requires activation of automatic backups so if your DB System has that feature turned off, you will need to enable PITR.

To check if your DB System has PITR or automatic backups enabled, visit the DB System details page and look for the *Backup* section as shown in Figure 6-1.

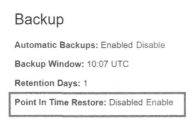

Figure 6-1. *Backup Settings – Disabled (DB System Details Page)*

To enable PITR on a DB System, click the *Enable* link as shown. This will open a new *Edit Backup Plan* dialog where you can configure the feature. You can set the backup retention period (in days), enable PITR by ticking the *Enable point in time restore* tick box, and choose the backup window. Once your settings are ready, you can click the *Save Changes* button to enable PITR and automatic backups (if applicable). Figure 6-2 shows the *Edit Backup Plan* dialog.

Edit Backup Plan

☑ **Enable Automatic Backups**
   Enables automatic backups. You must also specify a retention period, and select a backup window.

   Backup retention period *Optional*
   The Retention Period defines how long to store the backups, in days. ⓘ

   | 10 |

   ☑ **Enable point in time restore** ⓘ
      Enables you to restore from a DB system at a point in time.

☑ **Select Backup Window**
   The backup window start time defines the start of the time period during which your DB System is backed up.

Window Start Time

   | 10:07 UTC |

   ⚙ Show backup windows per region

   Save Changes   Cancel

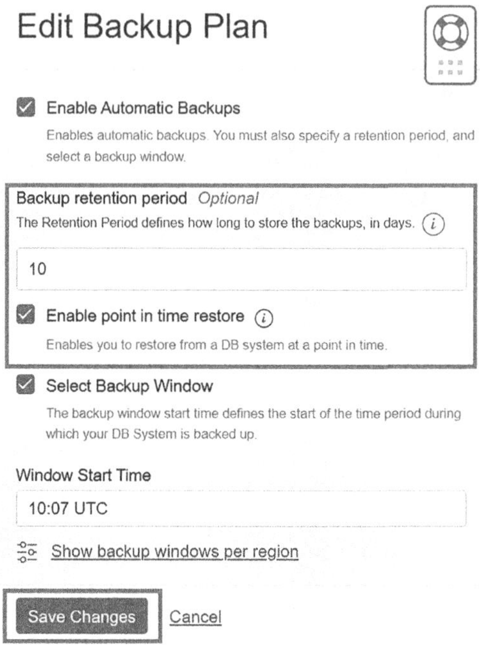

Figure 6-2. *Edit Backup Plan Dialog*

Note   If you have a DB System running MySQL 8.0.28, you will need to update to MySQL 8.0.29 at a minimum to use PITR. You can upgrade your DB System on the details page by clicking on the *Edit* link next to the MySQL version and choose the version you want to upgrade to from the list.

Once the changes are saved, the DB System will enter an update period so that the MDS automation can complete the changes to the configuration in the background. Once complete, you will see the automatic backups and PITR enabled as shown in Figure 6-3.

Figure 6-3. *Backup Settings – Enabled (DB System Details Page)*

If you want to enable PITR on a new DB System, you can complete the same parameters on the Create DB System dialog in the Backup section as shown in Figure 6-4.

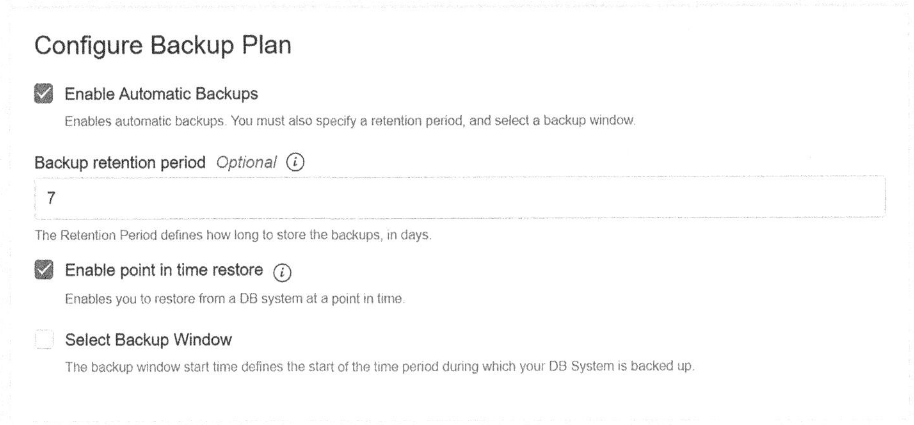

Configure Backup Plan

☑ **Enable Automatic Backups**
   Enables automatic backups. You must also specify a retention period, and select a backup window.

Backup retention period *Optional* ⓘ

> 7

The Retention Period defines how long to store the backups, in days.

☑ **Enable point in time restore** ⓘ
   Enables you to restore from a DB system at a point in time.

☐ **Select Backup Window**
   The backup window start time defines the start of the time period during which your DB System is backed up.

Figure 6-4. *Backup Settings (Create DB System)*

Finally, you can list your backups by selecting the Backups list on the Resources menu on the DB System details page as shown in Figure 6-5.

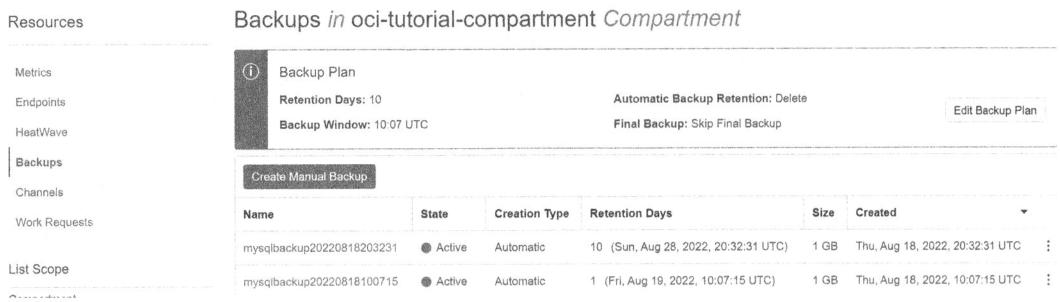

Resources

Metrics
Endpoints
HeatWave
Backups
Channels
Work Requests

List Scope

Backups *in* oci-tutorial-compartment *Compartment*

ⓘ Backup Plan
   Retention Days: 10   **Automatic Backup Retention:** Delete
   Backup Window: 10:07 UTC   **Final Backup:** Skip Final Backup   Edit Backup Plan

Create Manual Backup

Name	State	Creation Type	Retention Days	Size	Created	
mysqlbackup20220818203231	● Active	Automatic	10 (Sun, Aug 28, 2022, 20:32:31 UTC)	1 GB	Thu, Aug 18, 2022, 20:32:31 UTC	⋮
mysqlbackup20220818100715	● Active	Automatic	1 (Fri, Aug 19, 2022, 10:07:15 UTC)	1 GB	Thu, Aug 18, 2022, 10:07:15 UTC	⋮

Figure 6-5. *List of Backups (DB System Detail Page)*

Now that we know how to set up PITR, we can see a small demonstration on how to recover a DB System using PITR.

Recovery

Recovery of a DB System using PITR is very similar to recovery using any normal backup. The difference is in how you select the backup. If you choose to recover using a PITR entry, you will need to select the last backup from the list

To make this demonstration feasible, we will need to introduce an event from which we want to recover. A simple DROP DATABASE or similar SQL statement will suffice. In this case, I issued a `DROP DATABASE sakila`; command.

I did so by logging into a compute instance then launched MySQL Shell on the compute instance to connect to a DB System. I then issued the DROP command at approximately 21:06 UTC. I logged into the compute instance with the following command using the *public IP address* as shown on the compute instance details page:

```
ssh -i c:\users\cbell\.ssh\ssh-key-2022-08-16.key opc@150.136.69.126
```

From there, I logged into MySQL using MySQL Shell with the following and dropped the database:

```
[opc@connection-instance ~]$ mysqlsh --sql mysql_admin@10.0.1.226:33060
MySQL Shell 8.0.30

Copyright (c) 2016, 2022, Oracle and/or its affiliates.
Oracle is a registered trademark of Oracle Corporation and/or its
affiliates.
Other names may be trademarks of their respective owners.

MySQL  10.0.1.226:33060+ ssl  SQL > DROP DATABASE sakila;
Query OK, 23 rows affected (0.1493 sec)
```

Ok, now we have our event. Now, we can attempt to restore to a point prior to 21:06 UTC. We can do so by clicking on Restore to New DB System using the context menu for the backup in our list as shown in Figure 6-6. If you have more backups from which to choose, you should choose the one dated most recently before the event from which you want to recover.

Backups *in* oci-tutorial-compartment *Compartment*

ⓘ	Backup Plan					
	Retention Days: 10		Automatic Backup Retention: Delete			Edit Backup Plan
	Backup Window: 10:07 UTC		Final Backup: Skip Final Backup			

Create Manual Backup

Name	State	Creation Type	Retention Days	Size	Creati	View Details	
mysqlbackup20220818203231	● Active	Automatic	10 (Sun, Aug 28, 2022, 20:32:31 UTC)	1 GB	Thu, A	Restore to new DB system	⋮
mysqlbackup20220818100715	● Active	Automatic	1 (Fri, Aug 19, 2022, 10:07:15 UTC)	1 GB	Thu, A	Edit	⋮
mysqlbackup20220817100755	◐ Deleted	Automatic	1 (Thu, Aug 18, 2022, 10:07:55 UTC)	1 GB	Wed,	Copy OCID	⋮

Figure 6-6. *Launching Restore to New DB System (Backups List on DB System Details Page)*

This launches a new dialog where you can change several parameters for the new DB System. The first section in the dialog concerns the backup settings as shown in Figure 6-7.

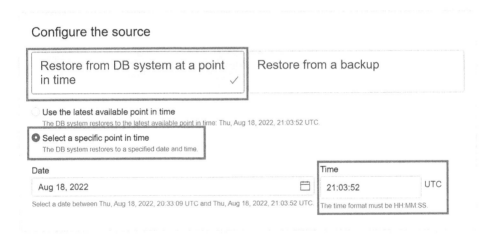

Figure 6-7. *Restore DB System from Backup (PITR)*

This is the area where you can specify that you want to restore to a specific point-in-time. Begin by clicking on the *Restore from DB System at a point in time*. Notice this allows you to choose the latest PITR period or a specific period. For this demonstration, we tick the *Select a specific point in time radio* button. Finally, you can enter a time period that occurs prior to your event. In this case, the last entry available is 21:03 UTC. Simply reduce the time shown by 5 minutes segments to reach your desired time period.

Once you click *Restore* button and the DB System is ready, we can log in and see that the *sakila* database is indeed present and the unwanted data change event has been recovered. Recall, there is much going on under the hood. MDS is restoring from the last known good backup and once restored, is applying the binary logs recorded since the backup. All this occurs without any intervention from the user. How cool is that?

Recall, we must first log into a compute instance prior to launching MySQL Shell using the *Private IP Address* of the restored DB System as shown in Figure 6-8.

Figure 6-8. *Private IP Address (Restored DB System via PITR)*

Listing 6-1 shows a test to ensure the sakila database is present.

Listing 6-1. Testing the Data (Restored DB System)

```
[opc@connection-instance ~]$ mysqlsh --sql mysql_admin@10.0.1.82:33060
Please provide the password for 'mysql_admin@10.0.1.82:33060':
****************
Save password for 'mysql_admin@10.0.1.82:33060'? [Y]es/[N]o/Ne[v]er
(default No): yes
MySQL Shell 8.0.30

Copyright (c) 2016, 2022, Oracle and/or its affiliates.
Oracle is a registered trademark of Oracle Corporation and/or its
affiliates.
Other names may be trademarks of their respective owners.

Type '\help' or '\?' for help; '\quit' to exit.
Creating a session to 'mysql_admin@10.0.1.82:33060'
Fetching schema names for autocompletion... Press ^C to stop.
Your MySQL connection id is 13 (X protocol)
```

```
Server version: 8.0.29-u2-cloud MySQL Enterprise - Cloud
No default schema selected; type \use <schema> to set one.
 MySQL  10.0.1.82:33060+ ssl  SQL > SHOW DATABASES;
+--------------------+
| Database           |
+--------------------+
| information_schema |
| mysql              |
| performance_schema |
| sakila             |
| sys                |
| world              |
+--------------------+
6 rows in set (0.0012 sec)
 MySQL  10.0.1.82:33060+ ssl  SQL > SELECT first_name, last_name FROM
sakila.actor LIMIT 10;
+------------+--------------+
| first_name | last_name    |
+------------+--------------+
| PENELOPE   | GUINESS      |
| NICK       | WAHLBERG     |
| ED         | CHASE        |
| JENNIFER   | DAVIS        |
| JOHNNY     | LOLLOBRIGIDA |
| BETTE      | NICHOLSON    |
| GRACE      | MOSTEL       |
| MATTHEW    | JOHANSSON    |
| JOE        | SWANK        |
| CHRISTIAN  | GABLE        |
+------------+--------------+
10 rows in set (0.0094 sec)
```

That's it! We now know how to restore a DB System to a specific 5-minute time period using point-in-time recovery.

Summary

Point-in-time recovery is one of those features, like automated backups, which can increase your ability to recover from data disasters and reduce your risk of data loss. PITR in MDS is automated and easy to set up. Recovery using PITR for your DB System is also easy to accomplish and works without any need to record complex system parameters or process binary log files. Once you've had a chance to use the feature and in the unlikely event you rely upon it to restore your systems to operation, you will appreciate the work Oracle has done to make a complex task simple in execution for DB Systems owners.

In the next chapter, we will learn about the options available to import and export your data to or from your MDS DB Systems.

CHAPTER 7

Data Import and Export

The DB System in MDS is clearly a very powerful and intriguing alternative to on-prem MySQL servers. We've seen how to create DB Systems and create backups, but what do you do when you want to get your own data into your new DB System? Or, if you want to use a copy of the data in your DB System to an on-prem development lab, how do you export the data?

Fortunately, there are methods for exporting your data and importing it to your DB System. As you will see, the process isn't complicated and works well for most use cases. However, if your data is very large and you have many gigabytes or terabytes of data, you may want to consider contacting Oracle's MySQL Sales team for more options for importing your data.

In this chapter, we will discover several ways we can migrate data to/from the cloud. But first, let's look at some of the concepts, strategies, and tools.

Overview

Oracle has ensured you don't have to start from nothing to populate your DB System. You can indeed copy your data from a local MySQL server to a DB System. Oracle uses several terms in the documentation including migrating and importing data. However, the process of copying your data to the cloud is called migrating while the operations for performing the migration are two processes named export and import.

In this section, we will see an overview of the tools and processes used for migrating data from your on-prem MySQL server to your DB System in MDS.

Migrating Data to MDS

The recommended process to migrate your data into MDS involves the use of the MySQL Shell to first export your data using one of several strategies for getting the exported

© Charles Bell 2023
C. Bell, *MySQL Database Service Revealed*, https://doi.org/10.1007/978-1-4842-8945-7_7

data to your DB System and then import the data using MySQL Shell. We will see the strategies for getting the data to your DB System in the next section.

MySQL Shell has several methods (also called utilities) for exporting data and one for importing data. These methods are found in the Java module named `util`, which is included as part of the MySQL Shell. To use the methods, you must be in the JavaScript mode. We can set the mode when we start MySQL Shell with the `--js` option or you can switch to JavaScript while in the shell with the `/js` shell command. When you start the shell in JavaScript mode or switch to the mode, you should see a prompt like the following:

```
MySQL  localhost:33060+ ssl  JS >
```

Note   We saw the MySQL Shell in Chapter 3 and if you have been following along with the examples in the book, you should have MySQL Shell installed. If not, visit the documentation at `https://dev.mysql.com/doc/mysql-shell/8.0/en/` for how to download and install the MySQL Shell.

The following briefly describes the methods for importing and exporting data. We list the required and option parameters (shown in square brackets). While these appear to be JavaScript methods (and they are), they execute a utility under the hood. Hence, Oracle calls these methods "utilities":

- `util.dumpInstance(outputUrl[, options])`: Use this utility to export all compatible databases (schemas) from the MySQL server. By default, the utility exports users, events, routines, and triggers.

- `util.dumpSchemas(schemas, outputUrl[, options])`: Use this utility to export a list of databases (schemas) from the MySQL server. Thus, you can use this to export one database (schema) at-a-time or export a portion of your databases for migrating to MDS.

- `util.loadDump()`: Use this utility to import the files from the `dump*()` methods.

This is a partial list of the utilities available in MySQL Shell. For a complete list of utilities, see `https://dev.mysql.com/doc/mysql-shell/8.0/en/mysql-shell-utilities.html`. The documentation includes a section devoted to the dumping (exporting) data utilities. We will see some of these utilities in action in a later section. But first, we must discuss the strategies for getting the exported data to your DB System for import.

Tip See `https://dev.mysql.com/doc/mysql-shell/8.0/en/mysql-shell-utilities-dump-instance-schema.html` for more information about using the `dumpInstance()` method.

Data Transfer Strategies

As mentioned, there are three ways to get your exported data to your DB System for import. The fastest is using another OCI resource called ObjectStore as the target from MySQL Shell where the shell copies the data directly to an ObjectStore bucket. A slower method is to use an intermediate Compute instance where you copy the data to the Compute instance then import it. The slowest method is to set up a Bastion Service to connect your PC to your DB System where the data is read from your PC when imported.

Recall from Chapter 2, ObjectStore is a storage resource that allows you to treat a set of files and an object. ObjectStore permits you to place the files (objects) in a container called a bucket. Thus, when you use MySQL Shell to export to ObjectStore, you will be exporting the data files into a bucket and then later reading those files from the bucket during import.

So, which method is best? That depends on your setup and how you've configured your OCI resources. However, the recommended method is to use ObjectStore. Be advised using ObjectStore to place the exported data in a bucket can lead to a small cost if you leave the files in the bucket (ObjectStore is a paid resource).

WHAT ABOUT OTHER PHYSICAL BACKUP TOOLS?

While it is possible to use certain physical backup tools like MySQL Enterprise Backup (MEB) to take a backup of your on-prem MySQL and restore it on an MDS DB System, the procedure is complex and requires intimate knowledge of MySQL data file storage, the DB System configuration, as well as a valid license for the tool that can be used in OCI. Thus, using a physical backup tool to import your on-prem data is not recommended.

Compatibility Concerns

While you are unlikely to encounter problems when migrating your data to MDS, there are some considerations you should heed concerning compatibility between your on-prem MySQL servers and MDS.

Security

Primarily, there are some restrictions concerning security that may not be present on your on-prem server. Fortunately, the dump utilities in MySQL Shell can detect such issues, and in some cases, make your database (schema) compatible during the export by altering the SQL `CREATE` statements. You can enable this feature by specifying the `ocimds:true` option when you launch (call) the `util.dumpInstance()` method in MySQL Shell. These are added as a JSON document. For example, to supply the `ocimds` and `dryRun` options for the `util.dumpInstance()` call, you would use the following command:

```
util.dumpInstance(".\test",{ocimds:true,dryRun:true});
```

This option instructs the MySQL Shell dump utility to run compatibility checks on your databases. If there are any issues found that cannot be automatically fixed, you will see a detailed report of those issues that includes strategies and examples on how to fix them.

Tip   It is strongly recommended to use the `ocimds:true` and `dryRun:true` options when using the dump utility in MySQL Shell for the first time. This will give you an opportunity to see and fix any potential issues before starting the migration.

To use the automatic correction feature in the dump utility, you must pass the `compatibility=<list>` option providing one or more of the following compatibility checks overrides (entered as strings) in a comma-separated list when you call the method. For example, `util.dumpInstance(...compatibility:["force_innodb", "strip_definers"}...)`:

- `force_innodb`: modifies the `ENGINE=` clause to use `INNODB`. This ensures all tables are dumped with `CREATE TABLE` statements to use the InnoDB storage engine. MDS supports only the InnoDB storage engine.

- `strip_definers`: removes the `DEFINER=<account>` clause from views, routines, events, and triggers.

- `strip_restricted_grants`: removes those privileges from `GRANT` statements that are not used by MDS. These include `RELOAD`, `FILE`, `SUPER`, `BINLOG_ADMIN`, and `SET_USER_ID`.

- `skip_invalid_accounts`: skips any user accounts that do not have passwords.

- `strip_tablespaces`: removes the `TABLESPACE=<>` option from the `CREATE TABLE` statements.

- `create_invisible_pks`: adds primary keys to tables without them. MDS requires primary keys for high availability.

- `ignore_missing_pks`: permits tables without primary keys. Use only if you do not intend to use the high availability feature for DB Systems.

Tip   For more information about these options and compatibility checks, see `https://dev.mysql.com/doc/mysql-shell/8.0/en/mysql-shell-utilities-dump-instance-schema.html`.

Let's look at an example of using the compatibility feature.

In this example, we have a MySQL server version 8.0.23 running on a local PC. There are several databases on the server some of which are the sample databases as shown in Listing 7-1.

Listing 7-1. Example: On-prem Server Databases

```
MySQL  localhost:33060+ ssl  SQL > SHOW DATABASES;
+--------------------+
| Database           |
+--------------------+
| animals            |
| contact_list1      |
| contact_list2      |
| contact_list3      |
```

```
| greenhouse         |
| information_schema |
| library_v1         |
| library_v2         |
| library_v3         |
| mysql              |
| performance_schema |
| plant_monitoring   |
| sakila             |
| sys                |
| test               |
| world              |
| world_x            |
+--------------------+
```

Notice the sakila, world, and world_x are sample databases from Oracle.

To run the dump utility as a dry run and run the compatibility checks, we use the following command. Notice we must switch to the JavaScript mode to use the command. Also, the location or destination is required, but we will use a local subfolder named test as shown (no files will be created since it is a dry run):

```
util.dumpInstance(".\test",{ocimds:true,dryRun:true})
```

Once we run that command, we will see a list of all the compatibility issues. Listing 7-2 shows an excerpt of some of the types of errors and warnings you may see.

Listing 7-2. Checking for Compatibility (Issues Found)

```
dryRun enabled, no locks will be acquired, and no files will be created.
Acquiring global read lock
Global read lock acquired
Initializing - done
13 out of 17 schemas will be dumped and within them 43 tables, 8 views, 10
routines, 6 triggers.
4 out of 7 users will be dumped.
Gathering information - done
All transactions have been started
Locking instance for backup
```

Global read lock has been released
Checking for compatibility with MySQL Database Service 8.0.28
NOTE: Database test had unsupported ENCRYPTION option commented out
NOTE: Database world_x had unsupported ENCRYPTION option commented out
NOTE: Database library_v3 had unsupported ENCRYPTION option commented out
NOTE: Database library_v2 had unsupported ENCRYPTION option commented out
...
NOTE: Database world had unsupported ENCRYPTION option commented out
NOTE: Database contact_list2 had unsupported ENCRYPTION option commented out
NOTE: Database plant_monitoring had unsupported ENCRYPTION option commented out
NOTE: Database library_v1 had unsupported ENCRYPTION option commented out
...
NOTE: Database contact_list1 had unsupported ENCRYPTION option commented out
NOTE: Database greenhouse had unsupported ENCRYPTION option commented out
NOTE: Database contact_list3 had unsupported ENCRYPTION option commented out
NOTE: Database animals had unsupported ENCRYPTION option commented out
ERROR: Table 'library_v1'.'books_authors' does not have a Primary Key, which is required for High Availability in MDS
...
ERROR: View animals.num_pets - definition does not use SQL SECURITY INVOKER characteristic, which is required (fix this with 'strip_definers' compatibility option)

ERROR: One or more tables without Primary Keys were found.

   MySQL Database Service High Availability (MDS HA) requires Primary
   Keys to be present in all tables.
   To continue with the dump you must do one of the following:

   * Create PRIMARY keys in all tables before dumping them.

MySQL 8.0.23 supports the creation of invisible columns to allow
creating Primary Key columns with no impact to applications. For
more details, see https://dev.mysql.com/doc/refman/en/invisible-
columns.html.
This is considered a best practice for both performance and
usability and will work seamlessly with MDS.

* Add the "create_invisible_pks" to the "compatibility" option.
  The dump will proceed and loader will automatically add Primary
  Keys to tables that don't have them when loading into MDS.
  This will make it possible to enable HA in MDS without
  application impact.
  However, Inbound Replication into an MDS HA instance (at the time
  of the release of MySQL Shell 8.0.24) will still not be possible.

* Add the "ignore_missing_pks" to the "compatibility" option.
  This will disable this check and the dump will be produced
  normally, Primary Keys will not be added automatically.
  It will not be possible to load the dump in an HA enabled MDS
  instance.

Compatibility issues with MySQL Database Service 8.0.28 were found. Please
use the 'compatibility' option to apply compatibility adaptations to the
dumped DDL.
Validating MDS compatibility - done
Util.dumpInstance: Compatibility issues were found (RuntimeError)

Here we see a number of errors. Most of them have to do with objects that do not
use the SQL SECURITY INVOKER characteristic. The report tells us to use the strip_
definers compatibility option. We also see issues with missing primary keys, but since
we won't be using the high availability feature, which isn't a problem. To do, we use the
ignore_missing_pks compatibility option. Other things cited include commented out
encryption clauses, which can be fixed during the migration.

If we run the command again but this time provide the compatibility options as
suggested with the following command (formatted for easier reading), we will get a
much shorter report. We also use the strip_restricted_grants compatibility option
to fix user accounts with incompatible grants (not shown in listing):

```
util.dumpInstance(".\test",
    {
        ocimds:true,
        dryRun:true,
        compatibility:[
            "strip_definers",
            "ignore_missing_pks",
            "strip_restricted_grants"
        ]
    }
)
```

Once we use this new command, we will get a much cleaner report as shown in Listing 7-3.

Listing 7-3. Checking for Compatibility (No Issues Found)

```
dryRun enabled, no locks will be acquired, and no files will be created.
Acquiring global read lock
Global read lock acquired
Initializing - done
13 out of 17 schemas will be dumped and within them 43 tables, 8 views, 10
routines, 6 triggers.
4 out of 7 users will be dumped.
Gathering information - done
All transactions have been started
Locking instance for backup
Global read lock has been released
Checking for compatibility with MySQL Database Service 8.0.28
...
NOTE: One or more tables without Primary Keys were found.

    This issue is ignored.
    This dump cannot be loaded into an MySQL Database Service instance
    with High Availability.

Compatibility issues with MySQL Database Service 8.0.28 were found and
repaired. Please review the changes made before loading them.
```

247

```
Validating MDS compatibility - done
Writing global DDL files
Writing users DDL
Writing DDL - done
Starting data dump
0% (0 rows / ~83 rows), 0.00 rows/s, 0.00 B/s uncompressed, 0.00 B/s
compressed
```

Here, we see a report where all critical compatibility issues are resolved. You can then proceed and remove the `dryRun:true` option.

Older MySQL Versions

There is one more compatibility issue to consider: the MySQL version. The minimum version supported for migration is MySQL 5.7.9. However, if you have a version older than the current version offered in MDS (currently 8.0.29), you should consider running the MySQL Shell Upgrade Checker Utility to see a report of potential issues with your migration. See the MySQL Shell User Guide – Upgrade Checker Utility (`https://dev.mysql.com/doc/mysql-shell/8.0/en/mysql-shell-utilities-upgrade.html`) for more information on this utility.

Now that we have learned a little about the data migration process, we can see examples of the methods to learn how to use them. In the following sections, we will see examples of export and import in action by migrating data from our local MySQL server to a DB System first then revisit the processes for migrating data from our DB System to our local MySQL server. As you will see, each process requires use of the export and import mechanisms and we will see a variety of ways to complete the process. This gives you options to getting your data into MDS that you can tailor to your needs.

If you want to follow along with the examples in the next sections, you should prepare your local MySQL server to contain only the *sakila* and *world* databases. If you include other databases, you may need to adjust the commands shown. You can find these sample databases and how to install them on `https://dev.mysql.com/doc/index-other.html` under the *Example Databases* heading.

Migrating Data to MDS

When migrating data to MDS, we must choose one of the three methods for moving the exported data to MDS. Recall, these include using an ObjectStore bucket, uploading the exported data to an intermediate Compute instance, and uploading the exported data directly to our DB System via a Bastion gateway. This section demonstrates migrating data to MDS using each mechanism. As you will see, all use the MySQL Shell to export and import data.

Using an ObjectStore Bucket

The first method to export our data from our local MySQL server will use the ObjectStore as an intermediate storage for the exported data. We will use the MySQL Shell on our local MySQL server to create an export of the data, which we will place in ObjectStore and then access that data from our MDS DB System for the import again using MySQL Shell.

In order to use the ObjectStore bucket option to upload the exported data, you must first configure your PC to permit use of the OCI CLI. This is because the mechanism and automation will require use of your security credentials during the process. We will need to configure our system to allow automated access to the objects in your OCI tenancy. However, you should consider the potential security implications of storing your OCI CLI access credentials on your PC. You only need to set up your PC once and unless your SSH key changes, you will not need to change the configuration.

Caution   Once you configure your PC for automated access to certain objects in your tenancy, you should ensure the security on your PC is sufficient to prevent unauthorized access to protect your OCI credentials.

Configure Your PC for OCI CLI Access

There are two things you will need to configure your PC to access your OCI objects via the API: (1) you will need an SSH key pair that you will upload the public key to your OCI account, and (2) you will need to create a special OCI configuration file that contains your account information. If you have an SSH key pair that you have already created, you can use that, but the following demonstrates how to create an SSH key pair and upload it to your OCI account.

> **Tip**   The following examples show how to generate the SSH key pair on Windows. If you use a Mac or Linux, see `https://docs.oracle.com/en-us/iaas/Content/API/Concepts/apisigningkey.htm#Required_Keys_and_OCIDs` for examples of the platform-specific commands for generating keys.

First, we need to create an SSH key pair, but we will place the keys in a special folder in our use account. Open the Windows PowerShell (or terminal) and create a folder named .oci in your user directory and change to the directory as shown:

```
PS C:\Users\cbell> mkdir %HOMEDRIVE%%HOMEPATH%\.oci
PS C:\Users\cbell> cd %HOMEDRIVE%%HOMEPATH%\.oci
PS C:\Users\cbell\.oci>
```

Next, we will generate the SSH key pair starting with the private key, then generate the public key. Note that you will be asked to provide a password for the key. Be sure to choose a password that differs from your MySQL administrative password and that you will remember as you will need to use it to access the keys. The following commands show you how to create the keys. The commands are shown in bold:

```
PS C:\Users\cbell\.oci> openssl genrsa -out oci_api_key.pem -aes128
-passout stdin 2048

Generating RSA private key, 2048 bit long modulus (2 primes)
......................+++++
....+++++
e is 65537 (0x010001)
Enter pass phrase for oci_api_key.pem:
Verifying - Enter pass phrase for oci_api_key.pem:

PS C:\Users\cbell\.oci> openssl rsa -pubout -in oci_api_key.pem -out oci_
api_key_public.pem
Enter pass phrase for oci_api_key.pem:
writing RSA key
```

Note   Mac and Linux system require the keys have a special set of permissions. You will need to run the command `chmod go-rwx ~/.oci/oci_api_key.pem` to set the permissions correctly for these platforms.

We will be uploading the public key to our OCI account. We can do so by either uploading the public key or by pasting in the text of the key. In this example, we will paste the text so we can show the contents of the key with the `type` command as shown. Notice the output is obscured for security. Your own key will appear similar but with different values:

```
PS C:\Users\cbell\.oci> type oci_api_key_public.pem
-----BEGIN PUBLIC KEY-----
12039812039u10293012983912839128309128309812039810-923801928309182
12039812039u10293012983912839128309128309812039810-923801928309182
12039812039u10293012983912839128309128309812039810-923801928309182
12039812039u10293012983912839128309128309812039810-923801928309182
12039812039u10293012983912839128309128309812039810-923801928309182
12039812039u10293012983912839128309128309812039810-923801928309182
UQIDAQAB
-----END PUBLIC KEY-----
```

Now that we have our keys generated, we can add the key to our OCI account. From the OCI console, open your account settings by clicking on your use icon in the upper-right corner and choose *My Profile*. Then, in the Resources list, choose API keys as shown in Figure 7-1.

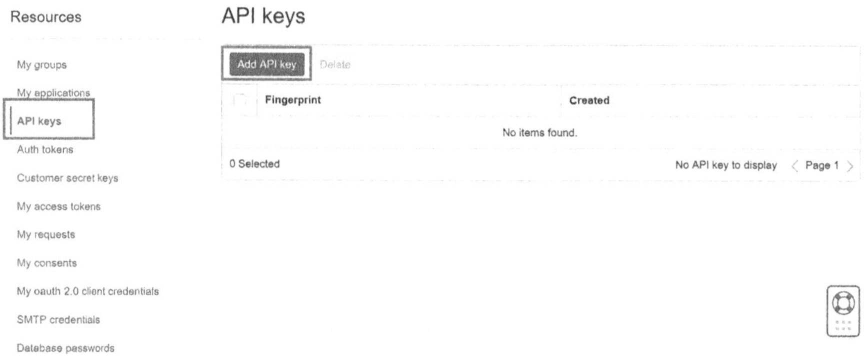

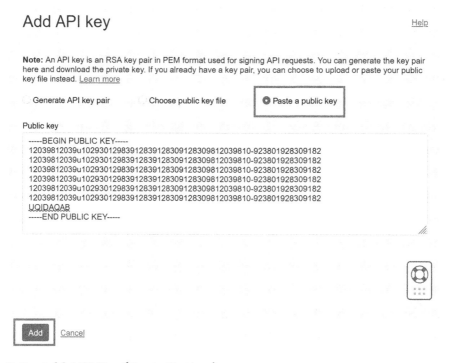

Figure 7-1. *API Keys (My Profile)*

Next, click the *Add API key* button as shown in Figure 7-1 to add a new key. On the next screen, choose the *Paste a public key* option then copy the text shown from the type command including the sections marked with - - - - - - - -...- - - - - - - - - and paste into the text box then click the *Add* button.

Add API key   Help

Note: An API key is an RSA key pair in PEM format used for signing API requests. You can generate the key pair here and download the private key. If you already have a key pair, you can choose to upload or paste your public key file instead. Learn more

   ○ Generate API key pair   ○ Choose public key file   ● Paste a public key

Public key

```
-----BEGIN PUBLIC KEY-----
12039812039u102930129839128391283091283098120398l0-923801928309182
12039812039u102930129839128391283091283098120398l0-923801928309182
12039812039u102930129839128391283091283098120398l0-923801928309182
12039812039u102930129839128391283091283098120398l0-923801928309182
12039812039u102930129839128391283091283098120398l0-923801928309182
12039812039u102930129839128391283091283098120398l0-923801928309182
UQIDAQAB
-----END PUBLIC KEY-----
```

   Add   Cancel

Figure 7-2. *Add API Key (Paste Option)*

Once you click the Add button, you will see a dialog that shows you the configuration file you need to create on your PC. Figure 7-3 shows an example of the output you can expect with certain parameters masked for security.

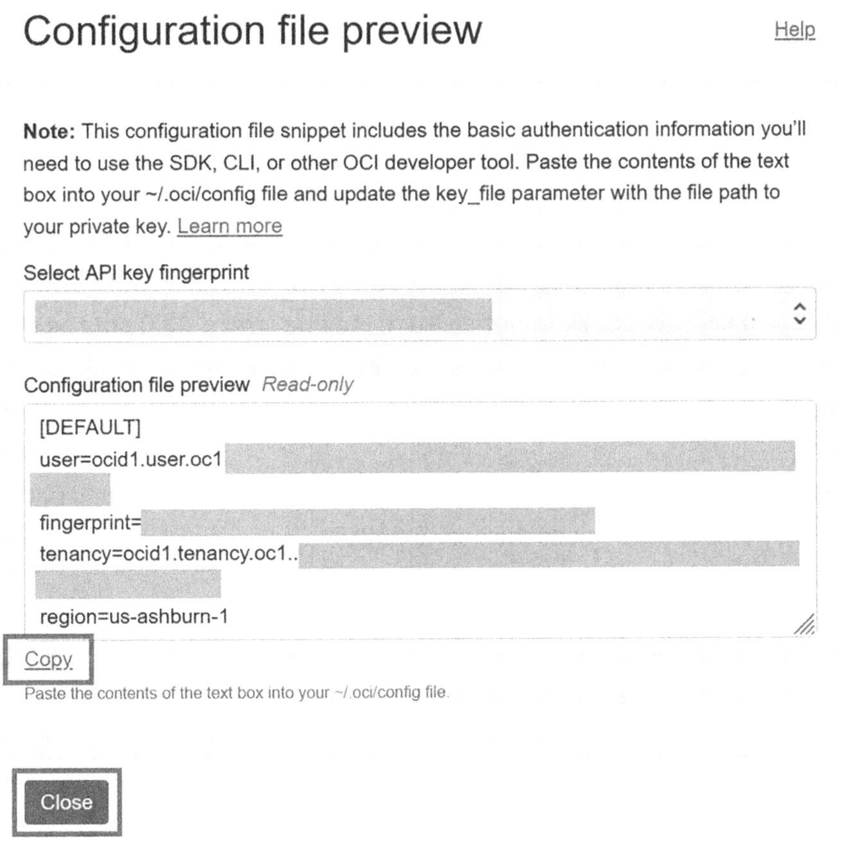

Configuration file preview Help

Note: This configuration file snippet includes the basic authentication information you'll need to use the SDK, CLI, or other OCI developer tool. Paste the contents of the text box into your ~/.oci/config file and update the key_file parameter with the file path to your private key. Learn more

Select API key fingerprint

Configuration file preview *Read-only*

```
[DEFAULT]
user=ocid1.user.oc1

fingerprint=
tenancy=ocid1.tenancy.oc1..

region=us-ashburn-1
```

Copy
Paste the contents of the text box into your ~/.oci/config file.

Close

Figure 7-3. *Sample OCI Configuration File Contents (Add API Key)*

Notice the API key is shown with a fingerprint, which is a special hash of the key unique to that key. We will be using the fingerprint in the configuration file we will create in the next step.

In fact, we will use the *Copy* link to copy the contents of the sample configuration file and paste it into a file named config that we will place in the .oci folder we created earlier. Open a new file with your favorite text file editor and paste the text into the file and save it as HOMEDRIVE%%HOMEPATH%\.oci. Once that is done, click the *Close* button. You should now see your API key fingerprint in the list as shown (obscured for security) in Figure 7-4. Note that the key shown may vary.

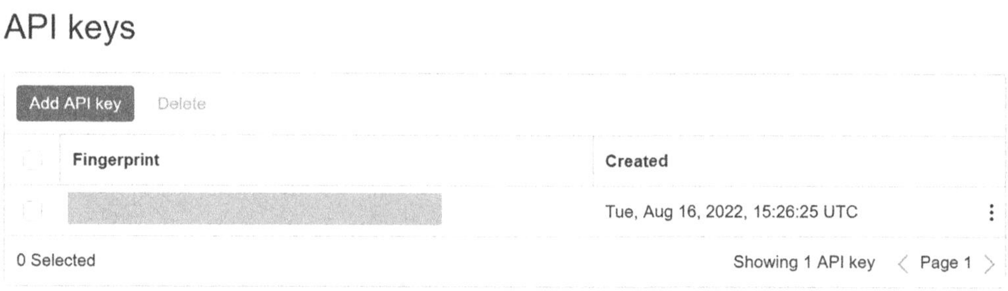

API keys

Figure 7-4. *API Key List (My Profile)*

Ok, we're almost done. There is one more thing we need to add to the config file. We must set the key location (path) of our SSH keys. Open the configuration file (HOMEDRIVE%%HOMEPATH%\.oci) and notice there is a line with a TODO note as shown below. Here, we will replace the <> with the path where the SSH keys are located:

```
key_file=<path to your private keyfile> # TODO
```

At the bottom of the file, replace the path as shown using your specific path on your PC to your SSH keys. Be sure to use the actual path:

key_file=**C:\Users\cbell\.oci\oci_api_key.pem**

Once you have made the changes, save, and close the file. We can test that our configuration is working by installing the OCI command line interface (CLI). We will be using the OCI CLI to test in this chapter but will use the OCI CLI in Chapter 8 to demonstrate how to script your MDS operations.

Install and Test the OCI CLI

To install the OCI CLI, we will use the PowerShell on Windows. Similar commands are available for other platforms. Be sure to open the PowerShell with administrator privileges. Note that the installation process enables auto-complete when running an installation script. You must enable the RemoteSigned execution policy, which is the first command. The next command changes the PowerShell to use TLS 1.2. The following command downloads the installer script file, and the last command executes the installation script (with prompts). Listing 7-4 shows a sample execution of the required commands (shown in bold). Your output may vary depending on what Python packages you may have installed. Also, note that we use the default paths for all installations. Portions omitted for brevity.

Listing 7-4. Installing OCI CLI (Windows 11)

```
PS C:\WINDOWS\system32> Set-ExecutionPolicy RemoteSigned
Execution Policy Change
Do you want to change the execution policy?
[Y] Yes  [A] Yes to All  [N] No  [L] No to All  [S] Suspend  [?] Help
(default is "N"): A
PS C:\WINDOWS\system32> [Net.ServicePointManager]::SecurityProtocol = [Net.
SecurityProtocolType]::Tls12
PS C:\WINDOWS\system32> Invoke-WebRequest https://raw.githubusercontent.
com/oracle/oci-cli/master/scripts/install/install.ps1 -OutFile install.ps1
PS C:\WINDOWS\system32> iex ((New-Object System.Net.WebClient).
DownloadString('https://raw.githubusercontent.com/oracle/oci-cli/master/
scripts/install/install.ps1'))

...
-- Verifying Python version.
-- Python version 3.7.5 okay.

===> In what directory would you like to place the install? (leave blank to
use 'C:\Users\cbell\lib\oracle-cli'):
-- Creating directory 'C:\Users\cbell\lib\oracle-cli'.
-- We will install at 'C:\Users\cbell\lib\oracle-cli'.

===> In what directory would you like to place the 'oci.exe' executable?
(leave blank to use 'C:\Users\cbell\bin'):
-- The executable will be in 'C:\Users\cbell\bin'.

===> In what directory would you like to place the OCI scripts? (leave
blank to use 'C:\Users\cbell\bin\oci-cli-scripts'):
-- The scripts will be in 'C:\Users\cbell\bin\oci-cli-scripts'.

===> Currently supported optional packages are: ['db (will install cx_
Oracle)']
What optional CLI packages would you like to be installed (comma separated
names; press enter if you don't need any optional packages)?:
-- The optional packages installed will be ''.
-- Trying to use python3 venv.
```

```
-- Executing: ['C:\\Program Files (x86)\\Microsoft Visual Studio\\
Shared\\Python37_64\\python.exe', '-m', 'venv', 'C:\\Users\\cbell\\lib\\
oracle-cli']
-- Executing: ['C:\\Users\\cbell\\lib\\oracle-cli\\Scripts\\python.exe',
'-m', 'pip', 'install', '--upgrade', 'pip']
Collecting pip
  Downloading https://files.pythonhosted.org/packages/1f/2c/
d9626f045e7b49a6225c6b09257861f24da78f4e5f23af2ddbdf852c99b8/pip-22.2.2-
py3-none-any.whl (2.0MB)
     |████████████████████████████████| 2.0MB 930kB/s
Installing collected packages: pip
  Found existing installation: pip 19.2.3
    Uninstalling pip-19.2.3:
      Successfully uninstalled pip-19.2.3

...

===> Modify PATH to include the CLI and enable tab completion in PowerShell
now? (Y/n): y
--
-- ** Close and re-open PowerShell to reload changes to your PATH **
-- In order to run the autocomplete script, you may also need to set your
PowerShell execution policy to allow for running local scripts (as an
Administrator run Set-ExecutionPolicy RemoteSigned in a PowerShell prompt)
--
-- Installation successful.
-- Run the CLI with C:\Users\cbell\bin\oci.exe --help
VERBOSE: Successfully installed OCI CLI!
```

Tip   If you use a different platform, see https://docs.oracle.com/en-us/
iaas/Content/API/SDKDocs/cliinstall.htm for installation details.

Next, close the PowerShell and reopen it (to pick up the installation path changes) and execute the following command. This is a simple OCI CLI listing command to list ObjectStore buckets for the `oci-tutorial-compartment` we created earlier. You will need to use the OCID for that compartment as shown (obscured for security). You may not have any created, so your output may differ. If the command executes without errors, your PC is now configured correctly for use with the OCI CLI, and you can proceed with the export example. Notice you may be required to enter the password for your SSH keys more than once:

```
PS C:\Users\cbell> oci os bucket list --compartment-id=ocid1.compartment.oc
1..1290387120983120928301982309128309128309182398
Private key passphrase:
Private key passphrase:
{
  "data": [
    {
      "compartment-id": "ocid1.compartment.oc1..
        aaaaaaaawzwb45t3lutkqvyhofxh3ai26e5oli2a4q6efbh25g3llqwys7pa",
      "created-by": "ocid1.user.oc1..
        aaaaaaaabbufd2sc7d6r2gojlnx3xeaenpesx5yu4clxi2eovyjf46jpopeq",
      "defined-tags": null,
      "etag": "2eec575a-80d0-42d2-9ab0-70c3b6a86ce3",
      "freeform-tags": null,
      "name": "test-bucket",
      "namespace": "idj5psxg6enz",
      "time-created": "2022-08-16T17:03:10.148000+00:00"
    }
  ]
}
```

Note   If this command returns an error, be sure to visit the online installation instructions for the OCI CLI (`https://docs.oracle.com/en-us/iaas/Content/API/SDKDocs/cliinstall.htm`) and correct the installation. You will need the OCI CLI in order to use ObjectStore with export and import.

Notice we have one bucket in the list. The JSON output format is used by default for the OCI CLI commands to return data.

Let's continue with our example export from MDS. Recall, the above steps (creating SSH keys, uploading the private key, creating the configuration file, and installing the OCI CLI) can be done once for each PC you plan to use with exporting data with ObjectStore (or using the OCI CLI).

Create the ObjectStore Bucket

Next, we need to create an ObjectStore bucket to store our data in from the export. In this example, we will create a bucket in the `oci-tutorial-compartment` named `mysql-data-bucket`. Begin by logging into OCI and choosing Storage | Buckets from the menu. You will see the ObjectStore bucket page as shown in Figure 7-5. Be sure to select the correct compartment from the list as shown.

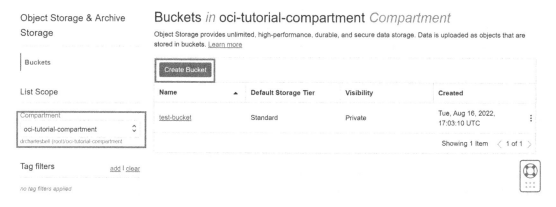

Figure 7-5. *ObjectStore Bucket List*

To create a new bucket, click the *Create Bucket* button and replace the bucket name with `mysql-data-bucket` on the create bucket dialog as shown in Figure 7-6. We can use the defaults for the other options listed. More specifically, we will use the standard bucket tier and the standard Oracle-managed encryption keys. Yes, buckets are encrypted by default. Nice.

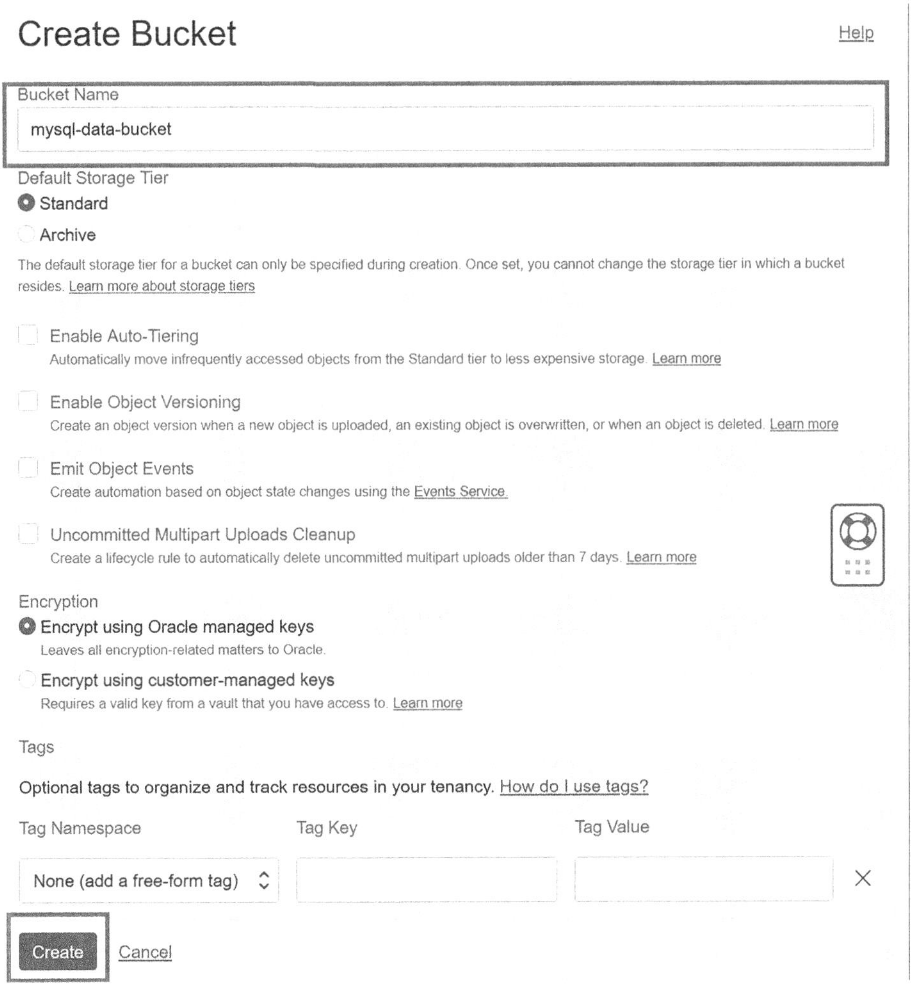

Create Bucket

Help

Bucket Name

mysql-data-bucket

Default Storage Tier
- ● Standard
- ○ Archive

The default storage tier for a bucket can only be specified during creation. Once set, you cannot change the storage tier in which a bucket resides. Learn more about storage tiers

☐ Enable Auto-Tiering
  Automatically move infrequently accessed objects from the Standard tier to less expensive storage. Learn more

☐ Enable Object Versioning
  Create an object version when a new object is uploaded, an existing object is overwritten, or when an object is deleted. Learn more

☐ Emit Object Events
  Create automation based on object state changes using the Events Service.

☐ Uncommitted Multipart Uploads Cleanup
  Create a lifecycle rule to automatically delete uncommitted multipart uploads older than 7 days. Learn more

Encryption
- ● Encrypt using Oracle managed keys
  Leaves all encryption-related matters to Oracle.
- ○ Encrypt using customer-managed keys
  Requires a valid key from a vault that you have access to. Learn more

Tags

Optional tags to organize and track resources in your tenancy. How do I use tags?

Tag Namespace	Tag Key	Tag Value
None (add a free-form tag) ⌄		

[Create] Cancel

Figure 7-6. *Create Bucket Dialog*

When ready, click the *Create* button to create the bucket. You should now see the bucket in the list for the compartment. We are now ready to export our data from our local MySQL server using this new bucket.

Export to an ObjectStore Bucket

Now we are ready to export our data from our local MySQL server. If you have not created a DB System to test with, do so now. Create a standard DB System that meets the storage requirements for your data. If you want to follow along with this tutorial, we will use a DB System with the name `oci-tutorial-mysql`, which we used earlier in the book.

We will also be using an intermediate compute instance (named connection-instance) to connect to our DB System rather than creating a Bastion or VPN gateway. Recall, you will need to install the MySQL Shell on that compute instance to connect to your DB System. See Chapter 4 for more details on creating and configuring the compute instance.

Return to your local MySQL server and open the MySQL Shell and connect to it. You can use the JavaScript option using the command shown below:

```
C:\Users\cbell>mysqlsh -uroot -p –js
```

Next, we will execute the util.dumpInstance() method providing a prefix for the bucket data (use mds-test) along with the ObjectStore information in a JSON string that includes the bucket name (osBucketName), threads, the MDS data compatibility switch (ocimds) set to true, and the compatibility options discussed earlier where we will strip restricted grants, definer clauses, missing primary keys, and invalid accounts. The following shows the format of the method call:

```
util.dumpInstance("bucketPrefix", {osBucketName: "mds-bucket", threads: n,
ocimds: true, compatibility: ["strip_restricted_grants", "strip_definers",
"ignore_missing_pks", "skip_invalid_accounts"]})
```

Ok, let's run the method and see what happens. Listing 7-5 shows the output of running the method to dump the databases on our local MySQL server to the ObjectStore bucket we created earlier (mysql-data-bucket).

Listing 7-5. Exporting Data from Local MySQL Server

```
MySQL  localhost:33060+ ssl  JS > util.dumpInstance("mds-test",
{osBucketName: "mysql-data-bucket", ocimds: true, compatibility: ["strip_
restricted_grants", "strip_definers", "ignore_missing_pks", "skip_invalid_
accounts"]})
Please enter the API key passphrase: **********
Acquiring global read lock
Global read lock acquired
Initializing - done
2 out of 6 schemas will be dumped and within them 19 tables, 7 views, 6
routines, 6 triggers.
```

1 out of 4 users will be dumped.

Gathering information - done

All transactions have been started

Locking instance for backup

Global read lock has been released

Checking for compatibility with MySQL Database Service 8.0.29

NOTE: Database `sakila` had unsupported ENCRYPTION option commented out

NOTE: Function `sakila`.`get_customer_balance` had definer clause removed

NOTE: Function `sakila`.`get_customer_balance` had SQL SECURITY
characteristic set to INVOKER

NOTE: Function `sakila`.`inventory_in_stock` had definer clause removed

NOTE: Function `sakila`.`inventory_in_stock` had SQL SECURITY
characteristic set to INVOKER

NOTE: Function `sakila`.`inventory_held_by_customer` had definer
clause removed

NOTE: Function `sakila`.`inventory_held_by_customer` had SQL SECURITY
characteristic set to INVOKER

NOTE: Procedure `sakila`.`rewards_report` had definer clause removed

NOTE: Procedure `sakila`.`rewards_report` had SQL SECURITY characteristic
set to INVOKER

NOTE: Procedure `sakila`.`film_in_stock` had definer clause removed

NOTE: Procedure `sakila`.`film_in_stock` had SQL SECURITY characteristic
set to INVOKER

NOTE: Procedure `sakila`.`film_not_in_stock` had definer clause removed

NOTE: Procedure `sakila`.`film_not_in_stock` had SQL SECURITY
characteristic set to INVOKER

NOTE: Database `world` had unsupported ENCRYPTION option commented out

NOTE: Trigger `sakila`.`ins_film` had definer clause removed

NOTE: Trigger `sakila`.`upd_film` had definer clause removed

NOTE: Trigger `sakila`.`del_film` had definer clause removed

NOTE: Trigger `sakila`.`customer_create_date` had definer clause removed

NOTE: Trigger `sakila`.`payment_date` had definer clause removed

NOTE: Trigger `sakila`.`rental_date` had definer clause removed

NOTE: View `sakila`.`staff_list` had definer clause removed

NOTE: View `sakila`.`staff_list` had SQL SECURITY characteristic set
to INVOKER
NOTE: View `sakila`.`customer_list` had definer clause removed
NOTE: View `sakila`.`customer_list` had SQL SECURITY characteristic set
to INVOKER
NOTE: View `sakila`.`film_list` had definer clause removed
NOTE: View `sakila`.`film_list` had SQL SECURITY characteristic set
to INVOKER
NOTE: View `sakila`.`sales_by_film_category` had definer clause removed
NOTE: View `sakila`.`sales_by_film_category` had SQL SECURITY
characteristic set to INVOKER
NOTE: View `sakila`.`nicer_but_slower_film_list` had definer clause removed
NOTE: View `sakila`.`nicer_but_slower_film_list` had SQL SECURITY
characteristic set to INVOKER
NOTE: View `sakila`.`sales_by_store` had definer clause removed
NOTE: View `sakila`.`sales_by_store` had SQL SECURITY characteristic set
to INVOKER
NOTE: View `sakila`.`actor_info` had definer clause removed
Compatibility issues with MySQL Database Service 8.0.29 were found and
repaired. Please review the changes made before loading them.
Validating MDS compatibility - done
Writing global DDL files
Writing users DDL
Running data dump using 4 threads.
NOTE: Progress information uses estimated values and may not be accurate.
Writing schema metadata - done
Writing DDL - done
Writing table metadata - done
Starting data dump
99% (52.58K rows / ~52.69K rows), 4.96K rows/s, 381.83 KB/s uncompressed,
95.16 KB/s compressed
Dump duration: 00:00:13s
Total duration: 00:00:14s
Schemas dumped: 2
Tables dumped: 19

```
Uncompressed data size: 3.23 MB
Compressed data size: 807.97 KB
Compression ratio: 4.0
Rows written: 52575
Bytes written: 807.97 KB
Average uncompressed throughput: 243.06 KB/s
Average compressed throughput: 60.78 KB/s
 MySQL  localhost:33060+ ssl  JS >
```

Notice there were some things changed during the export such as definer clauses and other compatibility issues corrected. Regardless, if you navigate to the ObjectStore bucket (mysql-data-bucket), you will see the data in the bucket.

To navigate to the mysql-data-bucket bucket contents, click on the OCI console menu and choose *Storage | Buckets* then click on the mysql-data-bucket link to open the bucket details page. Then, on the *Resources* menu, choose *Objects* and then expand the *mds-test* prefix by clicking on the >. You should see a list of files similar to those shown in Figure 7-7.

Objects

Name	Last Modified	Size	Storage Tier	
∨ 📁 mds-test	-	-	-	⋮
☐ @.done.json	Tue, Aug 16, 2022, 17:55:15 UTC	1.56 KiB	Standard	⋮
☐ @.json	Tue, Aug 16, 2022, 17:55:01 UTC	969 bytes	Standard	⋮
☐ @.post.sql	Tue, Aug 16, 2022, 17:55:01 UTC	240 bytes	Standard	⋮
☐ @.sql	Tue, Aug 16, 2022, 17:55:01 UTC	240 bytes	Standard	⋮
☐ @.users.sql	Tue, Aug 16, 2022, 17:55:01 UTC	1.23 KiB	Standard	⋮
☐ sakila.json	Tue, Aug 16, 2022, 17:55:02 UTC	1.84 KiB	Standard	⋮
☐ sakila.sql	Tue, Aug 16, 2022, 17:55:02 UTC	11.79 KiB	Standard	⋮
☐ sakila@actor.json	Tue, Aug 16, 2022, 17:55:04 UTC	672 bytes	Standard	⋮
☐ sakila@actor.sql	Tue, Aug 16, 2022, 17:55:03 UTC	875 bytes	Standard	⋮
☐ sakila@actor@@0.tsv.zst	Tue, Aug 16, 2022, 17:55:07 UTC	1.86 KiB	Standard	⋮
☐ sakila@actor@@0.tsv.zst.idx	Tue, Aug 16, 2022, 17:55:05 UTC	8 bytes	Standard	⋮
☐ sakila@actor_info.pre.sql	Tue, Aug 16, 2022, 17:55:03 UTC	687 bytes	Standard	⋮
☐ sakila@actor_info.sql	Tue, Aug 16, 2022, 17:55:03 UTC	1.78 KiB	Standard	⋮

Figure 7-7. *Objects in the mysql-data-bucket*

Ok, now we have our data in the bucket (so to speak), now we need to import it into our DB System but first, we must first configure our intermediate compute instance to use the OCI CLI like we did with our PC but instead of creating new API keys, we can simply upload the existing keys. We can also use the same configuration file with only one minor change. Nice.

Configure the Compute Instance

Begin by logging into the compute instance with the ssh command as shown below in one terminal (PowerShell) session. You can open a second one to perform the copies. Be sure to use the *public IP address* as shown on the compute instance details page:

```
ssh -i c:\users\cbell\.ssh\ssh-key-2022-08-16.key opc@150.136.69.126
```

On the compute instance, create the .oci folder using the command below:

```
$ mkdir .oci
```

On your PC (in another terminal), navigate to your `.oci` folder and copy the files to the compute instance. You will need to copy the config as well as the API keys as shown below. Notice we are using the SSH key we generated when we created the compute instance. The commands will not work if you do not have the correct key in your `.ssh` folder:

Caution   If you have lost the SSH key file, you will have to terminate and recreate the compute instance.

```
scp -i c:\users\cbell\.ssh\ssh-key-2022-08-16.key config
opc@150.136.69.126:~/.oci/
scp -i c:\users\cbell\.ssh\ssh-key-2022-08-16.key oci_api_key_public.pem
opc@150.136.69.126:~/.oci/
scp -i c:\users\cbell\.ssh\ssh-key-2022-08-16.key oci_api_key.pem
opc@150.136.69.126:~/.oci/
```

Next, return to the compute instance and edit the config file with the command nano ~/.oci/config. Change the key_file parameter on the last line to the following and save the file:

```
key_file=/home/opc/.oci/oci_api_key.pem
```

There is one more minor thing we need to do. We must create a pre-authenticated request for the ObjectStore bucket.

Create a Pre-Authenticated Request (PAR)

A pre-authenticated request (PAR) is an exclusive access token that permits access (read, read/write, write) to a bucket for a limited time. Using the OCI console, navigate to the ObjectStore list and open the details page for the bucket named `mysql-data-bucket`. On the bucket details page, navigate to the Pre-authenticated Requests in the Resources menu as shown in Figure 7-8.

Figure 7-8. *Pre-Authenticated Requests List*

To create a PAR, click on the *Create Pre-Authenticated Request* button. This will open a dialog similar to Figure 7-9. You can name the PAR (e.g., `par-import-mysql-data`), but you must set the *Access Type* to *Permit object reads* and tick the box for *Enable Object Listing*.

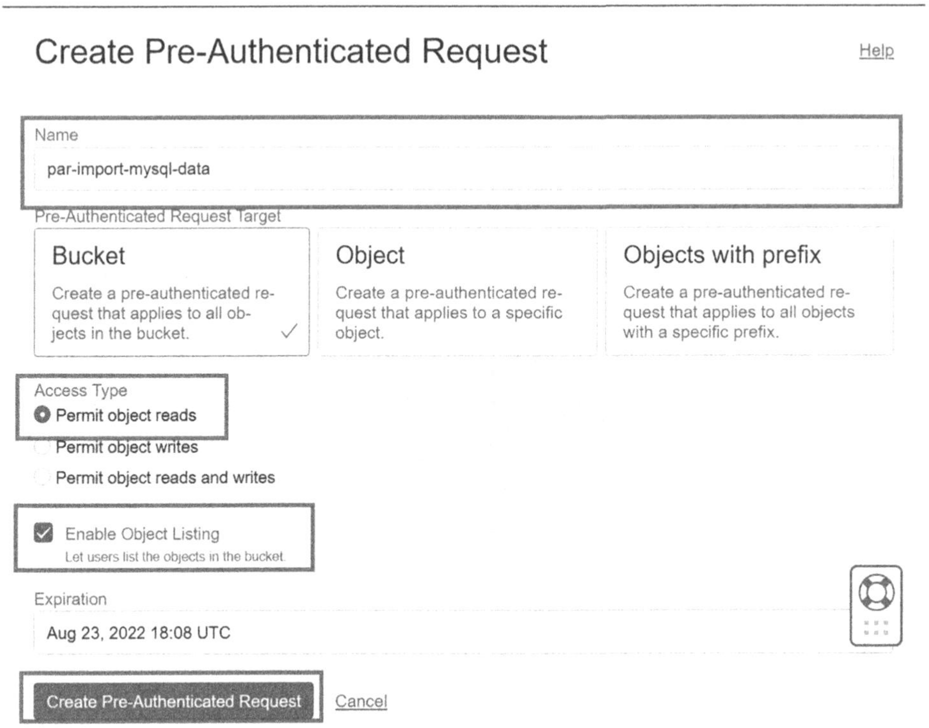

Figure 7-9. *Create PAR Dialog*

Notice you can also set the expiration. This is the date and time that the PAR expires. Any attempts to use the PAR after that date will result in an access denied error. When you are ready to create the PAR, click the *Create Pre-Authenticated Request* button.

OCI will then display a special dialog that requires careful attention. This dialog will present you with the PAR itself. This dialog is your one and only chance to copy the PAR string. If you close the dialog, you will not be able to retrieve the PAR again. You will have to create a new PAR. Figure 7-10 shows an example of the PAR dialog.

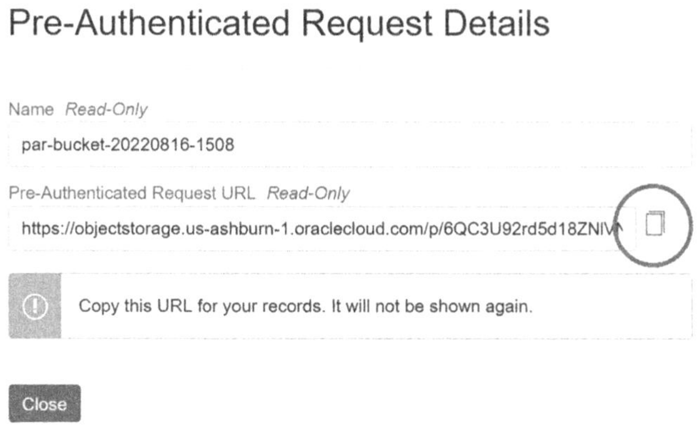

Pre-Authenticated Request Details

Name *Read-Only*

par-bucket-20220816-1508

Pre-Authenticated Request URL *Read-Only*

https://objectstorage.us-ashburn-1.oraclecloud.com/p/6QC3U92rd5d18ZNIV

ⓘ Copy this URL for your records. It will not be shown again.

Close

Figure 7-10. *PAR Dialog*

Be sure to copy the PAR and paste it into a file for safe keeping. Remember, while it is only valid for a limited time period, it should be protected like any other security access token.

Caution   You must copy the PAR from the dialog using the copy option shown. You will not be able to retrieve the PAR once you close the dialog.

Ok, now we are ready to run the import on our DB System.

Import from the ObjectStore Bucket into a DB System

Now that we have our compute instance properly configured and we have a PAR to use in the import, we can login to our DB System using our compute instance as demonstrated with the commands below. Once again, be sure to use the correct access points (IP) addresses for your compute instance and your DB System. Check the values by navigating to the correct detail pages in the OCI console:

```
PS C:\Users\cbell> ssh -i c:\users\cbell\.ssh\ssh-key-2022-08-16.key
opc@150.136.69.126
[opc@connection-instance ~]$ mysqlsh --sql mysql_admin@10.0.1.226:33060
```

Next, we can list the databases on the DB System as shown in Listing 7-6.

Listing 7-6. Test Database (Before Import)

```
MySQL  10.0.1.226:33060+ ssl  SQL > SHOW DATABASES;
+--------------------+
| Database           |
+--------------------+
| information_schema |
| mysql              |
| performance_schema |
| sys                |
+--------------------+
4 rows in set (0.0013 sec)
```

Now we can run the import. Recall, we can use the `util.loadDump()` method that requires a few parameters. We will pass the PAR as the first parameter and then the options list, which we need only a `progressFile`. You can name the file whatever you'd like. The following is an example of the command we will use:

```
util.loadDump("PAR_STRING_HERE", {progressFile: "progressFile"})
```

Tip   If you want to run the command to test it, you can add the dryRun: true option. This is strongly recommended for large or production data.

Ok, let's see this work! Switch to the JavaScript interface in the MySQL Shell, copy the command above replacing the PAR with the one you copied in an earlier step. Listing 7-7 shows the command running as a dry run to check for errors. Notice the PAR is obscured for security.

Listing 7-7. Dry Run Example

```
MySQL  10.0.1.226:33060+ ssl  JS > util.loadDump("https:...mysql-data-
bucket/o/mds-test/", {dryRun:true, progressFile:"progressFile"})
Loading DDL and Data from OCI prefix PAR=/p/<secret>/n/idj5psxg6enz/b/
mysql-data-bucket/o/mds-test/, prefix='mds-test/' using 4 threads.
Opening dump...
dryRun enabled, no changes will be made.
Target is MySQL 8.0.28-u3-cloud (MySQL Database Service). Dump was produced
from MySQL 8.0.29
```

```
Fetching dump data from remote location...
Listing files - done
Scanning metadata - done
Checking for pre-existing objects...
Executing common preamble SQL
Executing DDL - done
Executing view DDL - done
Starting data load
Executing common postamble SQL
0% (0 bytes / 3.23 MB), 0.00 B/s, 19 / 19 tables done
Recreating indexes - done
No data loaded.
0 warnings were reported during the load.
```

Ok, so there were no errors! Now, let's run the import without the dry run parameter as shown in Listing 7-8.

Listing 7-8. Importing the Data

```
MySQL  10.0.1.226:33060+ ssl  JS > util.loadDump("https.../mysql-data-
bucket/o/mds-test/", {progressFile:"progressFile"})
Loading DDL and Data from OCI prefix PAR=/p/<secret>/n/idj5psxg6enz/b/
mysql-data-bucket/o/mds-test/, prefix='mds-test/' using 4 threads.
Opening dump...
Target is MySQL 8.0.28-u3-cloud (MySQL Database Service). Dump was produced
from MySQL 8.0.29
Fetching dump data from remote location...
Listing files - done
Scanning metadata - done
Checking for pre-existing objects...
Executing common preamble SQL
Executing DDL - done
Executing view DDL - done
Starting data load
100% (3.23 MB / 3.23 MB), 2.15 MB/s, 19 / 19 tables done
Recreating indexes - done
Executing common postamble SQL
```

269

```
19 chunks (52.58K rows, 3.23 MB) for 19 tables in 2 schemas were loaded in
4 sec (avg throughput 2.15 MB/s)
0 warnings were reported during the load.
```

Excellent! It worked. Now, let's see if the import worked by checking the list of databases. Listing 7-9 shows the list of databases after import and a query to fetch some data.

Listing 7-9. Test Database (After Import)

```
  MySQL  10.0.1.226:33060+ ssl  SQL > SHOW DATABASES;
+--------------------+
| Database           |
+--------------------+
| information_schema |
| mysql              |
| performance_schema |
| sakila             |
| sys                |
| world              |
+--------------------+
6 rows in set (0.0011 sec)

MySQL  10.0.1.226:33060+ ssl  sakila  SQL > SELECT * FROM city LIMIT 5;
+---------+--------------------+------------+---------------------+
| city_id | city               | country_id | last_update         |
+---------+--------------------+------------+---------------------+
|       1 | A Corua (La Corua) |         87 | 2006-02-15 09:45:25 |
|       2 | Abha               |         82 | 2006-02-15 09:45:25 |
|       3 | Abu Dhabi          |        101 | 2006-02-15 09:45:25 |
|       4 | Acua               |         60 | 2006-02-15 09:45:25 |
|       5 | Adana              |         97 | 2006-02-15 09:45:25 |
+---------+--------------------+------------+---------------------+
```

If you see comparable results, congratulations! You've just migrated data from your local MySQL server to your DB System. If you see errors, check the MySQL Shell documentation for more information (https://dev.mysql.com/doc/mysql-shell/8.0/en/mysql-shell-utilities-load-dump.html).

If you must re-run the import, be sure to drop all databases created and use the resetProgress:true option parameter to force the progress to restart.

Now, let's explore an alternative process to export data. But first, be sure to drop the imported databases with the following commands on your DB System.

```
DROP DATABASE sakila;
DROP DATABASE world;
```

Using a Compute Instance

The second method to export our data from our local MySQL server will use a compute instance an intermediate storage. In this case, we simply perform the export on our local MySQL server placing the files on that system, copy them to the compute instance, then consume the data on the DB System. Before we begin, let us review how MySQL Shell exports data.

MySQL Shell exports data to local files with the util.dumpInstance() method in tab-separated value (file extension .tsv) files that are compressed by zstd (file extension .zst) to save space (gzip is also available as an option). You can also choose no compression but, if you are uploading to Object Storage, it is recommended to use the default.

Note   Large tables are chunked by default with a default chunk size of 32MB. Chunking can be disabled, but it is not recommended. You can improve import performance by importing the chunks by parallel threads.

If you export the data to a folder (e.g., on your local MySQL server), you will see several files for each database and table. For example, if your local MySQL server has the world_x database installed, you will see several files for the city table as follows:

```
world_x@city.json
world_x@city.sql
world_x@city@@0.tsv.zst
world_x@city@@0.tsv.zst.idx
```

Here, we see several files for the table. There is a `.json` file that contains information MySQL Shell needs to restore the table. The `.sql` file contains the CREATE TABLE and related SQL statements. The `.tsv.zst` files are the data and index in compressed tab-separated value files. You will see similar files for the other tables and databases.

Tip   The `zstd` utility source code is available for download from `https://github.com/facebook/zstd`. However, you will need to compile (build) the source code on your machine to use it.

Now that we understand what the data files look like, let us proceed with an example. We will once again use our local MySQL server with only the *sakila,* and *world* databases installed.

Export Data Using MySQL Shell

The first step is to run the `util.dumpInstance()` method to save the files to the local drive. In this case, we will use a different first parameter. Instead of passing in the bucket name and related parameters, we simply specify a folder (directory) to store the files and the same set of options as before. Since most of the commands are similar to the last method for migrating data to MDS, we omit some of the explanations and show less detail in the listings for brevity.

Begin by starting MySQL Shell and connecting to your local MySQL server using the JavaScript interface (`mysqlsh -uroot -p --js`). Listing 7-10 shows the export running with the notes and warnings omitted for brevity.

Listing 7-10. Export Data Locally (MySQL Shell)

```
MySQL  localhost:33060+ ssl  JS > util.dumpInstance("c:\\exported_data",
{ocimds:true, compatibility: ["strip_restricted_grants", "strip_definers",
"ignore_missing_pks", "skip_invalid_accounts"]})
Acquiring global read lock
Global read lock acquired
Initializing - done
2 out of 6 schemas will be dumped and within them 19 tables, 7 views, 6
routines, 6 triggers.
1 out of 4 users will be dumped.
```

```
Gathering information - done
All transactions have been started
Locking instance for backup
Global read lock has been released
Checking for compatibility with MySQL Database Service 8.0.29
...
Compatibility issues with MySQL Database Service 8.0.29 were found and
repaired. Please review the changes made before loading them.
Validating MDS compatibility - done
Writing global DDL files
Writing users DDL
Running data dump using 4 threads.
NOTE: Progress information uses estimated values and may not be accurate.
Writing schema metadata - done
Writing DDL - done
Writing table metadata - done
Starting data dump
99% (52.58K rows / ~52.69K rows), 0.00 rows/s, 0.00 B/s uncompressed, 0.00
B/s compressed
Dump duration: 00:00:00s
Total duration: 00:00:00s
Schemas dumped: 2
Tables dumped: 19
Uncompressed data size: 3.23 MB
Compressed data size: 807.97 KB
Compression ratio: 4.0
Rows written: 52575
Bytes written: 807.97 KB
Average uncompressed throughput: 3.23 MB/s
Average compressed throughput: 807.97 KB/s
```

If you navigate to the c:\\exported_data folder, we see all of our files as shown as an excerpt in Listing 7-11.

Listing 7-11. Listing the Exported Data Files (Windows 11)

```
C:\> cd exported_data

C:\exported_data> dir
 Volume in drive C is Local Disk
 Volume Serial Number is 3422-B048

 Directory of C:\exported_data

08/16/2022  04:23 PM    <DIR>          .
08/16/2022  04:23 PM             1,598 @.done.json
08/16/2022  04:23 PM               969 @.json
08/16/2022  04:23 PM               240 @.post.sql
08/16/2022  04:23 PM               240 @.sql
08/16/2022  04:23 PM             1,264 @.users.sql
08/16/2022  04:23 PM             1,886 sakila.json
08/16/2022  04:23 PM            12,073 sakila.sql
...
08/16/2022  04:23 PM               705 world@countrylanguage.json
08/16/2022  04:23 PM               959 world@countrylanguage.sql
08/16/2022  04:23 PM             8,721 world@countrylanguage@@0.tsv.zst
08/16/2022  04:23 PM                 8 world@countrylanguage@@0.tsv.zst.idx
             103 File(s)        888,396 bytes
               1 Dir(s)  36,038,184,960 bytes free
```

However, this is an extensive list that we can make life easier by compressing the files. You can use the Windows file explorer (or a zip application) to make a compressed file. Name the compressed file mysql_data.zip. We will upload this file in the next step.

Copy the Exported Data to the Compute Instance

First, login to your compute instance and create the directory exported data as shown below:

```
C:\exported_data> ssh -i c:\users\cbell\.ssh\ssh-key-2022-08-16.key
opc@150.136.69.126
[opc@connection-instance ~]$ mkdir exported_data
```

Next, navigate to the exported data folder and copy the mysql_data.zip file to the compute instance as shown below. Note that you will have to use the correct SSH key file and the public IP address of your compute instance:

```
C:\exported_data>scp -i c:\users\cbell\.ssh\ssh-key-2022-08-16.key mysql_
data.zip opc@150.136.69.126:~/exported_data.
mysql_data.zip                          100%  829KB 593.6KB/s    00:01.
```

Next, log into the compute instance again and unzip the files to a folder as shown below:

```
C:\exported_data>ssh -i c:\users\cbell\.ssh\ssh-key-2022-08-16.key
opc@150.136.69.126

[opc@connection-instance ~]$ rm mysql_data.zip
[opc@connection-instance ~]$ cd exported_data/
[opc@connection-instance exported_data]$ unzip mysql_data.zip
Archive:  mysql_data.zip
  inflating: @.done.json
...
extracting: world@city@@0.tsv.zst.idx
  inflating: world@country.json
  inflating: world@country.sql
  inflating: world@country@@0.tsv.zst
  inflating: world@country@@0.tsv.zst.idx
  inflating: world@countrylanguage.json
  inflating: world@countrylanguage.sql
  inflating: world@countrylanguage@@0.tsv.zst
  inflating: world@countrylanguage@@0.tsv.zst.idx
```

Import the Data on the DB System

The last step is to login to your compute instance again and launch MySQL Shell and import the data. Once again, we will not use the PAR parameters, rather, we will use the file path (/home/opc/exported_data). Listing 7-12 shows the transcript to running the util.loadDump() method. Notice the parameters used. We need only the path to the exported data. Cool!

Listing 7-12. Importing Data from Directory (MySQL Shell)

```
MySQL  10.0.1.226:33060+ ssl  JS > util.loadDump("/home/opc/exported_data")
Loading DDL and Data from '/home/opc/exported_data' using 4 threads.
Opening dump...
Target is MySQL 8.0.28-u3-cloud (MySQL Database Service). Dump was produced
from MySQL 8.0.29
Scanning metadata - done
Checking for pre-existing objects...
Executing common preamble SQL
Executing DDL - done
Executing view DDL - done
Starting data load
2 thds loading - 1 thds indexing / 100% (3.23 MB / 3.23 MB), 6.46 MB/s, 17
/ 19 tables done
Recreating indexes - done
Executing common postamble SQL
19 chunks (52.58K rows, 3.23 MB) for 19 tables in 2 schemas were loaded in
1 sec (avg throughput 3.23 MB/s)
0 warnings were reported during the load.
```

To be certain the import worked correctly, let's check the list of databases and perform a query on one of the tables. Listing 7-13 shows the commands used to briefly test the import.

Tip   You should always perform robust, comprehensive tests on any product data imported in any manner. Simply checking to see if the databases are present and you can run a query is a good, initial test but not sufficient for quality assurance purposes.

Listing 7-13. Checking the Import

```
MySQL  10.0.1.226:33060+ ssl  SQL > SHOW DATABASES;
+--------------------+
| Database           |
+--------------------+
| information_schema |
| mysql              |
| performance_schema |
| sakila             |
| sys                |
| world              |
+--------------------+
6 rows in set (0.0010 sec)

 MySQL  10.0.1.226:33060+ ssl  SQL > USE world;
Default schema set to `world`.
Fetching table and column names from `world` for auto-completion... Press
^C to stop.

MySQL  10.0.1.226:33060+ ssl  world  SQL > SELECT code, name FROM country
LIMIT 5;
+------+-------------+
| code | name        |
+------+-------------+
| ABW  | Aruba       |
| AFG  | Afghanistan |
| AGO  | Angola      |
| AIA  | Anguilla    |
| ALB  | Albania     |
+------+-------------+
5 rows in set (0.0048 sec)
```

While the steps seem simpler, and they are, this method is slower than the ObjectStore method since we have to copy the files manually. The next and final example bypasses the upload to the compute instance and instead allowing us to upload the data direct to the DB System.

Using a Bastion Gateway

The third method to export our data from our local MySQL server uses a Bastion gateway to connect our PC directly to our DB System. This means we no longer need to copy or upload the data for the import; MySQL Shell can read the data from our PC.

This method is slower than the other two methods due to the Bastion gateway and network layers and, more importantly, it has two potential issues: (1) the Bastion gateway is a paid service, and (2) the data you are copying must fit on the DB System storage in addition to the size of the data to be imported. Thus, it may require storing up to twice the amount of data; once for the exported data and a second time once the data is imported. This has the potential of creating an issue for smaller DB System storage sizes or for larger data. However, most initial data loads should not be an issue if you size your DB System initially to handle the exported data.

The steps in this method are similar to the previous method except that we must set up our Bastion server first, then export the data on our local MySQL server, and then import the data from our PC. Let's see a demonstration.

Setup the Bastion Service

Recall, we set up a Bastion gateway in Chapter 4 under the *Create a Bastion Service* heading. While once again the commands to do the export and import are similar, in this method we are creating access from our PC directly to our DB System so the exported data can be copied directly to the DB System for importing.

We will use the same process described in Chapter 4 to set up a Bastion Service. however this time we will need two port forwarding sessions; one setup for port 3306 and the other setup for port 33060 because MySQL Shell will use both ports during the import. Recall, we will be using the IP address of our DB System and you will either need to create an SSH key pair or reuse a pair that you created earlier. Figure 7-11 shows the Bastion Service setup with two port forwarding sessions.

MySQLBastion

Edit   Add tags   Move resource   Delete bastion

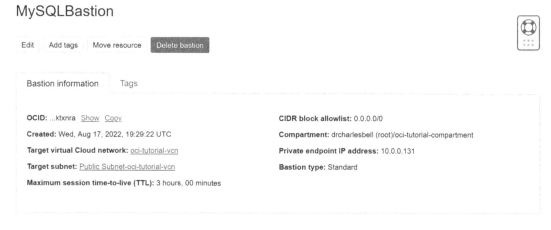

Bastion information   Tags

OCID: ...ktxnra Show Copy

Created: Wed, Aug 17, 2022, 19:29:22 UTC

Target virtual Cloud network: oci-tutorial-vcn

Target subnet: Public Subnet-oci-tutorial-vcn

Maximum session time-to-live (TTL): 3 hours, 00 minutes

CIDR block allowlist: 0.0.0.0/0

Compartment: drcharlesbell (root)/oci-tutorial-compartment

Private endpoint IP address: 10.0.0.131

Bastion type: Standard

Sessions

Create session

Name	Session type	Target resource	Target port	Username	State	Session TTL	Started ▼	
Session-20220817-1547	Port forwarding	10.0.1.226	3306	-	● Active	3 hours, 00 minutes	Wed, Aug 17, 2022, 19:49:13 UTC	⋮
Session-20220817-1540	Port forwarding	10.0.1.226	33060	-	● Active	3 hours, 00 minutes	Wed, Aug 17, 2022, 19:42:05 UTC	⋮

Figure 7-11. *Bastion Service Sessions (For Importing Data from PC)*

Tip   If you need to see the steps in detail, see the section entitled *Create a Bastion Service* in Chapter 4 for setting up a Bastion Service.

Export Data Using MySQL Shell

The next step is to run the util.dumpInstance() method to save the files to the local drive. In this case, we will use a different first parameter. Instead of passing in the bucket name and related parameters, we simply specify a folder (directory) to store the files and the same set of options as before. This is the same step we used in the last method, so we will show only the command used. If you are following along, you need not run this step again since the exported data should be on your PC. The command needed is shown below for clarity:

```
util.dumpInstance("c:\\exported_data", {ocimds:true, compatibility:
["strip_restricted_grants", "strip_definers", "ignore_missing_pks", "skip_
invalid_accounts"]}
```

Start the Bastion Service SSH Sessions

Once the Bastion Service is running and the two port forwarding sessions are enabled, you must start the port forwarding on your PC. You will need to execute the sample SSH command for each session. Recall, we can copy the basic SSH command by clicking on the context menu for each session and choose *Copy SSH command*.

Once each command is copied, you can paste it into a PowerShell (terminal) replacing the placeholder portions marked with <> with the correct data. For example, the following show the two commands used to open a port forwarding session for ports 3306 and 33060 on a Windows 11 PC:

```
ssh -i <KEY> -N -L 3306:10.0.1.226:3306 -p 22 ocid1.bastionsession.MASKED...
ssh -i <KEY> -N -L 33060:10.0.1.226:33060 -p 22 ocid1.bastionsession.MASKED...
```

On Mac or Linux, you can execute the commands with the & directive to run the commands in the background. On a Windows PC, you will need to use a different mechanism in PowerShell. You can use the Start-Job command with the -ScriptBlock option as shown below:

```
Start-Job -ScriptBlock {ssh -i <KEY> -N -L 3306:10.0.1.226:3306 -p 22
ocid1.bastion...}
Start-Job -ScriptBlock {ssh -i <KEY> -N -L 33060:10.0.1.226:33060 -p 22
ocid1.bastion...}
```

Ok, now that we have our Bastion setup, we can import the data.

Import the Data on the DB System

The last step is to login to your compute instance again and launch MySQL Shell and import the data. We will use the file path to the exported data on our PC (c:\\exported_data). Listing 7-14 shows the transcript to running the util.loadDump() method. Notice the parameters used. We need only the path to the exported data. Nice.

Listing 7-14. Importing Data from Directory (MySQL Shell)

```
MySQL  127.0.0.1:33060+ ssl  JS > util.loadDump("c:\\exported_data")
Loading DDL and Data from 'c:\exported_data' using 4 threads.
Opening dump...
Target is MySQL 8.0.28-u3-cloud (MySQL Database Service). Dump was produced
from MySQL 8.0.29
Scanning metadata - done
Checking for pre-existing objects...
Executing common preamble SQL
Executing DDL - done
Executing view DDL - done
Starting data load
100% (3.23 MB / 3.23 MB), 97.63 KB/s, 19 / 19 tables done
Recreating indexes - done
Executing common postamble SQL
19 chunks (52.58K rows, 3.23 MB) for 19 tables in 2 schemas were loaded in
55 sec (avg throughput 174.73 KB/s)
0 warnings were reported during the load.
```

To be certain the import worked correctly, let's check the list of databases and perform a query on one of the tables. Listing 7-15 shows the commands used to briefly test the import.

Listing 7-15. Checking the Import

```
MySQL  127.0.0.1:33060+ ssl  JS > \sql
Switching to SQL mode... Commands end with ;
 MySQL  127.0.0.1:33060+ ssl  SQL > SHOW DATABASES;
+--------------------+
| Database           |
+--------------------+
| information_schema |
| mysql              |
| performance_schema |
| sakila             |
| sys                |
```

```
| world                |
+--------------------+
6 rows in set (0.0737 sec)
MySQL  127.0.0.1:33060+ ssl  SQL > SELECT title, release_year FROM sakila.
film LIMIT 4;
+------------------+--------------+
| title            | release_year |
+------------------+--------------+
| ACADEMY DINOSAUR |         2006 |
| ACE GOLDFINGER   |         2006 |
| ADAPTATION HOLES |         2006 |
| AFFAIR PREJUDICE |         2006 |
+------------------+--------------+
4 rows in set (0.0620 sec)
```

While the steps seem simpler, and they are, this method is slower than both the ObjectStore and compute instance method since we have to import the data from our PC through the Bastion Service.

Now that we've had a good introduction to migrating data to a DB System, let's look at the reverse: migrating data from MDS to our PC.

Migrating Data from MDS

When importing data from MDS, we must choose one of the three methods for moving the exported data to MDS. Recall, these include using an ObjectStore bucket, uploading the exported data to an intermediate Compute instance, and uploading the exported data directly to our DB System via a Bastion gateway.

Migrating from MDS follows the same mechanism described above only in reverse. Thus, we will see only the smaller details as we work through the same three mechanisms demonstrated in the last section. If you need more detail such as setting up an ObjectStore bucket or a Bastion Service, please refer to the previous sections.

If you executed any of the previous examples, be sure to prepare your local MySQL Server by dropping the *sakila* and *world* databases before you attempt the import.

The following sections briefly demonstrate each of the mechanisms for importing data from MDS.

Using an ObjectStore Bucket

The first method to import our data from MDS to our local MySQL Server will use the ObjectStore as an intermediate storage for the exported data. We will use the MySQL Shell on our DB System to create an export of the data, which we will place in ObjectStore and then access that data from our local MySQL Server for the import again using MySQL Shell.

Prepare Your PC

If you have not executed the previous example of migrating data from your PC to MDS, go back and make sure you prepare your PC and your compute instance with the correct OCI API configuration file and SSH keys. See the sections *Configure Your PC for OCI CLI Access* and *Install and Test the OCI CLI* above for more details.

There is one more thing we must do on our PC. We must set the local_infile global variable in MySQL to ON. This is turned off by default and you will want to turn it off again after you have finished the backup. When logged into your local MySQL server, execute the following command:

```
set @@global.local_infile=ON;
```

Listing 7-16 shows the command in action.

Listing 7-16. Turn on local_infile (local MySQL server)

```
MySQL  localhost:33060+ ssl  SQL > SHOW VARIABLES LIKE '%local%';
+---------------+-------+
| Variable_name | Value |
+---------------+-------+
| local_infile  | OFF   |
+---------------+-------+
1 row in set (0.0033 sec)

 MySQL  localhost:33060+ ssl  SQL > SET @@global.local_infile=ON;
Query OK, 0 rows affected (0.0009 sec)

 MySQL  localhost:33060+ ssl  SQL > SHOW VARIABLES LIKE '%local%';
```

```
+---------------+-------+
| Variable_name | Value |
+---------------+-------+
| local_infile  | ON    |
+---------------+-------+
1 row in set (0.0032 sec)
```

Create the ObjectStore Bucket

Next, we need to create an ObjectStore bucket to store our data in from the export. In this example, we will create a bucket in the oci-tutorial-compartment named mysql-data-bucket. Begin by logging into OCI and choosing Storage | Buckets from the menu. You will see the ObjectStore bucket page.

Recall, to create a new bucket, click the *Create Bucket* button and replace the bucket name with mysql-data-bucket on the create bucket dialog. If you created this bucket earlier, you could reuse it, but you must delete all of the files first. You can do so by either deleting the bucket and recreating it or by deleting the folder mds-test by choosing *Delete Folder* from the context menu as shown in Figure 7-12.

Figure 7-12. *Deleting Objects in a Bucket*

Export to ObjectStore Bucket

Now we are ready to export our data from our DB System. If you have not created a DB System to test with, do so now and be sure to install the *sakila* and *world* databases or any other databases you want to use. Create a standard DB System that meets the storage requirements for your data. If you want to follow along with this tutorial, we will use a DB System with the name oci-tutorial-mysql, which we used earlier in the book.

Recall that we will need to use an intermediate compute instance to login to our DB System with MySQL Shell. You can use the same compute instance as before using SSH to connect then you can launch MySQL Shell as shown below:

```
PS C:\Users\cbell> ssh -i c:\users\cbell\.ssh\ssh-key-2022-08-16.key
opc@150.136.69.126
[opc@connection-instance ~]$ mysqlsh --sql mysql_admin@10.0.1.226:33060
```

Next, we will execute the `util.dumpInstance()` method providing a prefix for the bucket data (use `mds-test`) along with the ObjectStore information in a JSON string that includes the bucket name (`osBucketName`), threads, the MDS data compatibility switch (`ocimds`) set to `true`, and the `compatibility` options discussed earlier where we will strip restricted grants, definer clauses, missing primary keys, and invalid accounts. Listing 7-17 shows the output of running the method to dump the databases on our DB System to the ObjectStore bucket we created earlier (`mysql-data-bucket`).

Listing 7-17. Exporting Data from Local MySQL Server

```
MySQL  10.0.1.226:33060+ ssl  JS > util.dumpInstance("mds-test",
{osBucketName: "mysql-data-bucket", ocimds: true, compatibility: ["strip_
restricted_grants", "strip_definers", "ignore_missing_pks", "skip_invalid_
accounts"]})
Please enter the API key passphrase: **********
Acquiring global read lock
Global read lock acquired
Initializing - done
2 out of 6 schemas will be dumped and within them 19 tables, 7 views, 6
routines, 6 triggers.
4 out of 7 users will be dumped.
Gathering information - done
All transactions have been started
Locking instance for backup
Global read lock has been released
Checking for compatibility with MySQL Database Service 8.0.30
...
Compatibility issues with MySQL Database Service 8.0.30 were found and
repaired. Please review the changes made before loading them.
Validating MDS compatibility - done
```

```
Writing global DDL files
Writing users DDL
Running data dump using 4 threads.
NOTE: Progress information uses estimated values and may not be accurate.
Writing schema metadata - done
Writing DDL - done
Writing table metadata - done
Starting data dump
99% (52.58K rows / ~52.68K rows), 0.00 rows/s, 0.00 B/s uncompressed, 0.00
B/s compressed
Dump duration: 00:00:01s
Total duration: 00:00:01s
Schemas dumped: 2
Tables dumped: 19
Uncompressed data size: 3.23 MB
Compressed data size: 807.97 KB
Compression ratio: 4.0
Rows written: 52575
Bytes written: 807.97 KB
Average uncompressed throughput: 2.90 MB/s
Average compressed throughput: 726.36 KB/s
```

Ok, now we have our data in the bucket, we can import the data into our local MySQL server, but first we need to create a PAR. Refer to the section *Create a Pre-Authenticated Request (PAR)* above to create a read PAR so we can use that on our local MySQL Server to import the data.

Remember, be sure to copy the PAR and paste it into a file for safe keeping. Remember, while it is only valid for a limited time period, it should be protected like any other security access token.

Caution   You must copy the PAR from the dialog using the copy option shown. You will not be able to retrieve the PAR once you close the dialog.

Ok, now we are ready to run the import on our local MySQL server.

Import from ObjectStore Bucket into Local MySQL Server

Be sure to drop the databases you have exported from the DB System on your local MySQL server before continuing. Once that is done, we can run the import. Recall, we can use the `util.loadDump()` method that requires a few parameters. We will pass the PAR as the first parameter and then the options list, which we need only a `progressFile`. You can name the file whatever you'd like. The following is an example of the command we will use:

```
util.loadDump("PAR_STRING_HERE", {progressFile: "progressFile"})
```

Ok, let's see this work! Switch to the JavaScript interface in the MySQL Shell, copy the command above replacing the PAR with the one you copied in an earlier step. Now, let's run the import without the dry run parameter as shown in Listing 7-18.

Listing 7-18. Importing the Data

```
MySQL  localhost:33060+ ssl  JS > util.loadDump("https://objectstorage.
us-ashburn-1.oraclecloud.com/p/5SX2LLcQ4wsQ30SdXVwrstyFu6jGnBADU3441TJpT1-
jIIeKVryac5ko3MFpGa38/n/idj5psxg6enz/b/mysql-data-bucket/o/mds-test/",
{progressFile: "progressFile"})
Loading DDL and Data from OCI PAR=/p/<secret>/n/idj5psxg6enz/b/mysql-data-
bucket/o/mds-test/, prefix='mds-test/' using 4 threads.
Opening dump...
Target is MySQL 8.0.29. Dump was produced from MySQL 8.0.28-u3-cloud
Fetching dump data from remote location...
Listing files - done
Scanning metadata - done
Checking for pre-existing objects...
Executing common preamble SQL
Executing DDL - done
Executing view DDL - done
Starting data load
1 thds indexing - 100% (3.23 MB / 3.23 MB), 444.85 KB/s, 19 / 19
tables done
Recreating indexes - done
Executing common postamble SQL
```

```
19 chunks (52.58K rows, 3.23 MB) for 19 tables in 2 schemas were loaded in
33 sec (avg throughput 376.69 KB/s)
0 warnings were reported during the load.
```

Excellent! It worked. Now, let's see if the import worked by checking the list of databases. Listing 7-19 shows the list of databases after import and a query to fetch some data.

Listing 7-19. Test Database (After Import)

```
MySQL  localhost:33060+ ssl  SQL > SHOW DATABASES;
+--------------------+
| Database           |
+--------------------+
| information_schema |
| mysql              |
| performance_schema |
| sakila             |
| sys                |
| world              |
+--------------------+
6 rows in set (0.0019 sec)

 MySQL  localhost:33060+ ssl  SQL > SELECT name FROM world.city LIMIT 5;
+----------------+
| name           |
+----------------+
| Kabul          |
| Qandahar       |
| Herat          |
| Mazar-e-Sharif |
| Amsterdam      |
+----------------+
5 rows in set (0.0013 sec)
```

If you see comparable results, congratulations! You've just migrated data from your DB System to your local MySQL server. If you see errors, check the MySQL Shell documentation for more information (https://dev.mysql.com/doc/mysql-shell/8.0/en/mysql-shell-utilities-load-dump.html).

Since we are executing the import on our local PC, we can use an alternate form of the `util.loadDump()` method that does not require a PAR where we specify only the name of the folder, bucket name (`osBucketName`), and bucket namespace (`osNamespace`) parameters as shown below:

```
util.loadDump("mds-test", { osBucketName:"mysql-data-bucket",
osNamespace:"SECRET"})
```

When you run the method with these parameters, you will be asked for your SSH key password. You can find the bucket name and namespace on the bucket details page as shown in Figure 7-13.

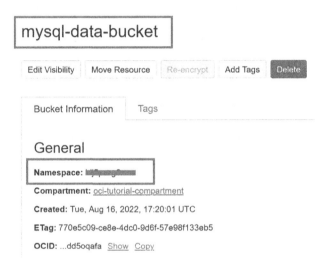

Figure 7-13. *Finding the Bucket Name and Namespace*

Using a Compute Instance

The second method to export our data from our DB System will use a compute instance for intermediate storage. In this case, we simply perform the export on our compute instance placing the files on that system, copy them to our local PC, then consume the data on our local MySQL server.

Export Data Using MySQL Shell

The first step is to run the `util.dumpInstance()` method to save the files to the local drive on the compute instance. Begin by creating an SSH session to login to the compute instance then create a folder named /home/opc/imported_data as shown below. Once created, start MySQL Shell using the JavaScript interface:

```
$ mkdir /home/opc/imported_data
```

Next, run the `util.dumpInstance()` method like we did with the migrate to MDS example except use /home/opc/imported_data for the location of the exported data. Listing 7-20 shows the export running with the notes and warnings omitted for brevity.

Listing 7-20. Export Data on Compute Instance (MySQL Shell)

```
MySQL  10.0.1.226:33060+ ssl  JS > util.dumpInstance("/home/opc/imported_
data", {ocimds:true, compatibility: ["strip_restricted_grants", "strip_
definers", "ignore_missing_pks", "skip_invalid_accounts"]})
Acquiring global read lock
Global read lock acquired
Initializing - done
2 out of 6 schemas will be dumped and within them 19 tables, 7 views, 6
routines, 6 triggers.
4 out of 7 users will be dumped.
Gathering information - done
All transactions have been started
Locking instance for backup
Global read lock has been released
Checking for compatibility with MySQL Database Service 8.0.30
...
Compatibility issues with MySQL Database Service 8.0.30 were found and
repaired. Please review the changes made before loading them.
Validating MDS compatibility - done
Writing global DDL files
Writing users DDL
Running data dump using 4 threads.
NOTE: Progress information uses estimated values and may not be accurate.
Writing schema metadata - done
```

```
Writing DDL - done
Writing table metadata - done
Starting data dump
99% (52.58K rows / ~52.68K rows), 0.00 rows/s, 0.00 B/s uncompressed, 0.00
B/s compressed
Dump duration: 00:00:00s
Total duration: 00:00:00s
Schemas dumped: 2
Tables dumped: 19
Uncompressed data size: 3.23 MB
Compressed data size: 807.97 KB
Compression ratio: 4.0
Rows written: 52575
Bytes written: 807.97 KB
Average uncompressed throughput: 3.23 MB/s
Average compressed throughput: 807.97 KB/s
```

Copy the Exported Data to Your Local MySQL Server

While logged into your compute instance, navigate to the exported data folder, and create a zip file of the data with the command below:

```
$ zip -r imported_data.zip ./imported_data/*
```

Next, log out of the compute instance and open a PowerShell (terminal) on your PC. We will be copying the mysql_data.zip file to your PC as shown below. Note that you will have to use the correct SSH key file and the public IP address of your compute instance:

```
C:\> scp -i c:\users\cbell\.ssh\ssh-key-2022-08-16.key
opc@150.136.69.126:~/imported_data.zip .
imported_data.zip                      100%  838KB   1.7MB/s   00:00
```

Next, return to your PC and unzip the files to a folder. On Windows, you can use the file explorer to locate the file, right-click on it and choose *Extract All....*

Import the Data on the DB System

The last step is to launch MySQL Shell on your PC and import the data. We will use the command below. Notice the parameters used. We need the path to the exported data and, since we're executing the import on our PC, we also need to add a path to the progress file option. The path must be a location where the user account has access to create and write files:

```
util.loadDump("c:\\imported_data", {progressFile: "c:\\imported_data\\
progressFile"})
```

Listing 7-21 shows the transcript to running the util.loadDump() method.

Listing 7-21. Importing Data from Directory (MySQL Shell)

```
MySQL  localhost:33060+ ssl  JS > util.loadDump("c:\\imported_data",
{progressFile: "c:\\imported_data\\progressFile"})

Loading DDL and Data from 'c:\imported_data' using 4 threads.
Opening dump...
Target is MySQL 8.0.29. Dump was produced from MySQL 8.0.28-u3-cloud
Scanning metadata - done
Checking for pre-existing objects...
Executing common preamble SQL
Executing DDL - done
Executing view DDL - done
Starting data load
2 thds loading - 1 thds indexing - 100% (3.23 MB / 3.23 MB), 6.23 MB/s, 17
/ 19 tables done
Recreating indexes - done
Executing common postamble SQL
19 chunks (52.58K rows, 3.23 MB) for 19 tables in 2 schemas were loaded in
3 sec (avg throughput 3.23 MB/s)
0 warnings were reported during the load.
```

Listing 7-22 shows the list of databases after import and a query to fetch some data.

Listing 7-22. Test Database (After Import)

```
MySQL  localhost:33060+ ssl  SQL > SHOW DATABASES;
+--------------------+
| Database           |
+--------------------+
| information_schema |
| mysql              |
| performance_schema |
| sakila             |
| sys                |
| world              |
+--------------------+
6 rows in set (0.0019 sec)

MySQL  localhost:33060+ ssl  SQL > SELECT first_name, last_name FROM
sakila.actor LIMIT 6;
+------------+--------------+
| first_name | last_name    |
+------------+--------------+
| PENELOPE   | GUINESS      |
| NICK       | WAHLBERG     |
| ED         | CHASE        |
| JENNIFER   | DAVIS        |
| JOHNNY     | LOLLOBRIGIDA |
| BETTE      | NICHOLSON    |
+------------+--------------+
6 rows in set (0.0012 sec)
```

Using a Bastion Gateway

The third method to migrate data from MDS uses a Bastion gateway to connect our PC directly to our DB System. Recall, we must set up the Bastion Service with two port forwarding sessions: one for port 3306 and another for port 33060 using the IP address of our DB System. If you have not set up a Bastion Service in the previous section, please refer to the sections *Setup the Bastion Service* and *Start the Bastion Service SSH Sessions* above for details.

Note that if you ran the previous example, you may need to delete the `imported_data` folder you created.

Export Data Using MySQL Shell

The next step is to run the `util.dumpInstance()` method to save the files to the local drive. In this case, we will use a different first parameter. Instead of passing in the bucket name and related parameters, we simply specify a folder (directory) to store the files and the same set of options as before. This is the same step we used in the last method, so we will show only the command used. If you are following along, you need not run this step again since the exported data should be on your PC. The command needed is shown below for clarity:

```
util.dumpInstance("c:\\imported_data", {ocimds:true, compatibility:
["strip_restricted_grants", "strip_definers", "ignore_missing_pks",
"skip_invalid_accounts"]}
```

Listing 7-23 shows the data export running on the compute instance connected via a Bastion gateway.

Listing 7-23. Export Data from DB System to Local PC

```
MySQL  127.0.0.1:33060+ ssl  JS > util.dumpInstance("c:\\imported_data",
{ocimds:true, compatibility: ["strip_restricted_grants", "strip_definers",
"ignore_missing_pks", "skip_invalid_accounts"]})
Acquiring global read lock
Global read lock acquired
Initializing - done
2 out of 6 schemas will be dumped and within them 19 tables, 7 views, 6
routines, 6 triggers.
4 out of 7 users will be dumped.
Gathering information - done
All transactions have been started
Locking instance for backup
Global read lock has been released
Checking for compatibility with MySQL Database Service 8.0.29
...
```

Compatibility issues with MySQL Database Service 8.0.29 were found and repaired. Please review the changes made before loading them.

Validating MDS compatibility - done

Writing global DDL files

Writing users DDL

Running data dump using 4 threads.

NOTE: Progress information uses estimated values and may not be accurate.

Writing schema metadata - done

Writing DDL - done

Writing table metadata - done

Starting data dump

99% (52.58K rows / ~52.68K rows), 7.38K rows/s, 512.03 KB/s uncompressed, 125.08 KB/s compressed

Dump duration: 00:00:11s

Total duration: 00:00:38s

Schemas dumped: 2

Tables dumped: 19

Uncompressed data size: 3.23 MB

Compressed data size: 807.97 KB

Compression ratio: 4.0

Rows written: 52575

Bytes written: 807.97 KB

Average uncompressed throughput: 271.98 KB/s

Average compressed throughput: 68.01 KB/s

Import the Data on Your Local MySQL Server

The last step is to launch MySQL Shell on your PC and import the data. We will use the command below. Notice the parameters used. We need the path to the exported data and, since we're executing the import on our PC, we also need to add a path to the progress file option. The path must be a location where the user account has access to create and write files:

```
util.loadDump("c:\\imported_data", {progressFile: "c:\\imported_data\\progressFile"})
```

Listing 7-24 shows the transcript to running the util.loadDump() method.

Listing 7-24. Importing Data from Directory (MySQL Shell)

```
MySQL  localhost:33060+ ssl  JS > util.loadDump("c:\\imported_data",
{progressFile: "c:\\imported_data\\progressFile"})

Loading DDL and Data from 'c:\imported_data' using 4 threads.
Opening dump...
Target is MySQL 8.0.29. Dump was produced from MySQL 8.0.28-u3-cloud
Scanning metadata - done
Checking for pre-existing objects...
Executing common preamble SQL
Executing DDL - done
Executing view DDL - done
Starting data load
2 thds loading - 1 thds indexing - 100% (3.23 MB / 3.23 MB), 6.23 MB/s, 17
/ 19 tables done
Recreating indexes - done
Executing common postamble SQL
19 chunks (52.58K rows, 3.23 MB) for 19 tables in 2 schemas were loaded in
3 sec (avg throughput 3.23 MB/s)
0 warnings were reported during the load.
```

Listing 7-25 shows the list of databases after import and a query to fetch some data.

Listing 7-25. Test Database (After Import)

```
MySQL  localhost:33060+ ssl  SQL > SHOW DATABASES;
+--------------------+
| Database           |
+--------------------+
| information_schema |
| mysql              |
| performance_schema |
| sakila             |
| sys                |
| world              |
+--------------------+
```

```
6 rows in set (0.0019 sec)

MySQL  localhost:33060+ ssl  world  SQL > USE world;
Default schema set to `world`.
Fetching table and column names from `world` for auto-completion... Press
^C to stop.

 MySQL  localhost:33060+ ssl  world  SQL > SELECT countrylanguage.
language, country.name FROM country JOIN countrylanguage on country.code =
countrylanguage.countrycode LIMIT 4;
+------------+-------+
| language   | name  |
+------------+-------+
| Dutch      | Aruba |
| English    | Aruba |
| Papiamento | Aruba |
| Spanish    | Aruba |
+------------+-------+
4 rows in set (0.0011 sec)
```

Ok, that's it! We have learned how to migrate data from our local PC to a DB System and from a DB System to a local MySQL server.

Summary

One of the challenges for getting started with any cloud-based service is getting your data from your on-prem storage (server or services) to the cloud. For developers and those planning their cloud-based systems, it is also important to be able to get your data out of the cloud. Whether for development, testing, quality control, replication, or simply off-cloud backup, export can be as important as import.

Cloud services that omit these facilities can make the import issue far larger an issue and more problematic than need be. While it is true this step is normally exercised only a few times or perhaps once when your solution goes into production, importing and exporting data should be a seamless integration when using the cloud service.

Getting started with MDS would be a lot more difficult if no import and export capabilities existed. Fortunately, we learned that the MySQL Shell provides some well-thought-out utilities for getting your data into (and out of) MDS.

In this chapter, we saw how to migrate our data from an on-prem MySQL server to a DB System in MDS. We also saw examples on how you could migrate your data out of MDS for use in your local environment.

We also learned three mechanisms for transferring your exported data to MDS; we can use the ObjectStore bucket (recommended, fast), upload our exported data to an intermediate Compute instance (slower), or use a Bastion Service to upload our exported data directly to our DB System (slowest, not recommended). If you're following along with your own on-prem MySQL data, you now have it migrated to MDS!

In the next chapter, we will learn about the high availability options to make your DB Systems more resilient and dependable.

High Availability

Database administrators and systems architects who manage infrastructures understand the need for building in redundancy while keeping maintenance chores to a minimum. One of the tools used to achieve this is a class of features that make the server or service available as much as possible. We call this high availability.

Not only is high availability a key factor in establishing robust, always ready infrastructures, but it is also a quality of robust, enterprise-grade database systems. Oracle has continued to develop and improve the high availability features in MySQL and has translated those capabilities to the MySQL Database Service (MDS).

High availability in MDS is accomplished through a feature in the DB System, which leverages a collection of components and automation built upon the long-term stability of MySQL Group Replication. Together, these components form the high availability feature for DB System in MDS.

In this chapter, we will discover what high availability is and how it can be used to achieve high availability using DB Systems in MDS. Let's begin with a brief tutorial on high availability.

Overview

High availability is easiest to understand if you consider it loosely synonymous with reliability – making the solution as accessible as possible and tolerant to failures either planned or unplanned for an agreed upon period. That is, it's how much users can expect the system to be operational. The more dependable the system and thus the longer it is operational equates to a higher level of availability.

High availability can be accomplished in many ways, resulting in various levels of availability. The levels can be expressed as goals to achieving some higher state of reliability. Essentially, you use techniques and tools to boost reliability and make it possible for the solution to keep running and the data to be available as long as possible

© Charles Bell 2023
C. Bell, *MySQL Database Service Revealed*, https://doi.org/10.1007/978-1-4842-8945-7_8

(also called uptime). Uptime is represented as a ratio or percentage of the amount of time the solution is operational.

You can achieve high availability by practicing the following engineering principles:

- *Eliminate Single Points of Failure*: Design your solution so that there are as few components as possible that, should they fail, render the solution unusable.

- *Add Recovery Through Redundancy*: Design your solution to permit multiple, active redundant mechanisms to allow rapid recovery from failures.

- *Implement Fault Tolerance*: Design your solution to actively detect failures and automatically recover by switching to a redundant or alternative mechanism.

These principles are building blocks or steps to take to reach higher levels of reliability and thus high availability. Even if you do not need to achieve maximum high availability (the solution is up nearly all the time), by implementing these principles you will make your solution more dependable at the least, which is a good goal to achieve.

RELIABILITY VS. HIGH AVAILABILITY: WHAT IS THE DIFFERENCE?

Reliability is a measure of how operational a solution is over time, which covers one of the major goals for high availability. Indeed, you could say that the ultimate level of reliability – the solution is always operational – is the definition of high availability. Thus, to make your solution a high-availability solution, you should focus on improving reliability.

High Availability in MDS

The high availability feature in MDS is built into the DB System. It uses group replication to provide secondary servers that can be used to provide continuity in the event something happens to render the primary unavailable. MySQL Group Replication is very robust and, for some, can be complex to set up and manage. However, Oracle's automation layer for MDS makes the configuration and management easy to set up and use. So much so that you do not need to know how group replication works to use it:

> **Tip**   See `https://dev.mysql.com/doc/refman/8.0/en/group-replication.html` for more information about MySQL Group Replication.

DB Systems with high availability enabled replicate data over a secure, managed, internal network, unconnected to the VCN subnet you configured for your DB System endpoint connection. However, DB Systems with high availability use more resources (e.g., memory, CPU processing, and networking bandwidth). Thus, the performance of networking throughput may differ from a DB System without high availability.

Since MDS uses group replication, you may encounter some of the terms used such as primary (the server instance responsible for read/write access to the data) and secondary (one or more servers used as standby), failover (when group replication detects that the primary has failed and a secondary is automatically selected as its replacement), and switchover (a manual switch of the primary role from the primary to a secondary).

MDS high availability is implemented using three DB Systems: one primary and two secondaries. This forms a minimal group that permits automatic failover. All data written to the primary is copied (replicated) to the secondaries making them available for failover or switchover.

When you enable high availability on a DB System, you can select the availability domain for the primary DB System and the secondary DB Systems are placed in two other availability domains making the system fault tolerant at the availability domain level (since the domains are separate supporting hardware). This is the preferred placement of the primary instance. The secondaries are placed automatically in the other two availability or fault domains.

You can choose to place the DB Systems using on the following methods:

- *Multiple Availability Domains with a Regional Subnet*: The primary and secondaries are placed in different availability domains.

- *Multiple Availability Domains with an Availability Domain-Specific Subnet*: The primary and secondaries are placed in different fault domains in the same availability domain.

- *Single Availability Domain Region*: The primary and secondaries are placed in different fault domains in the same availability domain.

How Does Failover and Switchover Work?

When group replication detects that the primary has failed (failover) or if the user initiates a manual switch (switchover), group replication will switch the primary role to a secondary. This action is called promotion of promoting a secondary to a primary.

Failover is automatic when group replication detects that the primary is no longer viable. When this occurs, one of the secondaries is selected and promoted to the primary resuming availability for client applications without data loss. Switchover on the other hand is initiated by the user, and once initiated promotes a secondary to the primary.

What Are the Conditions for Failover?

There are two main groups of incidents that can cause failover conditions: hardware and MySQL. Hardware failures include storage, network, availability domain, or host (VM host) incidents. MySQL failures include if the MySQL process stops, operating system crashes, MySQL instance is slow or taxed resulting in low performance, or group replication errors. All these incidents can cause conditions where group replication initiates a failover event.

Prerequisites

As mentioned, DB Systems with high availability use three DB Systems and thus will consume three times the disk storage, which also means your costs will be slightly higher again depending on shape and data storage sizes chosen. Aside from that, there is one other prerequisite for using high availability with DB Systems: primary keys.

Note Henceforth when referring to DB Systems with high availability enabled, we will use the terms HA and HA DB System.

If you want to enable HA on a DB System, your tables must have primary keys. This is essential for group replication to be able to correctly (and uniquely) identify rows in your tables. The following sections show you how to find tables without primary keys and strategies for adding primary keys without adding unnecessary complexity to your schema.

How to Find Tables Without Primary Keys

You can search the MySQL metadata to locate tables without primary keys. Listing 8-1 shows an SQL statement that you can use to mine the metadata database in MySQL. Notice we use the information_schema and the tables to find the table name and schema by joining that to the information_schema statistics table to find primary indexes, which indicates the table has a primary key. We also exclude the MySQL metadata databases.

Listing 8-1. SQL Statement for Locating Tables Without Primary Keys

```
SELECT t.table_schema, t.table_name
FROM information_schema.tables t
  LEFT JOIN (SELECT table_schema, table_name
             FROM information_schema.statistics
             WHERE index_name = 'PRIMARY'
             GROUP BY table_schema, table_name, index_name
             ) pks
  ON t.table_schema = pks.table_schema AND t.table_name = pks.table_name
WHERE pks.table_name IS NULL
  AND t.table_type = 'BASE TABLE'
  AND t.table_schema NOT IN ('mysql', 'sys', 'performance_schema',
  'information_schema');
```

Listing 8-2 shows the SQL statement execution where one table was found without a primary key.

Listing 8-2. Checking for Missing Primary Keys (SQL)

```
MySQL  localhost:33060+ ssl  SQL > SELECT t.table_schema, t.table_name FROM
information_schema.tables t
   LEFT JOIN (SELECT table_schema, table_name
              FROM information_schema.statistics
              WHERE index_name = 'PRIMARY'
              GROUP BY table_schema, table_name, index_name
              ) pks
    ON t.table_schema = pks.table_schema AND t.table_name = pks.table_
    name  WHERE pks.table_name IS NULL
```

```
    AND t.table_type = 'BASE TABLE'
    AND t.table_schema NOT IN ('mysql', 'sys', 'performance_schema',
    'information_schema');
```

```
+--------------+------------+
| TABLE_SCHEMA | TABLE_NAME |
+--------------+------------+
| no_keys      | t1         |
+--------------+------------+
1 row in set (0.0230 sec)
```

How to Add Surrogate Primary Keys

While you can easily use an ALTER TABLE SQL command to add a primary key to a table either by using one or more fields for the key or by adding an auto increment field to create a surrogate key. However, there is another way: invisible columns. In MySQL 8.0.23 and later, you can add a column to a table and make the column invisible (does not display in queries). In this case, the invisible column is a surrogate key for the table that satisfies the prerequisite for HA DB Systems.

The following shows an example of how to create an invisible column as a primary key for the table in the listing above using the ALTER TABLE statement. Notice we are adding an auto increment column as the primary key like we would normally but the INVISIBLE FIRST clause creates the invisible column:

```
ALTER TABLE no_keys.t1 ADD surrogate_key BIGINT UNSIGNED NOT NULL AUTO_
INCREMENT PRIMARY KEY INVISIBLE FIRST;
```

Listing 8-3 shows the structure of the altered table.

Listing 8-3. Example of ALTER TABLE with Invisible Surrogate Primary Key

```
MySQL  localhost:33060+ ssl  SQL > EXPLAIN no_keys.t1\G
*************************** 1. row ***************************
  Field: surrogate_key
   Type: bigint unsigned
   Null: NO
    Key: PRI
Default: NULL
```

```
  Extra: auto_increment INVISIBLE
*************************** 2. row ***************************
  Field: a
   Type: int
   Null: YES
    Key:
Default: NULL
  Extra:
*************************** 3. row ***************************
  Field: b
   Type: char(1)
   Null: YES
    Key:
Default: NULL
  Extra:
3 rows in set (0.0024 sec)
```

Tip   See `https://dev.mysql.com/doc/refman/8.0/en/invisible-columns.html` for more information about invisible columns.

Now that you understand the goals or requirements that high availability (HA) can solve, let's now discuss how you can set up your DB Systems to use the MDS high availability feature.

How to Set Up HA

Setting up HA on a DB System is very easy. You need only select the options to enable HA during DB System creation or enable HA on an existing DB System. The following sections demonstrate each condition.

Setup HA (Create DB System)

When you create a DB System, you have the option to enable HA. The following explains how to enable HA when you create a new DB System. We omit details that are the same for creating a standalone DB System so if you want to follow along, you may want to refer to the *Create a DB System* section in Chapter 4 for how to create a DB System.

Recall, we create a DB System by using the OCI cloud interface and selecting *Databases | MySQL | DB Systems* and clicking on the *Create DB System* button. Near the top of the dialog, you will see a section that allows you to choose between *Standalone, High Availability*, and *HeatWave*. To enable HA, choose the *High Availability* option as shown in Figure 8-1.

Standalone
Single-instance DB System
High Availability
Run a DB system with 3 MySQL instances providing automatic failover and zero data loss
HeatWave
DB System that allows you to enable HeatWave for accelerated query processing, suitable for running both OLTP and OLAP workloads

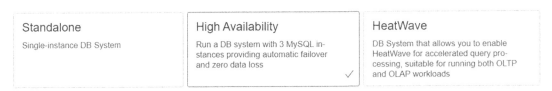

Figure 8-1. *Enable HA (Create DB System)*

Once you select *High Availability*, you will notice a subtle change to the configure networking section. The change is an additional paragraph that suggests choosing a VCN with a regional subnet to maximize the robustness of availability should a fault occur in one of the domains. Figure 8-2 shows the changes to this portion of the dialog.

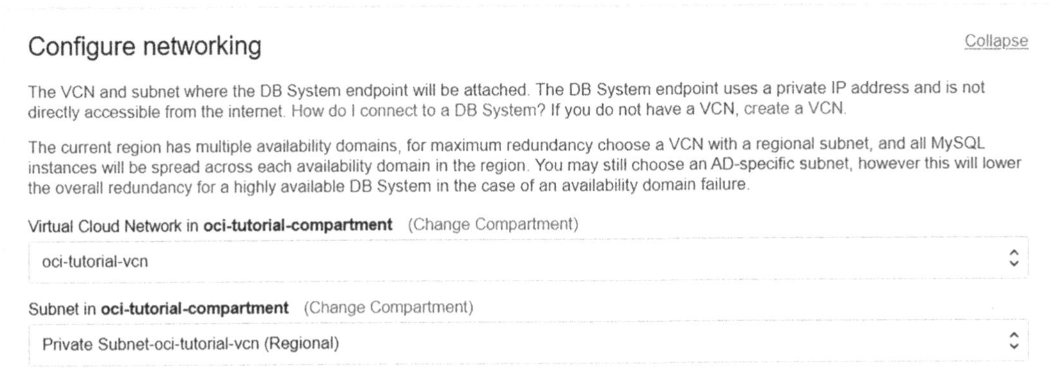

Configure networking
Collapse
The VCN and subnet where the DB System endpoint will be attached. The DB System endpoint uses a private IP address and is not directly accessible from the internet. How do I connect to a DB System? If you do not have a VCN, create a VCN.
The current region has multiple availability domains, for maximum redundancy choose a VCN with a regional subnet, and all MySQL instances will be spread across each availability domain in the region. You may still choose an AD-specific subnet, however this will lower the overall redundancy for a highly available DB System in the case of an availability domain failure.
Virtual Cloud Network in oci-tutorial-compartment (Change Compartment)
oci-tutorial-vcn
Subnet in oci-tutorial-compartment (Change Compartment)
Private Subnet-oci-tutorial-vcn (Regional)

Figure 8-2. *Networking Section (HA Enabled)*

You will also see a new section that allows you to choose the placement of the primary among the availability domains as shown in Figure 8-3.

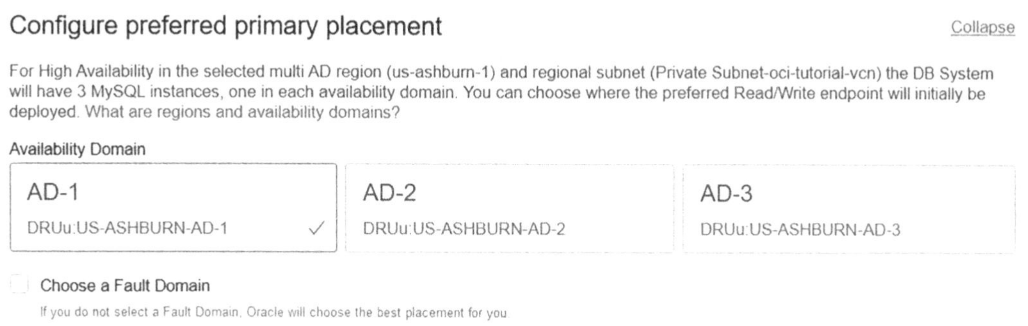

Configure preferred primary placement   Collapse

For High Availability in the selected multi AD region (us-ashburn-1) and regional subnet (Private Subnet-oci-tutorial-vcn) the DB System will have 3 MySQL instances, one in each availability domain. You can choose where the preferred Read/Write endpoint will initially be deployed. What are regions and availability domains?

Availability Domain

AD-1	AD-2	AD-3
DRUu:US-ASHBURN-AD-1 ✓	DRUu:US-ASHBURN-AD-2	DRUu:US-ASHBURN-AD-3

☐ Choose a Fault Domain
   If you do not select a Fault Domain, Oracle will choose the best placement for you

Figure 8-3. *Configure Primary Placement (HA Enabled)*

That's it! Once you complete the rest of the dialog (MySQL administrator information, shape, and data storage size) then click the *Create* button, your HA DB System will be created. Once the HA DB System is ready, you can view it like you would any other DB System.

There are also changes to the DB System details page starting with the summary, which shows the state of HA as shown in Figure 8-4.

High Availability

High Availability: Enabled ⓘ

High Availability Type: Multi-AD

Figure 8-4. *HA Enabled (DB System Details Page)*

Enable HA (Existing DB System)

Enabling HA on an existing DB System is accomplished by either using the context menu on the DB Systems list by choosing *Enable high availability*, choosing *Enable high availability* from the *More actions* menu, or by clicking on the *Enable* link next to the high availability section on the DB System details page as shown in Figure 8-5.

High Availability

High Availability: Disabled Enable (i)

Figure 8-5. *Enable HA (DB System Details Page)*

Once you click *Enable,* you will see a dialog that explains what MDS will do to convert your standalone DB System to an HA DB System. Figure 8-6 shows the enable HA dialog.

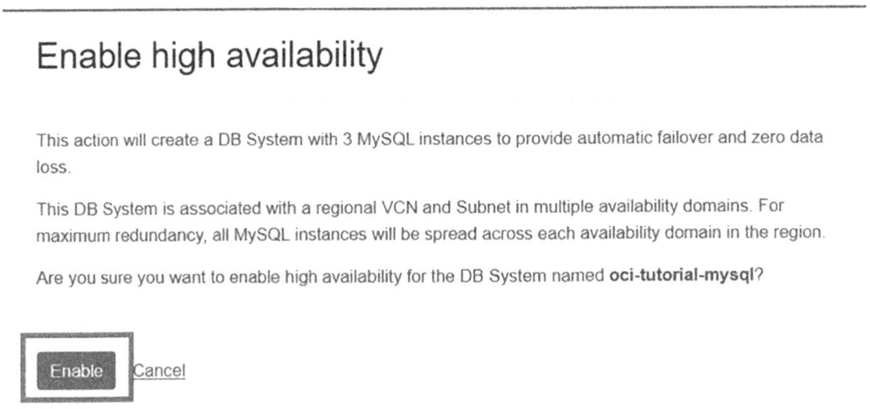

Enable high availability

This action will create a DB System with 3 MySQL instances to provide automatic failover and zero data loss.

This DB System is associated with a regional VCN and Subnet in multiple availability domains. For maximum redundancy, all MySQL instances will be spread across each availability domain in the region.

Are you sure you want to enable high availability for the DB System named **oci-tutorial-mysql**?

Figure 8-6. *Enable HA Dialog (Existing DB System)*

When you are certain you want to proceed, you can click the *Enable* button. The results will be the same as the previous example of creating an HA DB System.

Caution   While point-in-time recovery is available for standalone DB Systems, it is not available for HA DB Systems. Thus, you may need to turn off point-in-time recovery to enable HA on a standalone DB System.

However, if the shape you used for your standalone DB System is not compatible with MDS HA, you will see a dialog where you can choose a different shape. Simply choose a shape from the drop-down list then click the *Enable* button. Your data will not be erased, but you may incur additional charges for the new shape.

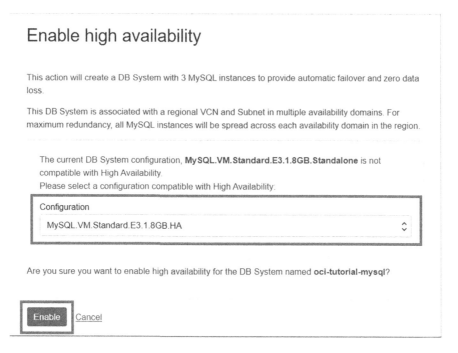

Figure 8-7. *Change Shape on Enable HA (Existing DB System)*

This process may take a few moments to run, so be prepared to wait until the HA feature is enabled on your DB System.

Note   Enabling HA on an existing DB System will increase cost because you will be adding two additional DB Systems and data storage for the secondaries. Fortunately, any additional networking loads for the HA feature support are not billed.

Disable HA (Existing HA DB System)

Surprisingly, you can disable HA on an existing HA DB System. Simply choose the *Disable* link on the DB System details page under the High Availability section as shown in Figure 8-8.

High Availability

High Availability: Enabled Disable (*i*)

High Availability Type: Multi-AD

Figure 8-8. *Disable HA (Existing DB System)*

Once you click on *Disable*, you will be asked to confirm the operation as shown in Figure 8-9. Once confirmed, click the *Disable* button on the dialog to disable HA on your DB System. This may take some time to complete.

Disable high availability

Are you sure you want to disable high availability for the DB System named **oci-tutorial-mysql**?

Disable   Cancel

Figure 8-9. *Confirm Disable HA*

How to Use MDS HA

Once again, failover will occur automatically, but if you want to perform a switchover, you can do so by either choosing the context menu on the list of DB Systems or choosing Switchover from the menu as shown in Figure 8-10.

DB Systems *in* oci-tutorial-compartment *Compartment*

Name	DB System State	Crash Recovery	Delete Protected	High Availability	HeatWave Cluster	HeatWave State	Created	
							Sun, Aug 21	
HA_Tutorial	● Active	● Enabled	Disabled	Enabled	Disabled	-	View Details	⋮
							Edit	
restored_PITR	● Deleted	● Enabled	Disabled	Disabled	Disabled	-	Start	⋮
							Stop	
test-mysql-restore	● Deleted	● Enabled	Disabled	Disabled	Disabled	-	Restart	⋮
							Switchover	
oci-tutorial-mysql	● Inactive	● Enabled	Disabled	Disabled	Disabled	-	Copy OCID	⋮

Figure 8-10. *Selecting Switchover (DB Systems List)*

You can also use the More Actions menu on the DB System details page and choose Switchover as shown in Figure 8-11.

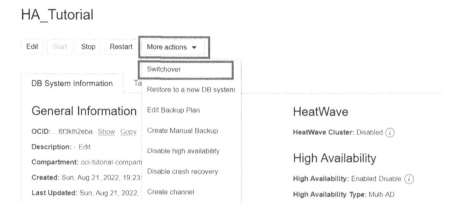

Figure 8-11. *Selecting Switchover (DB System Details Page)*

In either case, you will be presented with a dialog where you will need to choose the availability of fault domain of the secondary you want to promote as shown in Figure 8-12.

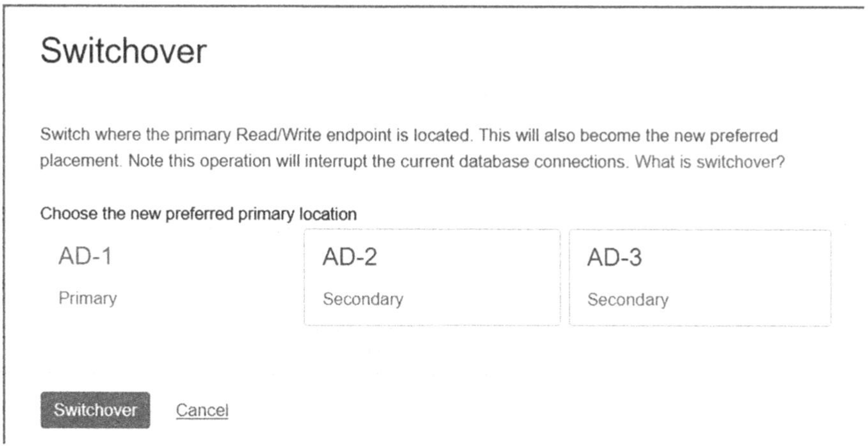

Switchover

Switch where the primary Read/Write endpoint is located. This will also become the new preferred placement. Note this operation will interrupt the current database connections. What is switchover?

Choose the new preferred primary location

AD-1	AD-2	AD-3
Primary	Secondary	Secondary

Switchover   Cancel

Figure 8-12. *Switchover Dialog*

Once you select a different availability domain and click the *Switchover* button, the status of the DB System changes to Updating, and the selected instance becomes the primary.

Limitations

There are a number of limitations for using HA DB Systems as listed below:

- *Backup*: You cannot restore a standalone DB System backup on an HA DB System.

- *HA Configuration*: You cannot change the configuration of an HA DB System. However, you can use a backup of an HA DB System to restore to a new HA DB System with a different HA configuration.

- *HeatWave*: You cannot use HeatWave on an HA DB System.

- *MySQL Version*: HA DB Systems must use MySQL 8.0.24 or later.

- *Point-in-Time Recovery*: You cannot use PITR on an HA DB System.

- *Rolling Upgrades*: When HA DB Systems are upgraded, rolling upgrades are used where each DB System (primary and secondaries) is upgraded that incur a brief downtime period before the new primary is available.

- *Secondary Access*: You cannot access the secondary instances directly, using MySQL Shell, or any other such client.

- *Shapes*: You must choose certain shapes available for HA and the maximum size of transaction is limited by shape. See the *Limitations* section at `https://docs.oracle.com/en-us/iaas/mysql-database/doc/high-availability1.html` for more information.

Advanced Topics

The HA features of MDS include two additional, advanced topics that bear mentioning. If your existing on-prem MySQL servers use replication and you want to replication to/from MDS, you can do so using features named inbound replication and outbound replication.

These features are designed to allow you to create a hybrid cloud solution where part of your MySQL solution may be on-prem and the rest in OCI (MDS). These technologies can also be used to synchronize data between on-prem and MDS MySQL servers.

Inbound replication uses a replication channel configured in MDS to copy transactions from an on-prem MySQL server (or another DB System elsewhere) called the source to a DB System called the replica. See `https://docs.oracle.com/en-us/iaas/mysql-database/doc/inbound-replication.html` for more information about setting up inbound replication.

Outbound replication does the reverse. It uses a replication channel configured in MDS to copy transactions from a DB System to an on-prem (or another DB System elsewhere) called the replica. The channel connects the DB System (source) to the replica and copies transactions from the source to the replica.

Summary

Achieving high availability with MDS is very easy. You can select it during the create operation or enable it later once you've used the DB System. Either way, Oracle has conquered the rather steep learning curve to get replication up and running and to manage it over time.

Thus, Oracle has improved upon MySQL Group Replication building upon its OCI feature set and success and folding in several other features to make an easier to learn and easier to maintain high availability solution. In fact, there is no reason not to use high availability on your DB Systems. While it does cost more since you are using more resources, the piece of mind of reliability and availability is well worth the minimal increase.

In the next chapter, we will see an overview of two additional technologies: the OCI command-line interface (CLI) and the OCI application programming interface (API). We have seen the CLI in Chapter 7, but we will see more about what is possible in the CLI including how to script certain actions that you can use in your development operations (DevOps) tasks.

CHAPTER 9

OCI Command-Line and Application Programming Interfaces

Thus far in this book we have used the OCI web-based console to work with OCI products and services. We saw how to set up our OCI account, create networking services, and create and configure DB Systems. If you are comfortable with the web-based console, you should consider continuing using it as every operation you need to perform is easy to find and most information can be found on a single page or a page with tabs.

However, what do you do if you want to write development operations (DevOps) procedures in the form of Bash (or similar) script files? What if you want to write those scripts in a programming language like Python? Further, what if you want to configure your PC to use only command-line access to manipulate objects in OCI? Fortunately, the answers for all these questions can be found in the command-line and application programming interfaces available for OCI.

In this chapter, we will see an overview of the capabilities of the command-line interface (CLI) and application programming interface (API) for working with OCI and MDS DB Systems.

Getting Started

One of the nice features of the OCI documentation is that Oracle often includes text that covers both web-based and CLI examples for working with OCI products and services. There are also examples where Oracle includes how to perform operations using the APIs, but those are often seen only in the API documentation.

© Charles Bell 2023
C. Bell, *MySQL Database Service Revealed*, https://doi.org/10.1007/978-1-4842-8945-7_9

You can use the CLI with very little effort on your part. In fact, if you have executed the examples in Chapter 7, you have already installed the CLI. Recall, we installed the CLI because MySQL Shell required it. However, what was not revealed was that the CLI is written using the Python OCI API. So, if you install the CLI, you've also installed the Python API. Nice!

In Chapter 7, we configured our PC for use with the CLI in the section entitled *Configure Your PC for OCI CLI Access*. This requires the following at a minimum, which applies to both the CLI and APIs. If you have not configured your PC yet, please refer to that section in Chapter 7 to configure your PC for use with the CLI and API:

- An SSH key used for signing API requests and the public key uploaded into your OCI account.

- Python 3 installed on a supported operating system.

Tip   See the CLI installation documentation at `https://docs.oracle.com/en-us/iaas/Content/API/SDKDocs/cliinstall.htm` for more information about installing the CLI.

Command-Line Interface (CLI)

The OCI CLI is a Python-based application that you can download and run from your PC. It represents an alternative to the web-based cloud console and is especially helpful for running repeated tasks or tasks you want to automate from your developer operations (DevOps) tools.

Interestingly, the CLI is built using the OCI APIs (SDK) and can show you what is possible for your own applications should you decide to use the API.

Install the CLI

Recall, we installed the CLI in Chapter 7 in the section entitled *Install and Test the OCI CLI*. If you have not installed the CLI yet, please refer to those sections to configure your PC and install the CLI.

Capabilities

The CLI is a macro-level interface for the Python API. As such, many of the operations available perform a set of tasks that would typically require several methods in the API. Fortunately, the CLI is designed with an eye for the operator. Thus, the operations are those that we think about when we work with OCI products and services.

The CLI works by providing a list of commands that each can have subcommands and parameters. The CLI main executable is named oci and invoked with the same name. A nice touch is you don't need to remember all of the command lists because the CLI has context help. For example, you can issue the oci command without parameters to get more information about all commands or help for a specific command with oci <command>. This also applies to subcommands. Listing 9-1 shows the help for the main commands excerpted for brevity.

Listing 9-1. CLI Help Example

```
C:\>oci
Usage: oci [OPTIONS] COMMAND [ARGS]...

  Oracle Cloud Infrastructure command line interface, with support for
  Audit, Block Volume, Compute, Database, IAM, Load Balancing, Networking,
  DNS, File Storage, Email Delivery and Object Storage Services.

  Most commands must specify a service, followed by a resource type and then
  an action. For example, to list users (where $T contains the OCID of the
  current tenant):

    oci iam user list --compartment-id $T


  Output is in JSON format.
...
Commands:
  iam                          Identity and Access Management Service
  raw-request                  Makes a raw request against an
                               OCI service
  session                      Session commands for CLI
```

setup	Setup commands for CLI
adm	Application Dependency Management
ai	Language
ai-vision	Vision
analytics	Analytics
announce	Announcements Service
anomaly-detection	Oracle Cloud AI Services
api-gateway	API Gateway
apm-config	Application Performance Monitoring Configuration
apm-control-plane	Application Performance Monitoring Control Plane
apm-synthetics	Application Performance Monitoring Synthetic Monitoring
apm-traces	Application Performance Monitoring Trace Explorer
application-migration	Application Migration
appmgmt-control	Resource Discovery and Monitoring Control
artifacts	Artifacts and Container Images
audit	Audit
autoscaling	Autoscaling
bastion	Bastion
bds	Big Data Service
blockchain	Blockchain Platform Control Plane
budgets	Budgets
bv	Block Volume Service
ce	Container Engine for Kubernetes
certificates	Certificates Service Retrieval
certs-mgmt	Certificates Service Management
cloud-guard	Cloud Guard and Security Zones
compute	Compute Service

compute-management	Compute Management Service
dashboard-service	Dashboards
data-catalog	Data Catalog
data-connectivity	Data Connectivity Management
data-flow	Data Flow
data-integration	Data Integration
data-labeling-service	Data Labeling Management
data-labeling-service-dataplane	Data Labeling
data-safe	Data Safe
data-science	Data Science
database-management	Database Management
database-migration	Oracle Database Migration Service
db	Database Service
dbtools	Database Tools
devops	DevOps
dns	DNS
dts	Data Transfer Service
em-warehouse	EmdwControlPlane
email	Email Delivery
events	Events
fn	Functions Service
fs	File Storage
fusion-apps	Fusion Applications Environment Management
goldengate	GoldenGate
governance-rules-control-plane	GovernanceRulesControlPlane
health-checks	Health Checks
iam	Identity and Access Management Service
instance-agent	Compute Instance Agent Service
integration	Oracle Integration
jms	Java Management Service
kms	Key Management
lb	Load Balancing
license-manager	License Manager
limits	Service Limits

log-analytics	LogAnalytics
logging	Logging Management
logging-ingestion	Logging Ingestion
logging-search	Logging Search
management-agent	Management Agent
management-dashboard	ManagementDashboard
marketplace	Marketplace Service
media-services	Media Services
monitoring	Monitoring
mysql	MySQL Database Service
network	Networking Service
network-firewall	Network Firewall
nlb	NetworkLoadBalancer
nosql	NoSQL Database
oce	Oracle Content and Experience
ocvs	Oracle Cloud VMware Solution
oda	Digital Assistant Service Instance
oma	Managed Access
onesubscription	OneSubscription
ons	Notifications
opa	OracleProcessAutomation
opctl	OperatorAccessControl
opensearch	OpenSearch Service
opsi	Operations Insights
optimizer	Cloud Advisor
organizations	Organizations
os	Object Storage Service
os-management	OS Management
osp-gateway	OSP Gateway
osub-billing-schedule	OneSubscription Billing Schedule
osub-organization-subscription	OneSubscription Gateway Organization's Subscription
osub-subscription	OneSubscription Subscription, Commitment and Rate Card Details

osub-usage	OneSubscription Usage Computation
resource-manager	Resource Manager
rover	RoverCloudService
sch	Service Connector Hub
search	Search Service
secrets	Vault Secret Retrieval
service-catalog	Service Catalog
service-manager-proxy	Service Manager Proxy
service-mesh	Service Mesh
speech	Speech
stack-monitoring	Stack Monitoring
streaming	Streaming
support	Support Management
threat-intelligence	Threat Intelligence
usage	Usage Proxy
usage-api	Usage
vault	Vault Secret Management
visual-builder	Visual Builder
vn-monitoring	Network Monitoring
vulnerability-scanning	Scanning
waa	Web Application Acceleration (WAA)
waas	Web Application Acceleration and Security Services
waf	Web Application Firewall (WAF)
work-requests	Work Requests

As you can see, there are a lot of commands! The one command we are interested in most is the mysql command. Listing 9-2 shows the help for the mysql (MDS) commands.

Listing 9-2. CLI mysql Help Example

```
C:\>oci mysql
Usage: oci mysql [OPTIONS] COMMAND [ARGS]...

  The CLI for the MySQL Database Service
```

Options:
  -?, -h, --help For detailed help on any of these individual
    commands, enter
                    <command> --help.

Commands:
  backup   A full or incremental copy of a DB System
                            which...
  channel   A Channel connecting a DB System to an
                            external...
  configuration   The set of MySQL variables to be used when...
  db-system   MySQL Database Service
  shape   The shape of the DB System.
  version   A supported MySQL Version.
  work-request   The status of an asynchronous task in the system.
  work-request-error   An error encountered while executing a work...
  work-request-log-entry   A log message from the execution of a work...

Similarly, if you wanted to see the help for the mysql backup command, you can issue the oci mysql backup command. Listing 9-3 shows the output of this command.

Listing 9-3. CLI mysql backup Help Example

C:\>**oci mysql backup**
Usage: oci mysql backup [OPTIONS] COMMAND [ARGS]...

  A full or incremental copy of a DB System which can be used to create a
  new DB System or recover a DB System.

  To use any of the API operations, you must be authorized in an
  IAM policy.
  If you're not authorized, talk to an administrator. If you're an
  administrator who needs to write policies to give users access, see
  [Getting Started with Policies].

Options:
  -?, -h, --help For detailed help on any of these individual
    commands, enter
                    <command> --help.

```
Commands:
  change-compartment  Moves a DB System Backup into a different
                      compartment.
  create              Create a backup of a DB System.
  delete              Delete a Backup.
  get                 Get information about the specified Backup
                      [Command...
  list                Get a list of DB System backups.
```

Notice how much information is included in the help. This is the quickest way to explore the CLI and for the most part you should not need to visit the longer, more detailed online documentation. This is why we started with the web-based console. Once you master that, all these terms will become clear, and you can easily find the command and parameters you need to script any supported operation.

The output of the CLI is JavaScript object notation (JSON), which most will find easy to read and use. For example, if you wanted to list the backups for a specific DB System, you would issue the following command without parameters adding the --help option to get more information:

```
oci mysql backup list --help
```

This produces the output in Listing 9-4 (reformatted for brevity). Notice the DB System option.

Listing 9-4. CLI mysql backup list Help Example

```
C:\>oci mysql backup list --help
"list"
******
* Description
* Usage
* Required Parameters
* Optional Parameters
* Global Parameters
* Examples

Description
===========
```

Get a list of DB System backups.

Usage
=====

    oci mysql backup list [OPTIONS]

Required Parameters
==================

--compartment-id, -c [text] The compartment OCID.

Optional Parameters
==================

--all Fetches all pages of results. If you provide this option, then you cannot provide the "--limit" option.

--backup-id [text] Backup OCID

--creation-type [text] Backup creationType Accepted values are: AUTOMATIC, MANUAL, OPERATOR

--db-system-id [text] The DB System OCID.

--display-name [text] A filter to return only the resource matching the given display name exactly.

--from-json [text] Provide input to this command as a JSON document from a file using the file://path-to/file syntax.

The "--generate-full-command-json-input" option can be used to generate a sample json file to be used with this command option. The key names are pre-populated and match the command option names (converted to camelCase format, e.g. compartment-id compartmentId), while the values of the keys need to be populated by the user before using the sample file as an input to this command. For any command option that accepts multiple values, the value of the key can be a JSON array.

Options can still be provided on the command line. If an option exists in both the JSON document and the command line then the command line specified value will be used.

For examples on usage of this option, please see our using CLI with advanced JSON options link: https://docs.cloud.oracle.com/iaas/Content/API/SDKDocs/cliusing.htm#AdvancedJSONOptions

--lifecycle-state [text] Backup Lifecycle State Accepted values are: ACTIVE, CREATING, DELETED, DELETING, FAILED, INACTIVE, UPDATING

--limit [integer] The maximum number of items to return in a paginated list call. For information about pagination, see List Pagination.

--page [text] The value of the *opc-next-page* or *opc-prev-page* response header from the previous list call. For information about pagination, see List Pagination.

--page-size [integer] When fetching results, the number of results to fetch per call. Only valid when used with "--all" or "--limit", and ignored otherwise.

--sort-by [text] The field to sort by. Only one sort order may be provided. Time fields are default ordered as descending. Accepted values are: displayName, timeCreated, timeUpdated

--sort-order [text] The sort order to use (ASC or DESC). Accepted values are: ASC, DESC

Global Parameters
==================
Use "oci --help" for help on global parameters.

"--auth-purpose", "--auth", "--cert-bundle", "--cli-auto-prompt", "--cli-rc-file", "--config-file", "--connection-timeout", "--debug", "--defaults-file", "--endpoint", "--generate-full-command-json-input", "--generate-param-json-input", "--help", "--latest-version", "--max-retries", "--no-retry", "--opc-client-request-id", "--opc-request-id", "--output", "--profile", "--query", "--raw-output", "--read-timeout", "--region", "--release-info", "--request-id", "--version", "-?", "-d", "-h", "-i", "-v"

Wow, that's a lot of information! We now know all we need to know to list the backups for a compartment or for a specific DB System (using the `--db-system-id` option).

Note   Some options are required while others are optional. Also, some provide with shortcuts. For example, `--compartment-id` and `-c` are the same option.

Now that we understand the basics of the CLI, let's look at some example operations that you can use right away with your DB Systems.

Example Uses

The following are some examples of using the CLI for common MDS operations ranging from simple listing of objects to creating objects. These are provided as examples and do not represent complete coverage of all MDS CLI commands. See the *For More Information* below for links to the documentation.

Caution   The parameters for the oci command must not use spaces. For example, `--param1=value` is valid, but `--param1 = value` is invalid and will lead to "invalid option" errors.

List Backups for a DB System

To list the backups for a DB System, we use the `--db-system-id` and `--compartment-id` options providing the OCID for each. Listing 9-5 shows how to formulate and execute the command. Notice that the output generated in JSON format. Notice also we used the `--lifecycle-state` option with the `ACTIVE` parameter to skip all backups that aren't active.

Listing 9-5. Listing Backups for a DB System

```
C:\>oci mysql backup list --compartment-id=ocid1.compartment.MASKED --db-
system-id=ocid1.mysqldbsystem.MASKED --lifecycle-state=ACTIVE
{
  "data": [
    {
      "backup-size-in-gbs": 1,
      "backup-type": "INCREMENTAL",
      "creation-type": "AUTOMATIC",
      "data-storage-size-in-gbs": 50,
      "db-system-id": "ocid1.mysqldbsystem.MASKED",
      "defined-tags": {
        "Oracle-Tags": {
          "CreatedOn": "2022-04-11T18:42:37.374Z"
        }
      },
      "description": null,
      "display-name": "mysqlbackup20220821100711",
      "freeform-tags": {},
      "id": "ocid1.mysqlbackup.MASKED",
      "lifecycle-state": "ACTIVE",
      "mysql-version": "8.0.29",
      "retention-in-days": 10,
      "shape-name": "MySQL.VM.Standard.E3.1.8GB",
      "time-created": "2022-08-21T10:07:11.725000+00:00"
    },
    {
      "backup-size-in-gbs": 1,
      "backup-type": "INCREMENTAL",
      "creation-type": "AUTOMATIC",
      "data-storage-size-in-gbs": 50,
      "db-system-id": "ocid1.mysqldbsystem.MASKED",
      "defined-tags": {
        "Oracle-Tags": {
          "CreatedOn": "2022-04-11T18:42:37.374Z"
```

```
        }
      },
      "description": null,
      "display-name": "mysqlbackup20220820100710",
      "freeform-tags": {},
      "id": "ocid1.mysqlbackup.MASKED",
      "lifecycle-state": "ACTIVE",
      "mysql-version": "8.0.29",
      "retention-in-days": 10,
      "shape-name": "MySQL.VM.Standard.E3.1.8GB",
      "time-created": "2022-08-20T10:07:10.149000+00:00"
    },
    {
      "backup-size-in-gbs": 1,
      "backup-type": "FULL",
      "creation-type": "AUTOMATIC",
      "data-storage-size-in-gbs": 50,
      "db-system-id": "ocid1.mysqldbsystem.MASKED",
      "defined-tags": {
        "Oracle-Tags": {
          "CreatedOn": "2022-04-11T18:42:37.374Z"
        }
      },
      "description": null,
      "display-name": "mysqlbackup20220818203231",
      "freeform-tags": {},
      "id": "ocid1.mysqlbackup.oc1.iad.MASKED",
      "lifecycle-state": "ACTIVE",
      "mysql-version": "8.0.29",
      "retention-in-days": 10,
      "shape-name": "MySQL.VM.Standard.E3.1.8GB",
      "time-created": "2022-08-18T20:32:31.588000+00:00"
    }
  ]
}
```

Note   You may be required to enter the password for your API SSH key.

Stop/Start a DB System

The next example shows how you can stop a DB System with the CLI. In this case, we need to use the `mysql db-system` command, pass the DB System OCID, and the `stop` operation. Listing 9-6 shows an example of this command.

Listing 9-6. Stopping a DB System

```
C:\>oci mysql db-system stop --db-system-id=ocid1.mysqldbsystem.MASKED --
shutdown-type=fast
{
  "opc-work-request-id": "ocid1.mysqlworkrequest.MASKED"
}
```

Notice the output is a work request id. This indicates an operation that is running and while we do not get a status, we can get more information about this work request including the status with the following command. Here, we use the `work-request` subcommand with the `get` operation to fetch the details of a work request with the OCID specified in the `--work-request-id` option:

```
oci mysql work-request get --work-request-id=<OCID>
```

Listing 9-7. Getting a Work Request Status

```
C:\>oci mysql work-request get --work-request-id=ocid1.
mysqlworkrequest.MASKED
Private key passphrase:
{
  "data": {
    "compartment-id": "ocid1.compartment.MASKED",
    "id": "ocid1.mysqlworkrequest.MASKED",
    "operation-type": "STOP_DBSYSTEM",
    "percent-complete": 100.0,
```

```
    "resources": [
      {
        "action-type": "RELATED",
        "entity-type": "mysqldbsystem",
        "entity-uri": "/dbSystems/ocid1.mysqldbsystem.MASKED",
        "identifier": "ocid1.mysqldbsystem.MASKED"
      }
    ],
    "status": "SUCCEEDED",
    "time-accepted": "2022-08-22T01:01:18.469000+00:00",
    "time-finished": "2022-08-22T01:02:39.135000+00:00",
    "time-started": "2022-08-22T01:01:22.935000+00:00"
  }
}
```

Notice we see a status of SUCCEEDED. If the work request were still running, we would see the appropriate status. This is how you can track your work requests with the CLI, and it is a common mechanism.

We can also get the information for the DB System we just stopped to ensure it is in a stopped state. Listing 9-8 shows the CLI command for getting the DB System information followed by fetches for the work request status.

Listing 9-8. Getting the DB System Information (stopped)

```
C:\>oci mysql db-system start --db-system-id=ocid1.mysqldbsystem.MASKED
{
  "opc-work-request-id": "ocid1.mysqlworkrequest.MASKED"
}

C:\>oci mysql work-request get --work-request-id=ocid1.
mysqlworkrequest.MASKED
{
  "data": {
    "compartment-id": "ocid1.compartment.MASKED",
    "id": "ocid1.mysqlworkrequest.MASKED",
    "operation-type": "START_DBSYSTEM",
    "percent-complete": 0.48333332,
```

```
  "resources": [
    {
      "action-type": "IN_PROGRESS",
      "entity-type": "mysqldbsystem",
      "entity-uri": "/dbSystems/ocid1.mysqldbsystem.MASKED",
      "identifier": "ocid1.mysqldbsystem.MASKED"
    }
  ],
  "status": "IN_PROGRESS",
  "time-accepted": "2022-08-22T01:09:46.862000+00:00",
  "time-finished": null,
  "time-started": "2022-08-22T01:09:56.948000+00:00"
  }
}

...

C:\>oci mysql work-request get --work-request-id=ocid1.
mysqlworkrequest.MASKED
{
  "data": {
    "compartment-id": "ocid1.compartment.MASKED",
    "id": "ocid1.mysqlworkrequest.MASKED",
    "operation-type": "START_DBSYSTEM",
    "percent-complete": 100.0,
    "resources": [
      {
        "action-type": "RELATED",
        "entity-type": "mysqldbsystem",
        "entity-uri": "/dbSystems/ocid1.mysqldbsystem.MASKED",
        "identifier": "ocid1.mysqldbsystem.MASKED"
      }
    ],
    "status": "SUCCEEDED",
    "time-accepted": "2022-08-22T01:09:46.862000+00:00",
```

```
    "time-finished": "2022-08-22T01:13:56.223000+00:00",
    "time-started": "2022-08-22T01:09:56.948000+00:00"
  }
}
```

Like start/stop, you can also delete DB Systems as well as list the DB Systems in a compartment. There are many more commands available for DB Systems. Follow the links below in the *For More Information* section to learn more about the commands.

Ok, let's look at one more example but this time we will use a complex operation: creating a new DB System.

Create a DB System

Creating a DB System requires a more complex set of parameters and options. In this case, we need, at a minimum, the compartment OCID, subnet OCID, shape name (not OCIDs), and availability domain name. We will add some more optional parameters, but let's start assuming we do not know the OCIDs for these objects. Never fear, we can list them with the CLI!

Listing 9-9 shows the command to list the compartments in your tenancy. Notice we use the iam command (Identity and Access Management) with the compartment subcommand and the list parameter to list all compartments in our tenancy.

Listing 9-9. List Compartments

```
C:\>oci iam compartment list
{
  "data": [
    {
      "compartment-id": "ocid1.tenancy.MASKED",
      "defined-tags": {},
      "description": "MASKED",
      "freeform-tags": {},
      "id": "ocid1.compartment.MASKED",
      "inactive-status": null,
      "is-accessible": null,
      "lifecycle-state": "ACTIVE",
      "name": "ManagedCompartmentForPaaS",
```

```
      "time-created": "2022-03-12T10:30:27.437000+00:00"
    },
    {
      "compartment-id": "ocid1.tenancy.MASKED",
      "defined-tags": {
        "Oracle-Tags": {
          "CreatedOn": "2022-04-15T20:11:23.394Z"
        }
      },
      "description": "Used for MySQL development",
      "freeform-tags": {},
      "id": "ocid1.compartment.MASKED",
      "inactive-status": null,
      "is-accessible": null,
      "lifecycle-state": "ACTIVE",
      "name": "mysql-development-compartment",
      "time-created": "2022-04-15T20:11:23.466000+00:00"
    },
    {
      "compartment-id": "ocid1.tenancy.MASKED",
      "defined-tags": {
        "Oracle-Tags": {
          "CreatedOn": "2022-03-11T19:40:29.719Z"
        }
      },
      "description": "Our first compartment!",
      "freeform-tags": {},
      "id": "ocid1.compartment.MASKED",
      "inactive-status": null,
      "is-accessible": null,
      "lifecycle-state": "ACTIVE",
      "name": "oci-tutorial-compartment",
      "time-created": "2022-03-11T19:40:29.794000+00:00"
    }
  ]
}
```

Listing the subnets for our compartment is a similar command except we can use the network command and subnet subcommand with the list option. We pass the compartment OCID with the --compartment-id parameter.

Listing 9-10.   Listing the Subnets for a Compartment

```
C:\>oci network subnet list --compartment-id=ocid1.compartment.MASKED
Private key passphrase:
{
  "data": [
    {
      "availability-domain": null,
      "cidr-block": "10.0.1.0/24",
      "compartment-id": "ocid1.compartment.MASKED",
      "defined-tags": {
        "Oracle-Tags": {
          "CreatedOn": "2022-03-11T20:27:33.457Z"
        }
      },
      "dhcp-options-id": "ocid1.dhcpoptions.MASKED",
      "display-name": "Private Subnet-oci-tutorial-vcn",
      "dns-label": "sub03112027061",
      "freeform-tags": {
        "VCN": "VCN-2022-03-11T20:25:54"
      },
      "id": "ocid1.subnet.MASKED",
      "ipv6-cidr-block": null,
      "ipv6-cidr-blocks": null,
      "ipv6-virtual-router-ip": null,
      "lifecycle-state": "AVAILABLE",
      "prohibit-internet-ingress": true,
      "prohibit-public-ip-on-vnic": true,
      "route-table-id": "ocid1.routetable.MASKED",
      "security-list-ids": [
        "ocid1.securitylist.MASKED"
      ],
```

```
    "subnet-domain-name": "sub03112027061.ocitutorialvcn.oraclevcn.com",
    "time-created": "2022-03-11T20:27:33.893000+00:00",
    "vcn-id": "ocid1.vcn.MASKED",
    "virtual-router-ip": "10.0.1.1",
    "virtual-router-mac": "00:00:17:38:7B:54"
  },
  {
    "availability-domain": null,
    "cidr-block": "10.0.0.0/24",
    "compartment-id": "ocid1.compartment.MASKED",
    "defined-tags": {
      "Oracle-Tags": {
        "CreatedOn": "2022-03-11T20:27:32.655Z"
      }
    },
    "dhcp-options-id": "ocid1.dhcpoptions.MASKED",
    "display-name": "Public Subnet-oci-tutorial-vcn",
    "dns-label": "sub03112027060",
    "freeform-tags": {
      "VCN": "VCN-2022-03-11T20:25:54"
    },
    "id": "ocid1.subnet.MASKED",
    "ipv6-cidr-block": null,
    "ipv6-cidr-blocks": null,
    "ipv6-virtual-router-ip": null,
    "lifecycle-state": "AVAILABLE",
    "prohibit-internet-ingress": false,
    "prohibit-public-ip-on-vnic": false,
    "route-table-id": "ocid1.routetable.MASKED",
    "security-list-ids": [
      "ocid1.securitylist.MASKED"
    ],
    "subnet-domain-name": "sub03112027060.ocitutorialvcn.oraclevcn.com",
    "time-created": "2022-03-11T20:27:32.987000+00:00",
    "vcn-id": "ocid1.vcn.MASKED",
```

```
      "virtual-router-ip": "10.0.0.1",
      "virtual-router-mac": "00:00:17:38:7B:54"
    }
  ]
}
```

Next, we need the MySQL shapes available. Since this list could be long, we will see a paged output that will require multiple calls to get the complete list. If you're like me, you don't have the patience for that, so we can use the --all parameter.

The command we need to get the list of shapes and their names requires using the mysql command and shape subcommand with the list option and the --compartment-id parameter as shown in Listing 9-11 (excerpted for brevity).

Listing 9-11. Listing the MySQL Shapes

```
C:\>oci mysql shape list --compartment-id=ocid1.compartment.MASKED --all
Private key passphrase:
{
  "data": [
    {
      "cpu-core-count": 1,
      "is-supported-for": [
        "DBSYSTEM"
      ],
      "memory-size-in-gbs": 8,
      "name": "VM.Standard.E2.1"
    },
    {
      "cpu-core-count": 2,
      "is-supported-for": [
        "DBSYSTEM"
      ],
      "memory-size-in-gbs": 16,
      "name": "VM.Standard.E2.2"
    },
    {
      "cpu-core-count": 4,
```

```
      "is-supported-for": [
        "DBSYSTEM"
      ],
      "memory-size-in-gbs": 32,
      "name": "VM.Standard.E2.4"
    },
    {
      "cpu-core-count": 8,
      "is-supported-for": [
        "DBSYSTEM"
      ],
      "memory-size-in-gbs": 64,
      "name": "VM.Standard.E2.8"
    },
    {
      "cpu-core-count": 1,
      "is-supported-for": [
        "DBSYSTEM"
      ],
      "memory-size-in-gbs": 8,
      "name": "MySQL.VM.Standard.E3.1.8GB"
    },
...
```

Ok, there is one more list we need: the name of the availability domain. To find the availability domains, we issue the iam command with the availability-domain subcommand and the list option providing the compartment OCID with --compartment-id parameter.

Listing 9-12. Listing Availability Domains

```
C:\ >oci iam availability-domain list --compartment-id=ocid1.
compartment.MASKED
{
  "data": [
    {
      "compartment-id": "ocid1.compartment.MASKED",
```

```
      "id": "ocid1.availabilitydomain.MASKED",
      "name": "DRUu:US-ASHBURN-AD-1"
    },
    {
      "compartment-id": "ocid1.compartment.MASKED",
      "id": "ocid1.availabilitydomain.MASKED",
      "name": "DRUu:US-ASHBURN-AD-2"
    },
    {
      "compartment-id": "ocid1.compartment.MASKED",
      "id": "ocid1.availabilitydomain.MASKED",
      "name": "DRUu:US-ASHBURN-AD-3"
    }
  ]
}
```

Next, we need some optional parameters. The following shows the options we will use and their parameters:

- `--admin-password <password>`: The password for the MySQL administrative user.

- `--admin-username <name>`: The username for the MySQL administrative user.

- `--data-storage-size-in-gbs <int>`: Size of the data storage (database drive) in GBs.

- `--display-name <text>`: A user-friendly name for the DB System.

- `--is-highly-available <bool>`: Specifies if the DB System is highly available.

There is one more option we should discuss – the option to have the operation wait for a specific state. We do this with the `--wait-for-state <state>` option and one of the states (`ACCEPTED`, `CANCELED`, `CANCELING`, `FAILED`, `IN_PROGRESS`, `SUCCEEDED`). You can specify this option multiple times to wait for multiple operations. This operation asynchronously executes the operation and uses a work request to track the progress. Multiple states can be specified, returning on the first state. If timeout is reached, a return code of 2 is returned. For any other error, a return code of 1 is returned.

Ok, now we are ready to form out command. The following is an example of the command. If you want to follow along, be sure to substitute your OCIDs instead of the masked OCIDs shown:

```
oci mysql db-system create \
    --compartment-id=ocid1.compartment.MASKED \
    --shape-name=VM.Standard.E2.4 \
    --subnet-id=ocid1.subnet.MASKED \
    --admin-password=MASKED \
    --admin-username=mysql_admin \
    --data-storage-size-in-gbs=50 \
    --display-name=MySQL_CLI_Create \
    --is-highly-available=false \
    --wait-for-state=FAILED \
    --wait-for-state=SUCCEEDED \
    --availability-domain=DRUu:US-ASHBURN-AD-2
```

Listing 9-13. Create DB System Example Command

```
C:\>oci mysql db-system create --compartment-id=ocid1.compartment.MASKED --
shape-name=VM.Standard.E2.4 --subnet-id=ocid1.subnet.MASKED --admin-
password=MASKED --admin-username=mysql_admin --data-storage-size-in-gbs=50 --
display-name=MySQL_CLI_Create --is-highly-available=false --wait-for-
state=FAILED --wait-for-state=SUCCEEDED --availability-domain=DRUu:US-
ASHBURN-AD-2
Private key passphrase:
Private key passphrase:
Action completed. Waiting until the work request has entered state:
('FAILED', 'SUCCEEDED')
{
  "data": {
    "compartment-id": "ocid1.compartment.oc1..
    aaaaaaaawzwb45t3lutkqvyhofxh3ai26e5oli2a4q6efbh25g3llqwys7pa",
    "id": "ocid1.mysqlworkrequest.oc1.
    iad.83fd016c-1083-4a3f-92b9-c7c583d40b44.
    aaaaaaaai3m2mauwmhp3ppbdjvtwq26xomazthrsqk6teguy73mofidayk5q",
```

```
    "operation-type": "CREATE_DBSYSTEM",
    "percent-complete": 100.0,
    "resources": [
      {
        "action-type": "CREATED",
        "entity-type": "mysqldbsystem",
        "entity-uri": "/dbSystems/ocid1.mysqldbsystem.oc1.iad.
        aaaaaaaay3d7ex7lnbvb24snjyvdg7mn6cx3qrezaq2nifq56ohdwmjk4owa",
        "identifier": "ocid1.mysqldbsystem.oc1.iad.
        aaaaaaaay3d7ex7lnbvb24snjyvdg7mn6cx3qrezaq2nifq56ohdwmjk4owa"
      }
    ],
    "status": "SUCCEEDED",
    "time-accepted": "2022-08-22T01:54:59.037000+00:00",
    "time-finished": "2022-08-22T02:08:05.671000+00:00",
    "time-started": "2022-08-22T01:55:13.888000+00:00"
  }
}
```

Ok, now the operation has returned, and it succeeded. If we visit the OCI console, we can find the DB System and display its details page as demonstrated in Figure 9-1.

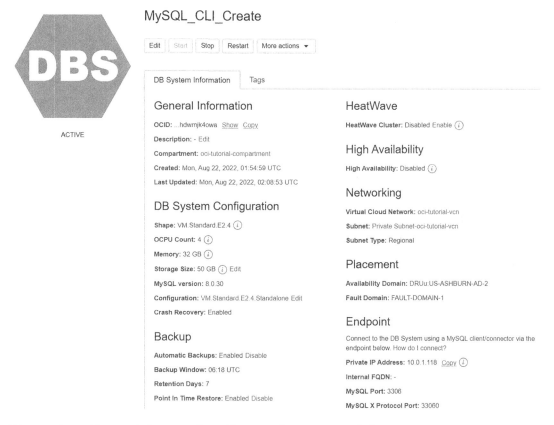

Figure 9-1. *New DB System Details Page (CLI Example)*

Finally, to clean up from this example, we can delete the newly created DB System with the following command as demonstrated in Listing 9-14. Notice you are asked to confirm the delete operation.

Listing 9-14. Deleting a DB System

```
C:\>oci mysql db-system delete --db-system-id=ocid1.mysqldbsystem.MASKED
--wait-for-state=SUCCEEDED
Are you sure you want to delete this resource? [y/N]: y
Action completed. Waiting until the work request has entered state:
('SUCCEEDED',)
```

```
{
  "data": {
    "compartment-id": "ocid1.compartment.oc1..
    aaaaaaaawzwb45t3lutkqvyhofxh3ai26e5oli2a4q6efbh25g3llqwys7pa",
    "id": "ocid1.mysqlworkrequest.MASKED",
    "operation-type": "DELETE_DBSYSTEM",
    "percent-complete": 100.0,
    "resources": [
      {
        "action-type": "DELETED",
        "entity-type": "mysqldbsystem",
        "entity-uri": "/dbSystems/ocid1.mysqldbsystem.MASKED",
        "identifier": "ocid1.mysqldbsystem.MASKED"
      }
    ],
    "status": "SUCCEEDED",
    "time-accepted": "2022-08-22T02:15:30.534000+00:00",
    "time-finished": "2022-08-22T02:18:02.293000+00:00",
    "time-started": "2022-08-22T02:15:32.565000+00:00"
  }
}
```

Now that we've seen a few of the more common operations including listing, creating, and deleting resources, let's look at the documentation available for the other MDS operations available in the CLI.

For More Information

The most valuable resource and indeed the starting point for your continued research into the CLI is the documentation at https://docs.oracle.com/en-us/iaas/tools/oci-cli/3.15.0/oci_cli_docs/. This documentation is listed by OCI product and service which includes every possible use of the CLI for those products and services. For example, the MDS portion of the documentation contains the following major sections. Links to the documentation for each section are included:

- *Backup*: Operations for working with backups including creating and listing (`https://docs.oracle.com/en-us/iaas/tools/oci-cli/3.15.0/oci_cli_docs/cmdref/mysql/backup.html`).

- *Channel*: Operations for working with replication channels for inbound and outbound replication (`https://docs.oracle.com/en-us/iaas/tools/oci-cli/3.15.0/oci_cli_docs/cmdref/mysql/channel.html`).

- *Configuration*: Operations on the set of MySQL server variables that configure the parameters of MySQL (`https://docs.oracle.com/en-us/iaas/tools/oci-cli/3.15.0/oci_cli_docs/cmdref/mysql/configuration.html`).

- *DB System*: Operations on DB Systems including all features such as high availability, HeatWave, and more (`https://docs.oracle.com/en-us/iaas/tools/oci-cli/3.15.0/oci_cli_docs/cmdref/mysql/db-system.html`).

- *Shape*: List operation to see available shapes (`https://docs.oracle.com/en-us/iaas/tools/oci-cli/3.15.0/oci_cli_docs/cmdref/mysql/shape.html`).

- *Version*: List operation to list the MySQL server versions available (`https://docs.oracle.com/en-us/iaas/tools/oci-cli/3.15.0/oci_cli_docs/cmdref/mysql/version.html`).

- *Work-Request*: Operations to list and get work requests for monitoring operations (`https://docs.oracle.com/en-us/iaas/tools/oci-cli/3.15.0/oci_cli_docs/cmdref/mysql/work-request.html`).

- *Work-Request-Error*: List operation to get more information about work request errors (`https://docs.oracle.com/en-us/iaas/tools/oci-cli/3.15.0/oci_cli_docs/cmdref/mysql/work-request.html`).

- *Work-Request-Log-Entry*: List operation to get more information from the work request log (`https://docs.oracle.com/en-us/iaas/tools/oci-cli/3.15.0/oci_cli_docs/cmdref/mysql/work-request-log-entry.html`).

Refer to the links above for more details about the CLI operations for these areas. You can also visit the OCI CLI main documentation at `https://docs.oracle.com/en-us/iaas/tools/oci-cli/3.15.0/oci_cli_docs/index.html` to see the complete list of the OCI CLI commands.

OCI APIs

Oracle provides APIs for almost every operation in OCI and MDS is no exception. Oracle also provides software development kits (SDK) that you can use to develop and deploy applications that interact with the OCI resources. Oracle provides SDKs for the following programming languages. Each SDK includes example code and documentation. Best of all, most SDKs are available via GitHub where you can contribute your own suggestions for improvements. The following show the SDKs available for OCI along with a link to the documentation for the SDK. If you want to use any of these SDKs for your applications, be sure to review the documentation and examples as you get started:

- *Java*: `https://docs.oracle.com/en-us/iaas/Content/API/SDKDocs/javasdk.htm#SDK_for_Java`

- *Python*: `https://docs.oracle.com/en-us/iaas/Content/API/SDKDocs/pythonsdk.htm#SDK_for_Python`

- *TypeScript and JavaScript*: `https://docs.oracle.com/en-us/iaas/Content/API/SDKDocs/typescriptsdk.htm#SDK_for_TypeScript_and_JavaScript`

- *.NET*: `https://docs.oracle.com/en-us/iaas/Content/API/SDKDocs/dotnetsdk.htm#SDK_for_NET`

- *Go*: `https://docs.oracle.com/en-us/iaas/Content/API/SDKDocs/gosdk.htm#SDK_for_Go`

- *Ruby*: `https://docs.oracle.com/en-us/iaas/Content/API/SDKDocs/rubysdk.htm#SDK_for_Ruby`

Since the Python SDK is popular and the Python language is easy to learn, we will look at a few examples of using the Python SDK. Before we jump into the Python API examples, let's discuss the MDS APIs briefly so that we understand the interfaces.

Each SDK has as part of its documentation an API reference, which is an extensive list of the APIs for each resource supported. For example, the Python SDK API reference is found at `https://docs.oracle.com/en-us/iaas/tools/python/2.79.0/api/landing.html`.

Now, let's take a brief look at the MDS API.

MDS API

The MDS API has five main components (or, more correctly, classes) that make up the interface. These include the following:

- `oci.mysql.ChannelsClient`: API for working with inbound and outbound replication.

- `oci.mysql.DbBackupsClient`: API for working with backups.

- `oci.mysql.DbSystemClient`: API for working with DB Systems.

- `oci.mysql.MysqlaasClient`: API for working with the MySQL client access (e.g. configuration, shapes, versions).

- `oci.mysql.WorkRequestsClient`: API for interactive with work requests.

In addition, the MDS API has five classes that have grouped some of the individual API methods and classes together for macro operations. These include the following:

- `oci.mysql.ChannelsClientCompositeOperations`: API for working with inbound and outbound replication.

- `oci.mysql.DbBackupsClientCompositeOperations`: API for working with backups.

- `oci.mysql.DbSystemClientCompositeOperations`: API for working with DB Systems.

- `oci.mysql.MysqlaasClientCompositeOperations`: API for working with the MySQL client access (e.g., configuration, shapes, versions).

- `oci.mysql.WorkRequestsClientCompositeOperations`: API for interactive with work requests.

It is often necessary to use multiple MDS API classes to achieve certain functions. Let's get a brief tour of the MDS API in Python using a few examples.

Example Uses

Using the OCI SDKs can be a little challenging when you first begin working with them. In this section, we will see how to get started by demonstrating the basics of how the Python SDK works. But first, let's install the Python SDK.

Note   You must have Python 3 installed on your PC. See the Python organization at `www.python.org/` for more details about installing Python on your PC.

Install the Python SDK

Before we can use the Python SDK, we must install it. Recall, we mentioned that the Python SDK is part of the OCI CLI, but it is installed in its own environment, so it is not accessible by a typical Python client. Fortunately, we can install the Python SDK alongside the OCI CLI without affecting either product. The following demonstrates how to install the Python SDK on Windows 11, but details for installing on other platforms or with other methods can be found at `https://docs.oracle.com/en-us/iaas/tools/python/2.79.0/installation.html`.

The command to install the Python SDK uses pip, which is installed automatically when you install Python:

```
pip install oci
```

Listing 9-15 shows an excerpt of this command running on Windows 11. Once it is complete, you have the Python SDK installed and can proceed. The output for your PC may vary from this listing depending on the other Python components installed on your PC.

Listing 9-15. Installing the Python SDK

```
C:\ >pip install oci
Collecting oci
  Downloading oci-2.79.0-py2.py3-none-any.whl (16.9 MB)
     |                                          |
                                                | 16.9 MB 6.8 MB/s
Collecting python-dateutil<3.0.0,>=2.5.3
  Downloading python_dateutil-2.8.2-py2.py3-none-any.whl (247 kB)
     |                                          |
                                                | 247 kB 6.8 MB/s
Collecting cryptography<=37.0.2,>=3.2.1
  Downloading cryptography-37.0.2-cp36-abi3-win_amd64.whl (2.4 MB)
     |                                          |
                                                | 2.4 MB 3.3 MB/s
Collecting pytz>=2016.10
  Downloading pytz-2022.2.1-py2.py3-none-any.whl (500 kB)
     |                                          |
                                                | 500 kB ...
Collecting certifi
  Downloading certifi-2022.6.15-py3-none-any.whl (160 kB)
     |                                          |
                                                | 160 kB 3.3 MB/s
Collecting circuitbreaker<2.0.0,>=1.3.1
  Downloading circuitbreaker-1.4.0.tar.gz (9.7 kB)
Collecting pyOpenSSL<=22.0.0,>=17.5.0
  Downloading pyOpenSSL-22.0.0-py2.py3-none-any.whl (55 kB)
     |                                          |
                                                | 55 kB 943 kB/s
Collecting cffi>=1.12
  Downloading cffi-1.15.1-cp39-cp39-win_amd64.whl (179 kB)
     |                                          |
                                                | 179 kB 3.3 MB/s
Collecting pycparser
  Downloading pycparser-2.21-py2.py3-none-any.whl (118 kB)
```

```
                                                                    | 118 kB 3.2 MB/s
Requirement already satisfied: six>=1.5 in c:\users\cbell\appdata\
local\programs\python\python39\lib\site-packages (from python-
dateutil<3.0.0,>=2.5.3->oci) (1.16.0)
Using legacy 'setup.py install' for circuitbreaker, since package 'wheel'
is not installed.
Installing collected packages: pycparser, cffi, cryptography, pytz, python-
dateutil, pyOpenSSL, circuitbreaker, certifi, oci
    Running setup.py install for circuitbreaker ... done
Successfully installed certifi-2022.6.15 cffi-1.15.1 circuitbreaker-1.4.0
cryptography-37.0.2 oci-2.79.0 pyOpenSSL-22.0.0 pycparser-2.21 python-
dateutil-2.8.2 pytz-2022.2.1
```

Getting Started

The basic layout of any Python SDK script begins with an import section where you import the getpass and oci modules. We need the getpass module because we must read the SSH key (called a passphrase) from the user (command-line).

This is followed by creating an instance of the oci.config class. This is an operation that reads your configuration file and prepares the SDK objects for use with your credentials. We then read and add the passphrase to the configuration file dictionary. Next, we connect to whichever API class we want to use and, if the connection is successful, we can proceed to make the API method calls.

Note   If you have not set up your PC to use the OCI CLI, please refer to Chapter 7 and finish that setup before attempting the API examples. The configuration file is required for access to MDS via the API.

Listing 9-16 shows the basic Python script you need to access the OCI API classes. The script is named basic_api.py.

Tip   If you are new to Python programming, you can visit www.python.org/ for how to download and install Python as well as tutorials and help getting started with Python. There are also many excellent books on Python and a few websites that can help you get started.

Listing 9-16. Basic Python API Script

```python
#
# MySQL Database Service
#
# Basic Python script for working with the MDS Python API
#
# Created by: Dr. Charles Bell
#

# Import the getpass module
import getpass
# Import the oci module
import oci

# Read your configuration file: be sure to provide a path if
# your configuration file.
config = oci.config.from_file()

# Read the passphrase from the user
pass_phrase = getpass.getpass("Enter the SSH key passphrase: ")

# Add the passphrase  to the config file dictionary.
config.update({'pass_phrase':pass_phrase})

# Initialize service client with default config file
mysql_client = oci.mysql.MysqlaasClient(config)

# Create an instance to the API module and call methods

# Check response codes as needed and exit
```

You can execute this script with the following command. You should see it run and then exit without errors. If it does not, check your configuration file and the Python SDK install to make sure everything is installed and configured correctly before proceeding:

```
python3 basic_api.py
```

Now, let's look at some of the examples we used in the CLI section to see how to accomplish the same using the Python SDK. Let's start by listing the MySQL shapes using the `oci.mysql.MysqlaasClient` class.

Listing the MySQL Shapes

To list the MySQL shapes, we use the `list_shapes()` method from the `oci.mysql.MysqlaasClient` class, which takes as a parameter the compartment id, which is common among many of the API methods.

Since we will be using he compartment id often, we can save it in an environment variable and read it from the Python script. To set an environment variable in macOS or Linux, use the `export` command as shown below:

```
export COMPARTMENT_ID=ocid1.compartment.MASKED
```

For Windows, we use the `set` command as shown below:

```
set COMPARTMENT_ID=ocid1.compartment.MASKED
```

You can read an environment variable in Python with the os module as shown below:

```
import os
COMPARTMENT_ID = os.getenv('COMPARTMENT_ID')
```

The call to the API to get the list of shapes is shown below::

```
list_shapes_response = mysql_client.list_shapes(compartment_
id=COMPARTMENT_ID)
```

This returns a list or ShapeSummary classes, which we can use to loop through the shapes and print the name, which is a lot cleaner (and fewer lines) than a JSON output like the CLI. You can find the description of the ShapeSummary class at `https://docs.oracle.com/en-us/iaas/tools/python/2.79.0/api/mysql/models/oci.mysql.models.ShapeSummary.html#oci.mysql.models.ShapeSummary`.

Ok, now let's look at the complete code. Listing 9-17 shows the completed code for this example. The file is named list_mysql_shapes.py.

Listing 9-17. List MySQL Shapes Script

```
import getpass
import os
# Import the oci module
import oci

# Read your configuration file: be sure to provide a path if
# your configuration file.
config = oci.config.from_file()

# Read the passphrase from the user
pass_phrase = getpass.getpass("Enter the SSH key passphrase: ")

# Add the passphrase  to the config file dictionary.
config.update({'pass_phrase':pass_phrase})

# Initialize service client with default config file
mysql_client = oci.mysql.MysqlaasClient(config)

# Get the compartment id from the environment
COMPARTMENT_ID = os.getenv('COMPARTMENT_ID')
# List the MySQL shapes
list_shapes_response = mysql_client.list_shapes(compartment_
id=COMPARTMENT_ID)

# Loop through the data and print the shape names only.
for shape_summary in list_shapes_response.data:
    print(shape_summary.name)
```

When you execute this code, you will see an excerpt of the list of MySQL shapes as shown in Listing 9-18.

Listing 9-18. Output of List MySQL Shapes Script

```
C:\Users\cbell>python list_mysql_shapes.py
Enter the SSH key passphrase:
VM.Standard.E2.1
```

```
VM.Standard.E2.2
VM.Standard.E2.4
VM.Standard.E2.8
MySQL.VM.Standard.E3.1.8GB
MySQL.VM.Standard.E3.1.16GB
MySQL.VM.Standard.E3.2.32GB
MySQL.VM.Standard.E3.4.64GB
MySQL.VM.Standard.E3.8.128GB
MySQL.VM.Standard.E3.16.256GB
MySQL.VM.Standard.E3.24.384GB
MySQL.VM.Standard.E3.32.512GB
MySQL.VM.Standard.E3.48.768GB
MySQL.VM.Standard.E3.64.1024GB
...
MySQL.VM.Optimized3.1.8GB
MySQL.VM.Optimized3.1.16GB
MySQL.VM.Optimized3.2.32GB
MySQL.VM.Optimized3.4.64GB
MySQL.VM.Optimized3.8.128GB
MySQL.VM.Optimized3.16.256GB
MySQL.HeatWave.BM.Standard.E3
```

Now, let's take the complexity up a bit. Let's see how to control DB Systems.

Stop/Start DB System

When working with DB Systems, we will use the `oci.mysql.DbSystemClient` class and its methods. To stop a DB System, we use the `stop_db_system()` method and to start a DB System, we use the `start_db_system()` method. As you can see, the API methods are often quite self-explanatory.

This example is a bit more complicated because we will have to provide a DB System id (OCID) in the form of another class named `stop_db_system_details()` for the stop or start operation. This class uses a model to populate the data. In this case, we need the DB System OCID and the shutdown type.

We are also going to make it a bit more complex by first listing the DB Systems in our compartment and select the one with a specific name. You may be amazed at how difficult it is to remember OCIDs, but it is much easier to remember a DB System name.

We'll display a list for the user to choose the DB System to control. To list the DB Systems, we use the `list_db_systems()` method and pass in the compartment id, which we have saved in an environment file.

In summary, we will import the libraries we need, read the configuration file, read the SSH key passphrase from the user, read the compartment id from the environment variable, then read the DB System name from the user. Once we have that information, we can call the method to list the DB Systems in the compartment, select one that matches the name, then either stop or start it.

Interestingly, these API methods do not return with a work request id like we saw with the CLI examples. Instead, the method waits until the operation is complete. Listing 9-19 shows the complete code for this example. The file is named `stop_db_system.py` Take some time to study it before moving on to the next example.

Listing 9-19. Control DB System Script

```python
import getpass
import os
import sys
# Import the oci module
import oci

# Determine which operation is requested: start/stop
if len(sys.argv) > 1:
    is_stop = sys.argv[1].upper() == "STOP"
    operation = "Stopping"
else:
    is_stop = False
    operation = "Starting"

# Read your configuration file: be sure to provide a path if
# your configuration file.
config = oci.config.from_file()

# Read the passphrase from the user
pass_phrase = getpass.getpass("Enter the SSH key passphrase: ")

# Add the passphrase  to the config file dictionary.
config.update({'pass_phrase':pass_phrase})
```

```python
# Initialize service client with default config file
db_client = oci.mysql.DbSystemClient(config)

# Get the compartment id from the environment
COMPARTMENT_ID = os.getenv('COMPARTMENT_ID')

# List the DB Systems
list_db_systems_response = db_client.list_db_systems(compartment_
id=COMPARTMENT_ID)

# Loop through the DB System Summary
db_systems = []
num = 1
print("DB Systems in Compartment")
print("-------------------------")
for db_system_summary in list_db_systems_response.data:
    if db_system_summary.lifecycle_state != 'DELETED':
        print("{0}: {1}".format(num, db_system_summary.display_name))
        db_systems.append(db_system_summary)

# If no DB Systems active, exit
if len(db_systems) == 0:
    print("No db systems to control.")
    exit(1)

# Get the name of the DB System to control
db_num = int(input("\nWhich DB System (int)? "))
print("\n{0} the DB System named '{1}'\n".format(operation, db_systems[db_
num-1].display_name))

# Perform the operation
if is_stop:
    db_system_response = db_client.stop_db_system(
        db_systems[db_num-1].id,
        stop_db_system_details=oci.mysql.models.StopDbSystemDetails(
            shutdown_type="FAST")
        )
```

```
    print(db_system_response.headers)
else:
    db_system_response = db_client.start_db_system(db_systems[db_num-1].id)
    print(db_system_response.headers)

print("Done!")
```

As you can see, the code it much more complex, but most of that is the Python code to gather the list of DB Systems and display them to the user to select one for the operation. Listing 9-20 shows the code running (formatted for easier reading). Notice we have a user-friendly albeit terse interface that may be more appealing and easier to use than the OCI console.

Listing 9-20. Output of the Control DB System Script

```
C:\Users\cbell>python control_db_system.py STOP
Enter the SSH key passphrase:
DB Systems in Compartment
-------------------------
1: oci-tutorial-mysql

Which DB System (int)? 1


Stopping the DB System named 'oci-tutorial-mysql'

{
    'Date': 'Mon, 22 Aug 2022 20:44:34 GMT',
    'opc-request-id': 'MASKED',
    'opc-work-request-id': 'ocid1.mysqlworkrequest.MASKED',
    'X-Content-Type-Options': 'nosniff',
    'Content-Type': 'application/json'
}
Done!
```

This script would make a good starting point for other operations you may want to perform on your DB Systems. Simply modify it to your needs!

The last example we will look at is the operation to create a new DB System. While the Python code may seem more complex, but it uses the same features of this example only with a more sophisticated Python programming style. However, there are more API methods, and the parameters are more complex.

Creating a DB System

Recall from the create DB System example in the CLI section that we needed several pieces of information in order to create the DB System. We repeat the required and optional parameters in the following list:

- `--compartment-id <id>`: The compartment id.
- `--shape-name <name>`: The shape name.
- `--subnet-id <id>`: The subnet OCID.
- `--availability-domain <name>`: The availability domain name to use.
- `--admin-password <password>`: The password for the MySQL administrative user.
- `--admin-username <name>`: The username for the MySQL administrative user.
- `--data-storage-size-in-gbs <int>`: Size of the data storage (database drive) in GBs.
- `--display-name <text>`: A user-friendly name for the DB System.
- `--is-highly-available <bool>`: Specifies if the DB System is highly available.

Recall from the CLI example, we used four CLI commands; one each to get the shape name, subnet id, and availability domain, and one to perform the create. This example using the Python API will do the same thing only in a single Python script.

Like the last example, we will display a simple user interface to allow the user to choose the items from the lists asking only for the display name and data size as prompts. We will also prompt for the MySQL administrative user and password.

Rather than go through line-by-line, let's summarize what we will be doing. We know we must get the subnet, shape, and availability domain so we will write methods to get that information using a helper method that presents a list to the user prompting her to choose one from the list. Thus, we will get these three data items from the user.

In doing so, we will explore more API classes including the `oci.core.VirtualNetworkClient`, `oci.mysql.MysqlaasClient`, and `oci.identity.IdentityClient` classes calling the appropriate methods for getting a list of those resources.

The optional parameters; MySQL administrator user and password, data storage size, and display name are read from the user with prompts. We also set the HA to disabled by default.

Once we have all the information, we use the `create_db_system()` method of the `oci.mysql.DbSystemClient` class to create the DB System. This method requires the population of a model named `oci.mysql.models.CreateDbSystemDetails`.

Finally, since the `create_db_system()` method returns immediately, we pole the DB System by fetching its details with the `get_db_system()` method passing in the OCID for the new DB System as returned in the `create_db_system_response.data.id` variable. We pole the DB System until its `lifecycle_state` equals ACTIVE. There are other methods for doing this including some helper methods in the OCI API, but those are a bit more advanced for those getting started. Polling the `lifecycle_state` is an acceptable initial solution if you want the script to execute and wait until the resource is ready.

That's about it. There are more nuances to this example especially the Python programming parts, but we leave those details to you to ponder as an exercise. There are no magical or arcane code constructs here, just normal Python code around the Python API for OCI.

Listing 9-21 shows the completed script. Take a few moments and read it so that you understand how it works. Don't worry about the Python details; they will come with experience working with Python.

Listing 9-21. Create DB Systems Script

```
import getpass
import os
import sys
import time
```

```python
# Import the oci module
import oci

# Global variables
# Get the compartment id from the environment
COMPARTMENT_ID = os.getenv('COMPARTMENT_ID')
config = None

# Helper function to display a list of items and let user choose one.
def get_selection(title, items):
    item_chosen = -1
    print("\n{0}\n".format(title))
    num = 1
    for item in items:
        # Display only the first column if item is a list
        if isinstance(item, list):
            print("{0:2}: {1}".format(num, item[0]))
        else:
            print("{0:2}: {1}".format(num, item))
        num += 1
    item_chosen = int(input("\nSelect the item in the list (int): "))
    return item_chosen - 1

# Get the subnet OCID
def get_subnet_ocid():
    # Initialize service client with default config file
    core_client = oci.core.VirtualNetworkClient(config)

    # List the subnets
    list_subnets_response = core_client.list_subnets(
        compartment_id=COMPARTMENT_ID,
        lifecycle_state="AVAILABLE"
    )
    # Loop through the data and get the subnet name + OCID
    subnets = []
    for subnet_summary in list_subnets_response.data:
        subnets.append([subnet_summary.display_name, subnet_summary.id])
    return subnets[get_selection("Choose a subnet:", subnets)][1]
```

```python
# Get the MySQL shape
def get_mysql_shape():
    # Initialize service client with default config file
    mysql_client = oci.mysql.MysqlaasClient(config)

    # List the MySQL shapes
    list_shapes_response = \
    mysql_client.list_shapes(compartment_id=COMPARTMENT_ID)

    # Loop through the data and get the shape names only.
    shapes = []
    for shape_summary in list_shapes_response.data:
        shapes.append(shape_summary.name)
    return shapes[get_selection("Choose a MySQL shape name:", shapes)]

# Get the availability domain name
def get_availability_domain_name():
    # Initialize service client with default config file
    identity_client = oci.identity.IdentityClient(config)

    # List the availability domains
    list_availability_domains_response = \
    identity_client.list_availability_domains(COMPARTMENT_ID)
    # Loop through the data and get the shape names only.
    ad_names = []
    for ad_summary in list_availability_domains_response.data:
        ad_names.append(ad_summary.name)
    return ad_names[get_selection(
    "Choose an availability domain:", ad_names)]

# Main function
def main():
    # Read your configuration file: be sure to provide a path if
    # your configuration file.
    global config
    config = oci.config.from_file()

    # Read the passphrase from the user
```

```
pass_phrase = getpass.getpass("Enter the SSH key passphrase: ")
# Add the passphrase  to the config file dictionary.
config.update({'pass_phrase':pass_phrase})

# Initialize service client with default config file
db_client = oci.mysql.DbSystemClient(config)

# We need to get three pieces of information:
# 1. Subnet OCID
# 2. MySQL shape name
# 3. Availability domain name

# Get the subnets for the compartment
subnet_ocid = get_subnet_ocid()

# Get the shape name
shape_name = get_mysql_shape()

# Get the availability domain
availability_domain_name = get_availability_domain_name()

# Get optional parameters
print("\nEnter optional parameters:\n")
display_name = input("Enter display name: ")
db_size = int(input("Enter DB size in GBs (e.g. 50): "))
mysql_admin_user = input("Enter MySQL administrator user name: ")
mysql_admin_passwd = getpass.getpass(
"Enter MySQL administrator password: ")
# Disable HA
is_ha = False

# Now, we create the DB System
create_db_system_response = db_client.create_db_system(
    create_db_system_details=oci.mysql.models.CreateDbSystemDetails(
        compartment_id=COMPARTMENT_ID,
        shape_name=shape_name,
        subnet_id=subnet_ocid,
        display_name=display_name,
        is_highly_available=is_ha,
```

```python
                availability_domain=availability_domain_name,
                admin_username=mysql_admin_user,
                admin_password=mysql_admin_passwd,
                data_storage_size_in_gbs=db_size,
              backup_policy=oci.mysql.models.CreateBackupPolicyDetails(
                    is_enabled=False),
            )
        )
    print("\nWaiting for DB System to be available.", end='')
    # Now, loop until the work request is done by watching
    # the DB System lifecycle state.
    db_system_ocid = create_db_system_response.data.id
    while True:
        get_db_system_response = db_client.get_db_system(
            db_system_id=db_system_ocid)
        if get_db_system_response.data.lifecycle_state == 'AVAILABLE':
            break
        else:
            print(".", end='')
            sys.stdout.flush()
            time.sleep(10)

    print("Done!")


# Direct execution to main if this module is executed directly
if __name__ == "__main__":
    main()
```

Now, let's see the code running. Listing 9-22 shows the output from running the script. Notice the lists of choices and the responses (edited for brevity).

Listing 9-22. Output from DB System Script

```
C:\Users\cbell>python create_db_system.py
Enter the SSH key passphrase:

Choose a subnet:
```

```
 1: Private Subnet-oci-tutorial-vcn
 2: Public Subnet-oci-tutorial-vcn

Select the item in the list (int): 1

Choose a MySQL shape name:

 1: VM.Standard.E2.1
 2: VM.Standard.E2.2
 3: VM.Standard.E2.4
 4: VM.Standard.E2.8
 5: MySQL.VM.Standard.E3.1.8GB
 6: MySQL.VM.Standard.E3.1.16GB
 7: MySQL.VM.Standard.E3.2.32GB
 8: MySQL.VM.Standard.E3.4.64GB
 9: MySQL.VM.Standard.E3.8.128GB
10: MySQL.VM.Standard.E3.16.256GB
11: MySQL.VM.Standard.E3.24.384GB
12: MySQL.VM.Standard.E3.32.512GB
13: MySQL.VM.Standard.E3.48.768GB
14: MySQL.VM.Standard.E3.64.1024GB
...
45: MySQL.HeatWave.BM.Standard.E3

Select the item in the list (int): 5

Choose an availability domain:

 1: DRUu:US-ASHBURN-AD-1
 2: DRUu:US-ASHBURN-AD-2
 3: DRUu:US-ASHBURN-AD-3

Select the item in the list (int): 3

Enter optional parameters:

Enter display name: TEST_API
Enter DB size in GBs (e.g. 50): 50
```

```
Enter MySQL administrator user name: mysql_admin
Enter MySQL administrator password:

Waiting...................................................
..................................................Done!
```

Take some time and experiment with this script for your own uses. You may find it helpful to getting your own automation in Python going for MDS.

However, in case you're curious, Figure 9-2 shows the DB System details page from the console.

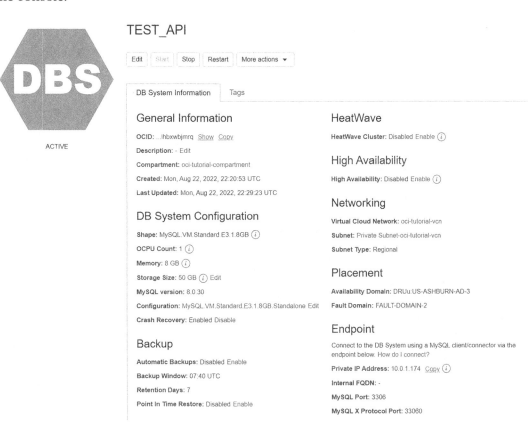

Figure 9-2. *New DB System Details Page (API Example)*

But wait, there is more. Let's add a bonus example for you to try on your own.

Delete a DB System

Your challenge is to take the control DB System script above and add the `delete` operation. To get started, you will need to use the `delete_db_system ()` method of the `oci.mysql.DbSystemClient` class. You can find the documentation for this method and an example Python script at `https://docs.oracle.com/en-us/iaas/tools/python/2.79.0/api/mysql/client/oci.mysql.DbSystemClient.html#oci.mysql.DbSystemClient.delete_db_system`. You should not have to add much to the control DB System script (`control_db_system.py`) to accomplish this task, but it will be a good exercise for those just starting out with Python and the API.

Well, that's our tour of the API! Although the tour of the MDS API and the Python SDK was brief, it should give you an idea of what is possible and the basis to begin researching your own Python applications to work with MDS resources.

Summary

When working with tens, hundreds, or thousands of DB Systems, performing maintenance operations on or working with the OCI web-based console may become tedious and somewhat slower than you'd like. That's where the CLI and APIs shine; they allow you to script common operations either in a Bash (or similar) script or in a Python code file that you can execute.

Either way, you will gain greater control and greater productivity when working with many OCI products and services and especially when your OCI operations become routine. In those cases, any improvement in productivity pays dividends. If these advantages appeal to you, I encourage you to read the online documentation for those areas you want to automate (script) first so that you can get acquainted with the mechanisms used. Once you've mastered the basics, you can branch out to explore more complex operations.

In the next chapter, we will learn some strategies and planning for migrating existing on-prem MySQL installations to MDS.

CHAPTER 10

Migrating to MDS

This book has covered a lot of material including a brief overview of the MySQL Database Service (MDS) including how to set up a DB System, perform backup and recovery, data migration to/from MDS, how to set up and use the high availability features, and we took a quick look at the OCI command line interface (CLI) and application programming interfaces (API). We saw demonstrations of most of these technologies so that you can get started using MDS in your environment.

However, this book represents an introduction to MDS and there is much more to MDS than what can be conveyed in an introductory text. For example, we have not discussed any strategies for planning and migrating your existing MySQL installations to MDS nor have we discussed some of the deeper topics such as getting more details about MDS features or troubleshooting tips should something go wrong.

In this chapter, we will discuss these topics so that you are prepared to begin planning and designing your MySQL infrastructure using MDS objects. As you will see, many of the tasks you may have used for planning your on-prem MySQL installations also apply to MDS.

One of the first things you should consider when thinking about and planning your migration to MDS is how to get help and what to do should something happen when using OCI and MDS. Let's look at that topic first.

Getting Help While Using OCI and MDS

When you begin working with recent technologies or new software, there is always a learning curve. The same is true with MDS and that's why you are reading this book – to get a jump on learning MDS so that you can start using it right away.

However, there will be cases where you will need to know more information about OCI and MDS. Indeed, this book does not and should not be considered a replacement for the documentation not only because the book doesn't cover every nuance but

© Charles Bell 2023
C. Bell, *MySQL Database Service Revealed*, https://doi.org/10.1007/978-1-4842-8945-7_10

also because Oracle is improving all of its OCI features weekly. Thus, if you want to keep updated on all of the features and the latest changes, you will need to check the documentation from time to time.

There are also times when things happen in OCI, and you will need to know about those. Fortunately, Oracle is good about keeping its customers well informed. Finally, you may also need some help troubleshooting should something go wrong. We will cover all these topics in this section.

Communication with Oracle

When you use OCI, you are using a massive distributed system that has so many components that operate behind the scenes that most customers are completely unaware of and that is really the point to using the cloud, isn't it? You need not worry about the details instead you rely on Oracle to provide services for you to consume in your own products and services.

However, despite the brilliant and hard-working army of engineers employed by Oracle, things sometimes go wrong. There could be an Internet outage, hardware failure, or some other localized incident that could cause temporary disruption in one or more services. Fortunately, these incidents are brief and often localized to a small portion of OCI.

Should something occur that Oracle detects could impact its customers, Oracle will send an email to customers alerting of the potential issue. Notice I mentioned potential because Oracle is proactive in its responses and often broadcasts notices of incidents that may affect customers. That should be reassuring to anyone who has used other cloud services in the past that simply stopped working with no explanation.

Should Oracle detect a situation that could affect you or some of your OCI objects, you will receive an email that describes the problem and lists any potential actions you may want to take. Figure 10-1 shows an excerpt of an email that I received when Oracle detected a latency issue with the ObjectStore services in my region. Fortunately, these emails are infrequent but should never be dismissed without considering the impact of the problems identified.

ORACLE' Cloud Infrastructure

Oracle Cloud Infrastructure Object Storage - Identified

Oracle Cloud Infrastructure Customer,

We've identified an issue with the Oracle Cloud Infrastructure (OCI) Object Storage service in the US East (Ashburn) region.

Customer Impact: Some customers may experience increased latency or failures when performing API calls to OCI Object Storage. This may also impact services which rely on Object Storage to perform their service management operations.

Production Event Notification

Start Time: June 14, 2022 22:00 UTC

Service(s): Oracle Cloud Infrastructure Object Storage
Tenant Name: ▓▓▓▓▓

What should I do if I am still having an issue?

Please contact support to create a Service Request and provide the Reference Number and Tenant ID shown below.

Reference Number: CN-742327
Tenant ID: ocid1.tenancy.oc1.▓▓▓▓▓▓▓▓▓

Visit the OCI Service Health Dashboard for current status information and to subscribe to notifications about interruptions to services in your region.

Figure 10-1. *OCI Potential Problem Alert Email*

Notice the email plainly describes the problem and the potential issues I could have experienced. In this case, it was higher latency problems. The email also includes links for getting more information and contacting Oracle support for additional help.

This also illustrates the need for anyone wanting to use MDS to become more familiar with the OCI technologies and services. In this case, it was a service that I was not using at the time, but as the email states, it could affect any other service that is built on top of ObjectStore. This is an excellent example and a good opportunity to learn more about OCI even if you do not recognize the service mentioned. We will discuss how to find out more about other OCI services and products in the next section.

Oracle also sends its customers emails when the problem is resolved. Figure 10-2 shows an example of an "all clear" email message from Oracle. Once again, Oracle provides links for you to find out more about the issue and a link to support if you need more help.

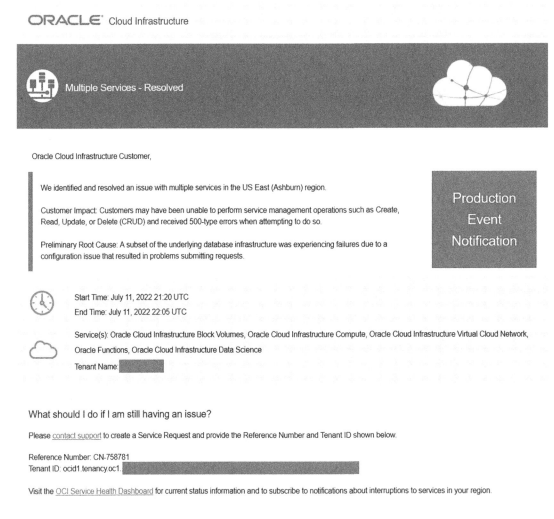

Figure 10-2. *OCI Problem Resolved Email*

Oracle also sends out regular emails about your usage and billing information. For example, you will receive an email prior to Oracle charging your account that provides a summary of your charges to date. The email includes your account (company) name, account number, the date and number of the invoice (transaction), amount billed, and a reference number.

Like the incident emails, you will also see links to Oracle's billing department should you need help and the email and phone number for someone you can contact. You can also find the details of your bill through the OCI console by clicking on your account icon in the upper-right corner and clicking *Analyze costs* under the *Usage* heading. This will present you with a dialog that you can use to see the cost incurred by day as well as a breakdown by service. Figure 10-3 shows an example from one of my experimental accounts (that has had little activity).

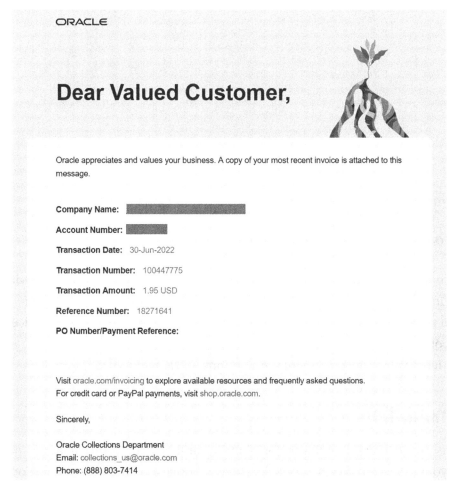

Figure 10-3. *Example OCI Billing Email*

Figure 10-4 shows an example of detailed billing for the same experimental account.

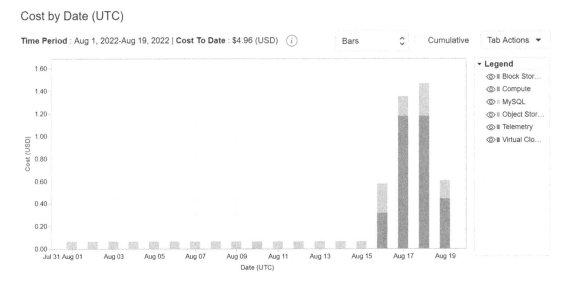

Figure 10-4. *Billing Usage (OCI Console)*

Notice you can manipulate the chart to show additional details or different views. The Tab dropdown control allows you to download the report as a PDF, comma-separated value (CSV) file, or just download the chart as an image. Those are nice touches your accounting personnel will appreciate.

Now, let's explore the documentation options for OCI and MDS.

Documentation

Oracle has provided documentation for all of OCI and MDS that you can access at a touch of your mouse. In the OCI console, you will notice a symbol with a question mark. This is the starting point for all of your documentation needs. At any point, you can click that icon and see a menu appear that will have content-specific links. For example, if you are working on a compute instance, you will see links for documentation for compute instance.

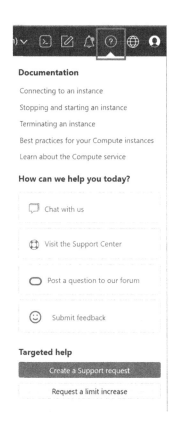

Figure 10-5. *Documentation Menu (OCI Console)*

Notice that you see links to specific tasks related to compute instances, which is very helpful when you want to learn how something works. Notice also you see links to support. You can open a chat window and talk to someone right away, go to the support center to do research on topics, post a question to the community forum, or submit feedback to support.

There are also buttons at the bottom that will include specific targeted tasks. In this example, we see buttons for creating a support request (a formal support ticket) and increasing your service limit. Recall, the service limit refers to how many of certain objects or services your account is permitted to use at one time. If you run over your limit, you can visit this menu and submit a request for an extension.

If you want general OCI documentation information, you can visit the main documentation at `https://docs.oracle.com/en-us/iaas/Content/home.htm` for the complete documentation on OCI. Here you will see a multi-column menu that you can use to find documentation on all OCI products and services. When you click on the *MySQL Database* link, you will be directed to the top of the MySQL (MDS) documentation as shown in Figure 10-6. From there, you can explore all of the topics for MDS.

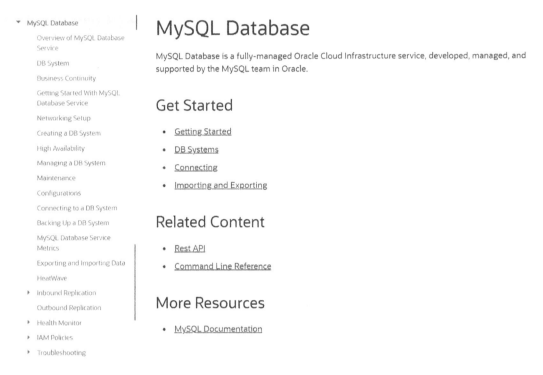

Figure 10-6. *MDS Documentation Home*

Notice at the bottom-right is a link to the MySQL documentation (for the server, MySQL Shell, etc.).

Tip   You may want to bookmark the MDS documentation page for future reference.

There is one more documentation item that could become critical for customers; the announcements page. On the OCI console, you will see a bell symbol. When you click on this, you will see the announcements page where you can monitor critical announcements about products and services you may use or be interested in as well as critical information about your account. Figure 10-7 shows the main announcements page.

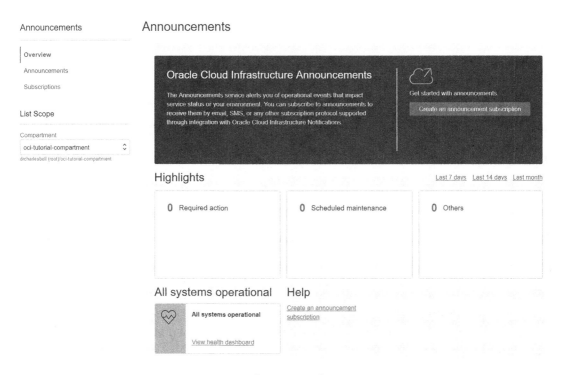

Figure 10-7. *Announcements Page (Overview)*

Notice you will see announcements from Oracle as well as highlights concerning any required actions, scheduled maintenance notices, or other notices. When any of these categories have entries, the small bell symbol on the OCI console will appear with a red dot to alert you to announcements.

Notice the Create an announcement subscription button on the right. This allows you to create a subscription to watch for certain announcements. For example, you may want to create a subscription to watch for ObjectStore incidents if you plan to perform critical operations with ObjectStore buckets. You can view your subscriptions on the subscriptions page by clicking the *Subscriptions* link on the *Announcements* menu to the left.

You can also receive details about any open incidents that may affect your account by clicking on the *Announcements* link under the *Announcements* menu on the left. This will open a view of the incidents related to your account including tools for setting date ranges to explore incidents in the past. Figure 10-8 shows an example of this page that shows an incident that was resolved. Notice there is a link to the incident, which will open the details that you can review if you need more information.

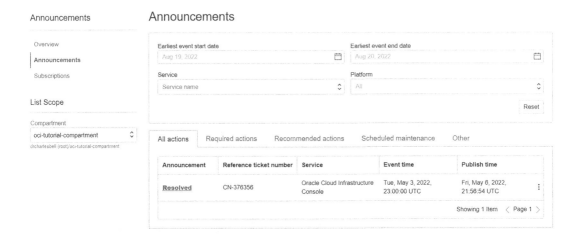

Figure 10-8. *Announcements Details*

Now that we know where the documentation is and the forms of communication Oracle uses to communicate, let's examine a topic you may need at some point: troubleshooting.

Troubleshooting

Oracle provides a comprehensive list of troubleshooting tips for all OCI products and services. This list is updated frequently as the products and services evolve and more innovations are found for helping customers with issues. For our purposes, there is a specific troubleshooting page for MDS at `https://docs.oracle.com/en-us/iaas/mysql-database/doc/troubleshooting.html`. Figure 10-9 shows the MDS troubleshooting page.

Tip   You may want to bookmark the MDS troubleshooting page for future reference.

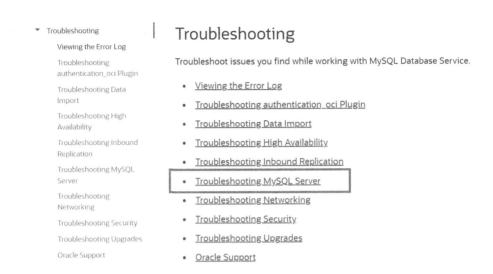

Figure 10-9. *MDS Troubleshooting Page (Documentation)*

You will find links to generic troubleshooting tips. However, notice in the center of the page is a link to the MySQL server troubleshooting page, which may be helpful if you have problems with MySQL unrelated to OCI.

Now that we have a complete view of the online help and documentation available to us from Oracle, let's discuss how to begin planning for migrating to MDS.

Examine Your DB System Needs

In this section, we will discuss the OCI-specific concepts and technologies that you must consider before planning your MDS solution. While you do not need to be concerned about the configuration of the MySQL server instance itself, since that is done for you by MDS, you must plan your databases with the same rigor you would for your on-prem MySQL servers. This planning will provide you vital information you will need for configuring your DB Systems.

Recall, we discussed planning database needs briefly in Chapter 4 as we created our first DB System, but there is more to consider. For instance, each DB System has a shape (size of CPU, memory) as well as a data size (size of data storage). Also, networking must be considered with regard to how you will make your DB Systems accessible. The following sections discuss each of these topics.

Shapes

You should consider carefully what shape you need to use. Smaller shapes typically cost less, but there could be considerable issues trying to use a shape that has fewer CPU cores than you need. Similarly, you should consider carefully how much memory you need to use. Be sure to consult with your system administration planners to ensure you choose shapes with sufficient CPU cores and memory. Figure 10-10 shows a partial list of the shapes available for DB Systems for the author's experimental account. Notice there are shapes that have 1, 2, 4, 8, 16, etc., CPU cores and the memory increases accordingly.

MySQL.VM.Standard.E3.1.8GB	Yes	1	8 GB
MySQL.VM.Standard.E3.1.16GB	Yes	1	16 GB
MySQL.VM.Standard.E3.2.32GB	No	2	32 GB
MySQL.VM.Standard.E3.4.64GB	No	4	64 GB
MySQL.VM.Standard.E3.8.128GB	No	8	128 GB
MySQL.VM.Standard.E3.16.256GB	No	16	256 GB
MySQL.VM.Standard.E3.24.384GB	No	24	384 GB
MySQL.VM.Standard.E3.32.512GB	No	32	512 GB
MySQL.VM.Standard.E3.48.768GB	No	48	768 GB
MySQL.VM.Standard.E3.64.1024GB	No	64	1 TB
MySQL.HeatWave.VM.Standard.E3	Yes	16	512 GB
MySQL.VM.Standard.E4.1.8GB	No	1	8 GB
MySQL.VM.Standard.E4.1.16GB	No	1	16 GB
MySQL.VM.Standard.E4.2.32GB	No	2	32 GB
MySQL.VM.Standard.E4.4.64GB	No	4	64 GB
MySQL.VM.Standard.E4.8.128GB	No	8	128 GB
MySQL.VM.Standard.E4.16.256GB	No	16	256 GB
MySQL.VM.Standard.E4.24.384GB	No	24	384 GB
MySQL.VM.Standard.E4.32.512GB	No	32	512 GB
MySQL.VM.Standard.E4.48.768GB	No	48	768 GB
MySQL.VM.Standard.E4.64.1024GB	No	64	1 TB

Figure 10-10. *Shapes Available for DB Systems*

The shapes listed are all virtual machines, but there are many more shapes you can choose from including those that support HeatWave and bare metal instances. Once again, generally speaking, the more cores and more memory the shape supports relates to the cost, but that is offset by the greater performance you gain from the "larger" shape. If performance is a concern, always aim for using a larger shape than what you consider would be minimal acceptance.

See the heading, *Supported Shapes*, at the following link for more information about shapes. `https://docs.oracle.com/en-us/iaas/mysql-database/doc/db-system.html`

Data Storage

Similarly, the database storage size needs careful consideration. Like shapes, smaller data storage sizes cost less, but larger sizes are implemented with RAID striping for better performance. You can choose any size from 50 GB and up. Be sure to consider if you are planning any data migration involving uploading or expanding data so that you ensure you have enough room for the imported data. You can increase the size of the data storage at a later date, but it is always best to plan for more at the onset.

See the section, *DB System Storage*, at the following link for more information about data storage options and considerations. `https://docs.oracle.com/en-us/iaas/mysql-database/doc/db-system.html`

Tip It is recommended to perform benchmark analysis during your testing to verify your environment's configuration has adequate performance for your application's requirements.

Networking

Recall that DB Systems are not accessible from the Internet. You will need to set up additional resources to bridge the networking gap such as Bastion Services, virtual private networks, Oracle FastConnect, or an intermediate compute instance. You should carefully consider these technologies when planning how you will incorporate your DB Systems into your applications.

There are also several limitations to consider regarding networking. The following lists a few of the details you will need to consider when planning your networking connectivity:

- Three IP addresses in each subnet are reserved for the networking service.

- DB Systems without high availability require three IP addresses: (1) the DB System's IP address, (2) compute instance, and (3) a separate IP address for MySQL server maintenance and upgrade tasks.

- DB Systems with high availability will also require up to seven IP addresses: one for the DB System's IP address, three for the compute instances hosting MySQL, and one for each MySQL server for maintenance and upgrade tasks.

See `https://docs.oracle.com/iaas/Content/Network/Concepts/overview.htm` for more considerations for planning networking requirements.

Planning Your DB Systems

Systems administration and planning are inseparable. That is, if you want to be successful. No more so than when planning cloud solutions. We must plan for how we want to set up, configure, and deploy our products and services in advance or face the perils of unexpected problems and delays. MDS is no exception to this policy, and you would do well to plan for how you want to use it in your environment.

The information in this section will provide you with insight into areas of planning specific to MDS DB Systems. You should consider this section an additional resource to use along with your established policies, practices, and tools for planning DB Systems. The following lists some of the key areas where deliberate planning is needed:

- Create separate user accounts for administration of your DB Systems and application access

- Configure the size of your data and use that to plan the size of your DB Systems

- Consider the size (CPU, memory) of your compute instance (for the DB System)

- Decide on a plan for upgrading to high availability

- Research all costs associated with all OCI services and create a spending projection to set expectations

- Plan your security carefully to ensure you protect your cloud resources

Most of these are things we have already discussed through the course of the book, but some may be new to you, especially if you have not used MySQL on-prem.

However, the most critical is planning the size and cost of your DB Systems. You should spend some time on these tasks as changing the size (shape) of DB Systems may not be trivial and could require some downtime to reconfigure. Fortunately, Oracle provides options to do this if you need to do so by taking a backup and restoring to a new DB System with a different shape and storage size. Spending time on planning and especially projecting your OCI costs in advance will help you control your spending while best meeting your needs. You will be surprised how must capability is available for lower costs, but this affordability can add up if you do not make a solid plan for growth.

Another critical area to consider is security. We discuss security in the next section.

Security Best Practices

Recall from earlier chapters that you must create accounts in OCI to divide the administrative and use functions. Recall also that it is recommended to create a separate user account(s) for use with your DB Systems either as user or application access. As such, there is a thorough list of security considerations. Since security is paramount for any solution, let us discuss several areas of security you should consider or plan to implement for your OCI solutions. The following lists and briefly describes the items you should investigate as you plan by category. Links are included for additional documentation:

- *Audit Services*: Employ audit services to view OCI API activities. See `https//docs.oracle.com/iaas/Content/Audit/Concepts/auditoverview.html`.

- *Data Masking*: You can protect your data using data masking to hide sensitive data. See *Data Masking* at `https//docs.oracle.com/en-us/iaas/mysql-database/doc/db-system.html`.

- *Deletion Plan*: Consider using a deletion plan to further protect your DB Systems from delete operations. See *Advanced Option Deletion Plan* at https//docs.oracle.com/en-us/iaas/mysql-database/doc/creating-db-system.html.

- *IAM Policies*: Use Identity and Access Management policies to control access. See *Required IAM Policy* at https//docs.oracle.com/en-us/iaas/mysql-database/doc/mysql-database-service-overview.html.

- *In-transit Encryption*: While data is encrypted at rest, you may want to use in-transit encryption to further protect your data. See *Data Security* at https//docs.oracle.com/en-us/iaas/mysql-database/doc/mysql-database-service-overview.html.

- *MySQL Authentication*: Use the authentication_oci plugin to map MySQL users to existing users and groups defined in the IAM service. See *Connecting to a DB System Using authentication_oci Plugin* at https//docs.oracle.com/en-us/iaas/mysql-database/doc/connecting-db-system.html.

- *MySQL Connection Control*: The MySQL Database Service supports connection-control plugin to provide a deterrent that slows down brute force attacks against MySQL user accounts. See *Plugins and Components* at https//docs.oracle.com/en-us/iaas/mysql-database/doc/db-system.html.

- *MySQL Password Validation*: Use the validate_password component to enforce password generation by setting rules for complexity and frequency of mandatory changes. See *Plugins and Components* at https//docs.oracle.com/en-us/iaas/mysql-database/doc/db-system.html.

- *MySQL Security*: Plan MySQL security features to control access to your data. See https//dev.mysql.com/doc/refman/8.0/en/access-control.html.

- *Networking Load Balancer*: Consider restricting access via the Internet to a specific or range of IP addresses and use in-transit encryption. Also, consider using the networking load balancer. See *Connecting to a DB System Using a Network Load Balancer* at `https//docs.oracle.com/en-us/iaas/mysql-database/doc/connecting-db-system.html`.

- *VCN Security Groups*: Use virtual cloud networking security groups or security lists of the VCN to restrict the authorized public IP addresses to a single IP address or a range of IP addresses. See *Adding Ingress Rules* Using at `https//docs.oracle.com/en-us/iaas/mysql-database/doc/networking-setup-mysql-db-systems.html`.

- *VCN Connection Restrictions*: You can configure your DB Systems to use private subnets of your VCN to restrict connections to either a VPN connection or use a Bastion Session. See *Bastion Session* at `https//docs.oracle.com/en-us/iaas/mysql-database/doc/networking-setup-mysql-db-systems.html` or *VPN Connection* at `https//docs.oracle.com/en-us/iaas/mysql-database/doc/networking-setup-mysql-db-systems.html`.

While the list contains terse descriptions, you should consider investigating each of the links for more detailed information for planning and implementing a secure MDS installation.

Summary

The task of planning an MDS installation is not overly complex but does require some forethought and a deliberate plan. Like any technology, we should start small with a simple experimental installation for testing as many aspects of the technology as possible. This includes not only the mechanics of setting up a DB System but also the specifics of configuring the networking and security for accessing and protecting your data. It also gives you an opportunity to ensure and learn how to connect your application to your DB System.

In this chapter, we learned some important considerations for planning your DB Systems including how to get help using the OCI documentation, where to go for additional help, and configuration considerations for shapes, disk storage, networking, and security.

This is an exciting time for MySQL users. Oracle continues to keep its promise to not only continue developing MySQL but also pouring resources into improving and expanding the feature set into the cloud, which is a game-changing technology that removes the burden (and expense) of building your own complex (and expensive) on-prem MySQL installation. For those that want to reduce costs and improve capabilities by leveraging cloud services, OCI and MDS should be your weapon of choice.

While already a capable and dependable service that is up to the challenge of fulfilling your database needs, keep a close watch on the Oracle Cloud Infrastructure for more excellent features, new MySQL services, and further refinement and updates to the MySQL Database Service.

Index

383

Printed in the United States
by Baker & Taylor Publisher Services